ALSO BY JEFFREY MEYERS

Inherited Risk: Errol and Sean Flynn in Hollywood and Vietnam
Orwell: Wintry Conscience of a Generation
Privileged Moments: Encounters with Writers
Hemingway: Life Into Art
Gary Cooper: American Hero
Bogart: A Life in Hollywood
Robert Frost: A Biography
Edmund Wilson: A Biography
Scott Fitzgerald: A Biography
Edgar Allan Poe: His Life and Legacy
Joseph Conrad: A Biography
D. H. Lawrence: A Biography
The Spirit of Biography
Manic Power: Robert Lowell and His Circle
Hemingway: A Biography
Disease and the Novel, 1880–1960
D. H. Lawrence and the Experience of Italy
The Enemy: A Biography of Wyndham Lewis
Katherine Mansfield: A Biography
Homosexuality and Literature, 1890–1930
Married to Genius
A Fever at the Core: The Idealist in Politics
Painting and the Novel
A Reader's Guide to George Orwell
The Wounded Spirit: A Study of Seven Pillars of Wisdom
Fiction and the Colonial Experience

Somerset Maugham

Somerset Maugham

A LIFE

Jeffrey Meyers

ALFRED A. KNOPF   NEW YORK

2004

THIS IS A BORZOI BOOK
PUBLISHED BY ALFRED A. KNOPF

Library of Congress Cataloging-in-Publication Data
Meyers, Jeffrey.
Somerset Maugham : a life / Jeffrey Meyers.—1st ed.
p.   cm.
Filmography: p.
Includes bibliographical references and index.
ISBN 0-375-41475-4
1. Maugham, W. Somerset (William Somerset), 1874–1965.
2. Authors, English—20th century—Biography.   I. Title:
Somerset Maugham.   II. Title.
PR6025.A86Z763 2004
823'.912—DC21   2003056187

Manufactured in the United States of America
First Edition

For Anthony and Sarah Curtis

Maugham reminds me of an old Gladstone bag covered with labels. God only knows what is inside.

—CHRISTOPHER ISHERWOOD

Contents

List of Illustrations		*ix*
Acknowledgments		*xiii*
Preface		*xv*

1.	Paris and King's School, 1874–1889	3
2.	Heidelberg and Medicine, 1890–1897	21
3.	*Liza of Lambeth* and Spain, 1897–1899	35
4.	Struggling Author, 1900–1904	47
5.	Bohemia and Fame, 1905–1908	58
6.	Sue Jones and Syrie, 1909–1915	76
7.	The Great War and Gerald Haxton, 1914–1916	96
8.	Secret Agent, 1916–1919	116
9.	Malaya and China, 1919–1921	134
10.	Dangerous Journeys, Dangerous Friends, 1921–1925	152
11.	Villa Mauresque, 1926–1928	166
12.	"Stately Homo," 1928–1929	184
13.	Reputations: *Cakes and Ale,* 1930–1933	196
14.	India and Eternal Youth, 1934–1938	217
15.	War Propaganda and Hollywood, 1939–1941	236

16. Yemassee and Haxton's Death, 1942–1944   254

17. Alan Searle and Art, 1945–1946   271

18. The Lizard of Oz, 1947–1950   288

19. Royalty and Honors, 1951–1955   299

20. The Old Party, 1956–1961   312

21. Family Values, 1962–1965   325

22. Afterlife   340

Notes   *353*

Maugham's Travels   *391*

Iconography   *393*

Bibliography   *395*

Filmography   *398*

Index   *401*

Illustrations

4 Robert Maugham (grandfather) *(Diana Marr-Johnson)*

6 Robert Ormond Maugham (father) *(Diana Marr-Johnson)*

8 Edith Maugham (mother) *(Diana Marr-Johnson)*

13 Rev. Henry Macdonald Maugham (uncle), c. 1880
(Diana Marr-Johnson)

Barbara von Scheidlin Maugham (aunt) *(Diana Marr-Johnson)*

The Vicarage, Whitstable *(King's School, Canterbury, Archives)*

14 High Street, Whitstable, 1890 *(King's School, Canterbury, Archives)*

17 Entrance to King's School *(Valerie Meyers)*

Maugham as a schoolboy, 1884 *(Diana Marr-Johnson)*

18 Maugham (first row, third from right) behind Leonard
Ashenden, King's School, 1885 *(King's School, Canterbury, Archives)*

20 Maugham (in chair, second from right) wearing scholar's gown,
King's School, 1889 *(King's School, Canterbury, Archives)*

26 St. Thomas's Hospital from across the Thames, 1939
(St. Thomas's Hospital, London)

28 Ward in St. Thomas's Hospital, 1890s *(St. Thomas's Hospital, London)*

33 John Ellingham Brooks

39 Adney Walter Payne

41 Maugham, author of *Liza of Lambeth,* 1897 *(Diana Marr-Johnson)*

75   *The Jester,* portrait of Maugham by Gerald Kelly, 1911
       (Loren Rothschild)

79   Sue Jones, portrait by Gerald Kelly

87   6 Chesterfield Street, Mayfair *(Valerie Meyers)*

88   2 Wyndham Place, Marylebone *(Valerie Meyers)*

89   43 Bryanston Square, Marylebone *(Valerie Meyers)*

93   Maugham and Syrie, 1920s

99   Gerald Haxton *(Diana Marr-Johnson)*

113   Leslie Howard and Bette Davis in *Of Human Bondage,* 1934

124   Sasha Kropotkin, portrait by Gerald Kelly *(Crawford Municipal Art Gallery, Cork, Ireland)*

127   Boris Savinkov before the Soviet tribunal, 1925

146   José Ferrer and Rita Hayworth in *Miss Sadie Thompson,* 1953

157   Maugham at Frederic Maugham's country house in Gloucestershire, c. 1923 *(Diana Marr-Johnson)*

161   Frederic Maugham as lord chancellor, 1938 *(Diana Marr-Johnson)*

173   Kenneth Clark *(Estate of Kenneth Clark, Margaret Hanbury, 27 Walcot Square, London SE11 4UB)*

188   Barbara Back

202   Hugh Walpole

231   Christopher Isherwood, early 1950s *(Don Bachardy)*

245   Glenway Wescott, Bill Miller and Maugham, early 1940s

257   Maugham and Robin Maugham, 1945 *(Diana Marr-Johnson)*

266   Maugham smoking cigarette and leaning on a desk, c. 1944 *(Loren Rothschild)*

272   Maugham with Bert Alanson, and Liza and Mabel Alanson, Yosemite National Park, 1945 *(Department of Special Collections, Stanford University Libraries)*

275   Alan Searle with Maugham, early 1950s *(Diana Marr-Johnson)*

284   Gerald Kelly painting Maugham
       Portrait of Maugham by Gerald Kelly, 1949 *(Loren Rothschild)*

285   Jacob Epstein sculpting Maugham, 1951 *(Diana Marr-Johnson)*

286 Graham Sutherland, portrait of Maugham, 1949 *(Loren Rothschild)*

292 Maugham seated on a sofa, with Mediterranean in background, 1947 *(Loren Rothschild)*

297 Maugham seated on floor in front of bookcase, 1950 *(Loren Rothschild)*

300 Maugham, "a pretty good likeness . . . in his old age," c. 1951 *(Loren Rothschild)*

302 Ann Fleming *(Mark Amory)*

309 Maugham on his eightieth birthday, "in my study & with all the books I have ever written," 1954 *(Loren Rothschild)*

310 Maugham at the villa; Picasso's *La Grecque* in the background, 1954 *(Loren Rothschild)*

314 Maugham with his dog Ching, on staircase of the villa, c. 1959 *(Loren Rothschild)*

316 Francis King, 1950s *(Francis King)*

321 Maugham and a fellow pupil, Charles Etheridge, King's School, 1958 *(King's School, Canterbury, Archives)*

323 Maugham and Winston Churchill, c. 1951 *(Loren Rothschild)*

329 Diana Marr-Johnson, Maugham's niece, May 2002 *(Valerie Meyers)*

333 Maugham smoking cigarette in brocaded dressing gown, c. 1963 *(Loren Rothschild)*

339 King's School garden, where Maugham's ashes are placed *(Valerie Meyers)*

148 Map: Maugham's Asia

Acknowledgments

I AM PLEASED to acknowledge the help I received while writing this book. My greatest debt is to Loren and Frances Rothschild, who allowed my wife and me to be the first biographers to study their great Somerset Maugham collection, and gave us splendid hospitality. Gill Drey was, as always, a generous host in London. Paul Pollak and Peter Henderson at King's School in Canterbury, and Elizabeth Serebriakoff at the medical library of St. Thomas's Hospital, were extremely helpful. Robert Calder and Stuart Hunt sent valuable information.

I had conversations about Maugham, long before I began work on this book, with several of his old friends, now gone: Alexander Frere, David Garnett, John Lehmann, David Posner, Peter Quennell, Frank Swinnerton and Rebecca West. For personal interviews I am grateful to Don Bachardy, Patrick Leigh Fermor, Francis King, Bluey Mavroleon and Diana Marr-Johnson.

For letters and phone calls about Maugham I thank the British Home Office, Peter Burton, John Edwards, Gregory Freidan, Alan Jutzi, John le Carré, Richard Nickson, Maugham's grandson Nicolas Paravicini, Frederic Raphael, Lord Rothschild, Burt Rubin and Taki Theodoracopulos. Many friends provided addresses and leads, articles and books, advice and encouragement: Paul Alkon, Mark Amory (for copies of Maugham's letters to Ann Fleming), Elena Balashova, Kate Bucknell, William Calder, Keith and Nora Crook, Anthony and Sarah Curtis (for unpublished BBC material), Quentin Curtis, Joseph Dobrinsky, Peter Firchow, Joseph Frank, Donald Hall, John Halperin (for interviews with Maugham's daughter and nieces), Carolyn Hillman, Nicholas Howe, Anthony Julius, Christian Kopff, Dan Laurence, Roger Louis (who invited me to try out my ideas in Texas), Martin Morland, Thomas Moser, Dr. Mario Papagni, David Stafford, Peter Viertel, Stanley Weintraub and Dennis Wills.

A number of contemporary authors kindly answered my query about what Maugham meant to them: Martin Amis, Anita Brookner, A. S. Byatt, Peter Carey, Margaret Drabble, Alan Hollinghurst, David Lodge, Muriel Spark, Paul Theroux (who also introduced me to the Rothschilds) and A. N. Wilson. I discuss their response in the last chapter.

I am grateful to the staffs of Stanford University and the Ransom Humanities Research Center at the University of Texas, where I did extensive research on Maugham; to Shrewsbury School and Keble College, Oxford (for Harry Philips); to Barry Pateman, Emma Goldman Archives, University of California, Berkeley (for Sasha Kropotkin); to the Bancroft Library, University of California, Berkeley, History and Archives Department, San Francisco Public Library, *San Francisco Examiner* and National Personnel Records Center (for Gerald Haxton); to the Bundesarchiv, Berlin and Bundesarchiv, Koblenz (for Joseph Goebbels). The following libraries answered queries and sent photocopies of Maugham's vast, unpublished correspondence: University of Arkansas; Bodleian Library; Boston University; British Library; University of California, Santa Barbara; Centre for Kentish Studies; Churchill College, Cambridge; Cornell University; Harvard University; Harvard University Archives; Hoover Institution; House of Lords; Huntington Library; University of Illinois; Imperial War Museum; Indiana University; University of Iowa; King's College, Cambridge; Library of Congress; London University; University of Michigan; Morgan Library; University of New Brunswick; New York Public Library; New York University and the Harold Acton Papers, Villa La Pietra, Florence (Marvin Taylor); Northwestern University; University of Oregon; Princeton University; Public Record Office (UK); Sotheby's (New York); University of South Carolina; University of Southern California; Southern Illinois University; Tate Gallery; Texas A & M University; University of Tulsa; Washington University, St. Louis; University of Western Australia; and Yale University. The library at the University of California, Berkeley, a major resource for all my work since the 1960s, has been enormously helpful.

As always, my wife, Valerie Meyers, assisted with the archival research, read and improved each chapter, and compiled the index.

Preface

SOMERSET MAUGHAM lived for nearly ninety-two years, wrote seventy-eight books and kept his faithful audience from the late Victorian era to the twenty-first century. He was obsessed by his critical reputation, carefully planned the pattern of his career and gradually phased out each of his literary genres. Somersault was adept at every kind of work he ever did: as an anthologist and as a writer of novels, stories, stage and screen plays, art and travel books, autobiographies, reportage and essays; and as a doctor, linguist, secret agent, war propagandist, government adviser, art connoisseur, philanthropist and presenter of his films.

Though Maugham's life and works have been intensively examined, my discovery of unpublished material and my research in the hitherto unknown Rothschild Collection have revealed a great deal of new information about his years at Heidelberg and on Capri; medical training at St. Thomas's Hospital; espionage in the South Seas; relations with Sasha Kropotkin and Boris Savinkov in Russia; condemnation by Joseph Goebbels; quarrels with D. H. Lawrence and Edmund Wilson; friendships with Noël Coward and Christopher Isherwood; knowledge of art and collection of paintings.

I have found his first childhood letter, in French; deciphered the mysterious Moorish sign he adopted as his personal symbol; and filled in the obscure background of his longtime lover Gerald Haxton. I describe the pervasive influence of Joseph Conrad on Maugham's works as well as his own powerful impact on George Orwell, Anthony Burgess and V. S. Naipaul. I show how his four mistresses and three lovers are portrayed in his work; and how Rose Crowley appears in *The Magician,* Harry Philips in *Of Human Bondage,* Barbara Back in *The Constant Wife* and Albert Arthur Kemp, the model for "Lord George," in *Cakes and Ale.*

Maugham, who really loved men but tried to love women, found it difficult to accept, even fought against, his deepest sexual feelings. Throughout his life he wavered uncertainly between his hidden desires and his wish for a respectable position in society. His repressed homosexuality was revealed in his strange analysis of El Greco and in the covert homosexual themes in three of his finest works: *The Circle, The Narrow Corner* and "The Kite." The struggle between sexual repression and artistic expression was at the heart of his personal and creative life.

Somerset
Maugham

1

Paris and King's School

1874–1889

THE EARLY DEATH of his parents and his consequent exile from home and country gave Somerset Maugham a wretched start in life. He shared Kipling's belief that "when young lips have drunk deep of the bitter waters of Hate, Suspicion, and Despair, all the Love in the world will not wholly take away that knowledge." "I had many disabilities," he wrote, looking back on his early days. "I was small; I had endurance but little physical strength; I stammered; I was shy; I had poor health. I had no facility for games." His miserable childhood left permanent scars, but provided rich material for the poignant, autobiographical *Of Human Bondage* and for the deeply moving *Cakes and Ale*. His stammer, a psychological and physical handicap, and his gradual awareness of his homosexuality made him furtive and secretive, and caused "an instinctive shrinking from my fellow men that has made it difficult for me to enter into any familiarity with them." A lifelong exile and wanderer, Maugham gave the impression of being icy, remote and arrogant. The love and affection, insight and sympathy that he repressed in everyday life were channeled into the creation of plays and stories. Maugham's teasing combination of passion and tenderness, coldness and cynicism was stamped on his life and work.

Maugham's family had for many generations been small farmers in the Lake District of northwest England. After his great-grandfather, ruined by the failure of a local bank during the Napoleonic wars, sent his son to

Robert Maugham (grandfather)

London, the family moved from agriculture into the learned professions. Maugham's grandfather Robert (1799–1862), educated at Appleby Grammar School, was articled as a solicitor in 1817 and later taken into partnership. In 1825 he helped found the Law Society—which was and still is "responsible for the education and examination of all articled clerks and the admission of all Solicitors in England and Wales"—and was its secretary from 1831 to 1856. In 1830 he also established a weekly newspaper, the *Legal Observer*, which "combined current professional news with reports of cases and articles of practical interest," and remained its editor and sole proprietor until 1856. Soon after leaving the newspaper he told a friend that "After 26 years daily labour & constant anxiety in conducting the *Legal Observer* I was not sorry to retire, & devote in future my whole time & best exertions to the interests of this Society. In the last No. of the *L.O.* I was authorised to give the inclosed [Report] as a 'flourish of trumpets,' on leaving the field." Maugham's active and energetic grandfather—whose motto was *In Finem Perseverans* (persevering to the end)—wrote many books, including a *Treatise on the Law of Attornies* (1825), that provided lawyers "with a text-book covering every aspect of their professional activities."[1]

This pillar of the legal establishment was capable of bizarre behavior. When a servant once handed him a dish of potatoes baked in their skins, he stopped carving the roast beef, picked up the offensive food and flung it at the pictures on the walls. Maugham, who twice in print recounts this iconoclastic story, gives no explanation of this eccentric behavior or the reactions of others at the table, who politely chose to ignore it. Why did his cook prepare potatoes in this way if he didn't like them? Did his grandfather feel a sudden antagonism to the family portraits or a need to liven up the dinner party? Did he, overworked and under pressure, seize this trivial occasion to vent his long-repressed rage? Or was it a mental aberration, preceding a nervous breakdown?

Maugham's father, Robert Ormond Maugham, was born in 1823. As an adventurous young man he traveled to Greece, Turkey and Asia Minor as well as to Fez, in Morocco. His home was filled with exotic objects he'd acquired en route: pottery from Rhodes, Tanagra statuettes and Ottoman daggers with richly decorated hilts. In 1848 the young Robert, following his father's profession but keeping clear of his influence, established his firm in Paris. He eventually built up a flourishing practice among the British expatriate community and accepted a semi-official appointment as legal adviser to the British embassy. Then, as now, "it was the custom for every British embassy to have an Honorary Legal Adviser, who earned prestige but not money, for giving legal advice about local issues, such as leasing embassy property or engaging a local lawyer if a British subject was accused of a serious crime. Issues of international law would go to the Foreign Office Legal Advisers." Robert opened an office opposite the embassy at 54, Faubourg St. Honoré, and worked there from early in the morning until seven at night.

A friend told Maugham that his grandfather was "the ugliest little man I ever saw"; and Maugham told his nephew Robin that his jaundiced-looking father was also "very ugly—almost a monster to look at, with a

Robert Ormond Maugham (father)

large, very yellow face and very yellow eyes." Maugham, fascinated and repelled by his father's appearance, discussed personal ugliness in several of his works. In *The Gentleman in the Parlour,* a record of his travels in Southeast Asia, a French governor admits that he's ugly and regrets that his ugliness has inspired ridicule rather than terror or respect. When people first see him they don't shrink from horror, which could be flattering, but burst out laughing. In Maugham's early fiction, however, women—like his mother—fall in love with repulsive men. In *Mrs. Craddock* the heroine exclaims to her fiancé that "when a woman loves an ugly man, they say his ugliness only makes him more attractive, and I shall love your faults as I love everything that is yours." And in "The Force of Circumstance," a wife tells her husband: "You're an ugly, little fat man, Guy, but you've got charm. I can't help loving you."[2]

Violet Hammersley, a childhood friend in Paris, saw the considerable charm beneath his father's forbidding appearance: "Mr. Maugham had a large, very sallow face one timidly explored, but when he took me on his knee to blow his watch open, I remember stealing over me a sense of complete safety and happiness." Maugham called his father "a very loving parent and wonderfully kind to children." But, infinitely closer to his beloved mother, he also told Robin that the remote and obsessively diligent lawyer "was a stranger to me when he was alive."[3] Like his grandfather and father, Maugham was hardworking, ambitious and successful, professionally competent and financially astute. Like his father, he became a cosmopolitan traveler and art collector. He also thought he was physically unattractive, but believed he could overcome that formidable disadvantage.

II

MAUGHAM'S MATERNAL GRANDFATHER, Major Charles Snell, served in India, where he died in 1841. After his death his wife, Anne, took her young daughter Edith, who "could prattle Hindustani much better than English," from India to England. The widow then moved to France, and supported herself by writing seventy novels and children's books in French. In 1863, the same year he opened his Paris law office, the forty-year-old Robert Maugham married the twenty-three-year-old Edith. They moved into an elegant apartment at 25, avenue d'Antin, facing the Champs-Élysées and close to the Rond-Point. Maugham, who often emphasized women's fine complexions in his letters and fiction, described his mother as "very small, with large brown eyes and hair of a rich reddish gold, exquisite features, and a lovely skin." When a lady friend asked his mother, who was very beautiful and attracted many charming young admirers, why she remained faithful to her ugly little husband, she smiled and gently answered that in all their married years he'd never hurt her feelings. She, presumably, was easily wounded and valued his kindness too much to hurt his feelings. Their first three sons were Charles Ormond (1865–1935), Frederic Herbert (1866–1958) and Henry Neville (1868–1904).

Violet Hammersley recalled the ominous atmosphere that surrounded the vivacious yet fragile young woman: "Mrs. Maugham was my god mother. She was lovely, with russet hair, brown eyes and a creamy complexion, and there was an air of romance and tragedy about her. My mother, who took me visiting with her of an afternoon, often had tea with

Edith Maugham (mother)

Mrs. Maugham. She would give me a doll dressed like a fisherwoman to play with ... while they talked in low and earnest tones. Mrs. Maugham died very young."[4]

Maugham later recalled an anecdote that concerned the power of ugliness and revealed his mother's sympathetic character. Like the question about Edith's fidelity to her husband, it suggests the cynical sexual mores of that expatriate Jamesian society: "The Lady Anglesey of that time, an American, was a pretty and agreeable woman, in spite of which Lord Anglesey ran away with a Frenchwoman. Mrs. Maugham, calling upon the disconsolate deserted marchioness, tried to console her by saying that he would surely regret it and come back to her before long. 'For I have met this Madame X and she is, I can assure you, as ugly as sin.' 'Oh, oh dear,' said Lady Anglesey, 'if she really is as ugly as that he will never come back.' "

William Somerset Maugham, Edith's youngest son, was born in the British embassy in Paris (to protect him from later conscription into the French army) on January 25, 1874. In that year the French Impressionists held their first exhibition, Wagner's *Götterdammerung* and Verdi's *Requiem* were first performed, Flaubert's *The Temptation of St. Anthony* and Hardy's *Far from the Madding Crowd* were published. Winston Churchill and Chaim Weizmann, G. K. Chesterton and Gertrude Stein, Robert Frost and Arnold Schönberg were born that year—and Maugham (who lived almost ninety-two years) outlived them all. Rooted in the nineteenth century but acutely sensitive to all the major artistic currents of the twentieth, he collected Impressionist art, frequented Wagner's operas in Bayreuth, was influenced by Flaubert's satiric style, wrote a novel about Hardy, and was a friend and exact contemporary of Churchill, whose parents were married that same year in the Paris embassy.

Maugham—an unusual name, rather like "Waugh" in spelling and sound—comes from Malham and Kirkby Malham in the West Riding of Yorkshire. "Somerset" came from his mother's ancestor General Sir Henry Somerset (1794–1862). Maugham disliked the name "William" and told Frank Swinnerton, who'd rehabilitated it in one of his novels, that he'd always regretted "owning" that silly name. In *Cakes and Ale* the autobiographical narrator, Willie Ashenden, who thinks his apparently respectable first name sounds ridiculous, also dislikes his second name and spends a good deal of time inventing others that seem more suitable. Influenced by Sir Walter Scott, he prefers the more elegantly polysyllabic Roderic Ravensworth and Ludovic Montgomery. In real life, Maugham compromised by publishing as "W. Somerset Maugham," reducing the name to an initial on the title page of his books. He encouraged friends to call him "Willie."

Impressionist paintings of the 1870s—Renoir's *Pont Neuf,* Degas' *Nursemaid in the Luxembourg Gardens,* Manet's *The Road Menders in the Rue de Berne* and Monet's *Rue Montorgueil Decked Out with Flags*—give a vivid idea of Parisian life when Maugham was a boy. His brother Frederic recalled that in those days the Champs-Élysées was elegant and residential: "there were no shops, no theatres, and I believe only one hotel for visitors. The broad avenue leading from the Rond-Point to the Arc de Triomphe was lined with private houses and luxurious apartments."

All the household servants as well as Willie's kind, reliable and deeply loyal nursemaid, with whom he shared a bedroom, were French. Every morning and afternoon in fine weather she took him out to play with his French friends on the Champs-Élysées. Like young Marcel in *Swann's Way* by Proust (born in Paris three years before Maugham), he might catch a glimpse of a favorite girl, "who continued to beat up and catch her shuttlecock until her governess, with a blue feather in her hat, had called her away."[5] Violet Hammersley, recapturing that long-faded atmosphere, remembered Willie—who took pleasure in fooling the gullible vendors—as both innovative and deceptive: "Being considered highly imaginative, he was allowed to invent what we should play. . . . [He] fascinated us by distributing false sous at the 'Kiosques' where paper windmills and coloured balloons and pieces of flat gingerbread pricked out in patterns were sold; or to the itinerant old woman with a tin strapped to her back out of which gaufrettes (wafer biscuits) were produced, powdered with icing sugar. These we ate as we sat on benches watching Guignol," the violent puppet shows that were Willie's first introduction to the theater. In the summers, the Maughams rented a villa in Deauville, a then unfashionable village on the Normandy coast. In the early 1880s, when Edith became sickly, she and Willie spent the winters in the milder climate of Pau, a health resort near the Pyrenees, in southwest France.

Born in Paris of a mother who'd lived there from early childhood, Willie spent his first ten years in France and—oddly enough—never seems to have visited England during that time. He always spoke French to the servants at home and was sent to a local French school. His father worked most of the time, his mother became a reclusive invalid and his three older brothers were at school in England. So his French was very good, but he had only a limited knowledge of English. On December 24, 1880, when he was nearly seven, Willie wrote his very first letter, to his parents—from whom, strangely, he was separated at Christmas. He wrote in a firm hand, in formal French rather than in English, and probably had his letter corrected by his nursemaid: "cher papa, chere maman. votre petit willie est heureux au jour de noel de vous exprimer ses meilleurs souhaits, et sa reconnaissante affection. croyez-moi, cher papa, chere maman, votre fils respectueux, willie maugham."[6]

In 1877, when he was three, Willie's older brothers left for Dover College. He was the adored youngest child and, except during the school holidays, the focus of his mother's love. When he was five, Edith gave birth to a stillborn infant. She also suffered from tuberculosis of the lungs, and Willie remembered the donkeys that stopped outside their door each day to provide her with fresh milk to build up her strength. Every morning, after she had taken her bath and was resting in bed, he was permitted to visit her. And when she invited lady friends for gossip and tea, he was asked to recite from memory a charming fable by La Fontaine.

Edith had been encouraged to have children on the theory, popular in those days, that childbirth was good for tubercular women. But the birth of her sixth son, who died the following day—on Willie's eighth birthday, January 25, 1882—weakened her both psychologically and physically. A few days later, on January 31, Edith, whose startling beauty had lit up the most elegant French salons, died at the age of forty-one. The death of his beloved mother had a tremendous emotional impact on the small child. He always remembered the melancholy atmosphere, silence and hopeless despair as the nurses passed through the sickroom, and retained a memory of the racking coughs, the spitting of blood, the sudden hemorrhages and the pale figure extended on her deathbed—no longer able to give him the Proustian good-night kiss. Edvard Munch's painting *Dead Mother and Child* (1899) portrayed this tragic atmosphere in the days when tuberculosis was pandemic.

Edith's long-expected yet shocking death forged in his mind the critical connection between love and suffering—a major theme in all his works. He believed that the only pure and selfless love was a mother's for her children, but that boys were better off when not "burdened" by too much parental love. The death of a truly affectionate mother was unbearable. Edith's death left him with a permanent sense of loss, and made him feel both guilty and bitter. His early experience of disease and death motivated his decision to become a doctor, but his anger and sense of abandonment developed into suspicion and hostility to women.

D. H. Lawrence, with whom Maugham would later tangle in Mexico, was himself shattered by his own mother's death. He expressed his guilt with a repulsive reptilian metaphor that suggested his life had been permanently poisoned: "I think I loved my mother more than I ever shall love anyone else. You do not know how much we were to each other. And these days crawl over me like horrid tortoises." Writing self-reflectively about Stendhal, Maugham observed that "most children, when they grow up, forget their grievances. Stendhal was unusual in that at fifty-three he harbored his old resentments." An invalid during his childhood, idealized after her early death, Edith always remained perfect—and unattainable— in his memory. At boarding school he used to hope that it was all a dream, that he would awake one day and find himself once again at home with his mother. He often exclaimed that her death was a wound which had never entirely healed. Toward the end of his long life, his daughter recalled, "I was in his sitting-room when he told me to wait while he went upstairs. When he came down he was holding a long strand of his mother's hair— he'd kept it [along with her photograph on his bedside table] all those years. I was very moved but also appalled"—by the still bitter wound of her loss.[7] Willie inherited his mother's short stature, melancholy tempera- ment and tubercular lungs as well as her good taste, delight in luxuries and love of social life.

In June 1884, two and a half years after Edith's death, Robert Maugham died of stomach cancer at the age of sixty-one, and left each son a disappointing £150 a year. The orphaned Willie, aged ten, was sent to live with his paternal uncle in England. He'd suddenly lost his mother, his father and a devoted nursemaid, and had to adapt to a new language, family, home, country and school. After Edith's death he'd been taken out of his French school and given daily lessons by an Anglican clergyman whose church was connected to the embassy. Willie learned English by reading aloud from the police-court news in the *Evening Standard*—a far cry from the gentle fables of La Fontaine—and he always remembered the horrific details of the murder stories. His English, however, was still shaky, and in prep school he was ridiculed for mispronouncing the word "unstable" to rhyme with the Kentish town of Dunstable.

III

THE REVEREND HENRY MACDONALD Maugham (1828–97), Angli- can vicar of Whitstable, was, a parishioner recalled, "a stoutish well fed looking individual with a cross dangling on an ample breast and usually accompanied by his womenfolk." Maugham's brother Frederic called his uncle "a very narrow-minded and far from intelligent cleric . . . severe, pedantic, and bigoted," and felt he lacked sufficient warmth and sympathy to become a surrogate parent. Abruptly shifted from a luxurious to an austere home, Willie retained bitter memories of his uncle for more than fifty years. He called the penny-pinching, hypocritical vicar an incredibly lazy man who made his assistants do all the work of the parish. The vicar caustically told one of his curates, who had an unpleasant voice but loved to sing in church, that God would be better pleased if he praised Him only

Rev. Henry Macdonald
Maugham (uncle), c. 1880

Barbara von Scheidlin
Maugham (aunt)

The Vicarage, Whitstable

High Street, Whitstable, 1890

in his heart. His nobly born German wife, Sophie, a childless Hausfrau also in her fifties, was a strict, unsympathetic woman who rarely left the house except to go to church or visit the local shops.

Whitstable, on the North Sea coast of Kent, had a maritime atmosphere and a briny smell. The weatherboarded fishermen's houses were clustered in the narrow streets around the port and perched on the edge of the shingle beach. The town looked across the Thames estuary to the Isle of Sheppey and to the spectacular sunsets once painted by Turner. "It consisted of a high street," Maugham wrote, "in which were the shops, the bank, the doctor's house, and the houses of two or three coalship owners; round the little harbour were shabby streets in which lived fishermen and poor people." The working class went to the Dissenting Chapel and were studiously ignored, even condemned, by the intensely snobbish vicar. The town was famous for its delicious oysters, "one of the few things—the very few—[Maugham] liked about Whitstable."[8]

The shy and lonely Willie was forbidden, in that rigidly stratified society, to play with the children of "common" people. He was small and frail for his age, but cunning. "I wasn't even likeable as a boy," he later said. "I was withdrawn and unhappy, and rejected most overtures of sympathy over my stuttering and shyness." So he retreated into books and became, from an early age, a great reader: "Scott was considered rather improper reading for a child, but I read the whole of him before I was ten. I also read *The Arabian Nights*. I can see it now, in three large fat illustrated volumes. Expurgated, of course. I read Captain Marryat, and every novel Harrison Ainsworth ever wrote," as well as Lewis Carroll's *Alice* books.[9]

Sundays, devoted entirely to worship, were even more austere than the rest of the week. When the long and tedious church service finally concluded, the Maughams drove home in a carriage for their Sunday joint. Willie got half a boiled egg. After dinner, the vicar opened his prayer book to the appropriate place and instructed Willie to memorize the collect of the day and recite it at teatime. The household's religious routine gave Maugham a thorough knowledge of the Bible, and his works are richly laced with biblical allusions.

Like Melville's Billy Budd, Willie "was apt to develop an organic hesitancy, in fact more or less of a [stammer] or even worse." It was intensified by the death of his parents and exile from Paris, his harsh and loveless life with the vicar, the bullying of his classmates and cruelty of the oafish schoolmasters, and lasted to the very end of his life. One day, when Willie had to travel alone from London back to Whitstable, he joined the long third-class queue, but when the time came to ask for his ticket he could not state his destination. As he stood there stammering, two impatient men pushed him aside and exclaimed: "We can't wait all night for you. Stop wasting our time." He was forced to go back to the end of the line and start all over again, and never forgot that searing humiliation.

Maugham revealed his feelings about his own disability in an intensely personal passage on the novelist Arnold Bennett, whom he met in Paris in 1905: "Arnold was afflicted with a very bad stammer; it was painful to watch the struggle he sometimes had to get the words out. It was torture to him. Few realised the exhaustion it caused him to speak. What to most men is as easy as breathing was to him a constant strain. It tore his nerves to pieces. . . . [There was] the minor exasperation of thinking of a good, amusing or apt remark and not venturing to say it in case the stammer ruined it."[10] The extremely emotional language of this passage—afflicted, painful, torture, exhaustion, strain, tore his nerves, exasperation—conveys the constant frustration and agony of impaired speech. Willie's stammer had a profound effect on his character and prevented him from continuing in the family profession and becoming a lawyer. It made him a victim and intensified his introspection, turned him away from people and toward his artistic vocation.

IV

IN MAY 1885, after a year at a local academy, the eleven-year-old Willie—a little French boy, heartbroken by his parents' death—entered King's School in Canterbury. The oldest public school in England, it traced its origins to the fifth century, when Kent was a kingdom, and had endured for thirteen hundred years. It began as an abbey school, where the rudiments of learning were taught by Augustinian monks. After the dissolution of the cathedral monastery in 1541, it was refounded by Henry VIII as the King's School. Adjacent to Canterbury Cathedral and sharing its history, the school stands below its lofty towers and shares its sacred precincts. "There was a wonderfully cobwebbed feeling about their dizzy and intoxicating antiquity. . . . The whole atmosphere was strangely light and airy, full of the sound of bells and the cries of jackdaws floating around the great Bell Harry Tower of the Cathedral."

Maugham wrote that "the neighbouring clergy sent their sons there. It was united by a long tradition to the Cathedral: its headmaster was an honorary Canon, and a past headmaster was the Archdeacon. Boys were encouraged there to aspire to Holy Orders."[11] Willie, however, soon lost his faith in the Christian religion. The school had 180 students, and the distinguished old boys include Thomas Linacre (doctor to Henry VIII), the playwright Christopher Marlowe, the physician William Harvey, the aesthete Walter Pater, the novelist Hugh Walpole, Field Marshal Bernard Montgomery, the film directors Carol Reed and Michael Powell, the travel writer Patrick Leigh Fermor, the Buddhist Alan Watts and the art critic Edward Lucie-Smith.

The students in the junior school were mainly sons of the local clergy, officers of the local garrison, and manufacturers and merchants in the town. The cubicles in the dormitory, divided by polished pitch-pine partitions and enclosed by green curtains, contained a bed, a chair and a small basin on a washstand. The leaden diet consisted of "boiled beef, boiled cabbage, boiled onions, boiled carrots, boiled potatoes, and slabs of near-stale bread." But the senior boys, imitating the mode established at Eton,

Entrance to King's School

Maugham as a schoolboy, 1884

Maugham (first row, third from right) behind
Leonard Ashenden, King's School, 1885

dressed elegantly in a "black coat, black striped trousers, starched wing collar, and black tie, and a straw boater worn at a jaunty angle."

Young Willie, like his mother, spoke a foreign language better than he spoke English, and he found it especially difficult to become an English schoolboy. He'd never held a cricket bat or kicked a soccer ball and, in that homogeneous and conformist society, saw himself and was seen by others as a foreigner and outsider. His brother Frederic, a much more outgoing, athletic and self-confident boy, who was at Dover College with his brothers, recalled: "My life at Dover was very unhappy for the first year or two, for I was a shy and doubtless an unattractive boy with a slight French accent and no knowledge of games. My brothers and I were called 'frog-gies' since we came from Paris, and, I suspect, wore French clothes."[12] Willie went to King's, rather than to Dover, its athletic and academic rival, because it was only six miles from Whitstable.

During his four years at King's School Willie studied Greek, Latin, English, history, religion, mathematics and French (where he must have been the star of the class), but was not cunning enough to avoid mockery and humiliation. When a fierce master (an ordained minister, like all the teachers) asked him to translate a passage and he began to stammer, the boys burst out laughing and the master shouted: "Sit down, you fool. I don't know why they put you in this form." Seventy years later Maugham recalled his degradation and told Ann Fleming that "on his arrival at Can-terbury he had been placed in the fifth form but stuttered when doing a Latin *construe* and the master and boys laughed and he was demoted to the third form." He had the usual schoolboy crush on the handsome boy he called Rose in *Of Human Bondage,* as well as some adolescent love affairs. Late in life, after meeting an old man at the Garrick Club, he casually told his companion Alan Searle: "Oh, he's someone I went to bed with at King's." Maugham later condemned the poisonous atmosphere at the school, which engendered "class consciousness, clannishness and an intolerable conservatism. [It] attached an exaggerated value to sport and looked upon learning with suspicion."[13] Despite all the discouragement, he worked well in the lower forms and won prizes and scholarships.

Willie's schooling was interrupted when he developed a potentially dangerous case of pleurisy, and he left school before reaching the sixth form. Desperately unhappy both at school and in his uncle's house, he was delighted to return to his French milieu and spend the winters of 1888 and 1889 with an English tutor in Hyères, near the south coast, just east of Toulon. Though Maugham certainly hated King's School as a student, he later told the headmaster that, when he felt nostalgic, "I often come down to Canterbury and wander about the School buildings." He remained strongly attached to King's, became a generous benefactor and, in a strange twist of fate, finally had his ashes interred there.

Maugham's Parisian childhood gave him a dual viewpoint that made him feel estranged from both France and England. This sense of alien-ation, compounded with his debilitating stammer, isolated him from ordi-nary life at the same time that it forged his artistic spirit. He wrote:

*Maugham (in chair, second from right) wearing
scholar's gown, King's School, 1889*

The accident of my birth in France, which enabled me to learn French
and English simultaneously and thus instilled into me two modes of life,
two liberties, two points of view, has prevented me from ever identifying
myself completely with the instincts and prejudices of one people or the
other, and it is in instinct and prejudice that sympathy is most deeply
rooted; the accident of a physical infirmity, with its attendant nervous-
ness, separated me to a greater extent than would be thought likely from
the common life of others.

With his two native languages, his two nationalities, his two professions (doctor and writer) and his bisexuality, he was intensely aware of his
own dual character, and concerned with the problem of identity and self-
hood. Like his literary master Joseph Conrad, who called himself "a Polish nobleman, cased in British tar," Maugham could say: "Homo duplex
has in my case more than one meaning."[14]

2

Heidelberg and Medicine

1890—1897

AFTER TWO WINTERS in Hyères, where he was free to enjoy continental life and do as he wished, Willie had no desire to return to the restrictions and cruelties of King's School. His German aunt suggested a year at Heidelberg, where he could live comfortably as a student on his legacy of £150 a year. He jumped at the chance to escape from the vicarage and school, and she arranged for him to live at the pension of a friend.

In the nineteenth century, "the German universities were coming to be regarded as the research-centres of Europe, making rapid advances especially in three areas: natural sciences, biblical criticism, and idealist philosophy. German theatre, much influenced by the new Romantic reading of Shakespeare, was also being revived. . . . [And there was] strong German interest in mystical religious experience, vividly illustrated in the rediscovery of the Gnostic philosophy of Jakob Boehme and the visionary painting of Caspar David Friedrich." Thomas Carlyle and Ralph Waldo Emerson, who helped introduce German philosophy and literature to Anglo-American readers, did not attend a German university, but Coleridge, Longfellow, Pater, Henry Adams, William James and George Santayana had all studied in Germany. The influence of Prince Albert, and Queen Victoria's cult of her dead consort, had made England more responsive to German culture and customs, and introduced (for example) the German celebration of Christmas. The popular play *Old Heidelberg*

(1903), performed a decade after Maugham left the university and later filmed as *The Student Prince,* created the popular image of carefree academic life at the end of the nineteenth century.

After four sieges and battles in the seventeenth century, "little was left in the old town to bear witness to its departed glories." In Maugham's time, Heidelberg "consisted principally of one street three miles long, extending from the Railway Station to the Heilbronngate, the main buildings being . . . the Church of the Holy Ghost in the market-place, the Church of St. Peter, the University and the ruined castle." A pale blue haze from the chimneys hung over the jumbled roofs and tall spires of the churches, and the deep-chiming clocks and slow lilting dialect gave the town a pleasantly medieval air. Ancient signs, expressing the Germanic obsession with rules and prohibitions, quaintly announced: "it is forbidden to drive cows, oxen and other cloven-footed animals in the area."[1]

The riverine setting of Heidelberg, as Longfellow rapturously wrote in 1836, was extraordinarily attractive: "The town stands between steep and high mountains on the Neckar, just where the valley, before so narrow that you can almost throw a stone across, spreads out trumpet-mouthed into the broad plain of the Rhine. The change in the face of the landscape is sudden and beautiful,—no gradual transition, with broken and irregular hills, but the mountains go down with one grand sweep into the plain. Overlooking the town stand the ruins of a magnificent old castle,—the finest I have seen in Europe." Fifty years later, Maugham also "looked down upon the plain, a-quiver with the sun, stretching vastly before him: in the distance were the roofs of Mannheim and ever so far away the dimness of Worms. Here and there a more piercing glitter was the Rhine." The walks in the fir-clad hills above the old town satisfied the romantic and mystical longings of the *Wandervögel* and *Naturfreunden:* "The *Philosophenweg* is one of the loveliest walks in this part of the country. It begins from the banks of the Neckar, and wends its way up through the woods, finally losing itself in the network of paths which run through the *Odenwald.* . . . From the opposite bank, rising dimly out of the wisps of mist, the castle [as in Edinburgh and Prague] overshadows everything."[2]

The university—whose buildings were scattered all over Heidelberg and whose students ate their meals at the huge common *Mensa*—was renowned for classics, chemistry, medicine and law. There were many *Hörer,* or auditors, like Maugham, who were not formally enrolled for a degree, but paid a fee to attend lectures. Impressed by the barbaric and bloodthirsty dueling societies, whose members fenced without masks, Maugham "looked with awe at the students of the corps, their cheeks gashed and red, who swaggered about in their coloured caps." Their stiff manners were accentuated by the military dress, "the clicking of heels and the formal, cold voice they used for addressing strangers."

Instead of living (as in England) in a college, the sixteen-year-old Willie rented a room in a lodging house—similar to the one later described in Katherine Mansfield's *In a German Pension* (1911). Instead of following strict Oxford and Cambridge rules about tutorials, dining and curfew (enforced by the proctors and officious "bulldogs"), he was once again free to do exactly as he wished. The *Frau Professor* had two daughters and a son a few years younger than Willie. His cosmopolitan fellow students included a Chinese man, a Frenchman and "a tall, lanky New Englander who taught Greek at Harvard" and was portrayed as "Weeks" in *Of Human Bondage*.[3]

Willie found the Germanic *Stimmung* of Heidelberg—which emphasized order, cleanliness and obedience, enlivened by beer, tobacco and music—suited him perfectly. He took language lessons, went to the theater and opera, listened to the brass band play and watched the yellow-braided girls promenade round and round the *Stadtgarten*. He walked in the forest, skated in the winter, went swimming and canoeing in summer. He had endless and apparently profound conversations about art and literature, free will and determinism, love and death. He ate hearty meals and at night, exhausted by all this activity, fell into a heavy sleep between a downy cover and a feather mattress.

Absorbed as always in books, Willie read seriously in both French and German literature. His favorites in French were the *Maximes* of La Rochefoucauld, *La Princesse de Clèves* (which inspired his play *Caesar's Wife*), the tragedies of Racine, the novels of Voltaire, Stendhal's *Le Rouge et le Noir* and *La Chartreuse de Parme*, Balzac's *Père Goriot*, Flaubert's *Madame Bovary*, the works of Anatole France, the exotic tales of Pierre Loti and the well-crafted stories of Maupassant. He also came under the influence of Goethe, Schopenhauer and Ibsen. Though he knew nothing about music and had never heard any operas by Giacomo Meyerbeer, in 1891 he wrote a now lost centenary life of the once popular composer.

One of the luminaries of Heidelberg was Kuno Fischer (1824–1907), a philosopher and literary critic then at the height of his fame. The author of books on Shakespeare, Kant, Lessing, Goethe and Schiller, Fischer was a professor at the university for the last thirty-five years of his life. The students queued up early in order to get into his brilliant lectures, stood up when he entered the room and audibly shuffled their feet when they were displeased. Fischer, Maugham wrote, "was a dapper, short, stoutish man, neat in his dress, with a bullet head, white hair *en brosse*, and a red face. His little eyes were quick and shining. He had a funny, flattened snub nose. . . . His voice was powerful and he was a vivid, impressive, and exciting speaker." Schopenhauer's fashionable fin-de-siècle pessimism—which argued that human beings were victims of their own instincts, that free will and the afterlife were illusions—strongly attracted young Willie. Like the young hero in *Of Human Bondage,* "he believed that the world he was about to enter was a place of pitiless woe and of darkness."[4]

Willie first read Goethe's *Faust* and *Wilhelm Meister* (later the subject of a major essay) in Heidelberg. He once saw the mutton-chop-whiskered Ibsen (who died in 1906) drinking a glass of beer "in a café in Berlin. He came in and sat down at the table always reserved for him. His *Stammtisch.* I must say, he looked extremely angry, vexed, and disagreeable. But then, of course, he *was* all those things." Maugham, discussing drama in his book on China, tried to cut Ibsen down to size by asserting that he "uses the same plot over and over again. A number of people are living in a closed and stuffy room, then someone comes (from the mountains or over the sea) and flings the window open; everyone gets a cold in the head and the curtain falls."[5]

The impressionable Willie befriended the melancholy, pensive and poetical John Ellingham Brooks, ten years his senior. "After reading law at Cambridge, [Brooks] was called to the Bar, but soon left it, decided to become a writer and went to Heidelberg to learn German. . . . Brooks' dilettante approach to life was well matched by his handsome, finely-cut features, curly hair, pale blue eyes and a hesitant, wistful expression—perfection marred only by his shortness of stature." Brooks loved literature, and during their long walks together he introduced Willie to the most important contemporary English writers: the theological works of Cardinal Newman, the witty novels of George Meredith, the *Imaginary Portraits* of Pater, the rapturous poetry of Swinburne and FitzGerald's sensual translation of *The Rubáiyát of Omar Khayyám.*

Later on Maugham outgrew Brooks, who'd been his greatest social and intellectual influence. He conceded that he had charm, was devoid of envy and (like his own father) was unusually kind. But Maugham, hardworking and now successful, turned against him and scorned Brooks' touchiness, egoism, vanity and self-delusion. Maugham wrote that: "he is extremely sensitive and is hurt if you do not accept his own opinion of himself. He has a craving for admiration. . . . He was a man who saw nothing for himself, but only through a literary atmosphere, and he was dangerous because he had deceived himself into sincerity." Brooks, always intending to write, never actually wrote anything at all. Maugham gave him cameo roles as Hayward in *Of Human Bondage,* as Brown in *The Summing Up,* and described him under his own name in *A Writer's Notebook* and "Looking Back."

This precious aesthete and homosexual, who for years drifted in and out of Maugham's life, was his first lover. Unlike Brooks, who romanticized and idealized his sexual life, Maugham always felt fearful and guilty about being a homosexual and rejected the idea of a platonic, nonsexual male love. When discussing the illustrious French authors (Sainte-Beuve, Flaubert and the Goncourts) who gathered for dinner and conversation at Magny's, he wrote: "they talked of lesbianism and transcendental homosexuality—whatever that may mean."[6]

Willie's two years at Heidelberg, which had made him aware of the intellectual currents of Europe, were a richly formative experience. But in 1892 the eighteen-year-old, without parental guidance, still didn't know what to do with his life. After tasting freedom, he couldn't bear the idea of going to an English university, which he thought would be like going back to school. Though he certainly could have won a scholarship, he was eager to plunge into the real world and decided not to follow his three older brothers to Cambridge. He later regretted this decision and felt that more education would have helped him avoid a lot of mistakes. But on his ninetieth birthday, using his favorite quote from Job 1:7, he observed that he might have been right after all. Going to university would have steered him into the restricted life of a scholar: "Had I not stammered I would probably have had the same sort of classical education as others in my class of life. Instead of becoming a wanderer on the face of the earth, I would have gone to Cambridge as my brothers did and perhaps become a don and every now and then published a dreary book about French literature."

A family friend got him a position as clerk in an accountant's office in Chancery Lane. But he loathed the work, left after a month and in his first story, "A Bad Example," described this mechanical and supremely boring

St. Thomas's Hospital from across the Thames, 1939

job. He "manufactured from the office paper a pair of false cuffs to keep his own clean, and, having examined the nibs in both his penholders and sharpened his pencil, set to work. From then till one o'clock he remained at his desk, solemnly poring over figures, casting accounts, comparing balance-sheets, writing letters, occasionally going for some purpose or another into the clerks' office or into the room of one of the partners." Since literature was not an appropriate profession for a gentleman and he could not hope to support himself with his pen, he decided to become "a medical student because I could not announce to my guardian that I wished to be a writer."[7] After going to a crammer he passed the entrance examination—a considerable achievement, since he'd had no training in science—and on September 27, 1892 he entered St. Thomas's Hospital in London.

II

ON HIS EIGHTIETH birthday, in 1954, Maugham recalled the leisurely, socially stratified environment of late Victorian England, familiar to readers of Sherlock Holmes, that existed when he became a medical student.

It was "a world that knew nothing of 'planes, motor-cars, movies, radio, or telephones . . . a world that inadequately warmed itself with coal fires, lit itself by gas and paraffin lamps, and looked upon a bathroom as a luxury out of reach of all but the very wealthy. The well-to-do . . . drove in broughams and landaus, lesser folks in hansoms and four-wheelers."

In his early novel *Mrs. Craddock,* Maugham wrote that the boat from London to Greenwich "came to the tottering wharves of Millbank, and then to the footstool turrets of St. John's, the eight red blocks of St. Thomas's Hospital and the Houses of Parliament." The massive hospital still exists on the south bank of the Thames, facing Westminster Abbey and Big Ben. "It consists of eight separate blocks of solid Gothic architecture, joined together by a long corridor. The innumerable large rooms in the basement and on the ground floor serve as kitchens, laboratories, store-rooms, X-ray, Casualty and Outpatient Departments."[8] St. Thomas's, whose medical school had opened in 1871, was one of the best teaching hospitals in England. In 1860 the Florence Nightingale School, which under her direction became the model for training nurses, had been founded there. The first experiments with X-rays began in 1895—only a few months after Röntgen's discovery in Germany. Candles and gas were used for lighting throughout the hospital until electricity was finally introduced in 1900.

About ninety-five shy and confused young men, some of them graduates of Oxford and Cambridge, entered the school each year. The students began by reading N. C. Macnamara's textbook on *Diseases of Bones and Joints,* third edition (1887), and George Ellis' *Demonstrations in Anatomy: Being a Guide to the Knowledge of the Human Body Through Dissection,* eleventh edition (1890), by attending lectures in anatomy, and by dissecting and memorizing the parts of the human body in the laboratory. Maugham later recalled that "I was once obliged to study anatomy, a very dreary business . . . ; but one remark made by my teacher, when he was helping me in the dissection of a thigh, has always remained in my memory. I was looking in vain for a certain nerve and it needed his greater skill to discover it in a place in which I had not sought it. I was aggrieved because the text book had misled me. He smiled and said: 'You see, the normal is the rarest thing in the world.' " Willie took this lesson seriously in his writing career, and added that "it has entertained me not a little to discover the hidden oddity of men to all appearances most ordinary."

After passing his first exams in anatomy, biology and chemistry,

Ward in St. Thomas's Hospital, 1890s

Maugham went on to more interesting subjects. He studied William Walsham's *Surgery: Its Theory and Practice,* fourth edition (1892), and Sir William Osler's *The Principle and Practice of Medicine* (1892), attended lectures and gained practical experience in medicine, midwifery and surgery. He practiced bandaging on outpatients, learned auscultation and how to use a stethoscope, began dispensing drugs and took an exam in pharmacology. In 1894 he started his clinical training and took every opportunity to practice giving enemas to his fellow students. He spent six months with the house physician as medical clerk, first with outpatients and then on the men's and women's wards. His duties involved writing up case histories, making notes and performing tests as well as dressing wounds, taking out stitches and changing bandages. During operations, he handed instruments to the surgeons and washed away the blood. Thomas Eakins' *The Gross Clinic* (1875) portrayed these horrific procedures, which were not very different from those in Rembrandt's *Anatomy Lesson* (1633). Maugham also spent time treating injuries in the casualty wards, learned to use the ophthalmoscope and attended patients in the eye department. The work could be dangerous, and he caught septic tonsillitis from performing an autopsy on a badly decomposed corpse. Another student got blood poisoning after doing a postmortem and died within forty-eight hours. A friend who'd been absent for two days returned to find him naked and dead on a mortuary slab.

By 1896 Maugham began training in midwifery and practical obstetrics. The professor of gynecology expressed the typically disparaging attitude toward women, especially the impoverished residents of the filthy Lambeth slums that surrounded the hospital. He began his series of lectures by remarking that: "woman is an animal that micturates once a day, defecates once a week, menstruates once a month, parturates once a year and copulates whenever she has the opportunity."[9] In addition to attending cesarean births in the hospital, then rare and dangerous operations, Maugham also worked in the surrounding district, delivering an average of three babies a day in their Lambeth homes until he reached a grand total of sixty-three confinements in only three weeks.

The historian of St. Thomas's noted that the hospital did not provide obstetric services until late in the nineteenth century, and that the students received only minimal training:

> Lying-in cases had not been admissible in previous centuries because the governors were afraid of encouraging immorality. In the nineteenth century, however, during the reforms of the medical school, it was decided that the syllabus should include practical instruction in midwifery. . . . Students attended lying-in cases in their own homes, provided the cases were expected to be straightforward. The assistant obstetric physician was called in to difficult cases, as the students only received four months' training.

The young Maugham overcame the deep-rooted prejudice of his class, emphasized both by the professor of gynecology and by the hospital itself. He instinctively sympathized with the poor, undernourished and often brutalized women he treated. In the preface to his first novel, *Liza of Lambeth,* he described how students attended women in childbirth: "the messenger led you through the dark and silent streets of Lambeth, up stinking alleys and into sinister courts where the police hesitated to penetrate, but where your black bag protected you from harm." He was horrified to see children die of meningitis, and was particularly concerned about the fate of one woman, desperate to have a child, who risked a cesarean operation. When he came back to the ward and asked one of the nurses how the patient was progressing, he was told that she'd died—weakened like his mother—in childbirth. He was so shocked by this news that he almost burst into tears. Maugham also felt sorry for prostitutes, but his sympathy did not prevent him from patronizing them. One night in Piccadilly he picked up a whore, paid her a pound to spend the night with him—and got a dose of the clap.

In October 1897, after five years at St. Thomas's, Maugham passed his final examinations (the last one in surgery) and was awarded the diplomas of Licentiate of the Royal College of Physicians and Member of the Royal College of Surgeons. Though he never practiced medicine, he maintained a lifelong subscription to the *Lancet* and always completed the annual questionnaire of the British *Medical Directory*. When exasperated with doctors, he'd say that medicine had improved very little since Molière's time. A half century after graduating, he invoked his authority and reminded an American writer: "you forget that I was trained as a doctor. . . . *The modern contraceptive*. That's what has changed the world." And as late as 1961, still fully qualified as an L.R.C.P. and a M.R.C.S., he prescribed 100 Nembutal and 100 Oreden to his aged contemporary Lord Beaverbrook.[10]

While in medical school Maugham, always sensitive to suffering, rejected the influential ideas of Nietzsche, who'd connected physical and mental agony with the concept of genius and argued that pain was precious—that it enabled, indeed inspired, the artist to create. In *For Services Rendered* a character, speaking for Maugham, bitterly exclaims: "You doctors are a brutal lot and there's no end to the amount of pain you can bear in other people." When a friend's wife became seriously ill, he blasted inhumane doctors for allowing patients to endure pointless agony. And in his early novel *The Merry-Go-Round* Dr. Frank Hurrell, representing Maugham's point of view, attacks the theological idea that man is ennobled by pain and suffering. Pain, he says, "doesn't refine; it brutalizes. It makes people self-absorbed and selfish—you can't imagine the frightful egoism of physical suffering—querulous, impatient, unjust, greedy. I could name a score of petty vices that it engenders, but not a single virtue."

Maugham also rejected Christianity. His uncle had taught him to believe in miracles, and, like the hero of *Of Human Bondage,* as a boy he'd prayed to God to cure his agonizing stammer. He would wake up expecting to find himself transformed, and was always shattered to find that

God had either ignored his fervent petition or (even worse) lacked the power to help him. Reflecting on the suffering of children and the meaningless deaths he had seen in the hospital, he thought (like Ivan in *The Brothers Karamazov*) that the existence of evil contradicted the idea of a benign and omnipotent deity. In "The Judgement Seat" he stated that "if God cannot prevent Evil he is not all-powerful, and if he can prevent it and will not, he is not all-good."[11] In old age, without belief in the existence of God or the immortality of the soul, he faced death and oblivion with complete tranquility.

Maugham felt that his five years' training in a large London hospital, where he mastered the elements of science and learned everything he knew about human nature, had been a great help to him as a writer. When people were sick and fearful, they discarded their conventional masks and revealed their true selves. Later on, he wished he'd practiced medicine for a few years instead of writing the early books he eventually rejected: "It was idiotic. Absolutely idiotic. I could just as well have written at night and avoided the desperate financial struggle I had. I am sorry I abandoned medicine so soon."

Writing and medicine are not incompatible, and there is a long, distinguished tradition of doctors—from Conan Doyle to Walker Percy—who were authors.[12] After working all day at the hospital, Maugham walked across the river to his lodgings at 11 Vincent Square in Westminster. He bought a newspaper at Lambeth Bridge, and read it till his landlady served dinner. When ordinary men would have been completely exhausted, Maugham revved up for the most important part of the day. Deeply conscious of his ignorance and keen to educate himself, he read omnivorously. He studied serious books of philosophy and literature for two hours as a warm-up, saved the hardest work for last, and wrote novels and plays until bedtime. Writing about Chekhov, with whom he closely identified, he explained how the Russian author had made the most of his limited medical training: "After being qualified, he had never done more than three months' clinical work in a hospital and I surmise that his treatment of patients was somewhat rough and ready. But he had common sense and sympathy, and if he left nature to take its course, he probably did his patients as much good as a man with greater knowledge would have done." He quoted Chekhov's statement "Medicine is my lawful wife and literature only my mistress," but in his own life he reversed those priorities.[13]

III

DURING HIS SPRING holidays in 1894 Maugham went for the first
time to Italy. He rented a room on the Via Laura in Florence that gave
him, for only four lire a day, board, lodging and a view of Brunelleschi's
dome on the cathedral. Keen to master the language, he took a daily Italian lesson from the landlady's daughter. A friend who later lived with him
in Paris said Maugham was "a born linguist in spite of his slight stammer."
After dinner he went out looking for adventure, but still shy and silent,
though not quite as innocent (after his sexual experience with Brooks and
prostitutes) as he claimed to be, he returned home as virtuous as he'd
begun.

During his holidays of 1895, Maugham followed John Ellingham
Brooks to Capri, across the Bay of Naples. "The depravity of Tiberius, or
the salacity of Suetonius," wrote Anthony Burgess, "had left its mark on
an island all sodomy, lesbianism, scandal, and cosmopolitan artiness." The
natural beauty as well as the unnatural behavior—illegal in England but
permitted in Italy—had attracted many writers. In the nineteenth and
early twentieth centuries Ivan Turgenev, Axel Munthe, Gerhart Hauptmann, Norman Douglas, Maxim Gorky, Ivan Bunin and Rainer Maria
Rilke had visited and extolled the island. Conrad, who came to Capri in
1905, complained of the hot winds, violent contrasts and sexual scandals:
"This place here, this climate, this sirocco, this transmontana, these flat
roofs, these sheer rocks, this blue sea—are impossible. . . . The scandals of
Capri—atrocious, unspeakable, amusing, scandals international, cosmopolitan and biblical." D. H. Lawrence, who turned up in 1920, raged: "I am
very sick of Capri: it is a stewpot of semi-literary cats. . . . I can't stand this
island. I shall have to risk expense and everything, and clear out."[14]

Brooks represented everything that Lawrence hated about the place.
Although "Capri was very cheap, it was still too expensive for Brooks . . .
[who] lived on what he could scrounge." But in the spring of 1903, when
the American heiress and painter Romaine Goddard returned to Capri,
Brooks discovered the perfect solution to his financial problems. She
found him in a "worse financial state than usual, living in squalor and
slowly selling his possessions to buy food. She paid off his debts, put his
house in order, gave him enough to live on and, surprisingly, in view of her
own lesbian inclinations and his homosexuality, accepted his proposal of

John Ellingham Brooks

marriage." A year later, Romaine left Capri and "bought Brooks off with an allowance of £300 a year and the proviso that she never saw him again."

Maugham, quite at home in decadent Capri, shared a white-walled, flower-covered villa with Brooks and the homosexual E. F. Benson, who later wrote the popular and rather precious "Lucia" novels. Italian boys were paid to visit the house. Benson suggested the depraved side of Brooks' character and called him a dilettante "who, partly from laziness, partly from a flawless mental fastidiousness, made less of fine abilities and highly educated tastes than anyone I have ever known. . . . His mouth had a fine upper lip, priestlike and ascetic in character, but below was a full loose lower lip, as if the calls of the flesh had not yet been subdued. Hand-some though he was I found him sinister in appearance." Benson also recorded the sensual and aesthetic pleasures of the island in purple prose: "Long mornings of swimming through translucent waters interspersed with baskings in the sun, siestas, fresh figs, walks up to the top of Monte Solaro, home-comings in the glowing twilight, dinner under the vine per-gola, games of piquet in the café, strollings on to the piazza at night to look at the lights of Naples lying like a string of diamonds along the main with the sultry glow of Vesuvius behind."[15] Maugham loved swimming for hours, drying himself in the sun and then plunging once again into the warm, clear water.

Maugham's medical training destroyed his religious belief; but it turned him into a student of raw human nature, and taught him to observe closely, to adopt—like a surgeon with a scalpel—a cool, objective and clinical point of view. His emergent homosexuality, continued with Brooks on Capri, forced him to become reticent and secretive, to repress a vital part of his life. In all his important roles—exile, traveler, artist, homosexual, husband and spy—Maugham was to remain an alienated outsider.

3

Liza of Lambeth and Spain

1897–1899

IN 1897, when he finished medical school, the twenty-three-year-old Maugham was poor, shy and acutely aware of his physical shortcomings. Self-conscious about his height, he tended to cultivate friends who were also short. He had a wide, jutting, somewhat pugnacious, ape-like jaw. His voice was soft, and to overcome his stammer he spoke slowly and deliberately, with a rather musical effect. Throughout his life his accent remained Edwardian: rounded, unhurried and precise. Though he thought himself ugly, the young Willie struck at least one observer as "an unobtrusive, rather wary, unusually good-looking man."

He had read widely and written furiously in medical school. He had a strong desire to become a professional author, and believed his energy and ability would bring him success. He wanted to extend his travels, both to enhance his life and inspire his work. After five arduous years of medical training, he gave up a secure future to launch himself on a career of his own design. This crucial decision took a great deal of self-confidence and self-discipline. His determined, even ruthless ambition seemed motivated by a kind of revenge, a desire to take back from life all the joys and satisfactions stolen from him in childhood.

Troubled by his homosexuality, he tried to force an interest in women, and formed the habit of concealment. He was always on guard, inclined to repel the inquisitive. Analyzing his own reserved, egoistic, even tormented character in *Of Human Bondage,* he confessed that he was unable to become intimate with anyone. He shared "the English dread of sentimentality which keeps so tight a hold on emotion. . . . A fear of rebuff prevented him from affability, and he concealed his shyness, which was still intense, under a frigid taciturnity." Notorious for his sharp tongue and short fuse, he also "had a fiendish instinct for discovering other people's raw spots, and was able to say things that rankled."[1] A friend, noting the contradictions in his character, called him "abnormally reticent . . . remote and mysterious . . . too cold, too studied and self-conscious to be charming . . . a kindly, tolerant person who can be caustic and cruel without warning or provocation." Though unfailingly courteous, he was also (like his potato-hurling grandfather) given to sudden bursts of spleen. His sense of grievance and victimization was profound, and he told the photographer Cecil Beaton that "his temper was so violent that he could quite well imagine, in a moment of rage, killing someone."

He confessed that "something" in his personality antagonized many people, but never precisely defined what it was. His coldness, arrogance, clinical detachment, his desire for control and severe judgment of others were certainly unpleasant. Used to paying for services rendered, "he never expected people to be kind to him, and when they were, it surprised and moved him."[2]

Emphasizing the power of the will, Maugham wrote his artist-friend Gerald Kelly that "genius is a combination of talent and character, but character to a certain extent—I do not know how much, but I believe enormously—can be acquired." He later told a reporter: "I have more character than brains, and more brains than specific gifts [or talent]. It took me a long time to resign myself to making the best of what I had."[3] Maugham was as impatient and demanding with himself as he was with others. He admitted that when young he'd bang his fists on his desk in frustration and wish he had more brains to match his studiously acquired character. Fearful of the powerful emotions that threatened to overwhelm him, he tried to control his own life and the people around him.

Under the influence of Brooks and the aesthetes of the 1890s, Maugham began by writing in a flowery, precious and artificial manner. He studied the poetic books of the Bible—the Psalms and the Song of Solomon—and copied passages from the convoluted seventeenth-century prose of Richard Hooker and Jeremy Taylor. He trawled through the dictionary for unusual words and even put into his work the names of precious stones. "When I was your age," he later told a young disciple, Godfrey Winn, "I used to make out lists of beautiful-sounding words wherever I came upon them, and tried to work them into my writing, but the only effect was that all action was suspended, and I became a poor imitator of Pater."

He soon saw the light and gave up these decorative experiments. His first book had realistic content and a clear, straightforward style. Using the prose of Dryden, Swift and Cardinal Newman as his models, he set himself (as if he were studying Greek and Latin) "to learn how to write by taking passages from the English classics, copying them out, and then reproducing them from memory." Maugham's early life had been marked by sudden transformations: from adored child to lonely orphan, from French to English schoolboy. Now, with a dogged and dedicated effort, he changed from doctor to writer.

Maugham jump-started his work by thinking of the first two sentences he wanted to write while still in his morning bath. Like W. H. Auden (who also searched big dictionaries for arcane words) he believed that it was impossible to write while looking out at a view, and always sat down to work in front of a blank wall. He couldn't understand how Osbert Sitwell was able to write while traveling abroad and living in hotel rooms. Like Thomas Mann, he set himself a regular number of daily words (1,000 to 1,500), and faithfully wrote for three or four hours each morning when he was at home. In sixty years he produced an astonishing quantity of good work. He wrote in notebooks, in neat longhand, on the right-hand page opening. He edited it in red ink and made revisions on the left.

Maugham felt, after his early struggles and even before he'd achieved fame, that he was born to write, that writing came as naturally to him as swimming to a fish. He loved the actual process of writing, and when the going was good—as it usually was—he couldn't get the words down fast enough. Like many writers, he believed the subconscious mind enhanced the creative act and "does the really difficult work. I sit down with a fountain pen and unlined paper and the story pours out."[4] Maugham thought that writing, like drinking, was an easy habit to form and a difficult one to break. It was more an addiction than a vocation. He became so absorbed with the characters of his plays, stories and novels that when he stopped for the day, he was impatient of rest and eager to begin his work again. "When you're writing," he remarked, "when you're creating a character, it's with you constantly, you're preoccupied with it, it's alive." But when

you stop writing and "cut that out of your life, it's a rather lonely life."
Aloof from other people, he immersed himself in his own creations, and
his imaginary characters became so vivid that the real world seemed rather
shadowy.

Maugham needed an ample store of information for his mind and
imagination to work upon. He kept notebooks all his life and recorded
(sometimes dictated) his impressions while traveling. In London he used
the British Museum for research and had books sent from the London
Library when living abroad. Distance from the firsthand source of his fiction, he found, actually made the process of writing more vivid and
intense: "When an author is living in the scene of his story, perhaps
among the people who have suggested the characters of his invention, he
may well find himself bewildered by the mass of his impressions. . . . But
absence will erase from his memory redundant details and inessential
facts."

Maugham never suffered from writer's block. He was hardworking,
hasty, always driven and sometimes careless. His rapidly written work may
have seemed facile and superficial, but he insisted that he'd worked very
hard when revising his manuscripts: "Over and over again I have spent a
whole day writing and rewriting a single page and in the end left it, not
because I was satisfied with it, but because I could do no better."[5] Always
the pragmatist, Maugham applied himself, did his best and (even when
dissatisfied) published it anyway.

II

DESPITE HIS SHYNESS and his acerbic personality, Maugham enjoyed
social life and was a loyal friend. When he finished his medical training in
1897 he moved in with Adney Walter Payne, and shared a series of flats
and houses with him for the next twenty years. The son of a music-hall
impresario, Payne was educated at the City of London School and Heidelberg University, where he and Maugham first met. He qualified as a barrister and chartered accountant, but in 1910 he took over his father's
interests and devoted himself to the theater. The good-looking, smartly
dressed lawyer-producer handled Maugham's financial affairs and passed
on to his quiet roommate the minor actresses, secretaries and shop girls—
as well as, perhaps, young boys—he had taken to bed. Payne had great
charm, and "in spite of a steely precision of mind and an unalterable

Adney Walter Payne

determination to obtain his objectives, he was one of the most likeable of men and in manner suggested the country gentleman rather than the theatre manager." He was highly successful, and when he died in 1949 left an estate of £145,000. Maugham dedicated his first book, *Liza of Lambeth,* to Payne, inscribed it "Adney/with the author's love" and later referred to him as "the dear companion of my lonely youth." Payne later married a Hungarian woman, whom Maugham disliked, and the two old friends drifted apart.

Another important early influence was the shadowy Brooks-like aesthete and older mentor, Wentworth Huyshe—a homosexual, like Maugham's brother Henry, who'd introduced them. Huyshe took Willie to exhibitions and museums in London, showed him the world of art and inspired him with new ideas. In a letter to Huyshe sent with the handsome first edition of *Liza of Lambeth,* which had a stylish drawing of the heroine incised on the front cover and the name of the book on the title page in red letters, Maugham modestly wrote: "I can never forget how kind you were to me when I was stupid boy. . . . I can honestly say I owe a very great deal to you."[6]

The third formative influence was the homosexual autobiographer and successful travel writer Augustus Hare (1834–1903). He was born in

Rome, had (like Maugham) a dreadfully unhappy childhood, and had been educated at Harrow and Oxford. Hare, who moved in high society, gave Maugham his first glimpse of the manners and rituals of a Victorian country house. He taught the quiet young writer to set down the requisite number of words each morning, to observe carefully when traveling and dining out, to run a strict, well-regulated household, and to cultivate the famous, the wealthy and the powerful.

In 1896, shortly before he was taken up by his sexual, aesthetic and social mentors—Payne, Huyshe and Hare—Maugham sent two stories to the London publisher Fisher Unwin. He liked the stories, but said they were too short for inclusion in his Pseudonym Library and urged Maugham to write a novel. Never one to waste time, Maugham began work on *Liza of Lambeth* ten minutes after receiving the letter. Conrad and Ford, who satirized the rather crude and money-grubbing Unwin in *The Inheritors* (1901), described him as rather thin, with peaked grey hair: "He had even an anxious expression. . . . 'I . . . eh . . . believe I published your first book. . . . I lost money by it, but I can assure you that I bear no grudge—almost a hundred pounds. I bear no grudge.' . . . He had no idea that I might feel insulted." Unwin's nephew conceded that "his difficulty in personal relations was the tragedy of Fisher's business life." Maugham received neither an advance nor royalties on the first 750 copies of his novel. He felt that Unwin had taken advantage of his youth, inexperience and eagerness to get his first book published. He later told his agent that Unwin, who managed to pay him only £20 in royalties for the first edition of his very successful novel, "did me thoroughly in the eye."

Unwin's reader, the always perceptive Edward Garnett, immediately saw the honesty and accuracy of the novel, despite its depressing conclusion, and urged him to publish this promising new author. Referring to the original title, he observed:

> *A Lambeth Idyll* is *a very clever realistic study of factory girl and coster life.* The women; their roughness, intemperance, fits of violence, kindheartedness, slang—all are done truthfully. Liza and her mother Mrs. Kemp are drawn with no little humour and insight. The story is a dismal one in its ending, but the temper and tone of this book is wholesome and by no means morbid. The work is *objective,* and both the atmosphere and the environment of the mean district are unexaggerated.[7]

Maugham, author of Liza of Lambeth, *1897*

Liza of Lambeth, still in print after more than a hundred years, expresses not outrage but sympathy for the oppressed working class. Maugham's medical training and obstetric experience, his observation of the effects of illness, of the way women faced pain and the certain prospect of death, gave considerable power to his sharp portrayal of slum life. Liza "was a young girl of about eighteen, with dark eyes and an enormous fringe, puffed-out and curled and frizzed, covering her whole forehead from side to side, and coming down to meet her eyebrows. She was dressed in brilliant violet, with great lappets of velvet, and she had on her head an enormous black hat covered with feathers." When an Italian organ-grinder plays in the street, the audacious Liza "lifted her skirts higher, brought in new and more difficult movements into her improvisation, kicking up her legs." She's courted by the bashful young Tom, but on a bank holiday picnic in the country falls for the manly, married Jim Blakeston. They meet secretly, but are discovered, and she gets pregnant. In one of the great theatrical scenes in the short novel, Liza (who's constantly observed by her neighbors) is assaulted in the crowded street by Jim's wife, who—in a feral rage—spits in her face and beats her bloody:

> The blows came down heavy and rapid all over her face and head. She put up her hands to cover her face and turned her head away, while Mrs. Blakeston kept on hitting mercilessly. . . . [She] attacked Liza madly; but the girl stood up bravely, and as well as she could gave back the blows she received. The spectators grew tremendously excited. . . . They swayed about, scratching, tearing, biting, sweat and blood pouring down their faces, and their eyes fixed on one another, bloodshot and full of rage. The audience shouted and cheered and clapped their hands.[8]

This brutal street fight leads to Liza's miscarriage, septicemia and death.

Liza is swiftly transformed from a jolly girl wearing violet stockings and turning cartwheels to a battered drab—dying, comatose, unaware of Tom and Jim at her bedside. Jim, not an evil Victorian seducer, wants to leave his wife and marry Liza. Liza's mother has only two ambitions in life: to get as drunk as possible and to appear respectable in the eyes of her lady friends. When she learns that Liza is dying, she shows no emotion, but insists on a proper funeral. Liza's early death saves her from the typical fate of Lambeth women: backbreaking factory work, annual childbearing, beatings by drunken husbands and premature old age.

In June 1898 the *St. Thomas's Hospital Gazette* mentioned the publication of Anderson's *Deformities of Fingers and Toes,* a textbook written by one of their own doctors. In the same issue it proudly announced that Maugham's novel "has achieved a great and well-deserved success. It deals with one aspect of Lambeth life in a powerful and perhaps lurid way: the uncompromising vigour of both plot and style will appeal strongly to all lovers of realism." Joseph Conrad, another Unwin author and friend of Garnett, noted the novel's narrow scope and its clinical point of view: "It is certainly worth reading—but whether it's worth talking about is another question. . . . There is *any amount* of good things in the story and no distinction of any kind. It will be fairly successful I believe—for it is a 'genre' picture without any atmosphere and consequently no reader can live *in* it. He just looks on—and that is just what the general reader prefers." But Conrad underrated this youthful novel, which has a vivid heroine, a compelling atmosphere and a poignant theme.

Fifty years after its first publication George Orwell, who'd described industrial slums in his own work, reviewed a reprint of the novel. He praised Maugham's social realism and forceful simplicity, his depiction of "slum life in the nineties—a period when vast areas of every great town were dirty, dangerous, and poverty stricken to an extent that we can now hardly imagine." In 1948 the sixteen-year-old V. S. Naipaul, who knew about London slums only from reading Dickens, published his first work, a review of *Liza of Lambeth,* in his high school magazine in Trinidad. Maugham's blend of realism and pity, his aloof and disdainful attitude toward women, appealed to the young Naipaul:

> But what, I suppose, has rescued the novel from obscurity and has made it at least fit to be included in collected editions is the study of slum life. Maugham describes the slum people with a detachment that is not without humour. His novel is free from the social realism that has imposed itself on modern literature. The women, especially, are interesting. For them life is a messy monotony of motherhood and maulings. . . . The women accept blows as normal parts of their existence.[9]

Maugham's second novel, *The Making of a Saint* (1898), abandoned contemporary realism and took an unfortunate detour into historical fiction. The now forgotten critic Andrew Lang—an escapist who admired Robert Louis Stevenson's romantic fiction, *Kidnapped* (1886) and *The Master of Ballantrae* (1889)—advised young writers, lacking contemporary experience, to write historical novels. Maugham had just written a powerful novel based on his own medical experience. But he followed Lang's foolish notion and based his next book on the 1487 insurrection in Forlì, a town between Florence and Ravenna, in Machiavelli's *History of Florence* (1525). Machiavelli's brief but vivid account suggested the dramatic possibilities of the brave and bloodthirsty heroine. After her husband, the feudal count of Forlì, is murdered by the conspirators,

> the people who hated the count for his avarice and cruelty speedily sacked his house and took the Countess Caterina and her children prisoners. The fortress, which the castellan refused to give up, remained to be captured before the enterprise was entirely successful, and the people demanded of the countess that she should order the castellan to yield. She promised to do this if they would permit her to enter the fortress, and as hostages for

her good faith they might keep her children. The rebels relying on her word permitted her to enter the fortress, but as soon as she was within she threatened them from the walls with torture and death in revenge for the murder of her husband. They replied by threatening to take the lives of her children, to which she replied that she could still bring forth others. . . . As soon as the countess recovered the government of the town, she avenged the death of her husband with every kind of cruelty.

The loyal Edward Garnett was enthusiastic about Maugham's unreadable novel—filled, like a costume drama, with warfare, pillage, sword fights and grisly executions. He praised its vivid characters and re-creation of the early Renaissance: "Mr. Maugham is going *strong*. Nothing is more difficult than for an Englishman to deal with Latin character and temperament and make them move and act in their own environment . . . but Mr. Maugham does make his people real living Italians. . . . The novel promises to be a strong unusual piece of work, full of vigour . . . and shows Mr. Maugham has plenty of talent left in him to start on so new a tack."[10] Maugham later thought it was "a very poor novel," and when his major works were reprinted, he suppressed it. His historical novels, rubbing against the grain of his natural talent—the direct observation of contemporary experience—were all bogus, wooden and inert, filled with clichés of plot, character and style.

III

AFTER PUBLISHING *Liza of Lambeth* in September 1897 and passing his medical exams the following month, Maugham fulfilled a longstanding ambition. Establishing a dominant pattern in his life—constant travel and prolonged residence abroad—he went to live in Seville for sixteen months. Maugham had a talent for languages. He'd learned Greek and Latin at school, French in Paris, German in Heidelberg, Italian and Russian on Capri, and now studied Spanish in Seville. In *The Land of the Blessed Virgin: Sketches and Impressions in Andalusia* (1905), his account of his first visit to Spain, he joyfully wrote that the country had liberated him from all imprisoning ties: "To myself Seville means ten times more than it can mean to others. I came to it after weary years in London, heartsick with much hoping, my mind dull with drudgery; and it seemed a land of freedom. There I became at last conscious of my youth."

Maugham lived on the Calle Guzmán el Bueno in the elegant Santa Cruz district, socialized with the British vice-consul, Edward Johnston, and dedicated *Orientations* (1899) to Johnston's wife. He grew a mustache, puffed Filipino cigars, strummed the guitar, wore a black, wide-brimmed Córdoba hat and swaggered down the narrow, sinuous Sierpes like a true hidalgo. He described the Moorish fortress, the cathedral with its famous belltower, La Giralda, the hospital and jail as well as the squalid gypsies and grotesque beggars. To extract the essence of Andalusian life, he repeatedly returned to the bullfights, though that grim spectacle filled him with loathing and horror. In those days, before the picadors' horses wore protective padding, they were frequently gored and spilled their entrails onto the hot sand.

At a time when few Englishmen visited Spain, Maugham wanted to see the very heart of the region, "that part of the country which had pre-served its antique character, where railway trains were not, and the horse, the mule, the donkey were still the only means of transit. . . . I set out in the morning early, with saddle-bags fixed on either side and poncho strapped to my pommel. A loaded revolver, though of course I never had a chance to use it, made me feel pleasantly adventurous." He traveled alone and in considerable discomfort through the wild, deserted and impoverished countryside. On a journey of 150 miles, he rode northeast through Carmona and La Luisiana to Écija, and then back to Seville through Marchena and Mairena. He also traveled to Ronda, Córdoba, Granada, Jerez, Cádiz and Tangier in Morocco.

Maugham tried to interpret the Spanish character for an English audi-ence. His main sources were Théophile Gautier's *Journey to Spain* (1845), Richard Ford's *Handbook for Travellers in Spain* (1845), Stanley Lane-Poole's *The Moors in Spain* (1893), the current Baedeker and his firsthand experi-ence. He made generalizations which tended to reinforce clichés about the country: the Andalusian character (after nearly eight hundred years of Moorish occupation) is rich with Oriental strains; a realistic attitude to life is "the most conspicuous of Spanish traits"; Spain is highly traditional, a stronghold of antiquated customs, a place of somberness and gravity. The girls are beautiful in youth, often ugly in middle age. The people are lazy and vain, the food—thin soups, tough steaks, revolting sauces, disgusting innards and rancid oils—abominable.

The Spanish-American War, which finally destroyed the Spanish empire, was then being fought in Cuba. With a doctor's clinical eye

Maugham described the wounded soldiers, sent home to die: "what struck me most was the deathly colour; for their faces were almost green, while round their sunken eyes were great white rings, and the white was ghastly, corpse-like." This objective writing clashed with the remnants of his ornate and stilted style, especially when he tried to describe passion. Speaking of his beloved—who may have been a young man—Maugham gushingly wrote: "It was not love I felt for you, Rosarito; I wish it had been; but now far away, in the rain, I fancy (oh no, not that I am at last in love) but perhaps that I am just faintly enamoured—of your recollection." His description of a sexual encounter with a prostitute in Granada was much more convincing. When she took off her clothes he was shocked to find she was only thirteen and had been driven to sell herself by hunger. He paid her, but could not bring himself to have sex with her.

The paradoxical theme of the book—as in Baudelaire's "Voyage à Cythère" and Huysmans' *Against the Grain*—is that the traveler's idealistic expectations are inevitably destroyed by actual experience: "It is much better to read books of travel than to travel oneself; he really enjoys foreign lands who never goes abroad; and the man who stays at home, preserving his illusions, has certainly the best of it. How delightful is the anticipation as he looks over time-tables and books of photographs, forming delightful images of future pleasure! But the reality is full of disappointment, and the more famous the monument the bitterer the disillusion."[11] Yet Maugham's awareness of the negative aspects of travel never stood in the way of his own obsessive journeys. He makes a neat point, but does not really subscribe to it.

D. H. Lawrence made travel writing subjective by emphasizing the author's personal experience and point of view: what he saw and what happened to him. Maugham kept his intimate feelings—his friendships, loves and longings—quite hidden. He seemed to be watching an operatic spectacle instead of actually participating in the life around him. Mérimée's *Carmen* and Manet's paintings had revealed Spain's powerful influence on French culture in the nineteenth century. Gerald Brenan and Robert Graves moved to Spain after the Great War, and the Spanish Civil War aroused passionate feelings, but English writers did not really discover the country until well after World War II. Maugham anticipated this interest and—between Richard Ford's *Handbook* in 1845 and Gerald Brenan's *South from Granada* in 1957—wrote the best English travel book on Spain.

4

Struggling Author

1900–1904

WHEN HE RETURNED from Spain Maugham moved back in with Walter Payne, who had been reading his work and lending him money. He lacked the means to be a man about town, but picked up the threads of his London social life, played bridge and poker, and joined the Bath Club, where he could swim in the pool. After the tawny landscapes of Spain and the old-fashioned, traditional life of Seville, he looked at England with a fresh, analytical eye. The novels and plays he wrote in these years show his keen observation of the English middle and upper class. With discipline and determination he found the self-confidence to sit alone in the empty flat and get down to work.

Despite the success of *Liza of Lambeth,* Maugham could not, and perhaps did not want to, repeat its narrow focus and pared-down style. His next novels were satirical, and more ambitious in scope and theme. He was fascinated by social and sexual relationships, and his sharp outsider's eye diagnosed society's malaise. Maugham often chose disquieting themes that would be treated more successfully by others. His audience was not always ready for his pioneering books, and his style and approach were still uncertain.

Maugham's first work after returning to London was *The Hero* (1901), a novel with a suburban setting. It begins with the return of a disillusioned wounded soldier from the Boer War in South Africa (still being fought from 1899 to 1902, as Maugham was writing). The bitter struggle with a fierce guerrilla enemy forms the topical background to the hero's revulsion against his family's values and customs. James Parsons' arrival is announced by telegram to his eager parents and fiancée, Mary Clibborn, who expect a great deal from him. When serving as a colonel in the Indian army, his father had trapped some hostile tribes and unwisely shown them mercy, and they had massacred his men. His career ended with a dishonorable discharge; and he counts on his son—mentioned in dispatches, wounded and recommended for the Victoria Cross—to compensate for his disgrace. When James arrives home, however, he's pale and thin, strange and silent, withdrawn and alienated. He shocks the family by defending the Boers' behavior in the war and by admitting that he'd enjoyed killing men in battle. He's lost his religious belief, and feels unable to marry.

Maugham does not describe the war (vividly reported by Churchill and other correspondents in the daily press), or James' specific act of bravery under fire, nor use his war experience to deepen his character. James confesses that a friend "was killed because I tried to save him" and doesn't believe he deserves the V.C. After a promising start, the novel becomes static and filled with conventional situations and characters: young hero and doting girlfriend, degraded father and self-effacing mother who are "cruel in their loving kindness."

The Hero satirizes the petty and prejudiced, stifling and snobbish society of a small Kentish village. Maugham zeroes in on the unpleasant character of Mary, James' self-righteous fiancée. She's hopelessly ignorant, yet rigidly opinionated; priggish, yet aggressively virtuous, she nurses wounded soldiers, but makes them uncomfortable and disobeys the doctor's orders. A complete killjoy, she believes the village girls ought—for their own moral and spiritual welfare—"to be utterly miserable." James' parents, Mary's family and the vicar all pressure him to marry her. James' psychological trauma and resulting conflict becomes narrowly focused on whether he'll marry his fiancée or give himself to a widow in London. Unlike the unctuous Mary, she's a sexually experienced lover whose mere touch makes him "mad with passion." Realizing that he doesn't love Mary (and probably never did), James breaks their engagement. But when he gets enteric fever and she nurses him devotedly, he proposes again and is again accepted.

Finally, as he begins to hate her and find her physically repellent, James decides to shoot himself rather than be forced to marry her. In another nasty twist, Mary's mother, who's been cruel to her and has become her sexual rival, convinces herself that James has shot himself because he loved *her.* Maugham scarcely develops the promising subject of the novel: the return of an alienated and traumatized hero, or the true sexual and social struggle within James—his loathing of domesticity and fear of women. The resolution is more depressing than tragic. Maugham later told his agent that "it was one of my earliest novels, it was not a success when it came out, and I don't believe it has any merit at all."[1] But his judgment was too severe. *The Hero* is as good as *The Explorer* (1908), which has a similar theme and which he later reprinted, and is much better than his late historical novels.

After publishing his first three books with Unwin (including *Orientations,* a weak collection of stories, in 1899), Maugham moved to Hutchinson for *The Hero.* He then brought out *Mrs. Craddock* (1902) with Heinemann, where he remained for the next sixty years. Heinemann, as penny-pinching as Unwin, was at least amenable to discussion: "If young authors stood up to him and wrung better terms out of him, he would laugh heartily and say, 'Well, you're not a bad business man.' "

Like *The Hero, Mrs. Craddock* portrays a disillusioned lover and the conflict between desire and duty. Maugham gives the subject a fresh look by switching the sex of the main character, but goes far beyond *The Hero* in treating the conflict between sexual desire and social constraints. Bertha Ley is a willful, independent young woman who gets trapped in a miserable marriage. Brought up in Europe by a rackety father, she inherits his neglected estate in Kent and falls in love with her tenant farmer, the "intensely masculine" Edward Craddock. Drawn to his farmyard odor (subtly contrasted to that of the vicar, Mr. Glover, "a somewhat feminine edition of his sister, but smelling in the most remarkable fashion of antiseptics"), Bertha aggressively courts him, and outrages her genteel neighbors by marrying him—only to realize she's made a terrible mistake. The ox-like, practical Craddock turns out to be an unresponsive lover. Bertha needs a man with intellectual interests, but he's hopelessly dense, ignorant, callous, selfish, pompous and socially pretentious. Ironically, her neighbors, unaware of his true character, praise his work on the estate and think he's a splendid husband. Bertha becomes pregnant and gives birth to a stillborn child, "naked and very small, hardly human, repulsive, yet very pitiful." The loss of her child leads to the loss of her religious faith, and in a scene that shocked contemporary readers she calls God "either impotent or cruel. . . . It's God who needs my forgiveness—not I His. . . . If God made me suffer like that it's infamous. . . . How can you imagine Him to be so stupid, so cruel?"

The novel shifts direction when Bertha leaves Craddock, goes to Italy and falls in love with her younger distant cousin, Gerald Vaudrey, who's described in a distinctly androgynous fashion: "He was quite a boy, very slight and not so tall as Bertha, with a small, girlish face. He had a tiny nose, but it was very straight, and his somewhat freckled complexion was admirable. His hair was dark and curly; he wore it long, evidently aware that it was very nice." Torn between instinct and convention, Bertha reluctantly returns to her husband, who tactfully agrees not to make any sexual demands. Like D. H. Lawrence's lonely and sexually starved Connie Chatterley gazing at her naked self in a mirror, Bertha expresses her newly awakened passion by swimming naked in the sea: "Timidly, rapidly, she slipped off her clothes, and looking round to see that there was really no one in sight, stepped in; the wavelets about her feet made her shiver a little, and then with a splash, stretching out her arms, she ran forward, and half fell, half dived into the water. . . . It was an unknown pleasure to swim unhampered by a bathing-dress."

When Craddock suddenly dies and Bertha is finally free, she expresses Maugham's negative view of marriage: "husband and wife know nothing of one another. However ardently they love, however intimate their union, they are never one; they are scarcely more to one another than strangers." The intoxication of love is inevitably followed by bitter disappointment. But if Bertha has a right to choose for herself, she must also have the right to change her mind when that choice turns out to be wrong. Maugham punishes Bertha by making her baby die, and conveniently kills off Craddock in a riding accident. Dead babies, accidents and suicides crop up rather too often in Maugham's (as in E. M. Forster's) early novels.

Maugham not only challenged sexual conventions by arguing for Bertha's right to sexual gratification. He also dared to describe a marriage between an upper-class woman and a lower-class man and declared that sexual pleasure was essential for happiness. *Mrs. Craddock* was considered scandalous at the time, and Maugham had to take out shocking passages before Heinemann would agree to publish it. These deleted passages, restored in the 1955 edition, included Bertha's condemnation of God after her baby is stillborn and the frank expression of her adulterous sexual desire: "her very flesh cried out, and she trembled at the thought that she could give Gerald the inestimable gift of her body. . . . She did not try to hide her passion now, she clasped him to her heart. . . . Their kiss was rapture, madness; it was ecstasy beyond description, complete surrender."

Mrs. Craddock, for all its faults, is a trailblazing novel. D. H. Lawrence was influenced by the striking scene where Bertha experiences the sudden revival of her old passion as she washes her husband's dead body: "The touch of the cold flesh made her shudder voluptuously: she thought of him taking her in his strong arms, kissing her on the mouth. She wrapped him in the white shroud and surrounded him with flowers. They placed him in the coffin, and her heart stood still." A decade later, Lawrence brilliantly developed this passage in "Odour of Chrysanthemums" (1911).

The novel continued to haunt Lawrence, who took up Maugham's subject in his late masterpiece *Lady Chatterley's Lover* (1928) (Connie Chatterley's surname incorporates Bertha's). But Lawrence, who wanted to reclaim heterosexual love and place it at the center of civilization, argues against Maugham's conclusions. Maugham gave an unconvincing description of sexual passion: "Bertha, desire burning within her like a fire, had flung herself into her husband's arms, loving as the beasts love—and as the gods."[2] Lawrence, by contrast, set out to describe the real thing, using the dialect of the gamekeeper Mellors to express the tenderness and physical responsiveness of the lovers. Like Maugham's, his novel was bowdlerized for many years. While Maugham emphasized the social contrast between the couple and the disastrous results of a highborn woman's love for a working-class man, Lawrence's great novel uses his lovers to argue for a radical change in consciousness and for the triumph of life over the destructive forces of the modern world. He goes beyond the lovers themselves to consider the rigidity of the class structure, the horrors of industrialism, the effects of war and the decayed state of English civilization. Maugham's Craddock becomes a country squire, while Lawrence's Mellors remains loyal to his background and class. In Maugham's novel the result of love is a stillborn child and sexual revulsion. Lawrence's ends with Connie's pregnancy as sexual love transcends class through the "democracy of touch."

The Merry-Go-Round (1904), Maugham's third Edwardian novel, is more complex but less interesting than *Mrs. Craddock.* Miss Polly Ley, Bertha's outspoken aunt, reappears in this book. With epigrammatic wit she defies

a rich spinster, yet inherits her great wealth. Her main function is to provide a loose link to three stories of love gone sour. The first concerns a
frustrated intellectual who's trapped into marriage after seducing an
attractive barmaid. After she gives birth to a stillborn child (another punishment for lovers who cross class barriers) and commits suicide, he's free
to marry the wealthy widow. The second portrays a middle-aged spinster
who defies her father to marry a young and idealistic invalid who eventually dies of tuberculosis. The third describes the squalid liaison of a jaded
married woman and her equally cynical and worthless lover. The novel
shows once again that marriage, inspired by passion, soon becomes a
deadly trap.

This melodramatic and long-winded novel—a striking contrast to the
sharp focus of *Liza of Lambeth*—is marred by a convoluted plot, flat dialogue and purple prose. Maugham mechanically introduces a profusion of
characters, narrates many of the episodes retrospectively rather than
directly and cannot make the love affairs interesting or convincing. The
humane Dr. Frank Hurrell, who observes rather than participates in the
action, speaks for Maugham. (He, too, has caught a septic inflammation
while performing an autopsy.) He voices Maugham's intense desire to cut
loose from civilization and travel to exotic lands: "My whole soul aches for
the East, for Egypt and India and Japan; I want to know the corrupt, eager
life of the Malays and the violent adventures of the South Sea Islands. . . .
I want to see life and death, and the passions, the virtues and vices, of men
face to face, uncovered."[3] All three middle-class novels express Maugham's
fear and homosexual distrust of love, marriage and childbirth.

After being swindled by Fisher Unwin, Maugham hired an agent,
William Morris Colles, who handled his early novels and plays until after
the publication of *The Merry-Go-Round*. Born in 1855, Colles graduated
from Cambridge, was admitted to the Bar in 1880 and launched his firm
nine years later. He was "a big, burly, bearded lawyer, with a wheezy infec-
tious laugh—a sort of well-spoken, decent-minded, entirely respectable,
nineteenth-century Falstaff." When Maugham's novel didn't sell (Conrad's
Nostromo, Hudson's *Green Mansions* and Jack London's *The Sea-Wolf* were
also published that year), he wrote to Colles blaming its poor reception on
his agent's failure to push the book rather than on its all-too-obvious
weaknesses: "With regard to *The Merry-Go-Round* I think we must agree to
differ; I do not wish to break into recriminations; but I cannot help think-

ing that what is obvious to me now, your experience might have suggested to you then, namely, that when a publisher does not like a book and has made up his mind that it will not sell, one might just as well throw it in the Thames as let him publish it."[4] In 1904 Maugham switched to J. B. Pinker, a sturdy, lively man with pink cheeks and a pronounced Scottish burr—dapper, bow-tied and rather pleased with himself. Pinker, whose clients included James, Wilde, Conrad, Wells, Arnold Bennett and Stephen Crane, knew how to recognize talent and get the best deal for his authors.

II

IN THE 1890s, when the dominant playwrights were Oscar Wilde and Henrik Ibsen, Maugham wrote plays as well as novels. Wilde provided brilliantly witty entertainment; Ibsen, depicting the conflict between moral and social duty, the theater of ideas.[5] Oscillating between social satire and serious drama, Maugham was influenced by both.

Maugham's early comedies reflected the high spirits of his youth. He wrote them all very easily and with professional skill: one week (with weekends off) for each act and a fourth week to revise. He remembered the pleasure of writing them, and had no trouble finding a subject. He always had half a dozen plays in his head, "and when a theme presented itself to me it did so divided into scenes and acts, with each 'curtain' staring me in the face." In the preface to his *Collected Plays,* written forty years later, Maugham declared that he wrote them according to a formula. The theater managers, he said, wanted a comedy "with as much drama as it could carry, for the public liked a thrill; with a little sentiment, for the public liked to feel good; and a happy ending." So he gave audiences what they wanted and wrote lighthearted, amusing Wildean comedies of manners, with a touch of Scribe and Sardou. He was steeped in French as well as English drama, and followed the example of Dumas, who believed the most dramatic events took place behind closed doors. One manager told Maugham he would produce his first play "if I would write in twenty-four more epigrams. Those were the days when Wilde had made the epigram-studded play popular. Epigrams were no trouble for me. I wrote two dozen in an hour."[6]

Maugham's characteristic mixture of self-deprecation and pride made it all sound so easy. He thought "the difficulty of play-writing has been much exaggerated," certainly followed the current conventions and used plots that were often as timeworn as his characters. But his enormous success as a playwright cannot merely be attributed to pleasing the audience. He believed that the playwright had to have a distinct knack, "the dramatic instinct" for writing lines that get over the footlights. With his extraordinary ability to create characters, dialogue and situations that held and moved the audience, Maugham became the most successful dramatist of his time.

Maugham had a dark, stoic view of life, but his lucrative comedies encouraged him to turn away from the suffering and tragedy of his novels. He leavened the conventions of comedy and farce with his bitter, worldly perceptions, and balanced his cynically drawn characters with the physical nuance and verbal color of the actors of the day. In his novels Maugham created some of the nastiest harridans in literature; in his plays the heroines might be scheming manipulators, but they were always redeemed by their charm and intelligence.

Lady Frederick was Maugham's first significant play, first success on the London stage and first to be performed in New York. It was written in 1903 and produced four years later. Lady Frederick, a beautiful Irish widow with an enchanting brogue, a dubious reputation, huge gambling debts and no money, charms the young, wealthy Lord Charles Mereston. (Maugham must have enjoyed teasing his stuffed-shirt older brother by appropriating his name.) After a series of dramatic transactions involving debtors, suitors, blackmail and a bundle of incriminating letters, Lady Frederick reveals her high principles by deciding to discourage Charles for good. The conflicts of youth and age, love and money go back to the conventions of Restoration comedy, the frivolity and wit to Oscar Wilde; and the older woman's renunciation of a younger man's love echoes the tragic theme of Dumas' *La Dame aux camélias* and Hofmannsthal's *Der Rosenkavalier*.

Maugham drew on the acid misogyny of Jonathan Swift's poem "The Lady's Dressing Room" to stage the renunciation scene. In Swift the young lover is appalled by seeing his lady perform her repulsive toilette:

> Thus finishing his grand Survey,
> The Swain disgusted slunk away,
> Repeating in his am'rous Fits,
> Oh! Caelia, Caelia, Caelia shits.

In Maugham's play, however, the lady reveals not only the subterfuges of cosmetics, but also her courage, her generosity and her independent spirit. In a scene that shocked contemporary audiences and that many actresses refused to play, Lady Frederick invites Charles into her dressing room early in the morning to see what her skin and hair really look like without the help of makeup and a skillful lady's maid. "You don't for a moment suppose," she informs him, as he makes an awkward escape, "I should have let you into these horrible mysteries of my toilette if I had any intention of marrying you?"[7]

When *Lady Frederick* was accepted and immediately went into rehearsal, Maugham was traveling in Sicily. Unable to wait for the £20 that had been sent to pay his fare back to England, he took a ship from Palermo and arrived in Naples with only five shillings in his pocket. He wrote a check for his ticket on a ship to Marseilles, cashed another for £5 and won twenty-five shillings in the ship's sweepstakes. This got him to Paris and then to London, with a shilling left for a cab to reach the theater—just in time. The play, put on to fill a gap of a few weeks, ran for a year.

Maugham had tried for many years to get theater managers interested in his work, but nobody wanted it. After the success of *Lady Frederick,* when producers suddenly became interested, he pulled his old plays out of the drawer and gave audiences a string of up-to-date sparkling comedies. Many modern playwrights—Strindberg, Wilde and Chekhov as well as Beckett, Genet and Tennessee Williams—also wrote fiction. But only Maugham—whose stories and chapters in novels often end with a dramatic curtain line—rewrote the same plot for a different genre, turning plays into novels or novels into plays. His play *A Man of Honour* (1898), for example, became part of *The Merry-Go-Round* (1904), another part of which resurfaced as the play *Grace* (1910). Except for the play *Lady Frederick* and the dramatization of his story "The Letter," none of these mediocre works became a success in a different genre, and contemporary readers and audiences found them tediously familiar.[8]

Maugham found comedies difficult to rehearse. He was familiar with all the jokes and could no longer see how anyone might possibly find them amusing. But his plays took him out of his isolated study and put him into close contact with the theatrical world. He had to help choose actors and actresses, work with producers and directors, go to rehearsals and make last-minute changes in the script. He also had to endure the intense anxiety of opening night, which would determine whether the play was a critical success or a humiliating failure, whether he'd become rich and famous or remain impoverished and obscure. Friends and relatives who accompanied Maugham to first nights recalled that though his hand might tremble a little, he remained sphinx-like and didn't show much emotion.

Maugham's failures were hard to bear, but his arduous struggle to achieve success had helped build his character and prove his courage. During his first decade as a professional writer, from 1897 to 1907, he never earned more than £100 a year, and the £3,000 he'd inherited from his father (paying, at 5%, £150 a year) had gradually evaporated. In those days of minimum income tax and low wages for servants, Maugham the promising young author was taken up by wealthy patrons who could afford to entertain on a grand scale. But on country-house weekends he didn't have enough money to tip the butler properly, and was painfully aware that his tattered pajamas and modest toilet articles created an unfavorable impression on the condescending servants.

III

THOUGH MAUGHAM HAD never been close to his older brothers, he felt a certain sympathy for Henry, who was a writer, an alcoholic and a homosexual. A peculiar and neurotic person, Henry would "never take a train and he'd never go in a funicular. He had a kind of *vertigo*. If he came to stay in the country, he would always arrive on a bicycle."[9] He was an eminently unsuccessful author of a travel book; of several plays, including a dramatized life of St. Francis of Assisi; and of two novels, including *Richard Hawkblood,* a wooden Italian romance that Maugham, through Pinker, helped to get published.

On July 27, 1904, suddenly called to Henry's flat, Maugham witnessed a ghastly scene. Henry had drunk a bottle of corrosive nitric acid, though not enough to kill him instantly, and had been lying alone and in agony for three days. Maugham knew from his medical experience exactly what he had endured, and recognized the symptoms of poison: violent shuddering, imperceptible pulse, dilated eyes; chattering teeth, drawn lips and bluish face. Henry had been vomiting blood and was covered with strange spots, and his limbs twitched convulsively. Maugham rushed him to St. Thomas's, and, unable to save him, watched him die. Years later he remembered Henry's fate when describing the suicide of the captured spy

Chandra Lal, in *Ashenden*. To avoid execution, Lal poisoned himself with prussic acid, which left behind a distinct odor of almonds.

Henry's dreadful death reminded Maugham that he might share the same fate. To write for a living courted failure and poverty; to be homosexual risked one's freedom and reputation. But his ruthlessness and ingenuity as an author derived in part from his willed ambition. He wrote play after play about sexual and social entanglements, but became more careful than ever to conceal his own sexual life.

5

Bohemia and Fame

1905–1908

THE TRIALS OF Oscar Wilde took place in 1895, while Maugham was a medical student. In 1885 the Criminal Law Amendment Act had made sodomy a felony, punishable with penal servitude from a minimum of ten years to a maximum of life. The commission between two males of "any act of gross indecency" was punishable with two years' imprisonment and hard labor. Frank Harris, a connoisseur of illicit sexual behavior, said that after Wilde's arrest in 1895 "every train to Dover was crowded; every steamer to Calais was thronged with members of the aristocratic and leisured classes, who seemed to prefer Paris, or even Nice out of season, to a city like London where the police might act with such unexpected vigour." The Napoleonic Code in France did not make adult homosexuality a crime, and the Continent was undoubtedly more tolerant than England.

Wilde's two-year imprisonment established a pattern of persecution that forced homosexuals to go underground for more than eighty years and cast a shadow over Maugham's life. The law remained in force until the Wolfenden Report of 1957 advised that (as before 1885) "homosexual behaviour between consenting adults in private should no longer be a criminal offence." This recommendation was adopted in the Sexual Offences Act of 1967. Homosexuality had been a crime in England from the time Maugham was eleven years old and remained so until two years after his death.

Both Maugham and his friend Noël Coward—fearful of exposure and persecution—were deeply affected by Wilde's fate. The American author Glenway Wescott said that "Willie's generation lived in mortal terror of the Oscar Wilde trial." One of Coward's friends recalled that the Oscar Wilde trial "stuck in his craw. . . . He once [said,] 'I'm not going to court.' He was absolutely petrified about that sort of thing. . . . That ate into his soul."[1] The fear of social condemnation and judicial punishment forced homosexual writers to devise new strategies in their art. They often disguised homosexual characters as women in order to express their ideas in a public way.

Maugham showed his interest in and sympathy with Wilde, a major influence on his comedies, by forming friendships with several of Wilde's close friends. He knew Robert Ross and Robert Hichens, and briefly edited a magazine with Laurence Housman. He saw a good deal of Ada Leverson, a witty and popular novelist who'd helped Wilde after his arrest and sheltered him between trials. In *The Limit* (1909) Leverson portrayed Maugham as the successful playwright Hereford Vaughan and emphasized the attractive aspect of his personality: he was more "secretive and mysterious than blatant and dashing, and this, of course, made him, on the whole, more interesting to women."

Maugham was closest to the engaging Reggie Turner, the illegitimate son of the owner of the London *Daily Chronicle*. A wealthy Jewish homosexual, he wrote minor novels and belonged to the English set in Florence. He was "large-nosed and small-headed, with eyelids that blinked accidentally as well as deliberately. He was also excellent company, given to mimicry of sermons and the repartee that Wilde favored." Turner was also the model for Algy Constable in Lawrence's *Aaron's Rod:* "Algy was small and frail, somewhat shaky. . . . [His] nose trembled a little, and his eyes blinked. . . . He can be most entertaining, most witty, and amusing." Maugham, meeting him once in Paris, remarked, " 'You know my first editions are getting quite rare,' to which Reggie replied—'Ah, it's my *second* editions which are almost impossible to procure.' "[2]

II

BY 1905 MAUGHAM had become weary of keeping up his end when summoned to endless dinners in Mayfair and to weekends at the country houses of the rich and powerful. He longed for a more Bohemian life in the city where he'd grown up and had always associated with the Eden of his early childhood. In February he went to Paris with the twenty-four-year-old Harry Philips—who'd been to Shrewsbury School and left Oxford after a term at Keble—as his secretary, companion and lover. Douglas Goldring called the young Philips "quite the most dazzling figure for charm, good looks, and brilliant wit that I had ever encountered." They rented a tiny fifth-floor flat at 3, rue Victor Considérant, close to the Lion de Belfort monument (now the Denfert-Rochereau Métro Station) and with a view of Montparnasse Cemetery. The Lion memorialized the fortress in which French forces held out against the Prussians in the war of 1870–71.

Philips later wrote that Maugham's habits were always regular (if not rigid) and that Maugham, formerly tutored by Brooks, Hare and Huyshe, now assumed the role of artistic mentor: "His time table appeared the same. After he had breakfasted he wrote hard till about 12:30. He drank very little & we had no aperitifs except on Sunday when we sometimes went to the Café de Paris & sat sipping a grenadine or some simple drink until taking a most inexpensive lunch. He would, after that, take me to the Louvre or other museums." Philips also mentioned that in adult life (as in childhood) Maugham "enjoyed the [violence of the] 'Grand Guignol' plays—particularly one called *'la dernière torture.'*" Philips, who later married, also explained why he parted from the suspicious and calculating Maugham: "His cynicism distressed me & being a person who has always acted on impulse—I found it difficult to live with someone who believed that no one did anything without a motive."[3]

In Bohemian Paris Maugham broke out of his chrysalis and began to meet artists and writers who would soon become famous. They gathered in the evenings at the cheap Chat Blanc restaurant on the rue d'Odessa for animated conversation, esoteric discourse and intellectual battles. Roderick O'Conor, a silent Irishman who'd known Gauguin in Brittany, was cold, biting and virulent. He appears as Clutton in *Of Human Bondage,* "long and desperately thin, his huge bones seemed to protrude from his body; his elbows were so sharp that they appeared to jut out through the arms of his shabby coat. His trousers were frayed at the bottom, and on each of his boots was a clumsy patch." Claiming both humor and genius, "he spoke with solemnity, and his colossal, misshapen nose made what he said very quaint." O'Conor took an immediate and obvious dislike to Maugham, whose mere presence at their communal dinner table seemed to provoke him. When Maugham praised the Parnassian poet Hérédia, whose *Trophées* Brooks had been translating on Capri, O'Conor attacked him and they had a violent argument. (Their mutual hostility did not prevent Maugham from buying, in the 1920s, three of O'Conor's undistinguished still lifes.)[4]

By contrast, Maugham formed an enduring friendship with the equally irritable Irishman Gerald Kelly, whom he probably met through his brother Charles at a summer house near Paris. Kelly, five years younger than Maugham and just as short, was the son of the vicar of Camberwell, just south of the Thames. He went to Eton and Trinity College, Cambridge, and began painting in South Africa while convalescing from an illness. Clive Bell, the Bloomsbury art critic who also belonged to their circle, explained why Maugham was drawn to Kelly. He spoke correct and fluent French and was "a man of wit, culture and ideas, far better-educated and more alert than the majority of his companions in the quarter."

Other friends noted Kelly's scintillating conversation as well as his sharp tongue and peevish temperament: "Kelly was articulate par excellence, a brilliant talker both in public and in private, with an educated, humane, clubable, gentlemanly, Edwardian manner. . . . Undoubtedly, Kelly was a charmer, both in speech and in his letters, and of indomitable spirit, but he was often petulant and tactless. Hardly five feet six inches in height, he darted in thought and action at most things." Fifty years after their first meeting, when Kelly had been knighted and become president of the Royal Academy, Maugham recalled that the artist "was then a short, slender young man in his early twenties with a mass of untidy black hair, regular features and fine, eager eyes behind great round spectacles. He had a nervous vitality and that exuberant loquacity which we tongue-tied English look upon as a characteristic of the Irish. He was as violent in his enthusiasm for what he liked as he was violent in his denunciation of what he didn't."[5]

Maugham immediately disliked O'Conor and and was drawn to Kelly (though the two Irishmen had temperamental affinities). His feelings toward his fellow stammerer Arnold Bennett, a more obvious rival, were more complex. Maugham first felt jealous and hostile when Kelly introduced Bennett—with his receding chin, drooping mustache, rabbit teeth and high quiff of hair—but eventually came to respect him. They got off to a bad start when Maugham, whose French was extremely good, mistakenly called a napkin-ring an *anneau* instead of a *rond*. When Bennett, whose knowledge of French was rudimentary, had the nerve to correct him in his Midlands drawl, Maugham was furious. Kelly recalled that everyone was greatly amused "at the look of rage on Willie's face."

In his diary of March 3, 1905, Bennett, misled by his manner, called Maugham "lethargic." He also noted Maugham's characteristic control, his very deliberate way of never exceeding his limits:

> Somerset Maugham came up for tea. He has a very calm, almost lethargic demeanour. He took two cups of tea with pleasure and absolutely refused a third; one knew instantly from his tone that nothing would induce him to take a third. He ate biscuits and *gaufrettes* very quickly, almost greedily, one after the other, without a pause, and then suddenly stopped. He smoked two cigarettes furiously, in less time than I smoked one, and solidly declined a third. I liked him.

Maugham later called Bennett an extremely lovable man whose gauche peculiarities could be endearing: "Arnold was good company, and I always enjoyed spending an evening with him, but didn't very much like him. He was cocksure and bumptious, and he was rather common."[6] Bennett had a French mistress who was unusually well read and liked writers, and happened to have two nights free each week. Bennett urged Maugham to take up the slack and make use of her services. Maugham had already been a sexual stand-in for Walter Payne, was repelled by Bennett's attempt at intimacy and found his proposal "rather cold-blooded."

In contrast to his generous, if condescending, attitude toward Arnold Bennett, Maugham frequently attacked a superior artist, Henry James, whose technique and style were antithetical to his own. Maugham knew James personally and perceived his covert homosexuality. Keenly aware of James' weaknesses and limitations, Maugham called him a "trifle absurd" and didn't believe he had the qualities needed to write great books. Though James was extremely prolific and even dictated his last works, he was—unlike Maugham—not criticized for writing too much. As an older rival and darling of the highbrows, who'd established his reputation well before Maugham began to write, James had to be cut down to size.

A great theatergoer, Maugham happened to be present on the notorious first night of James' play *Guy Domville,* in 1895. Following the custom of the time, the author was brought onstage to take a bow. Greeted with a surprising outburst of boos and catcalls, James retreated like a wounded animal. Maugham, whose plays were far superior to James', never forgot that public humiliation. He bluntly told a theatrical friend: "Do you know why Uncle Henry's plays don't succeed? I'll tell you why. I've read them all. They're lousy, that's why they don't succeed."

Maugham thought that James, like the prototypical aesthete, didn't actually live but only observed life through a window. Instead of portraying the powerful rise of America, one of the crucial events of the nineteenth century, he merely recorded the trivial proceedings at tea parties in English country houses and exercised "his extreme subtlety on the anaemic passions of the fashionable world." Musing perhaps on James' "obscure hurt" and on the vague but practical utensil that created the wealth of Chad Newsome in *The Ambassadors,* Maugham wondered how James' ethereal and introspective characters actually coped with their physiological needs. A perennial outsider himself, Maugham felt that James was even more alienated from British society. James had lived in England for forty years, but never managed to create a completely convincing English character.

In Maugham's view, James' famous convoluted style, so different from his own, revealed his absurd pomposity. James' infinitely qualified and involved periphrastics were forever circling, approaching, retreating and feinting. His tortuous attempt to find the exact word to express his all-too-refined feelings in speech mirrored the exasperating indirectness of his work. Talking to Maugham, and curious about a well-known actress, James found it difficult to phrase his question. Gesturing, finally, in desperation, he asked: "Is she, *enfin,* what you'd call if you were asked point-blank, if so to speak you were put with your back to the wall, is she a *femme du monde?*" Maugham's most serious criticism was that James, because of his remoteness from real life, was imperceptive when dealing with human emotions, that he lacked the necessary empathy to penetrate the thoughts and express the feelings of his characters. The result, Maugham argued, lacked probability and truth, and was purely literary.

On his first trip to America, in 1910, Maugham visited James in Cambridge, where he had gone after the recent death of his brother William. According to Maugham, James, estranged and forlorn in his native country, made a fantastic and unforgettable remark. " 'I wander about these great empty streets of Boston,' he said, 'and I never see a soul. I could not be more alone in the Sahara.' " Maugham's point was that ordinary people in a crowded city meant nothing to James, who—a stranger in both England and America—saw Boston as a depopulated wasteland. Maugham's view of James was influenced by his personal impressions. He didn't like James' style or content, and did not, like most others, feel awe and reverence for his older contemporary. By assuming a critical, even superior, attitude to James, Maugham enraged the highbrow critics, who took revenge by attacking him and undermining his reputation.[7]

In the summer of 1905, after a few months of Bohemian life in Paris, Maugham returned to hedonistic Capri, where many devotees had fled after Wilde's imprisonment. Maugham once told the critic Raymond Mortimer that on "weekends in the country he was occasionally asked to share a bed with some other young man. More often than not this led to a sexual encounter which, in Maugham's words, 'turned out to be very pleasant.' " There were more pleasant surprises before he even reached the blessed isle. He archly wrote Gerald Kelly that on the boat from Marseilles to Naples he'd met an Egyptian pasha who immediately succumbed to his charms and made outrageous proposals. Though Maugham, like the biblical Joseph and Richardson's Pamela, haughtily declined the overture, he was nevertheless pleased by the compliment. He also told the novelist Violet Hunt that gossip and scandal were pandemic in Capri (though he didn't mention his own adventures) and said he was taking a complete holiday from writing: "Capri is as charming as ever it was, the people as odd: everybody is very immoral, but fortunately not so dull as those who kick over the traces often are. Each foreigner has his little scabrous history, which far from being whispered into the willing ear, is shouted from the rooftops. . . . All the morning I bathe; after luncheon I sleep till tea-time, then wander among the interminable vineyards, in the evening read or look at the moon."[8]

III

STILL HOPING FOR his first critical and financial success, Maugham immediately began work on his next novel. In the awkwardly titled *The*

Bishop's Apron (1906), which suggests an ecclesiastic in the kitchen and was dedicated to Harry Philips, Trollope meets P. G. Wodehouse. The unappealing hero Theodore Spratte, a fifty-year-old widower and canon of a fashionable London church, is worldly and ambitious. The story concerns his courtship of a rich widow, Mrs. Fitzherbert; his restless intrigues to obtain a bishopric; and, when the widow reveals she'll lose her income if she remarries, his final capture of a brewer's wealthy daughter.

In this drawing-room comedy in the form of a novel, all the characters are satirized. Spratte, a pompous snob and arch-Tory who condescends to women, is egoistic, arrogant and repulsive. But the farcical plot enables him to get everything he wants as he slithers toward episcopal preferment and produces a son who inherits his brother's title. Onstage the one-dimensional characters, carried along by the conventions of comedy, might be mildly amusing, but the novel makes tedious reading and (apart from his historical fiction) is Maugham's worst book. Since the first printing was less than 1,500 copies and it was never reprinted (nor even published in America), it is now one of Maugham's rarest books.[9]

The Explorer (1907) is loosely based on the adventures of the Welsh explorer H. M. Stanley (1841–1904), who found Dr. Livingstone in the depths of the Congo. Alec McKenzie, an old Etonian who has defeated Arab slave-traders in Africa and enabled Britain to claim a territory larger than the United Kingdom, causes tremendous excitement at home. "No such enthusiasm," Maugham writes, "had been aroused in England since Stanley returned from the journey which he afterwards described in *Darkest Africa*." Since Maugham had never been to Africa, he worked up the tropical material from books, and his generic sentences sound distinctly secondhand: "behind those gaunt rocks fierce battles were fought, new lands explored, and the slavers beaten back foot by foot."

The operatic themes of love versus honor and the obstacles to marriage emerge when the brave young man returns to England from the colonies. As in *The Hero,* which also has flashbacks to Africa, a disgraced father (this time imprisoned for fraud) seeks redemption through the career of his son, George. A touch of Victorian melodrama creeps in when the father, released from prison, is handed a bouquet of flowers by his daughter, Lucy: "He took them with trembling hands and pressed them to his heart, then he buried his face in them, and the tears ran afresh, bedewing the yellow flowers." On the campaign in Africa, George, "rotten-through-and-through," had disgraced himself by cowardly behavior. Alec, after sacrificing the treacherous George to save the other men, is falsely accused of cowardice. Alec has promised George not to tell Lucy what really happened, and cannot defend himself.

In *The Explorer,* a mediocre yet quite readable novel, Maugham imitated Conrad. His description of the tropics comes straight out of *Heart of Darkness* (1899): "Her eyes were dazzled with the torrid African sun, and she felt the horror of the primeval forest"; and his account of the *folie d'Afrique* (with its allusion to Proverbs 16:31) echoed Conrad's Kurtz: "Men seemed to go mad from a sense of power, to lose all the restraints which had kept them in the way of righteousness."[10] And, as in Conrad's novella, Alec had to lie to an Intended about the horrible behavior of her beloved hero in Africa.

The Magician (1908), a flawed but intriguing novel, is the story of Oliver Haddo, a character based on Aleister Crowley, whom Maugham met through Gerald Kelly in Paris. The son of a rich brewer and Plymouth Brother who left him a substantial fortune, Crowley, a self-styled Satanist, claimed to be a reincarnation of the Great Beast in Revelation 11:7, "that ascendeth out of the bottomless pit [to] make war against them, and shall overcome them, and kill them." After the Great War he settled in Sicily with a group of disciples. But rumors of drugs, orgies and magical ceremonies involving the sacrifice of infants led to his expulsion from Italy and earned his long-sought reputation for evil. He married Kelly's pretty sister Rose under strange circumstances. She was engaged to one man and involved with another, yet eloped with Crowley the day after they met. She came under his evil influence, and was the model for Margaret Dauncey in *The Magician.* Nuit, his daughter by Rose, died of typhoid fever in Rangoon at the age of two. Both Rose and his second wife, Maria Teresa, became alcoholics and were committed to insane asylums.

In *A Moveable Feast,* when Hemingway spots "the gaunt man in the cape with the tall woman [who] passed us on the sidewalk" in Paris, a friend tells him: "That's Aleister Crowley, the diabolist. He's supposed to be the wickedest man in the world." Yeats, who tangled with Crowley in mystical circles, called him " 'a person of unspeakable life,' already embroiled in homosexual scandal." Maugham told Christopher Isherwood that "he hadn't known many really evil men. The only two he could think of offhand were Aleister Crowley and Norman Douglas," who was a notorious pedophile.[11] Maugham took an instant dislike to Crowley, though Crowley interested and amused him, and in the novel made Oliver

Haddo even more sinister and ruthless. Crowley really was an accomplished big-game hunter and mountaineer, and had climbed K2, the second-highest peak in India, without using oxygen. But he was a liar and a fake, and when he claimed to be starving and urgently cabled a request for £25, Maugham refused.

In 1907 Maugham sent the completed novel to J. B. Pinker with a note that harshly concluded that it "is very dull and stupid; I wish I were an outside Broker, or [the popular novelist] Hall Caine, or something equally despicable." He also told Kelly about the difficulty of getting it into print. It was originally accepted, printed and advertised by Methuen. The head of the firm then read it, broke into a cold sweat and swore that publication of such an outrageous work would ruin Maugham as well as the publisher. Maugham thought of having it appear anonymously, but finally persuaded Heinemann to bring it out.

In *The Magician* Arthur Burdon, an established young English surgeon on a study trip to Paris, visits his fiancée, Margaret Dauncey. A vivacious and exquisitely beautiful art student, she lives with her friend Susie Boyd. Burdon, with an unusual capacity for suffering, fears that something terrible will occur to spoil their happiness. Their nemesis is the extremely tall and obese Oliver Haddo. Educated at Eton and Oxford, he speaks with fake grandiloquence, is consumed by a lust for evil knowledge and has formidable powers of magic. He makes a horse tremble by touching it, feels no pain when bitten by a snake and sets water on fire. His evil ambition is to create living beings, and he succeeds in making human blood and grotesque homunculi.

When Margaret's dog bites Haddo and he kicks it, Burdon beats and kicks him in retaliation. Haddo doesn't resist, but plots revenge. The novel describes Haddo's magic power over Margaret and the tragedy that results when—like Philip Carey in *Of Human Bondage*—she becomes mesmerized by the lover she hates: "Her contempt for him, her utter loathing, were alloyed with a feeling that aroused in her horror and dismay. She could not get the man out of her thoughts. All that he had said, all that she had seen, seemed . . . unaccountably to absorb her." In a fascinating scene Margaret, corrupted by Haddo's evil, takes "horrible delight" when Susie weeps over her frustrated love for Burdon.

Haddo casts a spell on Margaret and persuades her to marry him. But he agrees (as Crowley originally did with Rose Kelly) not to consummate the marriage because he needs a virgin for his monstrous experiments.

(Burdon could deflower her to ruin her satanic value, but is too much of a gentleman to do so.) After Burdon discovers that Haddo has murdered Margaret, he kills him and burns down the house where all the evil has occurred: "as he spoke it seemed that the roof fell in, for suddenly vast flames sprang up, rising high into the still night air; and they saw that the house they had just left was blazing furiously."

The Magician's hypnotic villain comes straight out of Revenge tragedy and Gothic fiction. As in Edgar Allan Poe's stories and Mary Shelley's *Frankenstein,* there's a mad scientist, a spooky mansion, bizarre experiments, a quest for divine (or diabolical) powers, a House of Usher–like destruction (brought about by both psychological and architectural stress) as well as the heroine's split personality. "There seem to be two persons in me," Margaret tells Burdon, predicting her fate, "and my real self, the old one that you knew and loved, is growing weaker day by day, and will soon be dead entirely." Ironically, Margaret does not seem sexually desirable to Burdon until Haddo has awakened her passion.

Though Crowley claimed "Willie's harmless as a wad of sterilized cotton,"[12] he was wounded by Maugham's satire. He retaliated by reviewing the novel in the London *Vanity Fair* (December 1908) under the byline "Oliver Haddo," pointing out Maugham's plagiarism from books on magic and from the fantastic experiments on animals in H. G. Wells' *The Island of Dr. Moreau* (1896). Since the books on magic were all mumbo jumbo and added nothing to the novel, the criticism fell flat. When Maugham's English and American publishers were planning his *Collected Works* in 1934, he told Nelson Doubleday that he'd been ashamed to let *The Making of a Saint, Orientations, The Hero* and *The Bishop's Apron* be reissued in their present form, and that he didn't want to spend a year revising them. But in 1956 he rightly changed his mind about *The Magician* and brought it out with a new preface. *The Explorer* and *The Merry-Go-Round* were not included in his *Collected Works* until after his death.

IV

WITH ASTONISHING VERSATILITY Maugham had written novels on many different, and sometimes topical, subjects: slum life and the oppression of women; the traumatic effects of the Boer War; marriage that attempted to transcend class barriers; ecclesiastical careerism; the slave trade in Africa; and black magic. None of them had made any money, and very few authors have ever achieved success after writing so many poor books. As late as 1907, when he had nearly exhausted his funds, he was prepared to return to medicine, enroll in a refresher course and sign on as a ship's doctor, which would have provided a steady income and allowed him to roam the world.

After slogging away on seven novels, a collection of stories and a travel book in the difficult and penurious decade since *Liza of Lambeth,* Maugham suddenly had a lucky break. In 1908 *Lady Frederick* was finally put onstage and became a surprising success. The following year *Mrs. Dot* and *Jack Straw*—which H. L. Mencken described as "labored epigrams strung upon a thread of drawing-room adultery"—as well as the stage version of *The Explorer* were also produced. In 1909 Maugham had four plays running at the same time—a first in British theatrical history—and thirty-five thousand people saw them every week. Walter Payne, glancing through a sporting paper, found photographs of two racehorses named Lady Frederick and Mrs. Dot. A cartoon in *Punch* showed Shakespeare, in doublet and hose, hunched over, biting his thumb and gazing enviously at the advertisements for Maugham's plays.

Maugham wrote brilliant parts for actresses. In a speech praising the talent and hard work of Marie Tempest, who starred in *Mrs. Dot,* he explained that her fine performances "are due not only to her natural gifts, which are eminent, but to patience, assiduity, industry and discipline. Without these it is impossible to excel in any of the arts." He was now in great demand, popular actors begged him for parts, and he told Gladys Cooper that he was going to collect all the lines that had been cut and make a new play out of them. The actor Ernest Thesiger, a mannered homosexual, "once complained that Somerset Maugham never sent him anything." Maugham replied: "B-but, I am always writing p-parts for you, Ernest. The trouble is that somebody called Gladys Cooper *will* insist on p-playing them."[13]

Maugham, who'd done without money for a long time but felt it was essential to happiness, was fond of saying that "money is like a sixth sense without which you cannot make a complete use of the other five." His American publisher George Doran noted that once he was courted by publishers and producers and got the upper hand, he was "a shrewd bargainer, with a proper and equitable appraisal of the value of his work for magazine or book publication or for the stage." A serendipitous windfall occurred in 1908, when the American producer George Tyler gave him a huge check for a year's option on *Lady Frederick*. Unable to put the play on, Tyler complained: "All I ever got out of it was the privilege of giving Maugham his first cocktail and paying him a thousand good dollars when he needed them in the worst way."[14] In a short time Maugham went from earning £100 a year to making several hundred a week. His instant and overwhelming theatrical success enabled him to live, like his father, as a gentleman.

The director Basil Dean found him remote, rather disdainful and apparently uninterested in the preparation of his plays: "Throughout the rehearsals he remained withdrawn, neither helpful nor destructive, never offering advice unless it was asked for. I think he found the whole business tiresome and the actors' arguments rather petty." But the actress Irene Vanbrugh saw the lively—even joyous—side of his character: "He would come constantly to rehearsals, looking very immaculate. He had a clear-cut personality and complete control of himself except for a slight stammer. He was a gay dancing partner and I have memories of a barn dance with him about midnight on the polished floor of Covent Garden Theatre at a gala charity ball."[15] Harold Acton, who was surprised to find Maugham foxtrotting in Florence, agreed that he was a very good "tea-dancer."

The bitterness of Maugham's early failures soured his belated triumph. His transition from failure to success made him just as sharp-tongued with his associates and his theatrical agent Reginald Bright as he'd been with William Morris Colles. Only later, when he was well established and secure, did he become more temperate and polite. When he felt that a colleague had betrayed him, he swore to get even. His main American impresario was Charles Frohman, a chubby little Buddha in a huge fur coat. (He drowned, at the peak of his career, when the *Lusitania* was torpedoed in 1915.) In November 1908, Maugham called him a "perfect idiot" and told Bright: "I have long been aware that he knows far less about a play than the youngest call-boy at the most insignificant of his theatres. . . . If Marie Tempest does not like [his play *Penelope*] she will be a bitch." (Luckily, she *did* like it.) The following spring, Maugham continued to condemn Frohman, who was condescending and insisted he turn out frivolous comedies instead of more substantial drama: "I am sick of the whole theatrical business. It is all hideous and revolting. Why does Frohman want me to do a 'light play'? Does he think I care to go on repeating myself? . . . If he thinks I am only good enough to provide comic relief from the serious work of Granville-Barker and Galsworthy, he can keep his commissions to himself."

Maugham wrote twenty-nine plays (and did three translations from French and Italian) between 1897 and 1933. But when he brought out his *Collected Plays* in 1931–34, he included only eighteen of them. He omitted *The Man of Honour* (1898) as too immature, *The Tenth Man* (1909), which he didn't much like, and *Landed Gentry* for reasons he forgot. *Smith* (1909), a comedy that satirized heartless upper-class women and the casual anti-Semitism of the time, contained in the third act a tragic and shocking scene. While the bridge players are waiting for Cynthia Rosenberg, her husband calls up to say that their baby is ill and asks that she ring him back as soon as she arrives. Unwilling to disturb the game, Rose Dallas-Baker, the hostess, does not convey the message when Cynthia appears. Soon afterward, her husband calls again and Smith, the goodhearted maid, answers the telephone, takes the message and is forced to announce that the baby has died. Though Cynthia is appalled and Smith deeply affected, the other women are merely irritated:

FREEMAN [Rose's brother]:   Rose, you didn't refuse to tell Rosenberg
    where his wife was so that your bridge party shouldn't be upset?
ROSE: Good heavens, you don't suppose I knew the child was dying.
    Otto was always getting into a state about its health. The whole thing's
    a beastly nuisance.

Maugham's caustic description of how a beautiful, selfish and shallow society woman responds to the threat of death was brilliantly re-created in two greater works. At the end of Proust's *The Guermantes Way* (1921) the Duke and Duchess de Guermantes are on their way out to a ball when their close friend Charles Swann comes to tell them that he has a fatal disease and will soon be dead. Incapable of responding to his despair, the duchess turns away from him and, at her husband's bidding, coldheartedly returns to the house to change into red shoes that match her dress. In Evelyn Waugh's *A Handful of Dust* (1934), Brenda Last is told that "John" has died in an accident. Distraught at first, she believes the victim is her lover and is relieved to learn that her young son is dead.

Maugham's theatrical achievements made him a social success. A London hostess told the quiet, even silent Maugham that she was intrigued by his restless vitality. But his triumph, he soon discovered, might not last.

With three straight flops after *Smith,* he ironically told a friend: "It is rather a nuisance, for all the people who have asked me to dine and to stay on the strength of a success will now have to put up with me as a failure."[16]

V

MAUGHAM'S NEWFOUND FAME led, as it had three years before in Bohemian Paris, to important literary friendships. In a rather cryptic remark about James Barrie, whose confused sexuality made *Peter Pan* an ambiguous as well as popular play, Maugham later told the English critic Cyril Connolly that he'd known Barrie for thirty years and didn't much care for him. Barrie's fake-precious character gave him the creeps. Replying to a query about his relations with Bernard Shaw, Maugham said he'd once known him fairly well, but never actually had a conversation with him. Shaw did all the talking and Maugham (like most others) was never able to get a word in.

Max Beerbohm, a wit, dandy and aesthete, carried the spirit of the 1890s into the new century and maintained it for the rest of his life. A neat, dapper man with goggle eyes and a turned-up mustache, he'd favorably reviewed three of Maugham's plays. "I've never met a man with a culture so self-contained as Max," Maugham exclaimed. "I think he's hardly read a book since he left Oxford in the nineties—even the little Latin tags in his essays seem to smack of his Oxford days." Maugham told Harold Acton that Beerbohm "has frozen himself in time, and continues without doing a stroke of work to become more and more famous. And there I am, writing more and more novels, which people criticize and find worse than the last, and I don't know why the devil I'm doing it." When Maugham was dining with the short, bald, white-mustached and straw-hatted Beerbohm at his home in Rapallo, on the Italian Riviera, Max suggested they go see the great German playwright Gerhart Hauptmann. Like Ibsen, Hauptmann was a towering figure in European theater and won the Nobel Prize in 1912. They found the old man, with an aureole of white hair and a naked reddish face, surrounded by a circle of admirers who listened to his every word with rapt attention. Literary figures in England, Maugham realized, did not receive such adoration.

In 1908 Reggie Turner introduced Maugham to Shaw's colleague in the Fabian Society, H. G. Wells, then at the height of his fame. Never a stuffed shirt, Wells had an engaging personality. Maugham described him as fat and homely, with a thin squeaky voice, but noted that one of his mistresses had said his skin smelled like honey. "H.G. had strong sexual instincts," and often told Maugham that the physical "need to satisfy these instincts had nothing to do with love." Unlike most men, Wells never idealized women. Like Maugham, Wells would later, in his novel *Boon* (1916), ridicule Henry James. He also wrote easily and revised very little, and repudiated his early novels. Since Wells' characters existed only to express his own ideas, he seemed more like a pamphleteer than a novelist. Using exactly the same term that Maugham used to describe his own early books, Wells exclaimed: "They're as dead as mutton, you know. They all dealt with matters of topical interest and now that the matters aren't topical any more they're unreadable."[17] Wells later gave Maugham a set of his *Complete Works,* and on the title page drew a line from *"Works"* to a witty sketch of himself with bits of clockworks floating inside his body.

In early 1907 Maugham, still uncertain of his sexual tastes, began the first of four significant affairs with women. Violet Hunt, twelve years his senior, was the daughter of a painter and a novelist who had known Tennyson, Browning and Ruskin and been part of the Pre-Raphaelite circle. Violet was snobbish, intensely curious and uncontrollably impulsive, "a sensualist of the emotions," who has been compared to Moll Flanders and Molly Bloom. "Chattering with sublime disregard for practically everything, with distraught golden hair, [she was] obviously a beauty of the Edwardian era." She was called "a handsome witch . . . brilliant and caustic, [and] an aura of Pre-Raphaelite glory still flickered about her."

Maugham had met Violet in April 1902 when both wrote for an ephemeral art and literature magazine, *The Venture,* which he edited with the artist and writer Laurence Housman. Maugham was preceded in her affections by the notorious lesbian Radclyffe Hall and followed by Wells and, during a scandalous liaison, by the much-married and harried Ford Madox Ford. Violet had previously contracted syphilis from Oswald Crawfurd, a publisher at Chapman and Hall. But she was (like Ada Leverson) attracted to the secretive and mysterious Maugham, and told Rebecca West the painful tale of how she'd seduced him and found him "a fearfully emotional man, sexually."

Maugham and Violet remained good friends after their affair, which had strengthened his ego, fizzled out. She sent him her unpublished work, and he made constructive comments on its content and style. He told her that since they were both very clever, they found it difficult to remain silent, even (or especially) when they thought of bitter and wounding remarks. Always keen to keep up appearances, Maugham was willing to remain unaware of Violet's true opinion of him as long as she was kind to him when they met. With pointed irony, he dedicated *The Land of the Blessed Virgin* to Violet, who "could not imagine what in hell would be her business in such a country." Violet retaliated by dedicating her 1908 novel, *White Rose of Weary Leaf* (an even worse title than Maugham's), to him.

Alec Waugh recalled a moving incident during a literary dinner in 1922, after Violet's involvement with Ford had destroyed what remained of her reputation: "As the waiter bustled forward with their bills, Maugham picked up the two slips of paper. 'I think I can stand you a lunch, Violet.' . . . Maugham's gesture reestablished her as regards that gathering. He seemed to be saying to us all that she was not only an old friend, but the one person in the room of any consequence to himself."[18]

Maugham's fondness for Violet's artiness, cynicism and brains shone through his affectionate portrayal of her as Rose Waterford in *The Moon and Sixpence*. Rose, who could be malicious, was "torn between the aestheticism of her early youth, when she used to go to parties in sage green, holding a daffodil, and the flippancy of her maturer years, which tended to high heels and Paris frocks. . . . [She] was a cynic. She looked upon life as an opportunity for writing novels and the public as her raw material. . . . She combined a masculine intelligence with a feminine perversity, and the novels she wrote were original and disconcerting."[19]

Gerald Kelly's portrait of Maugham, *The Jester* (1911), was painted a few years after his affair with Violet and his triumphant success on the London stage. In front of a rich background, with three Oriental statues standing on a cabinet and the swirling pattern of a large Chinese screen, Maugham, in a dandyish 1890s pose, stares at the viewer. He sits, one leg crossed over the other, in a padded chair with wooden arms. Formally dressed in gray trousers, black coat and tie, and high top hat with a wide ribbon and curved brim, he rests his left hand on an upright cane. The somber colors are highlighted by his white gloves, handkerchief and shirt, by the light glinting off his highly polished shoes and his pale white face. His curled mustache, echoing the curve of the top hat, suggests his old arrogance and his newfound self-assurance. Kelly's most famous portrait captured a dazzling image of the theatrical man of letters.

The Jester, *portrait of Maugham by Gerald Kelly, 1911*

6

Sue Jones and Syrie

1909–1915

MAUGHAM SPENT MOST of his life living with men. But in the decade between 1905 and 1915 he had love affairs with four attractive and professionally accomplished women, and portrayed them in his work. Violet Hunt appeared as Rose Waterford in *The Moon and Sixpence,* the revolutionary princess Alexandra Kropotkin became Anastasia Leonidov in *Ashenden* and Lydia in *Christmas Holiday,* the actress Ethelwyn Sylvia (Sue) Jones inspired Rosie Driffield in *Cakes and Ale* and Gwendolyn Syrie Barnardo Wellcome was the model for Mrs. Tower in "Jane" and Lady Grayston in *Our Betters.* Violet (who overlapped with Sue) was twelve years older than Maugham; the others were considerably younger.

Maugham was intensely misogynistic well before he had affairs with Violet and Sasha, fell deeply in love with and proposed to Sue, and rather reluctantly married Syrie. In a notebook entry as early as 1896, when his experience was limited to impersonal observation and to prostitutes, he remarked that marriage had a negative effect on the character of the man (if not of the woman): "The usual result of a man's cohabitation with a woman, however sanctioned by society, is to make him a little more petty, a little meaner than he would otherwise have been." In an unusually passionate and revealing letter of about 1905 (Maugham rarely included the year when dating his letters) to Gerald Kelly, who had become unfortunately tied up with a woman, Maugham said he felt grateful that he was no longer entangled, did not have to endure a woman's exacting demands and could retain his precious freedom. Men had to suffer unreasonable sulks, absurd quarrels and agonizing jealousy if they allowed themselves to be bound hand and foot. Concluding a polemic worthy of Nietzsche or Strindberg, Maugham prayed that he would never again become a slave to passion.

In *The Constant Wife* he called free love the "most overrated amusement that was ever invented." In *Christmas Holiday* he quoted Lord Chesterfield's caustic denigration of sexual relations: "the pleasure is momentary, the position is ridiculous, and the expense is damnable." After visiting the South Seas, he vitriolically contrasted the frank sexuality of the natives to the mendacious, exploitative, egoistic and sadistic behavior of Western women—who were also disappointing in bed:

> They did not have in their sexual congress the obnoxious deceit and shrewdness of European women. . . . [They do not use sex] as a cruel and psychological weapon. . . . I prefer a free-loving, passionate woman to a frigid and selfish one, a promiscuous one to a stupidly virtuous female. . . . Her European white sister is invariably a boresome psychopath, a frustrated female plagued by Freudian neuroses, who imposes on any man who truly loves her, but whom she does not care for, as much cruelty as she is capable of. . . . The majority of women are physiological messes, and not many of them, for sex, are worth more than a fiver.[1]

After all these fulminations Maugham—like Oscar Wilde, André Gide and Siegfried Sassoon—married and had a child.

Despite his ingrained misogyny and homosexuality, the great love of Maugham's life was undoubtedly the warm, gentle, maternal, sexy Sue Jones. Born nine years after Maugham, the second daughter of the eminent playwright Henry Arthur Jones, the blond, blue-eyed Sue radiated a natural vivacity and, like Violet Hunt, had "a most amusing direct way of talking." She started her stage career as a teenager in one of her father's plays, and then acted in Beerbohm Tree's Shakespearean company. But her talent was limited, and she spent most of her time playing small parts in provincial theaters.

Sue married the theatrical manager Montagu Leveaux in 1902. In the summer of 1904, when she was separated from her husband but not yet divorced, Maugham met her at the garden party of one of his wealthy

London hostesses, Christina Steevens, to whom he gratefully dedicated *The Explorer.* Gerald Kelly—who also found Sue attractive, painted her twice and probably slept with her—hinted at her promiscuity: "She was one of the most delightful women I have ever known. I thought her wonderfully beautiful, but she had one failing. . . . She posed beautifully for the picture, so patiently, and both of us did our best, and I think Willie loved the portrait. I did several portraits of her—all, I felt, quite good. The picture was painted when I myself was very much under the influence of the great Whistler: but it really was like dear Sue."

In one Kelly painting, the full-lipped, broad-nosed, wide-eyed Sue is seated on a patterned chair. She's holding white gloves and wearing a white gown (a strong contrast to the black background) that flows from the extreme décolletage down to the carpet and covers her feet, sniffed at by a square-muzzled terrier. In another, Sue stands in the foreground, wraps a feathered shawl around her arms and wears another low-cut, long white dress. It reveals her swan-like neck and ample bosom, and cascades to the ground like classical drapery. She's tied a black bow to the base of her elaborate hairdo, tilts her head slightly back, half-opens her mouth and half-closes her eyes. The effect is less formal, more engaging than in the first portrait, and makes her seem vulnerable yet emotionally responsive.[2]

In his notebook of 1904 Maugham wrote rapturously of Sue's "ripe and abundant charms, rosy of cheek and fair of hair, with eyes as blue as the summer sea, with rounded lines and full breasts." He compared her to Rubens' Hélène Fourment, and she also resembled the luscious women in the paintings of Renoir. He later said that Sue, who'd played Peyton, the maid, had inspired his play *Penelope* (1908). The play ends as Penelope mocks the sexual desires of her unfaithful husband and, to arouse his jealousy and maintain his interest, goes off for a weekend with friends. A friend of Gerald Kelly, on the scene at the time, noted that Sue had "led a miserable life . . . & then met Willie, the only man she ever loved, thinks G.K. This did not keep her from continuing her promiscuous ways. Maugham hasn't changed her a bit. She has no compunctions about the feelings of people."

Sue enjoyed sex and went to bed with any man she fancied. Maugham desperately wanted to marry her, but was troubled by her notorious promiscuity and humiliated by the fact that all his friends had slept with her. (It would have been worse if she'd slept with his enemies.) In late 1913

Sue Jones, portrait by Gerald Kelly

he followed her to Chicago, where she was appearing in a road company. He overcame his doubts and finally proposed to her, and was shocked when she refused. She said she wasn't married and didn't love anyone else, loved Maugham with all her heart and believed that he loved her, yet couldn't marry him. Years later she told him that "she had just learned she was pregnant by another man. A casual thing, an accident. But there it was. . . . She never had the child. . . . She had a miscarriage. But our moment had passed." In December of that year she married her lover, Angus McDonnell, son of the Irish earl of Antrim, left the stage and remained with him until her death in 1948.

Maugham's loving portrayal of the rosy-complexioned Sue as Rosie Driffield in *Cakes and Ale* is his most sincere, sensual and passionate characterization of a woman. Its warmth and tenderness provides a striking contrast to his unconvincing attempts to express sexual feelings in his early novels: "There was something amazingly attractive in the way her virginal beauty ... contrasted with the stateliness of her gown. ... The skin under her eyes, faintly blue, was all dewy. ... Her lips, those very full red lips of hers, rested on mine long enough for me to be conscious of their shape and their warmth and their softness." Overcome by desire and gratitude, the young Willie Ashenden weeps when they begin to make love and rests his head on her breasts: "She rocked me back and forth as though I were a child in her arms." After she undresses, "when I put my hands on her sides I could feel the ribbing of the skin from the pressure of the corsets. ... Her waist was naturally small; though so well developed she was very slender; her breasts were straight and firm and they stood out from the chest as though carved in marble. It was a body made for the act of love. ... It was all silvery gold: and the only colour was the rosy pink of the hard nipples."[3]

II

SYRIE'S FATHER WAS the great Victorian philanthropist Dr. Thomas John Barnardo. Tiny, frail and almost totally deaf, Barnardo was born in Hamburg in 1845. His Jewish family left Germany, after a wave of anti-Semitic riots, when Barnardo was still a small child. They settled in Dublin, where he later converted to Evangelical Christianity and preached fervently in the slums. After briefly studying medicine in London (he never actually became a doctor), he planned to become a missionary and convert the heathen in the wilds of China. But he decided instead to rescue homeless children in his own country, and with typically demonic energy founded more than forty orphanages in London and throughout England.

Syrie (short for Sarah Louise) was born in 1879, one of seven children (of whom four survived), including a mentally retarded dwarf. Brought up in a strict and pious household amidst a horde of waifs and orphans, Syrie (nicknamed "Queenie") spent her Sundays reading the Bible and singing hymns. She played the organ while her father raised money in London churches, and never smoked or drank. Syrie first met Henry Wellcome, a Wisconsin-born chemist and pharmaceutical tycoon, at her parents' house in Surbiton, on the Thames, in 1899. They became engaged on a cruise up the Nile in 1901. Though Wellcome was twenty-six years older than she, his religious background, commitment to medical research and impressive wealth (which might be channeled into Barnardo's orphanages) made him seem the ideal husband. They married in 1901, and two years later had a mentally retarded son, whom they farmed out to a foster family. The marriage ended acrimoniously in Quito, Ecuador, in 1909 when Wellcome accused Syrie of adultery with an American financier. Like Maugham, he believed she was a "deeply immoral" woman. After their separation Syrie, who had a hot temper and sharp tongue, told a friend: "Ever since our marriage, the greater part of our time has been spent, as he well knows, in places I detested, collecting curios . . . sacrificing myself in a way I hated, both to please him and to gather curios."

Reacting against her pious background, Syrie had many lovers. The leader of the pack was Gordon Selfridge, another Wisconsin tycoon, who'd made his fortune in England by founding the huge Oxford Street department store that still bears his name. Like Syrie, the flamboyant Selfridge came from a puritanical family, but knew how to spend money. He took long holidays in Monte Carlo, gambled and owned racehorses, and was seen about town with glamorous and socially prominent women. A contemporary gossip columnist wrote that "Selfridge is as much one of the sights of London as Big Ben. With his black morning jacket, grey-striped trousers, white vest slip, pearl tie-pin and orchid buttonhole, he is a mobile landmark of the metropolis."

Maugham first met Syrie in late 1913, when he was still in love with Sue Jones, and she was married to Wellcome and involved with Selfridge. In February 1914, soon after Sue had rejected his proposal and married her Irish nobleman, Syrie and Maugham became lovers. The thin-lipped, large-nosed Syrie was more attractive than beautiful. She had fine brown eyes and lovely skin, was fashionably and expensively dressed, and wore large—but fake—emerald rings. Her biographer wrote that "Syrie was independent-minded, unreflective and brassy, qualities which must have once appealed to her [future] husband but gradually stood out more and more harshly against his own reticence."[4]

Maugham dined frequently at her house and was delighted to go to bed with her. Syrie—a divorcée, adulteress and kept woman—flattered him by declaring she was madly in love and surprised him by suggesting they have a baby. He gallantly (if rather passively) went along with her wishes, but she miscarried their first child. It's surprising that Maugham, a medical doctor with a knowledge of genetics, would risk a second pregnancy with the thirty-five-year-old Syrie, whose brother and only child were both physically impaired and mentally retarded, and who'd just had a miscarriage. Nevertheless, when she became pregnant again in late November 1914 he took her to Rome (Italy had not yet entered the war, and it was close to his favorite bolt-hole in Capri), where she could have their baby in secret. Though not cut out to be a father, he wanted to have a child.

Wellcome had settled only £2,400 a year on Syrie, and Selfridge had been paying for her luxurious house in Regent's Park. In 1915, when Syrie nobly refused Selfridge's offer to settle £5,000 a year on her (more than double Wellcome's sum), Maugham wrote a rather cryptic letter to Kelly, his closest friend and confidant, suggesting that Syrie was pregnant and had broken with Selfridge. The sordid situation shocked Maugham and made him extremely uneasy. He couldn't bring himself to praise or defend Syrie's behavior, though he saw that her impulse to be honest had finally destroyed the edifice of secrecy and lies on which her life was built. Unwilling to lie about his own feelings, Maugham hoped to be kind, firm and just. If that led to a break with Syrie, he would have no regrets.

The affair reached its crisis when Wellcome hired private detectives to follow Syrie. When he found proof of her adultery, Syrie tried to kill herself by swallowing a whole bottle of veronal pills. She'd deceived Maugham by telling him that Wellcome had given her freedom to do as she pleased. But, Wellcome's biographer stated, "there is certainly no evidence" for this highly improbable assertion in Wellcome's correspondence with his lawyers." When his detectives got wind of Syrie's pregnancy, which Maugham was particularly eager to keep out of the courts, Wellcome sued for divorce and named the conveniently well-off and unmarried Maugham, rather than Selfridge, as corespondent.

Sir George Lewis, a reliable old friend and Oscar Wilde's solicitor, told Maugham that Selfridge, to avoid becoming involved in the scandal, had broken with Syrie and that she, living well above her means, she was heavily in debt. "You're to be the mug to save her," Sir George warned. "You're cruelly trapped and you'd be a fool to marry her." Maugham certainly did not want to marry her but, remembering that he'd been orphaned as a small child, replied: "if I don't I shall regret it all my life. . . . I could not bear to think what [the child's] future would be if I didn't marry its mother."

Maugham had often tried to solve his problems by a change of locale. After Syrie's first and second pregnancies he'd fled to his old refuge in Capri. Ellingham Brooks, aware that Maugham was being trapped, feared that an unholy woman would invade their sanctuary and disrupt their homosexual life. The novelist Compton Mackenzie, who also lived on Capri, remembered Brooks in the summer of 1914 "coming along one day in a great flutter to say that Maugham had got himself involved with a married woman and that he was going to have to marry her. 'I don't know what I shall do if Maugham brings a wife to the [Villa] Cercola. I don't think Benson will like it at all either.' "[5]

Maugham was an unwilling bridegroom, but he had social as well as literary ambitions, wanted to conform to the prevailing mores and thought a "good" marriage would enhance his career. In his autobiographical *The Summing Up* (1938), he gave a naive but poignant account of what he expected in marriage. He hoped it would bring peace from the disturbance of chaotic and troublesome love affairs, provide a tranquil and settled existence, allow him all the time he needed to write and enable him to live a free yet dignified life. In fact, none of these hopes was ever realized. His love affair with Gerald Haxton, whom he met before Syrie became pregnant, inevitably caused tumultuous complications with his wife. She constantly interfered with, even prevented, his writing, and his life became more turbulent than ever. Seeking freedom, he found only bondage. His relations with Syrie left a residue of permanent hatred and, at the very end of his life, a legacy of scandal and recrimination. Maugham would pay dearly for his generous impulse and façade of marital respectability.

In a fascinating letter to Syrie, written in the 1920s and not published until 1962, Maugham frankly stated that he married her out of a strange mixture of compassion, guilt and self-sacrifice. But, he said, she knew quite well the true state of his feelings:

> I married you because I thought you loved me and I could not bear to think that in a life in which I did not find much to praise you should suffer for something which was innocent. I married you because I was prepared to pay for my folly and selfishness, and I married you because I

thought it the best thing for your happiness and for Elizabeth's welfare, but I did not marry you because I loved you, and you were only too well aware of that.[6]

After the painful experience of his own marriage, his comments on matrimony were vitriolic. In "The Escape" he insisted that nothing but immediate flight could save a man once a woman had decided to snare him. He told his friend Ann Fleming that the institution of marriage had completely lost its point and was appropriate only for communicants in the Anglican Church. In *The Summing Up* he regretted that he'd sacrificed himself to unworthy women (like Syrie) because he did not want to hurt them.

The awkward situation—emotional, moral, legal and financial—hastened to its climax. Maugham's only child Elizabeth (always called Liza, after the heroine of his first novel) was born illegitimately in Rome on September 1, 1915. The birth by cesarean section was difficult and dangerous, and Syrie wept when told she would be unable to have any more children. Wellcome divorced her in February 1916. Considering Maugham's frequent condemnation of marriage in his early novels and Syrie's all-too-obvious faults, it must have been very difficult indeed for him to marry her. But he did so, incongruously, in a sleazy ceremony in Jersey City, New Jersey, on May 26, 1917. He later remembered "standing with my bride-to-be before a justice of the peace—who first sentenced the drunk in front of us, then married us, then sentenced the drunk behind us." The happy couple went on their Jersey Shore honeymoon with their twenty-month-old baby and her nursemaid.

Compton Mackenzie, on the scene at Capri, ironically observed that the usually egoistic Maugham, moved by Liza's plight, had acted out of character: "It was the only time in his life that Willie behaved like a gentleman; the result was fatal."[7] Trapped by Syrie's pregnancy, Maugham incurred the wrath that Wellcome had originally felt for Gordon Selfridge. Selfridge, in turn, managed to pass her on to the unfortunate Willie, and escaped without paying a penny. Though Syrie loved Maugham, she made him intensely miserable, and marrying her was the greatest mistake of his life. Living with her confirmed his misogyny and deepened his already cynical attitude toward life, and he resolved in future to be wary of altruistic acts.

III

MAUGHAM'S TEN YEARS with Syrie were as arduous and exhausting as his decade of struggle for literary success. He was a sophisticated man of the world who had known Syrie for three years before he married her, yet he didn't learn what she was really like until, after their wedding, the fur began to fly. He lived with her on and off—mainly off—for a decade, saw that their characters and interests clashed, and soon came to hate her. He knew she was poorly educated, and found she was also ignorant and superficial, vain, materialistic and philistine. He called her "a foolish woman who has never been interested in anything really except social position. She is, and always has been, a snob"—though Maugham himself liked nothing better than entertaining royalty. When they lived in Switzerland after Liza's birth, Syrie, on her own for most of the time while he was absorbed in his writing, became irritable and quarrelsome. He would repeatedly tell her, "don't make me scenes," and was greatly relieved when she decided to return to England. In March 1916 he told his brother Frederic that "the future cannot have in store any worse harassment than I have undergone in the last eight months."

Syrie drove Maugham mad with her pleas for attention and hysterical outbursts. She complained that he compelled her to remain on the staircase and put her in mortal danger as bombs fell on London during the Great War. Though a bomb would have saved him the trouble of strangling her, Maugham would not have remained at her side if the danger had been great. In his bitter letter to Syrie he complained of how bored he was by her constant nagging, her obsession with the trivia of furniture and frocks, her intellectual limitations that left him starved for conversation. When Maugham and his friends discussed books, Syrie, feigning interest and in several tones of voice, would merely declare: "How extraordinary!" All she wanted to do, he lamented, was to buy expensive clothes and be fashionably dressed. Writing in January 1920, Maugham explained how he, like many others unhappily married, gradually adjusted and came to accept his miserable state: "In married life there are times when one feels things are so hateful that it is worthwhile doing anything to get out of it, but one goes on—for one reason or another—and somehow they settle down more or less, and one becomes resigned or makes allowances or what not, and time goes on and eventually things seem not so bad as they might have been."[8]

Their conflicts focused on four aspects of domestic life: their sexual relations, their houses, her decorating business and the way she brought up Liza. Maugham, of course, was familiar with Syrie's sordid past and she knew all about his homosexuality. He thought she understood that he could not, and they would not, have a normal sexual life. But her love grew as his hatred intensified, and he felt she'd betrayed their tacit agreement by making intolerable sexual demands. Thinking, no doubt, of Syrie, he wrote in *Of Human Bondage* (1915): "She was the sort of woman who was unable to realise that a man might not have her own obsession with sex." In *The Hour Before the Dawn* (1942) he observed: "I don't think sexual relations are very satisfactory unless they spring from mutual desire; unless they do that there's something rather humiliating about them for both parties." In this case, however, he felt more humiliated than Syrie. Maugham, who really loved men but tried to love women, found it difficult to accept, and even fought against, his deepest sexual feelings. In one of his most frequently quoted comments, Maugham, explaining his bisexuality and the failure of his marriage, exclaimed: "I was a quarter normal and three-quarters queer, but I tried to persuade myself it was the other way round. That was my greatest mistake."[9]

Maugham and Syrie moved frequently. They lived in four different and increasingly grand houses as both became more and more successful in their professions. They began by displacing Walter Payne, and lived in Maugham's modest but fashionable Georgian house at 6 Chesterfield Street, off Curzon Street, in Mayfair. After the war, in the spring of 1919, they shifted to a larger, four-story house at 2 Wyndham Place, off the Marylebone Road. Four years later they moved slightly south to a more impressive five-story house at 43 Bryanston Square. And in 1927 they transferred to even grander premises at 213 King's Road, near Oakley Street and the Albert Bridge, in Chelsea.

Syrie, a wonderful hostess, knew how to entertain. The cosmopolitan Osbert Sitwell recalled that the most interesting guests came from Maugham's world rather than hers: "Mrs. Maugham and her brilliant husband . . . were always particularly kind to the young and gifted. There in Wyndham Place, in the large beige-painted, barrel-vaulted drawing-room of this eighteenth-century mansion, their friends were privileged to meet

6 Chesterfield Street, Mayfair

all the most interesting figures connected with the world of art, literature, and the theatre in both England and America."

The great trouble, from Maugham's point of view, was that Syrie enjoyed all the benefits of living in these houses while he suffered all the inconveniences. He complained to the young writer Godfrey Winn that Syrie's friends, all strangers to him, had (like Penelope's suitors) occupied his home and depleted his stores: "I used to write all day in my house in Chesterfield Street, and come down to dinner dead tired and not knowing one of the guests in my own house, eating my expensive food. They had all been invited by my wife." On other occasions he had, with some embarrassment, to cancel invitations to his own friends when he belatedly discovered Syrie was giving yet another party.

Worse still, he sometimes found when returning from abroad that he no longer had a place to write. In the spring of 1919 Syrie appropriated his quiet study in Chesterfield Street and forced him to work in a small room overlooking the road. In March 1920 she rented their house on Wyndham Place, and cut him off from his study as well as from his essential books and papers. She offered him a small bed-sitter in a cheaper rented house, where he felt he was "too old to pig it" and was unable to write. On the

2 Wyndham Place, Marylebone

King's Road, Syrie—with no conception of an author's needs, despite all her years with Maugham—once again interfered with his work. Maugham paid all the bills, but often got shut out of his own house: "The Glebe Place annex [to the King's Road house] was intended for Maugham, so that he could have his own entrance and a private suite. He used it from time to time, but said that he found it less than satisfactory to have his workroom converted to the gents' cloak room whenever his wife entertained."[10] When Syrie gave a party, his orderly papers, if not put away, were disturbed, even stolen. It seems strange that Maugham would allow her to get away with this, but she usually took advantage of his travels to present him with a fait accompli. Reluctant to provoke hysterical scenes by opposing her, he preferred to accept the situation. She cared nothing about his work—except for the prestige it brought and the money it earned.

Syrie's interest in furniture and houses soon blossomed into a thriving enterprise. In 1923 she opened a fashionable interior-decorating business which, with all her social contacts, became an immediate success. Cecil Beaton, a mutual friend, caustically described how her innovative ideas had taken hold: "Syrie caught the 'no color' virus and spread the disease around the world. . . . [She] bleached, pickled or scraped every piece of furniture in sight. White sheepskin rugs were strewn on the eggshell-

43 Bryanston Square, Marylebone

surfaced floors, huge white sofas were flanked with white crackled-paint tables, white peacock feathers were put in white vases against a white wall. . . . Mayfair drawing rooms looked like albino stage sets." Another precious client, swept away by her designs, noted the destructive aspect of her business: " 'Syrie's,' on Duke Street, already a Mecca for the fashionable, was full of her plaster-cast palm tree décor, limed and whitened Louis Quinze pieces (mostly nineteenth-century reproductions, which didn't stop the outcry that Mrs. Maugham was ruining antique furniture)."[11] Syrie's white-on-white décor suddenly became the rage on both sides of the Atlantic, but the craze came to an end when her clients realized that white soon became soiled and needed constant cleaning. Nevertheless, she was instrumental in changing the way people furnished and decorated their homes. Dark, heavy, ornate Victorian and Edwardian interiors gradually gave way to the bright, open look of modern houses.

Maugham, watching from the sidelines, never missed a chance—in his stories, letters, conversations or memoirs—to put the knife into Syrie. In "Jane" (1923), he satirized Syrie as Mrs. Tower, who was "seized with the prevailing passion for decoration. . . . Everything that could be pickled was pickled and what couldn't be pickled was painted." Mocking the current cant, he added: "Nothing matched, but everything harmonized." He told a close woman friend, Barbara Back, who disliked Syrie almost as much as he did, that Syrie, after exhausting all her good taste in trade, had nothing left for life. Beverley Nichols, a disciple who later turned against Maugham, recalled him mocking her sycophancy and greed. "She is almost certainly on her knees to an American m-m-millionairess," he told Nichols, "trying to sell her a chamber p-p-pot." And at one of their dinner parties Maugham felt obliged to warn his guests "to hold tight to your chairs. They are almost certainly for s-s-sale."

In "Looking Back" he accused her of dealing unscrupulously, even illegally, with her clients, forcing them at times to take legal action to recover payment for a fake she'd fobbed off as an antique. She was almost sent to prison when her insurance company discovered she'd sold a valuable jade necklace, claimed it was stolen and put in for the loss. When Maugham warned or reproved her, she would "make me scenes," accompanied by bountiful tears, till three in the morning. No matter how often she wore him out, he still had to get up early and write sparkling dialogue. Syrie *was* reckless and irresponsible. In October 1922, while driving a car, she killed a woman on a bicycle, then used all her wealth and influence to bring in a verdict of accidental death.

Nichols, in his partisan defense of Syrie, conceded that Maugham was "terribly proud of being a father . . . and had a father's tenderness for [Liza]."[12] In his travel book on China, Maugham dropped his impersonal mask and, in a rare display of affection, described Liza, at the age of five or six, "very smart in the white squirrel I brought her from China, coming in to say good-bye to me. . . . I play trains with her while her pram is being got ready." He told her "a little story before she [went] to sleep" and fondly observed that "she looks really very nice in her pyjamas with her hair done up in two plaits."

After Maugham moved permanently to France in 1926 and wanted to preserve his tax-free status, he could spend only a limited amount of time in England. As the pretty little girl grew up into a teenager—she looked rather like the actress Geraldine Chaplin—his personal relations with her were confined to formal annual luncheons at Claridge's Hotel. "You can imagine what an ordeal it was for me," he told a friend, "and must have been for her, poor darling." Maugham took no part in bringing up Liza, who was mainly cared for by nannies. But he felt she had absorbed her mother's snobbery, superficiality and materialism, and he could not refrain from criticizing both Syrie's maternal possessiveness and Liza's immature dependence. Other people noticed the suffocating intimacy of mother and daughter. One of Syrie's friends remarked that Liza "and Syrie were *very very* close. In fact, at the time I thought far too much so. And I said to Liza, 'Really, you should try to detach yourself a little bit from your mother's apron-strings.' I told her I thought it was just a little bit ludicrous at her age. I mean, even after she married Vincent [at the age of twenty-one] she was absolutely in her mother's pocket."[13]

Syrie had many staunch defenders, including Osbert Sitwell and Noël Coward, both in her lifetime and, after Maugham's attack in "Looking Back" (1962), after her death. The intensely intellectual Rebecca West called Syrie "an extremely talented and original and entertaining person with a curious driving industry." She noted, though Maugham had insisted that Syrie took no interest in books, that she "was oddly well read." The condescending Lytton Strachey, who dined with the Maughams in the mid-1920s, sensed the strained atmosphere, the incongruity of their marriage and Maugham's manifest misery. He called Maugham "a hang-dog personage ... with a wife. Perhaps it was because I've eschewed such things for so long that I was amused—the odd mixture of restraint and laisser-aller struck me freshly—but eventually it's just that that becomes such a bore."

Bruce Lockhart, an astute spy who knew both Syrie and Maugham, took a very different view from Rebecca West. In his diary he noted: "Somerset Maugham is a peculiar man—has terrific inferiority complex, hates people, yet is a snob and cannot refuse a luncheon where he is to meet a countess. Life ruined by a wife who is coarse and irritating. Once he was having tea in his own house with a friend, when his wife came in. Her voice downstairs irritated him so much that he hid behind the sofa and stayed there until his wife had left again!" Lockhart is doubtless exaggerating, but there is no question Maugham found his wife intensely annoying.

Lockhart went off the rails, however, in retailing some gossip he probably picked up secondhand from Maugham's lover Godfrey Winn. Lockhart maintained that an unnamed woman (Barbara Back) was intimately involved with Maugham's strange sexual habits and had a stranglehold on him: "because of his homosexual nervosity he could not perform alone. The liaison was *à trois*. The third was Godfrey Winn! Maugham ... is a man who has tried everything: drugs, etc., but he has an iron self-discipline and is now master of himself."[14] This sordid tale collapses under close examination. Maugham's affairs with Violet Hunt, Sasha Kropotkin, Sue Jones and Syrie Wellcome proved that he was perfectly capable of heterosexual relations. Sue would not have continued their affair for eight years, nor would Syrie have married him and continued to make sexual demands, if he were not. In any case, he valued self-mastery and would never expose himself to the repeated humiliation of sexual impotence. If there is any truth to this story, Winn may have been alluding to a homosexual ménage à trois with Maugham and his lover, Gerald Haxton.

A professionally posed photo of Maugham and Syrie, taken about 1925, vividly exposed the unhappy relations observed by Strachey and Lockhart. The couple are in their sitting room, with a painting and flowers in the background and a Persian carpet (slightly rucked up) on the floor. Maugham, staring severely at the camera and leaning casually on Syrie's padded armchair, looks rather dashing in his full dark mustache, knotted polka-dot tie, waistcoat with looping gold watch chain and gray spats on highly polished shoes. Syrie, seated below him, is stylishly attired in black (with a fluffy white blouse and white stockings). She wears a turban-like hat, with a jeweled pin, pulled down to her eyes, fox fur draped around her shoulders, satiny dress and shoes with a strap. Heavily made up, her dark hair cut short, she also has a severe expression, and gazes into the distance as if to emphasize their separation. The effect is chilling.

IV

TWO PLAYS, one written shortly after Maugham met Syrie, the other while he was living with her in Rome and awaiting the birth of Liza, illuminate their relationship. The shift in tone from the earlier to the later play reveals his increasing disillusionment and bitterness. Maugham spent a winter on a farm in the Canadian West to get the proper background for *The Land of Promise* (1913). The play, which takes place in Manitoba, is a modern version of Shakespeare's *The Taming of the Shrew*. Unlike Polly Ley in *The Merry-Go-Round,* who challenges a rich spinster but still inherits her wealth, Norah Marsh, the devoted companion of a nasty old lady, receives nothing of her promised legacy. Left almost penniless and unable to find a job, she goes to her brother's farm on the Canadian frontier. Snobbish and genteel, she quarrels with his coarse wife. In a fit of obstinate pique and to escape once again from an intolerably humiliating position, she agrees to marry a rough farmer, Frank Taylor. After they move into a cabin worthy of Charlie Chaplin's *Gold Rush,* she fights with her husband and is shocked when he wants to sleep with her. In a sensational scene of

Maugham and Syrie, 1920s

marital rape he forces her into the offstage bedroom: "*A look of shame, fear, anguish, passes over her face, and then, violently, a convulsive shudder runs through her whole body.*"

The Land of Promise dramatizes class conflict between spinster and companion, two sisters-in-law, husband and wife. In a melodramatic twist of the plot, Norah unexpectedly inherits £500 and is offered a position in England just as Frank's crop is ruined and he loses the farm. Finally recognizing Frank's worth, she decides to stay and use her legacy to rescue him, choosing to join her husband in the struggle for existence rather than return to her old subservient though more comfortable life. Against all odds, she shows sympathy, generosity and love, and finds happiness. Billie Burke, who played Norah in the American production, called it "a beautifully written but dreary kind of play" whose portrayal of "the problems of Canadian farmers did not interest New York audiences."[15]

Our Betters (1915), one of Maugham's best plays, is a scorching satire that exposes shameful secrets beneath society's brilliant surface. It takes up Henry James' "international theme," the mating dance of rich American title hunters and vicious, money-grubbing European aristocrats. The only innocent character is Bessie Saunders, an American heiress who visits her corrupt sister Lady Grayston in England, rejects a lord's proposal and flees home before she can be dragged into the moral cesspool. Bessie is based on the wealthy London hostess Emerald Cunard (born plain Maud Burke in San Francisco), who in real life married the heir to the great shipping fortune.

Arthur Fenwick, an American war profiteer who's made a fortune in England and pays Lady Grayston's bills in return for sexual favors, is clearly based on Syrie's lover Gordon Selfridge. As one character remarks: "This is a strange house in which the husband is never seen and Arthur Fenwick, a vulgar sensualist, acts as host." Syrie, sharing Maugham's life when he wrote the play, is drawn and quartered as the hypocritical and rapacious Lady Grayston. One close friend caustically condemns her behavior: "there's something very like heroism in the callousness with which you've dropped people when they've served your turn. . . . What makes it more complete is that what you've aimed at is trivial, transitory and worthless." Another friend writes her off by stating: "I know her through and through, and I tell you that she hasn't got a single redeeming quality."

Gerald Haxton appears as the parasitic gigolo Anthony Paxton, "*a handsome youth of twenty-five, in beautiful clothes, with engaging manners and a charming smile.*" In the most shocking scene, the American-born duchess, who's keeping Paxton (as Fenwick is keeping Lady Grayston), sends the innocent Bessie—the moral gauge of the play—to discover Paxton and Grayston having sex in the tea house. Fenwick calls Lady Grayston a "slut," and the second act ends when she exclaims to Paxton: "You damned fool, I told you it was too risky." Maugham must have taken wicked pleasure in portraying Syrie and Gerald, the arch-rivals who hated each other, as lovers. The dramatist Garson Kanin rightly called *Our Betters* "an absolutely first-class play, with bite and satiric content, with matchless character-drawing, constant surprise and wit and grace and lucidity."[16]

Maugham, fascinated by the "pattern" of his life in both *Of Human Bondage* and *The Summing Up,* must have been struck by the cruel irony in his relations with Ethelwyn Sylvia Jones and Gwendolyn Syrie Wellcome. Sue's pregnancy (followed by a miscarriage) prevented her from committing herself to Maugham, who loved her deeply, and she married another man. Syrie's second pregnancy (following a miscarriage) while she was married to another man forced Maugham to marry her. *Our Betters* clearly reveals that he did not love and soon came to hate her. He never forgave himself for giving in to an ignoble and short-lived passion, and she inspired his most savage literary portraits.

7

The Great War and
Gerald Haxton

1914—1916

THE YEARS OF World War I were the most turbulent, eventful and complicated of Maugham's life. In 1914 he was forty, in his prime as a man and a writer. In 1915 he published his most personal and ambitious novel, *Of Human Bondage*. His unhappy relationship with Syrie consumed time and energy, and for months he wavered uncertainly between his homosexual desires and commitment to a respectable position in society. But for all his literary and social ambition, Maugham, motivated by patriotism and principle, was now driven in other directions. In the midst of his intense emotional and creative life he took on dangerous work that put him at the heart of the war, and went to France as an interpreter, ambulance driver and nurse. He spent the winter of 1914 witnessing some of the worst carnage, and in Flanders he met and fell in love with Gerald Haxton. Liza was born in September 1915 and, still the Edwardian gentleman, he married Syrie in May 1917. His life then took another turn. He was recruited by British Intelligence and worked as a secret agent in neutral Switzerland from September 1915 to the summer of 1916. Throughout these extraordinary upheavals he managed to write two plays: *Our Betters* and *The Unattainable*.

Maugham joined the Red Cross and was sent to northern France to help with the massive casualties from the First Battle of Ypres. Billeted in a small house with an old merchant and his wife, whose sons were serving in the French army, he had a tiny room with a large canopied bed, and a view of the cobblestoned courtyard and red sloping roof. Pleased by the English officer who spoke excellent French, his hosts were cordial and eager to please. Though the work was taxing and stressful, Maugham found relief from his own anxieties in the disciplined routine behind the lines. "What was so pleasant in the Red Cross," he told Violet Hunt, "was that you did what you were told and had no responsibility. I suppose just that is the attractiveness of the monastic life. And your work done, you idle for the rest of the day."

The drivers began work at seven in the morning since, so close to the front, it was too dangerous to be outside at night. The narrow paved roads had deep trenches of mud on both sides. When the heavy, jolting ambulances were forced off the road by a military convoy, they got bogged down and needed a team of horses to pull them out. When Maugham was looking at the ruins of the magnificent Cloth Makers' Hall in the Grande Place of Ypres, a German shell blew up the wall where he'd been standing, and he narrowly escaped death.

Driving ambulances, he met the Cambridge-educated literary critic Desmond MacCarthy, learned and worldly, who would later write favorable estimates of his work. Obsessed, like Maugham, by an "uncomfortable curiosity" about the wounded soldiers they transported, MacCarthy "watched in each case to see where the bloody bandage would come, hoping it would not be across the stomach or face." Maugham later remembered a frantic, inhuman scene that recalled the description in *A Farewell to Arms* of Hemingway's experience as an ambulance driver on the Italian front. After a skirmish, the Germans were advancing and Maugham's unit had to evacuate the wounded men as fast as possible: "All through the night the ambulance cars, without lights, drove back and forth, and the wounded cried out to be taken, and some died as they were being lifted onto the stretchers and were thrown on the heap of dead outside the door, and they were dirty and gory, and the church stank of blood and the rankness of humanity."[1] One young man kept screaming, "I don't want to die," and didn't stop screaming till he did.

Like Walt Whitman, who'd dressed wounds in the American Civil War, Maugham dealt directly with the worst casualties: the shell-shocked, the dying and the dead. This was a totally different experience from treating patients at St. Thomas's and in the slums of Lambeth. Instead of one poor woman dead in childbirth, he now saw thousands of maimed and dead young men. Tending three hundred wounded in an improvised hospital, he dressed the raw burnt skin of screaming victims, incinerated amputated limbs and lined up corpses on the floor. "I have never seen such wounds," he exclaimed. "There are great wounds of the shoulder, the bone all shattered, running with pus, stinking; there are gaping wounds in the back; there are wounds where a bullet has passed through the lungs; there are shattered feet so that you wonder if the limb can possibly be saved."

After a retreat in which the French were badly cut up, he found a pile of corpses: some soldiers were dead when they arrived at the hospital; others had died before they could be treated. "Packed close together in every kind of grotesque attitude, their uniforms filthy with mud and blood, [and] strangely contorted, as though they had died in agony," they seemed more like things than men.[2] Yet he noticed that their white hands, with all the blood drained out of them, were "elegant." A glutton for experience, Maugham collected traumas, polished them up and laced his books with them. These dreadful spectacles confirmed his atheism. He could never believe in a God who could permit such pointless suffering.

II

THIS VIVID INTERLUDE of Maugham's life proved fateful. Soon after his arrival in France he met an American member of his ambulance unit, Gerald Haxton, who for the next thirty years would be his closest friend and sexual companion. A vital, adventurous, wild and reckless young man, Gerald fascinated him. Like Hemingway's protagonists in *A Farewell to Arms,* they fell in love amidst the danger and excitement of war.

Haxton was born in San Francisco on October 6, 1892. His birth certificate was destroyed in the San Francisco earthquake of 1906 and nothing has been known about him before he stepped into Maugham's life in October 1914. But it is now possible to shed some light on his ambiguous background and wayward character. His father, Henry Haxton—a prominent reporter and editor on the *San Francisco Examiner,* a friend of Ambrose Bierce and of Robert Louis Stevenson's stepson, Lloyd Osbourne—was a rather raffish, caddish Englishman. Gerald's mother, Sara Thibault, came from a wealthy, cultured and socially prominent family who played an

Gerald Haxton

important part in early California history. She held the same position in San Francisco society that Maugham's mother had had among the English colony in Paris. Sara was friendly with the novelist Gertrude Atherton, "belonged to one of the most exclusive circles of the 'four hundred' " elite families—the Crockers and the Sharons—and was considered a beauty as well as "the finest pianiste in local society."

The youthful Henry was, like Gerald, a rogue and fortune hunter. After he'd become famous as a journalist, but was still married to an actress, Agnes Thomas, he "overwhelmed Sara with flowers and worshipped at the shrine." When they married, her friends asked: "What happened to the first Mrs. Haxton?"—who'd conveniently disappeared. Keen to get publicity for the paper, Henry did some heroic stunts in the cold waters of San Francisco Bay:

> [When] a fisherman was wrecked in a storm and marooned on a rock . . . outside the Golden Gate, the Coast Guard, finding the seas too rough, elected to let the man cling there until morning if he could.
>
> Hearst and some of his younger men, among them George Bruton

and H.R. Haxton, hired a tug and steamed out to the scene. Haxton, a powerful swimmer, disrobed and carried a line to the chilled fisherman, who was hauled into the tug, bundled into blankets and taken to the *Examiner* office. There he was given hot coffee while an artist sketched him along with Hero Haxton for an exclusive story. . . .

Haxton [also] took a ride in the *Oakland* . . . accompanied by a reporter and an artist. Near Yerba Buena Island, Haxton toppled off and howled for help, while his mates likewise bellowed as they observed and timed the rescue operations with a stopwatch. . . . The *Examiner* next morning poured sarcasm on the inefficiency of the crew, and pointed out that Haxton would have drowned several times over had he been a non-athletic old lady.

Henry had literary ambitions as well. In 1889 he published a story, "The Reverend John Craig," in a local journal, the *Overland Monthly*. This rather sentimental tale, about a clergyman who sails from San Francisco in a ship that is accidentally run down by a Dutch vessel and is picked up by a German boat, uncannily anticipated what later happened to Gerald.

Sara and Henry sailed to Europe soon after their marriage, traveled in Algeria and lived in Paris. A few months after Gerald was born, Sara—who had married late and may have given up hope of marrying at all—confessed that it seemed "silly to be having a baby at my time of life." The marriage did not last very long. After it broke up Sara moved to London and Henry, after leaving for New York, disappeared from her life. He may, like Gerald, have been a heavy drinker and gambler who'd spent most of her money. In any case, her family's wealth seems to have dried up by the time Sara reached England and she had to survive in straitened circumstances. Sara's letters to Louise Sharon, a wealthy San Francisco friend who lived in Paris, revealed a conventional, sentimental, religious, timid and sickly woman. She read a lot, and sympathized with Louise's intense suffering during the serious illness of her children. She had just enough to live on, couldn't even afford to visit Paris and was often forced—with many protestations of gratitude—to borrow money from Louise.

Sara's San Francisco obituary noted that "her home in London always extended a welcome to her California friends," but she had few visitors. Writing from her flat at 5 Queens Road in St. John's Wood, North London, on January 1, 1901, she told Louise: "I am leading the dullest and most monotonous of lives, but I dare say it's good for me." Two years later she thanked her benefactor by saying: "I have my rooms pretty, and had many many treats for Gerald, and for myself too, solely from your great kindness." The following month, the single parent confessed that she was not quite sure what to do with her son:

> These days I am much worried and perplexed about Gerald's education. One has to decide, apparently while boys are still so young, about their career and fix upon the methods to fit them for it. English schools are splendid in many ways and I'm sure can help to give and develop in Gerald many qualities that he needs, but on the other hand the conservative spirit is almost paralysing, and I get quite wild sometimes thinking how I am wasting time for the boy.[3]

Sara never remarried and ended her life bedridden and in constant pain. She died in London in 1923, cut off from Gerald, who by then was unable to enter the country.

Gerald, the spoiled only child of a doting mother, had grown up without the support of a father and received no help from Sara's once prominent family in San Francisco. Like a shabby, on-the-make character in a novel by Henry James, he was a rootless young man, living on his wits, when he met Maugham. Beverley Nichols said Haxton's French was impeccable and described him as "slightly built, with a shock of fair hair and a retroussé nose and wide grey eyes of a deceptive candour." Another writer met Haxton on a ship in 1922 and wrote that his "blond hair stood up from his head like the bristles upon a military brush and he seemed very careless in his dress and in his entire demeanor." His skin was scarred from acne, which he tried to disguise with heavy makeup. Maugham, attracted to the louche side of Gerald, spoke of himself when he told Barbara Back that Haxton looked rough and some people "fancied" that side of his character.

Though Maugham loved Haxton, he was well aware of the faults that were part of his devil-may-care attraction. In *Our Betters* the American duchess who's keeping the vain and spoiled Paxton (as Maugham kept Gerald) declares: "He's a liar, a gambler, an idler, a spendthrift, but in his way he is fond of me."[4] In that play Tony Paxton complains (as Gerald did) of his luxurious enslavement. He can't call his soul his own, is dependent on the duchess for money and wants his own car so he doesn't have to borrow one of hers when he wants to drive a friend to the golf course. In his story "The Ant and the Grasshopper" Maugham also portrays Haxton as the charming and unscrupulous Tom Ramsay, who embarrasses his respectable older brother by defaulting on his debts and breaking the law: "He was a most amusing companion and though you knew he was perfectly worthless you could not but enjoy his society. He had high spirits, an unfailing gaiety and incredible charm."

In a much-quoted passage in *The Summing Up* (repeated in "Looking Back"), Maugham emphasized Haxton's dashing and debonair social gifts, his talent for striking up an instant friendship with all sorts of people when they traveled the world together and his ability to provide Maugham with stories to use in his fiction. But this was a misleading excuse for his sexual companion. Though Maugham was certainly less extrovert than Haxton, he was by 1914 a successful and famous author, much sought after and at ease in society, worldly and sophisticated, a great bridge player and easily able to meet anyone who took his fancy. Haxton may have sorted out the wits from the bores, but Maugham didn't actually need him to find the sources of his stories. Robin Maugham, who shared many sordid adventures with Gerald, was closer to the mark when he wrote that "his boisterous spirits could lift Willie from his occasional fits of gloom, his diligence saved Willie from all the minor irritations of travel."

Haxton, Maugham's evil genius, was decidedly not a gentleman. He did all the things Maugham never dared to do: getting drunk and using foul language, lying, sponging and gambling, homosexual cruising and pimping. Constantly skating on thin ice, he managed to escape almost every sticky situation. When his good luck failed, he would brazen his way out or use wealthy patrons to pay his bribes. Nothing worked, however, when he got into serious trouble on November 13, 1915. When his mother was living in London and Maugham was spying in Switzerland, Haxton and one John Lindsell were arrested by a snooping detective in a Covent Garden hotel and charged at the Old Bailey with six counts of gross indecency— the legal term for homosexual acts, excluding sodomy. Both men pleaded not guilty. With the help of skillful attorneys (possibly paid for by Maugham) they were acquitted on all counts on December 10.

The judge, however, was convinced of Haxton's guilt. Since Haxton had retained his American citizenship, he was registered as an undesirable alien, forced to leave the country and permanently banned. Foreigners had no right to remain in Britain; and the Home Secretary (especially in wartime) could exclude them without giving a reason. Frederic Maugham, who hated Haxton, may have used his influence as a leading barrister to get him deported. The circumstances of his arrest and possible entrapment seem suspicious, and his punishment, after he was declared innocent, was harsh. But he may have been working as a foreign spy and deported as a security risk. The case remains a mystery, for his files were closed in 1915 and later destroyed.[5] Though Maugham used all his power and influence, he was never able to rescind Haxton's status as an undesirable alien.

Gerald's unsavory trial, like his brother Henry's suicide, seemed to threaten Maugham's private life. He also risked ridicule, attack, persecution and jail, and had to be extremely careful and discreet. Robin later reported that his uncle, General Cecil Romer, "had been asked by an important official in the Home Office to warn my Uncle Willie that his homosexual activities in England must stop or he would be put into prison." Maugham's homosexuality, like his stammer, caused unceasing pain. His fear of being involved in a sexual scandal undoubtedly influenced his eventual decision to live permanently in France. Syrie, whom Maugham called unscrupulous, also had two close calls with the law: her attempt to defraud the insurance company and her fatal car accident. Competing with Gerald for Maugham's affections, she may well have used his prosecution and deportation to blackmail Maugham into marrying her. Though Syrie lost the emotional battle with Gerald, she won the great prize, became Maugham's wife and remained a thorn in his flesh until her death.

Maugham was living with Syrie in Switzerland when Haxton was deported from England and continued to stay with her, whenever he visited England, until their divorce in 1926. Though he had a foot in both sexual camps, he became increasingly bitter and misogynistic about Syrie, and relied on Gerald to cheer him up. He led a double life, split between theater, writing, home and London society with Syrie (who made endless "scenes" and demands for money), and strenuous, even dangerous trips to the South Seas and Indochina with Gerald, whose stimulating companionship was punctuated by reckless behavior.

III

AFTER HE MET Haxton, Maugham had no further heterosexual experiments. Apart from a few close friendships with women, he lived in—

indeed, created—an exclusively homosexual milieu. But he liked the respectable façade of marriage, always behaved discreetly and preferred cultured companions to rough trade. Maugham never struck perceptive observers, like the novelist Francis King, "as obviously homosexual. No one would have remarked of him: 'What an old queen,' or 'How camp can you be?'" Soon after he decided to live abroad, Maugham obliquely alluded to his sexual taste and explained that "my early years in France and other circumstances of my life have prevented me from ever feeling entirely at home in England." Letting his mask slip a bit in his late essays, he noted, when discussing A. E. Housman: "After all, the world won't come to an end because you can't go to bed with a soldier." He also referred to the "tea houses" where homosexuals made their furtive rendezvous and wryly remarked that "being an attendant in a public lavatory affords but a narrow view of human nature."[6] Constant travel and residence abroad enabled Maugham to enjoy much greater sexual freedom than he would have had in England.

Maugham and Haxton were not a monogamous couple. Both had sex with others when the opportunity arose, and Gerald even procured for his master. Writing to his principal confidante, Barbara Back, with whom he exchanged gossip for forty years, Maugham used unusually formal language when describing a sexual adventure. It was not a purely financial transaction, and since the object of his affection was not prepared to satisfy him without a decent meal and some pleasant chatter in the early part of the evening, a certain amount of courtship was involved. Sometimes an old friend like Emerald Cunard, mocking Maugham's temperate habits and obsession with his health, would be bold enough to refer publicly to his homosexuality: "Once, after dining with her, he prepared to leave at his usual early hour. 'But you can't go now,' she objected, 'the evening has only just begun.' 'I dare say, Emerald, but I have to keep my youth.' 'Then why didn't you bring him with you?' she asked. 'I should be delighted to meet him.'"

Maugham kept a tight rein on his social and sexual life. Influential and famous, older and wealthier than the financially dependent Haxton, he had no trouble establishing his dominance. He was attracted to androgynous and sexually ambiguous lovers, like the feminine Gerald Vaudrey in *Mrs. Craddock* and the boyish Mildred in *Of Human Bondage*. Male guests usually swam naked in the pool at Maugham's French villa, and Michael Swan recalled Maugham's bizarre and intimidating remark to a younger and presumably more potent man. Swan told Francis King "of the occasion when, round the swimming pool . . . Maugham pointed at his cock and said: 'Why don't you cut that off? You'd look even more attractive without it.' "

Though both men were promiscuous, Maugham—more attracted to Haxton than Haxton to him—preferred a longtime lover to a one-night stand. (Gerald stayed with him for thirty years and was replaced by Alan Searle, who remained for another twenty, till the end of Maugham's life.) Glenway Wescott, who had a lifelong relationship with Monroe Wheeler, told Maugham: "I am never as eager to have intercourse with a new lover as with one I have already enjoyed, again and again and again. Somewhat to my surprise, Willie said that oh, indeed, it was so for him as well." Maugham was particularly uninhibited with Wescott, who reported that "Maugham showed him that he still had . . . 'quite a respectable phallus.' "[7]

Wescott, a fund of information about Maugham's sexuality, recorded a rare example of one of Maugham's sexual-literary fantasies. "Last night in a dream," Maugham told him, "—you may scarcely believe it, but it is true—I dreamed that I went down on Shelley. I remember saying to myself that I mustn't try to bugger him; he wouldn't have liked that." The ethereal Shelley, rather than the more robust, bisexual Byron, was his obscure object of desire. On another occasion Wescott found Maugham gazing at Pavel Tchelichew's signs-of-the-zodiac illustrations for Wescott's *Calendar of the Gods,* which portrayed two men entwined in a sixty-nine position. Pretending to be sexually naive, Maugham remarked that, "having been struck by the beauty of it when he was here last, he had tried it and, alas, found it not perfectly feasible."[8]

Wescott (using a vivid image to illustrate Maugham's desire for control) mentioned that "Willie hated to be touched except by arrangement. If you touched him by surprise, he was like an oyster quivering when you pour lemon juice over it." By his own account, Maugham had been unwilling to sleep with the child prostitute in Granada. But he also confessed to Wescott that "his happiest sexual encounters had been with anonymous boys in far-off lands. The amorous high-point of his life had been a night on a sampan in Indochina." Robin—greatly favored by his uncle during Maugham's lifetime but severely critical of him after his death—said that Gerald supplied young boys who slipped quietly into the villa to spend the night with him. Alan Searle, in a sexual variant of the child-prostitute story, reported that in Mexico City in 1924, Gerald brought back to their hotel "a thin, large-eyed child who said he was fourteen. He undressed in Maugham's hotel bedroom, knelt to say his prayers, and crossed himself before getting into bed." Maugham, it seems, could resist little girls, but not little boys, with whom desire proved stronger than compassion.

The English mystic Gerald Heard, who met Maugham in America, believed "he was a man who could never get the two sides of his nature together." Rebecca West supposedly said that Maugham's "only pictur-esque quality was the decisiveness of his homosexuality"[9]—but this was surely a misprint for "deviousness." His homosexuality was carefully hid-den, and his outer calm and cautious reserve masked an inner struggle with his true nature. It took him forty years and an unhappy marriage to acknowledge that he was "three-quarters queer."

Maugham told Barbara Back that it was essential to be secretive about sexual matters. He felt that "there is hardly anyone whose sexual life, if it were broadcast, would not fill the world at large with surprise and horror." Elaborating this statement, which he may also have heard from his uncle or read in *Don Fernando,* Robin Maugham asserted that "in his private life he was at times a sadistic queer" and suggested that Maugham may have had something evil to hide. Robin also saw that the struggle between sex-ual repression and artistic expression was at the heart of Maugham's per-sonal and creative life: "I believe that if he hadn't been tortured by desires which in his heart he despised, he wouldn't have written as he did, and he wouldn't have written as excitedly."[10] Maugham's inner turmoil created the passionate energy that inspired his work.

IV

THE VERNACULAR STYLE of *Of Human Bondage* (1915), Maugham's first novel since *The Magician* (1908), marked a striking change from the mannered, mandarin prose of *The Land of the Blessed Virgin.* In contrast to the stylistic and technical innovations of the modernists—Joyce, Woolf, Pound and Eliot, born a decade after him—Maugham believed and was fond of repeating that the essence of good prose was simplicity, lucidity and euphony. He thought the obscure was too often mistaken for the pro-found, tried to write as clearly as possible and used a high proportion of monosyllabic words. He praised the sermons of John Tillotson, the sev-enteenth-century archbishop of Canterbury, as models of clarity and good sense: "He wrote simply and naturally, so that everyone understood his meaning. . . . It was like the conversation of a man of adequate learning who knew what he wanted to say and was at pains to say it clearly and correctly." The secret of the craft of writing, he explained, was to have common sense and stick to the point.

His own prose was rather flat and undistinguished; he stuffed his historical novels with scholarly research, and sometimes spoiled the freshness of his travel books with stale material from guidebooks. But as Gore Vidal noted, "once his own famous tone was set it would remain perfectly pitched to the end." Though sophisticated and worldly, he deliberately used clichés to match his narrator's diction with his characters' speech. He told effective stories in a language his readers could understand, and seemed to share his experiences with them. Graham Greene, in a shrewd essay, observed that Maugham sometimes seemed "a little bored and offhand," a little too detached.[11] Yet his fluent and readable style attracted a vast audience, and *Of Human Bondage* has enormous narrative power.

Maugham, like D. H. Lawrence, believed writing was a form of catharsis that could release him from agonizing memories of the past. Speaking of a writer in his story "The Human Element," Maugham stated that "when something has made him terribly unhappy, and he's tortured and miserable, he can put it all into a story and it's astonishing what a comfort and relief it is." Lawrence, in a famous letter, agreed that "one sheds one's sicknesses in books—repeats and presents again one's emotions, to be master of them."[12]

Of Human Bondage—more vivid, moving and convincing than anything else Maugham wrote—was exactly the cathartic work that summed up his past life and enabled him to go forward. The first version, "The Artistic Temperament of Stephen Carey," written in Seville in the late 1890s, was rejected by the publishers and put aside for fifteen years. In 1913 Maugham suspended his immensely successful career as a dramatist and returned to his autobiographical novel. He did so with a straightforward style, a keen sense of drama and a more mature point of view.

The first half begins with the death of Philip Carey's beloved mother after giving birth to a stillborn child; his forced move to the house of his selfish and hypocritical uncle, the vicar of Blackstable; and the cruelties he suffers at the King's School in Tercanbury, where middle-class parents pay high fees to have their children tortured and emotionally crippled. At school he is constantly humiliated, forced to show the boys his clubfoot, publicly called a cripple by one master and a "club-footed blockhead" by another. He falls in love with his classmate Rose, a recurrent name in Maugham's fiction for attractive male or female characters. When Philip returns after an illness, Rose brutally rejects him and calls him "a damned cripple." He endures another humiliating public examination of his clubfoot in medical school, when the surgeon remarks that Philip (the son of a doctor) has had an unsuccessful operation on his foot. Another operation, as an adult, also fails to cure his deformity.

The early part of the novel is solidly Victorian and follows the tradition of Dickens' *Great Expectations* and Butler's *The Way of All Flesh*: the drama of a gifted, sensitive and abused orphan child who overcomes disabilities and survives to adulthood. But Maugham also departs radically from this pattern by giving Philip a damning clubfoot, the symbol of his extended trial-by-degradation that forms a major motif of the novel. The book could have been called *Humiliation*.

Philip's handicap may have been suggested by several artistic and literary sources: José de Ribera's vividly grotesque painting *Boy with a Clubfoot* (1652), which Maugham often saw in the Louvre; the deformity of the equally hypersensitive Lord Byron, described by Edward Trelawny after Byron's death: "Both his feet were clubbed, and his legs withered to the knee. . . . This was a curse, chaining a proud and soaring spirit like his to the dull earth"; Charles Bovary's botched operation on the unfortunate Hippolyte's clubfoot in *Madame Bovary* (1857); and Rickie Elliott's lameness in E. M. Forster's *The Longest Journey* (1907). Philip's clubfoot stands for Maugham's stammer but, as Francis King has pointed out, it was also (as in Forster) "a metaphor for a graver disability."[13] (Maugham once sardonically remarked that they tried to make a musical out of *Bondage*, but gave it up because the clubfoot couldn't dance.)

Philip is shy, observant, inquisitive, honest, intelligent, sharp-tongued and witty. He cheers up a bereaved Anglican clergyman by telling him that a fire has destroyed the Wesleyan chapel, and earnestly prays for a harsh winter that will kill his ailing uncle and release his inheritance. In the course of the novel he moves from idealism to disillusionment, from the love of his lost mother to the love of a motherly wife. But the novel's main subject is Philip's masochistic urge, the "strange desire to torture himself . . . to do horrible, sordid things; he wanted to roll himself in gutters; his whole being yearned for beastliness; he wanted to grovel." Philip suffers from a series of degrading experiences: not only the miseries of his clubfoot and his schooldays, but also his abject poverty, his wretched job in an accounting firm, his relations with Mildred, his failed medical exams, his position as a shop-walker. He even becomes homeless and sleeps on the Thames Embankment. Philip observes the hypocrisy and absurdity of clergymen, teachers, doctors and bosses; he loses his religious faith; defies convention; longs (like Frank Hurrell in *The Merry-Go-Round*) to travel to Spain and the Far East; searches for aesthetic beauty, intellectual excitement and sexual freedom; and tries to escape the degradation of human bondage.

The Heidelberg and Paris chapters, in which Philip begins to reject convention and find a modicum of freedom, are enlivened by vivid and often satirical portraits of Maugham's actual friends and acquaintances. Hayward is based on Ellingham Brooks, Clutton on Roderick O'Conor, Lawson on Gerald Kelly, Cronshaw on Aleister Crowley. Philip's first mistress, the older Emily Wilkinson—with her bird-of-prey profile, affected French and arty airs, her worldliness, sophistication and seductiveness—has more than a hint of Violet Hunt. Maugham described Bohemian life on the Left Bank of Paris twenty years before the Lost Generation invaded the Closerie des Lilas. And Maugham is quite witty about Philip's straitlaced reaction to that eccentric world. When he observes some painters and models at an outdoor café, he hopes they "were not their lawful wives"; when "eager to do something characteristic," he felt absinthe was the only appropriate drink.

Three sources of acute anxiety haunt Philip in the Paris section and are finally resolved in the second half of the novel: the fear of artistic failure, the threat of death or suicide and the search for some meaning in human existence. Philip's (nonsexual) relationship with his fellow art student Fanny Price foreshadows his liaison with Mildred. Satirically named for the heroine of Jane Austen's *Mansfield Park,* a prim and disapproving poor relation at the Bertrams' country house, Maugham's Fanny is ugly, uncouth and untalented, ill-natured, disagreeable and starving. She finally hangs herself in despair and is discovered by the horrified Philip. Fanny's corpse is followed by the corpse of his aunt Louisa, the vicar's wife, and by the corpse he dissects in his anatomy class.

When discussing art in Paris Philip (like Maugham) admires Vermeer, Manet, Degas and Gauguin long before their reputations were established. But he's obsessed, for reasons never explained in this novel, by El Greco and by "the secret which he felt the mysterious painter held for him." Most important, Philip searches rather naively for "the meaning of life." Cronshaw magisterially tells him that it can be found in the "Persian carpets of the most exquisite hue and of a pattern the beautiful intricacy of which delights and amazes the eye. . . . Go and look at those Persian carpets [in the Cluny Museum], and one of these days the answer will come to you."[14]

Philip's sordid liaison with the waitress Mildred Rogers, the succubus who keeps returning to torment and wound him, dominates the second half of the novel, and runs parallel to his medical training and desperate poverty. Mildred is "tall and thin, with narrow hips and the chest of a boy. . . . She was very anaemic. Her thin lips were pale, and her skin was delicate, of a faint green colour." She's unspeakably common and vulgar, and Philip despises himself for loving her. He even dreams of cutting her throat and "knew enough anatomy to make pretty certain of getting the carotid artery." His groveling, tortured love for her, though completely irrational, is also completely convincing. A true masochist, he derives pleasure from humiliation. Every time he tries to get rid of her, she creeps back—under increasingly cruel and degrading circumstances—into his life. The more beastly she is to him, the more attached to her he becomes. As Lady Kastellan remarks in his story "A Casual Affair": "I know nothing more shattering than to love with all your heart . . . someone who you know is worthless."[15]

Maugham charts the stages of their mutual degradation. While Philip is slavishly courting her, Mildred suddenly announces she's going to marry a naturalized German called Emil Miller. But he turns out to be married, gets her pregnant and abandons her. Philip, as usual, takes up the slack and invites her and the baby to move into his small flat. When he introduces her to Harry Griffiths, his close friend in medical school, she steals Philip's money and runs off with Griffiths. After Griffiths abandons her, she becomes a prostitute and, with her baby, moves back in with Philip. When he rejects her sexual advances and exclaims, "You disgust me," Mildred, like his teachers and his schoolfriend Rose, calls him a cripple. She retaliates by using a hammer to destroy everything in his flat. Finally—like a stereotypical fallen woman in a Victorian melodrama—she contracts syphilis and, to Philip's horror, continues to ply her trade and infect her clients. Philip's mortifying relations with Mildred (which continue for 350 pages) exemplify the enslavement to passion suggested by the title.

The boyish Mildred does not resemble any woman in Maugham's life. But she's so indelibly lifelike that she must, like all the other major characters in the novel, be based on a real person. Harry Philips, Maugham's companion in Paris, revealed that "the real Mildred was a youth" and, with tantalizing suggestiveness, linked himself to her: "Mildred was a composite character & one incident in the book, *Of Human Bondage,* was undoubtedly an episode in our friendship not very creditable to me which he attributed to her. At the time I was somewhat ashamed as I realised that I had hurt his feelings more than I thought."[16]

By naming Philip's main rival for Mildred's love *Harry* Griffiths and changing the original first name of his hero from Stephen to *Philip* Carey, Maugham connects the two names and suggests that Harry Philips was indeed the model for Mildred. In the novel, Philip and Harry strengthen their male bond by having sex with Mildred, just as, before Maugham's marriage, he and Walter Payne had shared the same women. The sexual transformation of Harry Philips into Mildred shows that Philip Carey's constant need for humiliation and degradation was based on Maugham's homosexual desires and masochistic need to increase his pleasure by punishing himself for it. The "mysterious secret" of El Greco that so troubles Philip—as Maugham finally explains in his travel book *Don Fernando* (1935)—is homosexuality. After his painful break with Philips in 1905, Maugham—trying to believe that he was "three-quarters normal"—began the series of love affairs with women that culminated in fatherhood and marriage.

In *Of Human Bondage,* as in Lawrence's *Sons and Lovers* (1913), both heroes must have relationships with several different women before they can truly grow up. During a respite from Mildred, Philip has a brief, gratifying affair with Norah Nesbitt. Though she's worth ten Mildreds, he doesn't love her in the same obsessive way. He recalls Norah's "solicitude for his welfare and her interest in all that concerned him. She had loved him with a love that was kind and lasting, there was more than sensuality in it, it was almost maternal." Norah's maternal love leads Philip to Sally Athelny, whose unusual name recalls that of Adney Payne. His love affair with the even more maternal Sally and friendship with her kindly father take place during an idyllic summer of hop picking in Kent. The elusive pattern of Philip's life finally falls into place when he realizes the quite conventional desire "for a wife and a home and love" and marries the warm, responsive Sally. The novel—which opened on a gray, dull day, with heavy clouds and rawness in the air—ends with a shining sun.

This pleasant conclusion is undermined by Philip's conflicting desire to live a normal life and his overwhelming urge to suffer at Mildred's hands. Maugham himself, struggling with an outlaw passion, was attracted to philosophies that described man's life as a struggle between pure and impure, physical and spiritual. He took his title from part IV of Benedict Spinoza's *Ethics*—"Of Human Bondage, or the Powers of the Affects [Emotions]." Spinoza wrote that "Man's lack of power to moderate and restrain affects I call bondage." He argued that men are subjected to bondage when they allow the passions to operate in egoistic blindness, and can achieve freedom only in the "intellectual love of God"—which Philip had rejected long before he finally freed himself from Mildred.

Maugham had studied Schopenhauer's philosophy under Kuno Fischer at Heidelberg. His fiction was influenced by Schopenhauer's idea of man's bondage to "the Will," an inescapable, overwhelming emotional force that drives men from the cradle to the grave and is the source of all his desires and all his grief. To Schopenhauer, as Thomas Mann observed, "sex is of the devil, a diabolic distraction from pure contemplation; knowledge is that denial of sex." Maugham was also fond of Benjamin Constant's *Adolphe* (1816), the story of a passionate but irksome love affair, full of pain, self-deception and disillusionment. After his mistress dies Adolphe escapes from bondage, but begins to regret her loss and cannot enjoy his loveless freedom. Glenway Wescott noted that "Maugham—whenever anyone has fallen in love with him—offers the victim or beneficiary of love a copy of *Adolphe,* as you might give quinine to a friend going on a journey."[17]

Cronshaw had urged Philip to search for the meaning of life, which might free him from the pain of living, in the pattern of a Persian carpet. Though Maugham condemned Henry James, he also borrowed the metaphor from James' story "The Figure in the Carpet" (1896), where "a complex figure in a Persian carpet" stands for the overarching pattern in a famous writer's work—and his search for the meaning of life. Toward the end of Maugham's novel, Philip, after hearing that Hayward has died of enteric fever on his way to the Boer War, rather portentously exclaims that "Life had no meaning. . . . [Man] was born, he suffered, and he died. . . . Man by living served no end."[18]

Sinclair Lewis urged George Doran to publish *Of Human Bondage,* despite its great length. Desmond MacCarthy recalled Maugham working on his thick packet of proofs when they were sharing a room in wartime France, and noted that he made very few corrections. Theodore Dreiser,

Leslie Howard and Bette Davis in Of Human Bondage, *1934*

reviewing the book for the *New Republic* in December 1915, declared that Maugham was "a genius endowed with an immense capacity for understanding and pity," and called it a "profound and philosophic book."[19] Despite what Gore Vidal called his "ghastly flowering of self-pity," *Of Human Bondage,* Maugham's first mature piece of fiction, was a magisterial achievement.

V

AFTER LEAVING FRANCE in February 1915, Maugham rejoined Syrie in London and then took her to Rome to await the birth of their child. Haxton temporarily dropped out of his life, but resurfaced at the end of the year during his scandalous trial in London. In September Maugham went to live in Switzerland, where his knowledge of French and German came in useful, and spent the next year working for British Intelligence as a secret agent. He was recruited by Sir John Wallinger, a friend of Syrie, portrayed as "R." in *Ashenden,* the book of stories based on his experiences as a spy in Geneva and St. Petersburg. Syrie and Liza were with him for part of the year, providing an excellent domestic cover, and his profession as a writer enabled him to travel about and stay in hotels without attracting much notice. But his writing was more than a disguise, and while waiting for developments he sat down at his desk and got on with his latest play.

Since the documents concerning his work have always been kept secret, *Ashenden* is virtually the only evidence we have for Maugham's activities in Switzerland. In his preface Maugham wrote that "there will always be men, who, from love of adventure or a sense of duty, will risk a shameful death to secure information valuable to their country." His predecessor, unable to take the strain, had had a nervous breakdown, and his colleague in Lausanne had been imprisoned for two years by the Swiss authorities. For patriotic reasons Maugham refused to take pay, and those who accepted money thought him "damned foolish." Ashenden's English controller warned him, in a nicely balanced sentence: "If you do well you'll get no thanks and if you get into trouble you'll get no help." But Maugham, always greedy for new experiences, seemed to relish the chance to complicate his already immensely complicated emotional and intellectual life. The offer enabled him to get out of London, the scene of Syrie's divorce case, which had named him corespondent.

In *Under Western Eyes,* published five years before Maugham went to Geneva, Conrad described the prim and heartless city: "there was but little of spring-like glory in the rectangular railed space of grass and trees, framed visibly by the orderly roof-slopes of that town, comely without grace, and hospitable without sympathy. . . . He saw the green slopes framing the Petit Lac in all the marvellous banality of the picturesque made of painted cardboard."[20] Maugham, too, mentioned the unfriendly streets and silent houses; the absurd lake with its too blue water and the too snowy mountains. He stayed at the Hôtel Beau Rivage—a den of intrigue, filled with agents, spies, agitators and revolutionaries eager for action.

His main job was to give orders to, collect intelligence from and pay British agents in wartime Germany, then dispatch their information to headquarters in London. In addition to keeping his eyes open and writing his reports in code, he ran his own network, recruited new spies and sent them into enemy territory to find out about troops, munitions and morale. He made weekly visits to the market to get messages from an old woman who slipped across the Swiss border from France; and he crossed the French frontier every week to hand over his reports and get his orders.

Much of what Maugham described in *Ashenden* was close to the truth, and Ashenden himself is a wry self-portrait. Though much of his work was as dull and monotonous as a city clerk's, Maugham was more than a mere conduit of information. He carried a gun, had considerable life and death responsibility, and even planned to assassinate a king. One of his agents, called "the Hairless Mexican" in *Ashenden,* killed a woman who spied on him and murdered an innocent man whom he mistook for a German agent. Maugham tells the story of how Ashenden persuaded the mistress of an Indian agitator to help him. She lures Chandra Lal back to France, where he promptly takes poison to avoid interrogation. In his diary of the period, Inspector Basil Thomson of Scotland Yard noted the same story: "David Gullick returned yesterday from Switzerland. He had been at the same sanatorium as Anna Brandt and was very much in love with her. At his first interview he proposed a daring scheme for the capture of Chattopadya by luring him into France, on the understanding that, if he was captured, Anna would be set at liberty."

On February 8, 1916, Major Walter Kirke, chief of British agents in Switzerland, noting Maugham's complicated life, wrote that his employment was now formally at an end: "*Somerset Maugham* discharged but will examine the Swiss frontier on his own for John [Wallinger], but no expense to us to be incurred. Has been writing a play during his time in Switzerland and got into the Divorce Court. John is sending a new man." British Intelligence, run as a sort of club, relied on the brains and trustworthiness of amateurs.

In his World War II propaganda novel *The Hour Before the Dawn,* Maugham tried to define the perverse mind of the spy: "there was something in his nature, pitiless and rather dreadful, that made him take a peculiar pleasure in his secret work. Because his motives were pure he allowed himself to revel in the crooked ways in which, setting his wits against theirs, he strove to combat the wiles of his adversaries."[21] Maugham, reflecting on his own enjoyment of power, must have known that his chilling personal qualities, his remoteness, wariness and reticence, were useful on the job. Like all successful spies, he was secretive, devious and manipulative. His homosexuality, like that of the traitors Guy Burgess and Anthony Blunt, had taught him to be an undercover agent in both his life and his work.

8

Secret Agent

1916–1919

FOR TEN YEARS, between his marriage to Syrie and the purchase of his villa in France, Maugham lived out of suitcases, "going to and fro in the earth and walking up and down in it"—to use one of his favorite quotations from Job. Though London amused and contented him, he was often seized by restlessness. He said his resolute desire for a well-ordered life clashed with "his passion for living in the future; and no sooner was he settled in his work . . . than he had busied himself with arrangements for his travels." While the war raged on in Europe, in November 1916 Maugham fulfilled a long-standing ambition by traveling to Hawaii, Samoa and Tahiti. Reunited with Gerald Haxton, who'd narrowly escaped prison after his arrest and trial in London, Maugham found him, as Johnson said of Boswell, "a companion, whose acuteness would help my inquiry, and whose gaiety of conversation and civility of manners are sufficient to counteract the inconveniences of travel."

Like Philip Carey, Maugham "pictured to himself palm-trees and skies blue and hot, dark-skinned people, pagodas; the scents of the Orient intoxicated his nostrils."[1] On his journeys he always carried a large sack of books to fit every occasion and every mood, and was drawn to the South Seas by several writers. Herman Melville, who'd deserted from a whaling ship in the Marquesas Islands in 1841, wrote about the cannibal paradise in his autobiographical travel books *Typee* (1846) and *Omoo* (1847). Pierre

Loti published *Rarahu,* a novel about Tahiti, in 1879. Robert Louis Stevenson in 1888, Henry Adams in 1891 and Rupert Brooke in 1914 had all visited that lush green island. The French Post-Impressionist painter Paul Gauguin had lived in Tahiti, where he painted serenely beautiful figures and sensual landscapes. The South Seas legend had been firmly established by the end of the century.

Though Maugham had plenty of reasons for going away—not least, to escape from Syrie—it seems odd that he should abandon his work in Switzerland and go to the South Seas in the middle of the war. In fact, the impetus to set off at precisely this time was not personal. He was sent there as a secret agent. In a crucial passage in one of his letters, overlooked by scholars, he later explained: "The exotic background was forced upon me accidentally by the fact that during the war I was employed in the Intelligence department, and so visited parts of the world which otherwise I might not have summoned up sufficient resolution to go to."

Maugham was sent specifically to acquire vital information about Samoa. In "1884 Germany had staked out her claim to the northeastern quarter of New Guinea and also to the Bismarck Archipelago. The next year the Marshall and Solomon Islands were declared German possessions, and by the end of the decade Germany had come to an agreement with Great Britain and the United States concerning a condominium in the Samoan Islands." Germany had controlled Western Samoa until New Zealand occupied the island when war broke out in August 1914. The British had a strategic interest in Samoa, a turbulent and potentially troublesome island. The efficient German administration had been abruptly replaced by the government of New Zealand, and recent volcanic eruptions had caused severe damage. Discontented natives were protesting; tropical diseases were rampant. German businesses had been expropriated, but it was not clear who actually owned the money deposited in German banks on the island. Vital information was needed about the use of the island's powerful radio station, the threat of German military forces and installations, and the danger from German warships still cruising the Pacific.

This journey on His Majesty's Service began Maugham's addiction to exotic places. In *The Gentleman in the Parlour* (1930), his book on Southeast Asia, he defined his aesthetic of travel: "I travel because I like to move from place to place, I enjoy the sense of freedom it gives me, it pleases me to be rid of ties, responsibilities, duties; I like the unknown; I meet odd people who amuse me for a moment and sometimes suggest a theme for a composition; I am often tired of myself, and I have a notion that by travel I can add to my personality and so change myself a little."[2] He was always excited by the exhilaration of departure and the recourse to flight, by the opportunity to clear out and avoid obligations. Travel allowed him to relieve the strain of writing and the pressure to earn his living, to replenish his imaginative store and refresh his mind.

Maugham traveled for weeks, even months, at a time, when the only means of getting to remote places was on bug-infested steamers, crowded, rickety trains or bullock carts and donkeys. He often had to take loads of food and equipment with him. In his essay "Wordsworth in the Tropics," Aldous Huxley described the cultural barriers to the European understanding of tropical places, where the force of nature is "foreign, appalling, fundamentally and utterly inimical to intruding man." But Maugham had a restless, inquiring intelligence, and was quite prepared to put up with the indignities and hardships of travel for the thrill of new experiences. On a ten-hour trip to Samoa in an open boat, the forty-two-year-old Maugham reclined contentedly on the deck above the throbbing engine, resting his head on a sack of copra.

Henry James picked up the "germ" of a novel or short story at fashionable dinner parties in London. Maugham used drawing-room subjects for his plays, but his fiction was enriched by expeditions far beyond Europe. Very much the white man in a brown world, Maugham's comparative wealth enabled him to travel in style to European colonies. Like all true travelers, he also used the journey to explore himself, and exotic places heightened his own sense of identity. Like Kipling and Conrad before him, he was especially interested in "the effect of the climate and surroundings on the white people who for one reason or another had drifted there." In a letter of December 6, 1928, he wrote that travel stimulated his creativity: "When I went down to the South Seas I came across a great many types that were entirely new to me, and situations which appealed to my imagination. . . . I seemed to be entering upon an entirely new literary life, and after the war I deliberately travelled in search of this material."[3]

Maugham always wrote by hand and "liked to see how the words looked as he formed them with a pen." Though he composed nothing on his long trips to Asia and around the world, he "dictated great masses of notes" to Haxton, his companion and majordomo, who's not mentioned in the travel books. The time required to cover great distances and return home gave him an essential perspective on his exotic material. "It's only when you get away from a place that you can describe it," he said. "You recall the salient features and all the incidental details f-f-fall away."

In Apia, on Western Samoa, Maugham visited Robert Louis Stevenson's impressive residence and trekked up to his grave. Stevenson's Vailima, a magnificent house with redwood paneling, great hall, commodious verandah and thatched roof, stood three miles outside Apia, surrounded by deep ravines and clear waterfalls. Maugham also followed the slippery path through the overhanging jungle, listened to the shrill cries of tropical birds and climbed 1,500 feet to the top of Mount Vaea, where Stevenson's low rectangular tomb commanded a celestial view of both sides of the island and of the white surf pounding against the coral reefs.

Unlike his literary predecessors, Maugham emphasized the contrast between the romantic image of the South Seas and the disappointing reality. He was fascinated by the sullen, decadent white men trapped in a steamy landscape and by their relationships with the South Sea islanders. D. H. Lawrence, who passed through Tahiti a few years later, agreed with Maugham that the islands could no longer sustain their myth. The people, Lawrence wrote in one of his rages, were no longer the noble, sensual creatures of Gauguin's paintings, but ugly, false, spoiled and diseased: "Papeete is a poor sort of place, mostly Chinese, natives in European clothes, and fat. . . . I never want to *stay* in the tropics."[4]

Maugham was drawn to Tahiti because of Gauguin, and spent a month in early 1917 talking to people who had known him. Gauguin's work had interested him since 1905, when Roderick O'Conor, who'd known the artist at Pont-Aven in Brittany, told Maugham about him. O'Conor had lent Gauguin his studio in Paris and owned several of his impressive paintings and drawings. Talking to O'Conor about the eccentric and dazzlingly gifted painter, who'd died in 1903, made Maugham see the literary potential of Gauguin's life, and the idea of what was to become *The Moon and Sixpence* began to take shape in his mind.

Gauguin spent his childhood in Peru, then worked as a merchant seaman and lived in far-off places like Panama and Martinique. After a lucrative career as a stockbroker in Paris, he abandoned his Danish wife and five children and became an impoverished, unrecognized and embittered painter. Driven by a ferocious egoism, a combative personality and a contempt for traditional morality, he sponged off acquaintances and seduced the wife of his close friend Émile Schuffenecker (the model for Dirk

Stroeve in Maugham's novel). He led a Bohemian life in Paris and Provence (where he lived with Van Gogh), and spent the last twelve, relatively contented years of his life in Tahiti and the Marquesas. He lived with a succession of fourteen-year-old mistresses, and died prematurely of syphilis in a wild and remote tropical valley. Like Baudelaire's escape to Mauritius and Rimbaud's adventures in Abyssinia, Gauguin's legendary flight from the comforts of civilization to a primitive existence embodied the Romantic idea of the artist as a tormented pariah and victim who could not bear to live within the constraints of conventional society.

Gauguin reached the pinnacle of his creative powers in Tahiti. In that luxuriant setting his painting became more profound, his colors more striking, his composition more dramatic. In 1897 he painted his artistic and spiritual masterpiece, *D'où venons-nous? Que sommes-nous? Où allons-nous? (Where Do We Come From? What Are We? Where Are We Going?),* now in the Boston Museum of Fine Arts. Maugham alludes to this work, with deliberate vagueness, at the end of *The Moon and Sixpence:* "From floor to ceiling the walls were covered with a strange and elaborate composition. It was indescribably wonderful and mysterious. . . . It was tremendous, sensual, passionate. . . . It was the work of a man who had delved into the hidden depths of nature and had discovered secrets which were beautiful and fearful too."

In Tahiti Maugham tracked down in a remote hut Gauguin's *Eve in Paradise* (1898–99), which he'd painted on the glass panels of a door, and bought it for two hundred francs. Eve, in the guise of a black-haired, brown-skinned, full-breasted Tahitian woman, wears a white sarong and holds an oversized apple (or breadfruit). She stands next to a white, flowering tree that grows to her height and a white rabbit on a green field that crouches near her feet. A wavy, milky cloud covers her head and body like a shawl, and in the background three sharp-sailed boats float on a deep blue sea. The painting captures the harmony, peace and innocence of Eden before the Fall of Man. (In 1962 it was sold at Sotheby's for $104,700 and today would be worth millions.)

This trip to the South Seas not only set the pattern of Maugham's future journeys, where he combined a collector's passion for experience with the need to "change himself," but also solidified his ties to Haxton. Sailing from San Francisco to Honolulu on the outward journey he also had the luck to meet Bertram Alanson, who became one of his closest and most generous friends. "A tall, distinguished man who looked like a Spanish grandee," Alanson, three years younger than Maugham, came from a German-Jewish family in San Francisco. His father had owned coffee plantations in Guatemala, and Bert had grown up and gone to the university there. In 1907 he'd founded Alanson Bros. Investment Brokers, was tremendously successful and in 1930 became president of the San Francisco Stock Exchange. In 1924, at the age of forty-seven, he married the attractive Mabel Bremer, the divorced wife of a friend, and lived in splendor at 828 Francisco Street, with a stunning view of Alcatraz and the Bay. The devoted Bert handled Maugham's considerable American finances, as Walter Payne had once managed his English earnings. He turned a forgotten investment of $25,000 into more than a million dollars, and enabled Maugham to travel, live and entertain on a grand scale.

Though Maugham claimed to know nothing about business and wished he'd learned about it as an errand boy in Alanson's office, he was able to do Alanson an important service. Maugham told Bruce Lockhart (who later got the date wrong) that in August 1917 he met Alanson in San Francisco on his "way to Russia (Secret Service) *via* Siberia—Yank had big holding of roubles—wanted info. Maugham afraid in official position— sent telegram 'Rachel very ill recovery impossible.' Yank sold—made $200,000."[5] In mid-April 1917 Maugham and Gerald returned to San Francisco. On May 26 Maugham married Syrie in New Jersey.

That April America entered the war, and Haxton, urged on by a cable from his mother in England, enlisted in the U.S. Army. He was sent to France, was invalided out and returned to San Francisco. He then took a Japanese ship to a wartime job in Java, but on the way it was captured and scuttled by the German *Sea Wolf*. He spent the remainder of the war in a prison camp in Güstrow, east of Hamburg. By this time Maugham was in Russia, and when he heard that Haxton's ship had suddenly disappeared, he naturally assumed he was dead. After the war they were joyfully reunited.

II

"I AM GOING to Russia," Maugham dramatically announced in June 1917, "and shall be occupied there presumably till the end of the war." He'd taken some Russian lessons on Capri in 1905 from a hairy, dwarfish and desperately poor teacher from Odessa, who came to his villa each day. He found the Cyrillic alphabet daunting at first, but once he'd mastered the thirty-six strange letters the rest went smoothly. The grammar was easy, the sentence structure relatively simple and there were a great many recognizable foreign words. In a few months he knew enough to read the plays of Chekhov. This knowledge was very useful in his new undertaking. Once in Petrograd he continued to study the language and was soon fluent enough to conduct his business in Russian.

Incredibly, the relatively inexperienced Maugham "was chief agent in Russia for the British and American secret services during the crucial few weeks [i.e., months] preceding the Bolshevik coup of [October] 1917." The political situation in Russia—where he risked execution—was complicated and explosive, and his job was infinitely more difficult and dangerous than in Switzerland. Sir William Wiseman, director of British espionage in Russia, sent him there alone and with only $21,000 to pay his expenses, finance newspapers and buy arms. His task was to support the Kerensky government, prevent the Bolshevik revolution and keep Russia in the war against Germany. He had to work independently of the British and American embassies, and planned to blow up an Austrian ammunition factory and sacrifice many civilian lives. He stayed in Russia for only two and a half months, and his task, with hopelessly limited resources, was impossible. But if his mission had succeeded, Maugham could have changed the history of the modern world.

On July 28 Maugham sailed from San Francisco to Yokohama on a Japanese boat. On August 27 he took a train from Tokyo to Tsuruga, a port on the north coast of Honshu, sailed up the Sea of Japan to Vladivostok and then spent eleven days on the Trans-Siberian Railroad to Petrograd. In a train station along the way, he was moved by a soldier, scarred and blinded in the war, who played the accordion and sang in a powerful, sweet voice. In the preface to *Ashenden* he romanticized the vast landscape that he'd read about in so many Russian novels and that represented the last peaceful moment before he was thrown into the turmoil of revolution: "I felt the lonely steppes and the interminable forests; the flow of the broad Russian rivers and all the toil of the countryside; the ploughing of the land and the reaping of the ripe wheat; the sighing of the wind in the birch trees; the long months of dark winter; and then the dancing of the women in the villages and the youths bathing in shallow streams on summer evenings."[6]

In the spring of 1917—four months before Maugham reached Russia—Stalin had arrived in Petrograd from Siberia, Trotsky from America and Lenin (courtesy of the Germans) in a sealed train from Switzerland to the Finland Station. The situation was complex and extremely volatile. After the first revolution in March, Czar Nicholas II abdicated and Prince Lvov formed a government with the Socialist Alexander Kerensky as minister of justice. In June the Russian Black Sea fleet mutinied at Sebastopol, and Kerensky launched a counterattack against the Germans. In July, the Bolsheviks (always a threat to the democratic government) failed to seize power in Petrograd and, following Lvov's resignation, Kerensky took control.

The problems facing the government were overwhelming, indeed insoluble, the masses angry and violent: "A war with millions dead, food and supplies on a downward spiral, a people expecting, now that [the March] revolution had come, either the immediate transformation of their lives or an outlet for all their accumulated hatred and envy—these were the circumstances the Provisional Government had to master, and without constitutional authority, a secure basis of power or popular support, or strong, unified leadership." A Russian historian has emphasized the fatal weakness of the pro-war government—which Maugham was sent to support—and its failure to deal with the most serious economic, political and military problems:

> The Provisional Government lasted approximately eight months: from March 12 until November 7, 1917. Its record combined remarkable liberalism with an inability to solve pressing, crucial problems. . . . It proved unable to check inflation, restore transportation, or increase industrial production. In fact, the Russian economy continued to run rapidly downhill. . . . The government also made mistakes. It refused to recognize the catastrophic condition of the country and misjudged the mood of the people. . . . The crushing burden of the war and increasing economic dislocation made the position of the Provisional Government constantly more precarious.

Bruce Lockhart—an agent attached to the British embassy, who had the same mission as Maugham both with Kerensky before the revolution and with Lenin after it—simply declared that "the revolution took place because the patience of the Russian people broke down under a system of unparalleled inefficiency and corruption."[7]

In late August, using journalism as his cover, Maugham settled into his

Sasha Kropotkin, portrait by Gerald Kelly

cold and depressing room in the Hotel Europa. On September 5, soon after he reached Petrograd, he wrote Gerald Kelly (with deliberate vagueness) that he was doing the same work he'd done in Switzerland, though it was more varied and more responsible. The novelist Hugh Walpole, whom Maugham would later satirize in *Cakes and Ale,* was also in Russia and described the current atmosphere. Walpole had an elementary knowledge of the language, and in 1915 had worked with the Red Cross and been decorated by the Russian army for gallantry under fire. In 1916, as head of the British propaganda office, he wrote influential articles for the leading Petrograd newspapers. During the March revolution he heard "a terrific noise of firing and shouting; went to our windows and saw a whole revolutionary mob pass down our street. About two thousand soldiers, many civilians armed, motor lorries with flags." Walpole, noting that he and Maugham worked together in the fall of 1917, emphasized their swift change from high-minded hopes to disillusionment: "Very depressing those months were, when the idealism of some of us got some hard knocks, and when all our preconceived notions of Russia and the Russians fell to the ground one after the other."[8]

Maugham received help from two Russian friends: Alexandra (Sasha) Kropotkin and Boris Savinkov. The lively, dark-haired Sasha, daughter of the notorious anarchist Prince Peter Kropotkin, was born in England in 1887, during her father's years of exile. She grew up in the Socialist circles of William Morris and Bernard Shaw, who knew her as a child and called her a "most lovely girl." Gerald Kelly painted Sasha wearing a black, fur-trimmed dress, seated before a grayish-white background with classically stylized waves. She has curly hair parted down the middle, dangling ear-rings, large, wide-apart eyes, a thick nose and full, sensuous lips. Her expression suggests forcefulness and determination. Her father, who thought women should know self-defense, taught her fencing and later attempted to marry her off to his fellow anarchist Ivan Bakunin. Referring to Sasha in a letter to Maxim Gorki, Shaw wrote that "a little time ago a Russian lady, brought up as an extreme revolutionist [and alluding to the mission of Holy Russia], said to me with wild enthusiasm that the Rus-sians would give the world back its lost soul."

In the early years of the century, between Maugham's break with Harry Philips in 1905 and Sasha's marriage to the social revolutionary and jour-nalist Boris Lebedev in 1910, he had a short but amiable affair with her that concluded with friendly feelings on both sides. A princess and daugh-ter of a revolutionary who'd been sentenced to life imprisonment and had escaped from Siberia, Sasha had been a student at London University. She seemed to embody the Russian spirit at the time that England first discov-ered the Russian novelists, Diaghilev's ballet and the music of Stravinsky. Maugham wrote that Sasha, who appears in *Ashenden* as Anastasia Leonidov, "had fine eyes and a good . . . too voluptuous figure, high cheek-bones and a snub nose (this was very Tartar), a wide mouth full of large square teeth and a pale skin."[9] Intellectually as well as sexually attrac-tive, she served Maugham Russian tea in glasses and talked for hours about Marx and Gorki, fate, passion and the brotherhood of man. Maugham found her extremely intelligent, with an alarming love of intrigue and a lust for power.

Sasha returned to Russia with Lebedev in 1915; her father followed, two years later, when the czar fell. In a striking contrast to the dull, shabby life she'd been forced to lead in London, she was soon on intimate terms with Kerensky, and became Maugham's main liaison and translator. Maugham told Kelly that he'd seen a lot of Sasha, who was charming and helpful, energetic as well as impudent. She knew and had access to every important official and, by an extraordinary twist of fate, was now a powerful figure in Russia. But her fortunes changed once again when the Bolsheviks seized power and confiscated Peter Kropotkin's 250,000-acre estate in Tambov province. In 1919 Sasha was detained by the Cheka, and the following year caught typhoid fever. Lebedev, overworked and starving, suffered a nervous breakdown. After her father's death and state funeral in 1921, Sasha was finally allowed to emigrate and settled in New York.

In the last chapter of *Ashenden,* Maugham's Anastasia tries to help an American businessman, Mr. Harrington, whose negotiations have collapsed after the Revolution. Absurdly, he refuses to leave the country without his laundry. She warns him of the danger, but agrees to go with him and collect it. The Czech Emmanuel Voska, also working with Maugham at the time, confirmed that the story, in all its pathetic detail, was literally true, and claimed that he too had been on the scene: "On the way back from the laundry they had run into a street skirmish. In scurrying to cover they had become separated. Hadn't he come back to the hotel? I ran to the scene of the fight. I found him dead in the gutter, with his bundle of washing under him."[10]

Voska, who'd accompanied Maugham on the train across Siberia, also supported Kerensky's government, which was fighting the Hapsburgs who had oppressed the Czechs. Voska struck an English journalist as an unprepossessing fellow: "Thick set, of medium height, unshaven, grimy in appearance and in dress, with features of the semi-Tartar type." But Maugham was greatly impressed by the sound sense and determination of Voska's boss, the Czech leader Thomas Masaryk. He'd fought for his country's liberation from Hapsburg rule and in 1918 became the first president of Czechoslovakia. After the March revolution, Masaryk organized a 100,000-man Czech Legion from the Slavic prisoners of war in Russia, and during the civil war fought the Bolsheviks in Siberia.

Maugham's other close colleague and source of valuable information was the ruthless terrorist and underground man Boris Savinkov (1879–1925), who'd assassinated V. K. de Plehve, the oppressive czarist minister of the interior, in July 1904. His anonymous, firsthand descriptions in his novel *The Pale Horse* (1909) and in the *Strand Magazine* of July 1910 gave an insider's view of the same political murder that Conrad had vividly portrayed in the first chapter of *Under Western Eyes.* In February 1905, Savinkov also blew up the grand duke Sergius, uncle of the czar. (After the Revolution, the cross marking the spot where Sergius met his

Boris Savinkov before the Soviet tribunal, 1925

doom was removed by the Bolsheviks.) During Kerensky's regime, Savinkov—who'd first fought the czarists, then the Bolsheviks—was minister of war and governor-general of Petrograd. In 1918, he incited a rebellion in European Russia, captured the city of Jaroslavl on the Volga River and held it for two weeks.

Thomas Masaryk despised both Savinkov's ruthless violence and fanatical character. "Politically," he wrote, "he under-estimated the strength of Bolshevism; philosophically, he failed to realize the difference between a revolution and individual acts of terrorism. . . . Morally, he did not rise above the elementary notions of the blood feud." But Winston Churchill, impressed by his courage and daring in the fight against tyranny, described him as

> small in stature; moving as little as possible, and that noiselessly and with deliberation; remarkable grey-green eyes in a face of almost deathly pallor; speaking in a calm, low, even voice, almost a monotone; innumerable cigarettes. His manner was at once confidential and dignified; a ready and ceremonious address, with a frozen, but not a freezing composure; and through all the sense of an unusual personality, of veiled power in strong restraint.[11]

Maugham also found Savinkov resourceful and fearless. After his two political murders, Maugham wrote:

> He was finally arrested and sentenced to death. While awaiting his execution he was imprisoned at Sevastopol; and there, it was told me, such was the magic of his persuasive speech, he had induced his jailers to join the revolutionary ranks and contrive his escape. . . . [When I] suggested that it must have required immense courage to plan and commit those two dreadful assassinations, he shrugged his shoulders. "Not at all, believe me," he answered. "It is a business like another. One gets accustomed to it."[12]

III

THROUGH SASHA AND Savinkov Maugham saw a good deal of Alexander Kerensky (1881–1970), the head of the Provisional Government. He'd established his reputation as a young lawyer by successfully defending political prisoners. Young and idealistic, "his career was spectacular. Duma member and party leader at thirty-one, prime minister of Russia at thirty-six, permanent exile from his native land at thirty-six—his taste of power was brief. His flair for the melodramatic—there was much of the actor in Kerensky—and his supercharged emotionalism have led some to dismiss him as a shallow, flamboyant demagogue." Bruce Lockhart, describing his appearance, wrote that Kerensky's "face has a sallow and almost deathly pallor. His eyes, narrow and Mongolian, are tired. He looks as if he were in pain, but the mouth is firm, and the hair, cropped close and worn *en brosse,* gives a general impression of energy." The fundamentally decent but ineffective Kerensky met his nemesis in Lenin, who impressed Lockhart "by his tremendous will-power, his relentless determination" and his absolute ruthlessness. Lenin shot people, Kerensky did not—and executions were necessary to make the revolution succeed.

Maugham wrote about Kerensky in his notebooks, in *Ashenden* and in his secret reports to London. He was astonished, despite Kerensky's obvious weakness, by his meteoric rise to fame and power. Kerensky was a man of speech, not action, a leader whose vanity did not permit disagreement and whose colleagues were no more than toadies. Poorly educated and uncultured, without imagination or magnetism, he lacked physical and intellectual strength. Making endless speeches, he had lost control and ran about like a frightened hen. Maugham thought he looked strangely haunted and nervous, completely exhausted, unable to act and crushed by the burden of power. When Lenin was in hiding in Petrograd, Kerensky supposedly knew where he was but didn't dare to arrest him. Winter was approaching, famine threatened, the German army menaced Petrograd, the Russian army was mutinous, the masses wanted peace. As early as September 23, only a few weeks after he reached the capital, Maugham shrewdly warned his boss Sir William Wiseman that "Kerensky's government was losing power and probably could not last."[13]

In his reports to London Maugham stressed that it was impossible to combat German espionage and that the Bolsheviks would inevitably win: "Our agent reported the situation in Russia was entirely out of hand, and that no propaganda or organized support undertaken by the Allies could possibly stem the rising tide of Bolshevism." During their personal meetings, Kerensky seemed bitter, desperate and defeated. He asked Maugham why the London *Times* was so hostile to Russia, why the British kept their incompetent ambassador to Russia and why they'd failed to send the promised military aid. Kerensky exclaimed:

> I must make the Russian soldiers understand what they are fighting for. We haven't got boots or warm clothes or food. They have been fighting a year longer than England. They are tired out. We must give them something which will give them new heart and courage to go on. . . . The Allies must help us with guns and ammunition. When I go down to the front the generals say to me: "What are the Allies doing for us? They send us nothing." . . . It is very important that the [English] newspapers should treat Russia's affairs sympathetically.[14]

Five days before the Revolution, Vladimir Nabokov's father, chancellor of the Provisional Government, asked Kerensky about the threat of a Bolshevik revolt. Kerensky, who'd crushed General Kornilov's military rebellion in September, was hopelessly optimistic: " 'I would be ready to offer prayers for such an uprising to take place,' he replied. 'And are you sure that you will be able to cope with it?' 'I have more troops than I need. They will be crushed once and for all.' " But October 24 saw the outbreak of the Revolution and the ten days that shook the world. Hugh Walpole described the chaotic scene in his diary: "The latest news that Kerensky has defied the Bolsheviks and arrested their committee. . . . News in the morning that the Bolsheviks have the upper hand. . . . Firing in the

evening. Shelling of Winter Palace. . . . Whole town is in hands of Bolsheviks. . . . Putting barricades up in the streets. Saw the damage shells had
done to the Winter Palace."

Maugham, the secret agent of a reactionary government, had always
refused to treat with the Bolsheviks and was now a marked man. If captured by the Reds, who were shooting all their enemies, he would certainly
have been executed. On October 22, two days before the Revolution, he
hastily left for Stockholm and London with an urgent personal message
from Kerensky to the coalition prime minister, Lloyd George. Maugham
later said that Kerensky wanted Lloyd George to get rid of a Labour Party
politician who'd opposed the Provisional Government. Lloyd George
replied that if he dismissed the politician he'd have the entire party down
on him, and abruptly ended the interview.[15]

In January 1918 Maugham wrote Kelly that he'd had an exciting time in
Russia and was sorry he'd been recalled, but he had to deliver Kerensky's
message and get himself out of danger. He'd planned to return after a
week in London, but the Revolution broke out while he was en route to
England and everything he'd been striving for came to naught. On
December 5 Russia signed an armistice at Brest-Litovsk and pulled out of
the war against Germany. Keith Neilson pointed out that Maugham's
involvement "with British efforts in Russia reflected the fact that there
was no system in place to secure people with the requisite skills. [But] this
reliance on the gifted amateur did not prove ineffective." Maugham
believed, perhaps naively, that his mission might have succeeded. In 1933
he told Lockhart that if he'd been sent to Russia sooner, and with greater
resources and power, he could have made the "Bolshevik *coup d'état* impossible."[16] But the powerful tide of history ran against him.

Despite the considerable limitations imposed upon him, Maugham
showed great insight into the chaotic political events in Russia and the precarious state of the Provisional Government. An expert on espionage has
concluded that his reports, highly valued and seriously considered, were
immediately sent to the highest authorities:

> Maugham was more favored than most. He could not personally press his
> views on the American executive, but Wiseman ensured that his reports
> quickly reached the right quarter. Maugham was formally in authority
> over Voska, the one American agent who might have been considered
> [superior by the State Department]. . . . Unlike other sources of intelli-

gence, he gave due warning of Kerensky's infirmity, of Bolshevik strength, and of Polish and Czech possibilities [against the Hapsburg Empire]. . . . His findings were accurate compared with those of other contemporary reporters on the Russian scene; and, following Wiseman's brief, Maugham sensibly advised the Allies on political and financial methods which might enable them to "guide the storm" in East Central Europe. . . . But he was wrong in estimating that the Cossacks were at any time a national Russian force in the same sense that the Bolsheviks were.

Maugham's political activities and penetrating reports were so highly valued that the authorities wanted to send him back to Russia. His mission would have been to support the Cossack general who—with Allied soldiers, arms and money—was fighting both the Bolsheviks and the Germans. Another plan was to send him to Bucharest to keep Romania in the war against Germany. Both plans were abandoned when his health broke down.

Ironically, Maugham's plays continued to be performed in Soviet Russia after he'd barely managed to escape with his life. "In Russia not only was his work popular under the old régime, but continued to be performed in Moscow and the provinces." His plays were frequently staged after the Revolution, even as late as 1946, by several art theaters in Moscow and Leningrad. But in 1947 a decree was published "in *Culture and Life,* the organ of the Department of Propaganda and Agitation, drawing attention to the use of the Soviet stage for spreading '*bourgeois* reactionary ideology and morality.' " It particularly condemned Maugham's plays, and "called for prompt change of plans in many Soviet theaters."[17] Ten years later, the party line changed again and Maugham was rehabilitated as a reliable proletarian.

IV

MAUGHAM'S TUBERCULOSIS, which flared up in Switzerland, was aggravated by the harsh climate and lack of proper nourishment in Russia. His mother had died of the disease at the age of forty-two. In his adolescence his delicate lungs had forced him to spend the winters of 1888 and 1889 in Hyères, and tuberculosis had put him into a nursing home early in 1909. Now, at the age of forty-four, he was forced to give up his career as a spy. It was difficult to return to Davos or St. Moritz in wartime Switzerland, so he spent the long winters of 1917 and 1918 in a Scottish sanatorium at Banchory, on the River Dee, southwest of Aberdeen.

The sanatorium was built on the top of a hill and had a fine view of the snow-clad landscape. The theory was that rest in clean country air—whether sunlit or thick with falling snow—and a solid, well-balanced diet provided the best treatment and strengthened the patient. Maugham, with only a mild case, did not have to suffer the ghastly pneumothorax surgery described in Thomas Mann's *The Magic Mountain* (1924). He rose at eleven, went back to bed at four and drank three pints of milk every day. Like the other ambulatory patients, he sat on a deck chair well wrapped up in rugs in the outdoor verandah. He soon settled into a comfortable routine of reading, writing and playing bridge (his favorite pastime), walking, resting and eating. The high points of the day were the visits of the doctor and nurses as well as the rituals of weighing himself and taking his temperature. Some patients, who'd been there for many years, could survive only by staying in that hermetic atmosphere.

In January 1918 Maugham told Gerald Kelly that he was playing the role of Marguerite in *La Dame aux camélias*. He thought he'd hate the rigorous regimen and pathological ambiance. But he found (as in Mann's novel, where the smallest unit of time was a week) that time passed with surprising rapidity. He was devouring a great number of books, and also hoped to do some writing of his own. He noted that a low-grade fever and unconstrained atmosphere seemed to stimulate sexual passion (since death was a constant threat, the patients had little to lose), and told the American playwright Edward Knoblock:

> I think you would like this place. There is something that would appeal to your passion for the macabre in the way the tuberculars fall in love with one another. . . . You cannot imagine the effectiveness of threatening your beloved that you will have a hemorrhage . . . if she does not return a consenting ear to your entreaties. . . . One man came here and died four days later. I had quite a success with the remark that it seemed hardly worthwhile to come to Scotland for such a short time.[18]

Though the apex of one lung was thoroughly scarred, he completely recovered and was never again troubled by the disease.

Maugham used the Scottish setting for one of his most ambitious and penetrating stories, "Sanatorium" (1938). Ashenden, a patient like

Maugham, is a careful but emotionally detached observer of tangled relationships: the seventeen-year feud, as with two Highland clans, between Campbell and MacLeod; the love affair of the fatally ill ladies' man Major Templeton (who has the same name as the most interesting character in *The Razor's Edge*) and the pathetically sick beauty Ivy Bishop; and the conflict between Henry Chester and his healthy, devoted wife. On her monthly visits he's cruel and makes her weep, but is reconciled with her at the end. Maugham's characters realize that suffering is degrading rather than ennobling; that—as Templeton declares after defying the doctor and risking his life by marrying Miss Bishop—it's "better to have one's fling and take the consequences"; that love is more important than death.

Despite the war, entanglements with Syrie, love for Gerald Haxton, espionage and tuberculosis, Maugham continued to write plays. He wrote *Our Betters* in Rome, *The Unattainable* in Geneva, *Love in a Cottage* and *Home and Beauty* in the Scottish sanatorium. Mildly ill but well looked after, with plenty of time and no distractions, he found it a perfect place to work. In these grim surroundings, sitting up in bed as the cold blew in through his open window, wearing mittens as he took up his pen, Maugham wrote one of his wittiest and most inventive comedies.

Home and Beauty satirizes Maugham's own unhappy and inconvenient marriage. After the death in the war of her husband William, the spoiled and beautiful Victoria marries his best friend, Frederick. When William turns up alive after all, each man can hardly wait to surrender her to the other. Leicester Paton, a potential suitor and wealthy war profiteer, is partly based (like Arthur Fenwick in *Our Betters*) on Gordon Selfridge. The bizarre décor of Victoria's house, futuristic, "very modern, outrageous, fantastic," is another dig at Syrie's taste. After many complications, Victoria marries a famous Jewish divorce lawyer, A. B. Raham (Abraham), and Frederick and William toast their newfound freedom.

Home and Beauty, though comically antithetical to the dark mood of *Of Human Bondage,* expressed Maugham's distaste for Syrie and desire to get rid of her. "Sanatorium" portrayed the triumph of love, *Home and Beauty* the escape from bondage. After sacrificing his health and writing career during the war, and then spending many months to recover, Maugham hoped to return to his old way of life with his new companion. Their two-year wartime separation, Haxton's miraculous survival and his return from a watery grave strengthened their bond, and they remained together until Gerald's death, in 1944.

9

Malaya and China

1919–1921

As Maugham slowly recuperated from tuberculosis, the war was coming to an end and a shattered Europe also began to recover. Maugham's postwar period was productive and successful. Stimulated by his experiences in war and travel, and eager to get back to London life after his long rustication in Scotland, he wrote his best play, *The Circle*. Inspired by his South Seas journey, he completed one of his most famous novels, *The Moon and Sixpence,* and also brought out a fine collection of short stories. In both play and novel he dealt with an acutely personal theme: the choice between the orderly bourgeois existence and the precarious life of the artist. While the play is about love and the novel about art, the central characters in both yearn to escape from their stifling everyday lives, take risks and hurt others. There was always the deeper question, for Maugham, of how to be true to his own homosexual and creative nature. Deeply unhappy in his marriage, and not content to rest on his literary achievements, he would soon take another strenuous journey in search of new material.

The Circle, in many ways the quintessential 1920s play, is both sad and funny, with a serious theme expressed in witty, epigrammatic dialogue. Maugham places his characters in an emotionally complicated situation that forces them to examine their lives and acknowledge their weaknesses. Thirty years before the play opens, Kitty has abandoned her husband,

Clive, and five-year-old son, Arnold, and run off with Clive's best friend, Hughie Porteous, to live in Florence. Now, while visiting England, they've been invited to lunch by Arnold's wife, Elizabeth. Clive, once the victimized young husband, is now a cynical, vengeful man in late middle age. He gets wind of the impending visit and complicates matters by turning up at the house in time for lunch. Elizabeth, a lively young woman married to the dull Arnold, has romanticized the older couple who gave up all for love. But they turn out to be frivolous, quarrelsome and disagreeable. To complicate matters Teddie, a Malayan planter in search of a wife, wants Elizabeth to run away with him. Will Elizabeth escape as her mother-in-law had done with Hughie—and thus continue the cycle of emotional betrayal?

Kitty begs Elizabeth not to make the same pitiful mistake that she had made and warns her: "Men are very funny. Even when they are in love they're not in love all day long. They want change and recreation. . . . One sacrifices one's life for love, and then one finds that love doesn't last." (Tolstoy's Anna Karenina learned the same bitter lesson.) Clive (as spiteful as Alexei Karenin) echoes Maugham's criticism of Syrie. He caustically tells Kitty: "Women dislike intelligence, and when they find it in their husbands they revenge themselves on them in the only way they can, by making them—well, what you made me"—a betrayed and humiliated husband. Despite Arnold's sacrificial devotion, the conventional yet rebellious Elizabeth rashly ignores the good advice and drives off with Teddie. The choice is not simply whether to leave and be happy or stay and be sad, but whether to go away and risk unhappiness. "No one can learn by the experience of another because no circumstances are quite the same," and because romantic idealism exerts its perennial power. The lovers give in to their impulse, but are warned that their guilt-ridden life won't be any happier—how could it be?—than Kitty and Hughie's. The circle is the illusory dream of romance that first liberates and then ensnares the lovers, who are doomed to pursue the tragic pattern.

Arnold, abandoned as a man as he'd once been as a child, is the subtle clue to another theme of *The Circle*. Sensitive but uneasy with emotions, he condemns his mother for doing him irreparable harm and Hughie for ruining his father's life. He has a certain "*flair*. . . a passion for decorating houses" (always a black mark in Maugham's view). Most significantly, he exclaims that "a man marries to have a home, but also because he doesn't want to be bothered with sex and all that sort of thing." Apparently homosexual and perhaps impotent with Elizabeth, Arnold has driven her into Teddie's arms and—like Maugham with Syrie—is not entirely unhappy to see the last of her.

Maugham poignantly contrasts the love between Kitty and Hughie with Clive's selfishness and Arnold's lack of feeling. Time and exile have reduced the once youthful lovers to a pair of squabbling, petty, middle-aged dimwits, but they've retained their tender love for each other. Maugham gives his own views to Clive, the most flawed and unpleasant character, yet reveals that Clive has also been deeply hurt. Recognizing Maugham's impressive achievement, one drama critic has observed that he "was able to refine the technique of Society drama into the greater naturalism and subtler emotion of modern English drama, and in so doing to place himself among the most influential of the post-war playwrights."[1]

II

TWO OF MAUGHAM'S previous fictional characters, Frank Hurrell in *The Merry-Go-Round* and Philip Carey in *Of Human Bondage,* had longed to escape the bonds of civilization and go to the Far East. In *The Circle* the young lovers flee from an English country house to the Malayan jungle. *The Moon and Sixpence* (1919), his first commercially successful novel (the Great War had buried *Of Human Bondage*), reflected Maugham's own desire to abandon his wife and take off for the South Seas. The charismatic Charles Strickland, based on Paul Gauguin, gives up a respectable life in Europe to find his artistic destiny in Tahiti.

In this novel, as in two great contemporary works about the nature of imaginative genius—Thomas Mann's "Death in Venice" (1912) and Wyndham Lewis' *Tarr* (1917)—artistic powers are both a divine gift and a demonic curse that isolates and tortures the outcast. But Maugham does not focus on the artist's creative life. He simply asserts that Strickland is a great painter and describes his work only through the uncomprehending eyes of the narrator. The novel concentrates on the destructive effects of Strickland's personality—the sacrifice other people make for his art. He's at first torn between a sense of loyalty to his wife and children and a desire for personal freedom that will allow him to express the "disturbing vision in his soul." But Strickland, seeking a lost paradise, becomes "eternally a pilgrim, haunted by a divine nostalgia." Stimulated by his hatred of society, he is a monster of egoism, rebellion, promiscuity and ruthlessness who destroys the lives of all around him to satisfy his creative urge.

Like Conrad, Maugham used a first-person narrator who participates in the action. But unlike Conrad's perceptive Charlie Marlow in *Heart of Darkness* (1899) and *Lord Jim* (1900), his narrator is inexperienced, self-conscious and rather priggish, an observer with limited insight into Strickland's mind and art. As a trusted friend, he comforts Amy Strickland when Charles deserts her and commiserates with Dirk Stroeve after Strickland has ruined his life. The narrator's return to Amy at the end of the novel with news of her husband's death in Tahiti echoes Marlow's return to Kurtz's fiancée at the end of *Heart of Darkness* with news of his death in the Congo.

The novel has other Conradian echoes. In Conrad's *Lord Jim* the hero has committed a cowardly act and needs to recover his self-esteem. The trader Stein urges Jim not to hide from his past, and advises him to confront reality: "A man that is born falls into a dream like a man who falls into the sea. . . . The way is to the destructive element submit yourself, and with the exertions of your hands and feet *in* the water make the deep, deep sea keep you up."[2] Maugham imitates this passage when Strickland tells the narrator why he had to leave his wife in order to paint: "When a man falls into the water it doesn't matter how he swims, well or badly: he's got to get out or else he'll drown." Strickland, who cares nothing about what people think of him, ironically uses the same metaphor to explain his decision to abandon his family.

The Moon and Sixpence has three main settings—conventional London, Bohemian Paris and sensual Tahiti—each characterized by a different woman: the deserted wife, Amy Strickland; the abandoned mistress, Blanche Stroeve; and the faithful and obedient Ata. Maugham keeps the novel moving by frequently reversing the narrator's—and the reader's—expectations of what his characters will do. The narrator assumes that Strickland, an utterly conventional London stockbroker and family man, has run off with another woman. But when he finds him in a seedy Paris hotel he discovers that the runaway is living in squalor, not luxury, and has left his wife to dedicate himself to art. After the apparently colorless Strickland breaks free from his dull existence in London, he reveals his true self: callous, sarcastic and brutal. Maugham makes his hero less morally repulsive than Gauguin, who died of syphilis and whose mistress was fourteen, by portraying Strickland's faithful Ata as seventeen and having his hero die of leprosy.

The narrator has even more trouble understanding why the attractive Blanche ever married the buffoonish, untalented and sycophantic Dutch painter Dirk Stroeve. Only after Blanche—like Flaubert's Emma Bovary—has been deserted by her lover and scorched her throat by swallowing acid does he learn that she had been seduced and abandoned by a Roman prince, had been turned into the street while pregnant and had tried to commit suicide. Stroeve found her, rescued her and married her—and she could never forgive his sacrificial kindness. Blanche, who at first seems so devoted to Stroeve, hates Strickland for humiliating her husband and begs Stroeve not to bring the sick painter into their home. But she abandons her devoted husband for a brief and finally fatal affair with Strickland. Stroeve willingly submits to his power and allows Strickland to take his studio, his wife and finally his home. Out of this cruel liaison Strickland creates paintings that are "a manifestation of the sexual instinct."

At the beginning of the novel the narrator declares, "to my mind the most interesting thing in art is the personality of the artist," and his quest to understand the artist drives the action. When he quotes Kant's maxim "act so that every one of your actions is capable of being made into a universal rule," Strickland—his complete opposite in character, temperament and behavior—calls it "rotten nonsense." But the narrator—who condemns the artist's savage treatment of his family, friends and women—is deeply impressed by Strickland's complete contempt for what people think about him or his art. He grudgingly admires the disdain for convention and egomaniacal quest for freedom that have allowed Strickland to fulfill his artistic destiny, and confesses that he cannot fathom his personality. Seeking an explanation for the painter's actions, he asks himself "whether there was not in [Strickland's] soul some deep-rooted instinct of creation, which the circumstances of his life had obscured, but which grew relentlessly . . . till at last it took possession of his whole being and forced him irresistibly to action."

Stroeve immediately recognizes Strickland's genius and describes one of his paintings, which resembles Gauguin's dreamy *Nevermore* (1897, London, Courtauld Collection): "it was the picture of a woman lying on a sofa, with one arm beneath her head and the other along her body; one knee was raised, and the other leg was stretched out."[3] The narrator, by contrast, is remarkably imperceptive about the paintings. When Strickland unexpectedly offers to show them, the narrator—who thinks "descriptions of pictures are always dull"—reflects contemporary opinion, noting that Strickland draws very badly, uses crude colors and produces ugly paintings.

Nine years after Strickland's death, the narrator travels to Tahiti in order to trace his footsteps and reconstruct his life. One friend recalls that he'd seen Strickland's final masterpiece, which the blind artist himself could no longer see; and that after his death Ata, following his instructions, had burnt his house to the ground and turned his chef d'oeuvre into smoldering embers. Though Stroeve could not bring himself to destroy a painting by the man who had driven his wife to suicide, Strickland himself, believing he had finally realized his artistic vision, had ordered the destruction of his greatest work. He thus expressed his final contempt for the opinion of the world—and his desperate alienation.

The end of the novel doesn't reconcile the conflict between artistic impulses and ordinary responsibilities. The narrator suggests that great art exempts the artist from ordinary morality and that Strickland's art has justified his despicable life, even if his defiant destruction of his best work undercuts his achievement. But Strickland's leprosy and blindness seem to punish his ruthless behavior. Having suffered no guilt about the people he's destroyed in the course of his creative life, he's doomed himself to an agonizing end. The opposition of narrator and painter suggests the conflict in Maugham's own personality: between the conventional secure bourgeois and the ruthless creative artist who despises the norms of society.

When the novel appeared in 1919, European readers, who'd dreamed of escaping the carnage of war to an exotic paradise, responded enthusiastically. But Katherine Mansfield put her finger on the novel's weak spot when she criticized Maugham's superficial view of Strickland's creative imagination. "We are not told enough," she wrote. "We must be shown something of the workings of his mind. . . . The one outstanding quality in Strickland's nature seems to have been his contempt for life and the ways of life."

Despite its flaws, Maugham's theme made a powerful impression on two important American writers, both of whom recognized the original inspiration of the novel. Hart Crane exclaimed: "What a good job Somerset Maugham does in his *Moon and Sixpence*! Have just finished reading it at a single sitting. Pray take the time to read it if you haven't already. How far it follows the facts biographical to Gauguin, I am not able to say, but from what little I do know, it touches his case at many angles." Sherwood Anderson called it "a striking story" and told a friend that it "would help her understand him. It was based on Paul Gauguin's life; at the same time . . . it was a story he thought of writing."[4] The theme of the artist's escape was, for artists, irresistible.

III

MAUGHAM'S FIRST MATURE book of stories, *The Trembling of a Leaf* (1921), contained some of his finest work. He believed the short story demanded succinctness and compression, structure and form, and should be complete in itself. He defined the story as a "narrative of a single event, material or spiritual, to which by the elimination of everything that was not essential to its elucidation a dramatic unity could be given." This formula originated with Poe, the father of the modern short story. In his review of Hawthorne's *Twice-Told Tales* (1842), Poe insisted that every aspect of the story should contribute to its final impression: "Having conceived, with deliberate care, a certain unique or single *effect* to be wrought out, [the author] then invents such incidents—he then combines such events as may best aid him in establishing this preconceived effect. . . . In the whole composition there should be no word written, of which the tendency, direct or indirect, is not to the one pre-established design."

Technically, Maugham followed Maupassant, whose stories emphasized incident more than character, were tightly structured and stripped of nonessential details, with a clear beginning, a series of closely connected events and a swift, sometimes unexpected ending. When Maugham began writing stories, Maupassant was out of fashion, supplanted by Chekhov, who influenced the most original contemporary English writers: Mansfield, Woolf, Joyce and even Lawrence. Instead of plot and character, Chekhov emphasized the presentation of a quintessential event, a single significant scene that sums up a human life. He expressed character through symbolic objects, distillation of atmosphere and poetic evocations of mood; through subtle detail, precise phrasing and delicate observation. The fragmentary, loosely linked episodes conveyed the theme through suggestion rather than statement. In a *Writer's Notebook* entry of 1917 Maugham had praised the subtle Chekhov over the straightforward

Maupassant. But he later retracted this view and opposed the prevailing fashion in his fiction and criticism, and his successful stories were condemned by the avant-garde.

The strongest influence on Maugham's themes and settings, not only in *The Explorer* and *The Moon and Sixpence* but especially in the stories, is undoubtedly Conrad. It is interesting that though Maugham frequently attacked and denigrated his rivals James and Chekhov, he remained almost completely and cunningly silent about Conrad. He included Conrad's *Typhoon* in his anthology *Tellers of Tales* (1939), but ignored his tremendous achievement as a novelist and criticized him for being too long-winded: "Conrad rarely wrote anything but short stories, though, being a writer of exuberant verbosity, he often made them as long as most novels. He needed sea-room. He had little sense of concision." Maugham's anthology *Introduction to Modern English and American Literature* (1943) did not include any work by Conrad. Yet, after pioneering works by John Gordon (1940), F. R. Leavis and Muriel Bradbrook (both 1941), Conrad's reputation was on the rise. Just before appreciative books by Morton Zabel and Albert Guerard (both 1947) came out, Maugham mistakenly asserted: "Conrad is less read now and less admired than during his lifetime."[5] Like his comments on James, this criticism attempted to disguise his profound indebtedness to a far greater writer. It was bitterly resented by Conrad's admirers and damaged Maugham's reputation.

Maugham did, however, pay a halfhearted tribute to Conrad in his story "Neil MacAdam" (1932). The eponymous hero claims (quite impossibly) to know Conrad almost by heart and had expected to find in Malaya a land of "brooding mystery." When a Russian woman attacks (the violently anti-Russian) Conrad as a showy, rhetorical, affected, superficial and commonplace mountebank, MacAdam and Munro defend him. Alluding to the famous preface to *The Nigger of the "Narcissus,"* MacAdam declares: "There's no one who got atmosphere like Conrad. I can smell and see and feel the East when I read him. . . . I don't think it's a mean achievement to have created a country, a dark, sinister, romantic and heroic country of the soul." Yet Maugham gives the woman the last word. She calls Munro a sentimentalist and urges MacAdam to read the truly great Russian novelists: Turgenev, Dostoyevsky and Tolstoy.

The lives and works of Conrad and Maugham had significant similarities. Both were orphaned in childhood, learned French before they learned English and left their professions, sailor and doctor, to become writers. In search of fictional material, Maugham traveled to Malaya and Borneo, the settings of the stories in *The Casuarina Tree* (1926), which Conrad had visited in his maritime career. Maugham's characters, like Conrad's, are isolated and desperately lonely in remote Eastern outposts. Maugham described a "peculiar thrill, a strange primeval feeling"—similar to what Marlow felt when he pursued Kurtz up the river in the Congo— "that you get on a river in Borneo when you hear drums beating in a distant village." In *Heart of Darkness* Marlow contrasted the chaos and anarchy of the Congo with the security and order of England: "Here you all are, each moored with two good addresses, like a hulk with two anchors, a butcher round one corner, a policeman round another." In *Of Human Bondage,* Maugham borrowed Conrad's symbol and phrasing when he wrote that "Philip's rule of life" was to "follow one's instincts with due regard to the policeman round the corner."[6]

Conrad's first novel, *Almayer's Folly* (1895), set in Borneo, portrays the destruction of a white man by the East, by his own corrupt ambition and by his beautiful but treacherous half-caste daughter. Maugham said that the major theme of *The Trembling of a Leaf* was "the soul-eroding effects of succumbing to the sexual proclivities of native women." Writing about his second Borneo novel, *Outcast of the Islands* (1896), Conrad told his aunt: "I want to describe in broad strokes, without shading or details, two human outcasts such as one finds in the lost corners of the world." The themes of the novel are betrayal and retribution. Willems, like the hero of Maugham's *The Narrow Corner,* commits a crime and is sent to a remote tropical outpost. Married to a half-caste woman, overwhelmed by the hostile environment and by his sense of isolation, he becomes enslaved by his Malay mistress. Conrad not only provided the literary context of Maugham's Eastern fiction, but also invented the realistic espionage novel in *The Secret Agent* (1907), the model for Maugham's *Ashenden: or the British Agent* (1928).

Maugham's first-person narrator is aloof but charming, urbane and tolerant, commonsensical and ironic, with a keen eye for despicable behavior. A man of the world, at ease everywhere, he's dispassionate and never surprised by what people may do. He often begins by raising a provocative question that arouses the reader's interest, and introduces the main characters with a brief physical description. Typically, he hears a story from a stranger in an exotic place and retells it, shaping the events and characters, but rarely penetrating their inner lives. A character's surprising behavior, like the missionary's in "Rain," contradicts his external appearance and propels him to unexpected and extraordinary action. The stories are full of death and violence. "In my books I was always curious about how people were going to d-die," Maugham told a fellow writer. "It was fascinating to wait for the d-death of my hero or heroine. They grew more and more vivid and meaningful when I knew they were going to d-die."[7]

A contemporary observer, sneering at Maugham's success with the reading public, said: "Old Maugham, talking to a girls' school about the art of writing short stories, told them that the essential ingredients were religion, sex, mystery, high rank, non-literary language and brevity"—a grotesque parody of his actual practice in what was certainly an apocryphal event. In fact, there's little religion and few characters of high rank in his stories, and his best ones are quite long. His recurrent themes are the grief of unrequited love and the disastrous effects of self-deception. He took the title of one of his stories from F. H. Bradley's *Appearance and Reality*.

P. G. Wodehouse, who made a fortune from his technical mastery of the comic tale, also saw fit to mock Maugham's stories. Alluding to "A Casual Affair," he asked Evelyn Waugh, who actually admired Maugham's work: "How about old S. Maugham, do you think? I've been re-reading a lot of his stuff, and I'm wondering a bit about him. I mean, surely one simply can't do that stuff about the district officer hearing there's a white man dying in a Chinese slum and it turns out that it's gay lighthearted Jack Almond, who disappeared and no-one knew what had become of [him] and he went right under, poor chap, because a woman in England had let him down." But Angus Wilson, a younger homosexual novelist, appreciated how Maugham perceptively analyzed the hidden motives that animated his characters: "his most complex and economic narration is totally successful in giving the appearance of reality and ease to what is in fact a complete subjection of life to the discipline of art."[8]

The evocative title of Maugham's best collection of stories came from the French critic Sainte-Beuve, who wrote that "extreme happiness, separated from extreme despair by a trembling leaf, is that not life?" But the characters, vacillating between these emotional extremes, are usually overcome by despair. "Mackintosh," the story of two incompatible men who must work together on a remote Pacific island, was strongly influenced by Conrad's "An Outpost of Progress" (1898). In Conrad's tale, after a trivial quarrel about a bit of sugar, Kayerts shoots his unarmed companion,

Carlier, and is found hanging, with his tongue sticking out, when the long-overdue company steamer finally arrives. In Maugham's version, Mackintosh, a Scot, hates his vulgar superior Walker, an Irishman. Walker quarrels with the natives about his obsessive desire to build a road around the island, and Mackintosh allows his revolver to be stolen by an angry Samoan. When the Samoan shoots Walker, who asks Mackintosh to forgive the murderer, Mackintosh belatedly realizes that Walker was a good man. Overwhelmed by guilt and remorse, he shoots himself. Conrad expressed the dominant idea of both stories when he wrote: "contact with pure unmitigated savagery, with primitive nature and primitive man, brings sudden and profound trouble in the heart."

The theological title, "The Fall of Edward Barnard," is ironic, for the hero moves into rather than out of Eden. The self-serving and conventional narrator, Hunter Bateman, is sent, as in *Heart of Darkness,* to find a man who's disappeared into the wilderness. When the man refuses to return to civilization, Bateman must also lie to his Intended: "he had hidden nothing from her except what he thought would wound her or what made himself ridiculous." Edward Barnard, like the main characters in *The Hero* and *The Explorer,* is surrounded by scandal—his father's suicide, his uncle's imprisonment—and escapes from Chicago to Tahiti. The story presents two contrasting visions of personal happiness. Barnard, who defies convention and turns the values of Chicago upside down, wants to live in a tropical paradise. Bateman, who adheres to an unrealistically rigid morality, wants material success back home. As in *Of Human Bondage, The Moon and Sixpence* and *The Razor's Edge,* there's a love triangle between the hero, his best friend and the hero's girl, wife or fiancée (a situation which originated in Maugham's sharing lovers with Walter Payne). In the end Bateman marries Barnard's Chicago fiancée; and Edward, like Philip with Sally in *Of Human Bondage,* marries a local man's beautiful daughter. Edward Barnard's surname and his escape from his fiancée are also sly allusions to Maugham's escape from Syrie Barnardo with the disreputable Haxton.

By contrast, "Red," an inverted Samoan idyll, is a classic story of the transience of beauty and the tragedy of love. Maugham describes Red, an American sailor gone AWOL in Samoa, with the unusual rapture he reserves for androgynous men. Red had that "suave, feminine grace which has in it something troubling and mysterious. His skin was dazzling white, milky, like satin; his skin was like a woman's." After a brief romantic interlude with Sally, a native girl, he suddenly disappears—like Pinkerton in *Madama Butterfly* (1904)—and she pines away for him. The story is narrated by the Maugham-like Neilson: "Himself an ugly man, insignificant of appearance, he prized very highly comeliness in others. He had never been passionately in love, and certainly he had never been passionately loved." Abandoned by Red, Sally marries Neilson, though she doesn't love him, and takes care of him.

Many years later, a schooner stops at this obscure island. Its ugly old skipper crosses the log bridge to Neilson's house (which symbolizes the passage from the ideal past to the real present), and Neilson is shocked to find that this broken-down old tar is the once beautiful Red. Neither Red nor the equally decayed Sally (tropical versions of the decadent Kitty and Hughie of *The Circle*) recognize each other. Neilson had preserved the memory of the young lovers, frozen in an exquisite moment of time, like the figures on Keats' Grecian urn: "Forever wilt thou love and she be fair." He reflects that "perhaps they should thank the ruthless fate that separated them when their love seemed still to be at its height. They suffered, but they suffered in beauty. They were spared the real tragedy" of disillusionment.[9] Neilson's love for Sally has depended on this ideal vision. When he can no longer sustain this image to counteract the ravages of time, he leaves her and returns to Sweden.

"The Pool," one of Maugham's most vivid and ambitious stories, contrasts the Samoan and Scottish settings, the lush heat of the tropics and the cold granite of the highland stream. The narrator, whose compassion permeates the tale, is struck by the intimate revelation of another's heart: "I held my breath, for to me there is nothing more awe-inspiring than when a man discovers to you the nakedness of his soul." Lawson falls in love with a half-caste teenage girl whom he sees swimming in a jungle pool. He marries her and expects her to behave like a European woman, but she cannot fill this role and they quarrel bitterly. Hoping to repair his marriage, he takes her to his home in Scotland, but she leaves him and returns to Samoa. He follows her and begins to drink heavily, loses his job and becomes a derelict. When he whips her for infidelity, they experience sadomasochistic pleasure: "Perhaps then she was nearer loving him than she had ever been before." In a jealous rage, Lawson pursues her to the mysterious pool (the symbol of her unfathomable tropical nature) "with the madness of those who love them that love them not." Since Lawson can't live with her and loves her too much to live without her, he drowns

José Ferrer and Rita Hayworth in
Miss Sadie Thompson, *1953*

himself in the pool, and his body is discovered by her Samoan lover. The dominant Conradian motifs are unrequited love and the degeneration of the white man in the tropics. But the story also has the power of a Greek myth, of a mortal man led to his death by a water nymph.

Maugham based the characters in his most celebrated story, "Rain," on a real-life missionary and prostitute. He'd visited Iwelei, the red-light district of Honolulu, and taken notes on Miss Sadie Thompson, who was on the run from the San Francisco police. He'd also observed the two characters on the ship to Pago Pago, Samoa, and in a primitive lodging house where they were all marooned during an outbreak of measles. In the story, two doctors—Macphail, a sceptical and timid Scot who'd served in the war, and Davidson, a fanatical and brave American missionary—are doubly trapped by quarantine and unremitting rain: "It did not pour, it flowed. It was like a deluge from heaven, and it rattled on the roof of corrugated iron with a steady persistence that was maddening. It seemed to have a fury of its own. And sometimes you felt that you must scream if it did not stop." The unceasing downpour resembles Davidson's self-righteous pursuit of Sadie Thompson. As in Noah's flood, rain entraps the characters and punishes them for both carnal and spiritual sin.

Davidson's obsession focuses on Sadie's overt sexuality. Their emotional struggle has an unexpected outcome when the spirited whore uses her sexual power to destroy the religious maniac who's trying to send her to prison. (Mrs. Davidson's prurient interest in the sexual depravity of the natives reveals *her* sexual repression.) After sex with Sadie, Davidson, humiliated and horrified by his own degradation, cuts his throat. Sadie then contemptuously screams: " 'You men! You filthy, dirty pigs! You're all the same, all of you. Pigs! Pigs!' Dr. Macphail gasped. He understood."[10] Maugham had experienced this religious hypocrisy and tormenting sexual repression in his uncle's vicarage.

In her review of *The Trembling of a Leaf* the tough but incisive Rebecca West seemed exasperated with Maugham. She thought his "cheap and tiresome attitude towards life nearly mars these technically admirable stories. They are charged with a cynicism which one feels Mr. Maugham has stuffed into them to conceal his lack of any real philosophy," and felt his skill and inventiveness could not compensate for these radical defects. Reaching for a philosophical idea in "Edward Barnard," Maugham wrote that "perhaps even the best of us are sinners and the worst of us are saints." Graham Greene, who took up this religious paradox in *The Heart of the Matter* and *The Power and the Glory,* wrote that Maugham "has done more than anyone to stamp the idea of the repressed prudish man of God on the popular imagination." Alluding to *The Painted Veil,* "The Letter" and "Rain," Greene recognized that Maugham (like Kipling and Conrad) had impressed his themes and settings on his audience. For most readers, Greene wrote, Maugham "still primarily means adultery in China, murder in Malaya, suicide in the South Seas."[11] His vivid characters and poignant stories impressed millions of readers.

Maugham was shrewder than anyone else about the commercial possibilities of his work, but he did not see the dramatic potential of "Rain" and allowed two obscure writers to do the stage version. The American premiere of 1922, starring Jeanne Eagels, an intense beauty whose promising career was destroyed by erratic behavior and drug addiction, was a tremendous success. The strong-willed Tallulah Bankhead desperately wanted the part in the New York production of 1925. When Maugham cashiered her, she bitterly condemned him. In a letter to John Gielgud,

Maugham's Asia

CHINA

Peking
Tientsin

Shanghai

Yangtze River

Chungking

Mandalay
Hwang
Luk
Keng
Tung
TONKIN
Hanoi
Hong Kong
Pagan
Thazi
Taunggyi
Haiphong
BURMA
LAOS
Rangoon
Hue
SIAM
Danang
Lopburi
Bangkok
ANNAM
Angkor
CAMBODIA
(VIETNAM)
Phnom
Penh
Saigon
Kep
COCHIN
CHINA
South China Sea
Andaman Sea

MALAYA
SARAWAK
SUMATRA
Singapore
Kuching
BORNEO

who was directing one of his later plays, Maugham urged him to be ruthless about getting rid of actors: "Please remember not to be too kind about firing people if they seem unsuitable when you start work. My own experience in the theatre was that people who are not right for their roles at once never really get any better, no matter how much time the producer devotes to them."

Basil Dean, who produced the play in America, felt that Maugham exercised his right to reject actors in an arbitrary way: "In such matters of casting Maugham had the habit of pretending indifference until the last moment when he would suddenly pounce, with a decisive yea or nay that was usually an expression of personal like or dislike."[12] But in a letter of 1925 Maugham justified his decision by insisting that Bankhead was wrong for the part and complained that getting rid of her had caused him a great deal of trouble. He later called this decision his greatest professional mistake; and Bankhead triumphantly played the part in the New York revival of 1935. The film rights of the play were sold for $150,000 (of which Maugham received 25%), and he eventually earned a million dollars for the story and adaptations of "Rain."

I V

THE FIRST MODERN English author to write about Spain, Maugham was also the first to write about China. He went there before I. A. Richards and Peter Quennell visited the country in 1929 and 1931, before William Empson taught there in the late 1930s, before Auden and Isherwood, Osbert Sitwell and Harold Acton wrote about it. He traveled for four months in 1919–20, between the revolution of 1911 that overthrew the Manchu dynasty and the Shanghai revolution of 1927 that Malraux described in his novel *Man's Fate.* China's old civilization was being brutally swept away, but the country was ruled by a military dictatorship that imposed order and Maugham could go wherever he wished. He and Haxton took a ship north from Saigon, via Haiphong and Hong Kong, to Shanghai. They continued up the coast to Tientsin (now Tianjin) and inland to Peking. After seeing the Great Wall and exploring northern China to the edge of Mongolia, they returned to Shanghai and took a rough but romantic sampan 1,500 miles up the Yangtze River to Chungking, a walled city at the foot of a high mountain. They continued on foot, often completing as much as twenty miles a day. By early January they were back in Shanghai and in Hong Kong, an English crown colony off the coast of China, and enjoyed the spectacular view of the harbor from Victoria Peak.

The fruits of this adventurous journey were the travel book *On a Chinese Screen* (dedicated to Syrie), the play *East of Suez* (both 1922) and the novel *The Painted Veil* (1925). The title of his loosely structured, episodic travel book alludes to Eliot's "Prufrock," and the book offers a series of exotic images from an Oriental movie, "as if a magic lantern threw the nerves in patterns on a screen." Maugham never mentions his route or indicates where he is. Though traveling with Haxton, he claims to be alone. As he moves restlessly from place to place, he remains a detached and impersonal observer. He offers brief, impressionistic, sometimes satiric snapshots, with thumbnail physical descriptions of the people he meets and an ironic sting in the tail of his anecdotes. Maugham's not primarily interested in the Chinese, but in the English in China. Living in a time warp, permanent exiles with little desire to return to England, most of the old China hands don't know and don't want to know the Chinese. Their lives of quiet desperation reveal the emotional attrition and spiritual waste of the white man in the East.

Maugham memorably describes masters kicking old servants and barbers scraping the insides of eyelids; women hobbling on bound feet and newborn babies dropped down putrefying wells; cheerful and cosy opium dens (which also appealed to Greene and Malraux) and two executions by firing squad; a black pig walking across a ridge between flooded padi fields and a nameless "grey and gloomy city, shrouded in mist, [that] stands upon its rock where two great rivers meet so that it is washed on all sides but one by turbid, rushing waters." He responds to the Great Wall with a rhythmic adverbial tour de force:

> Solitarily, with the indifference of nature herself, it crept up the mountain side and slipped down to the depth of the valley. Menacingly, the grim watch towers, stark and foursquare, at due intervals stood at their posts. Ruthlessly . . . it forged its dark way through a sea of rugged mountains. Fearlessly, it went on its endless journey, league upon league to the furthermost regions of Asia, in utter solitude, mysterious like the great empire it guarded. There in the mist, enormous, majestic, silent, and terrible, stood the Great Wall of China.

Maugham took the title of *East of Suez,* set in Peking, from Kipling's "Mandalay": "Ship me somewhere east of Suez, where the best is like the worst," and the characteristic theme is the decay of moral standards in the Orient. In this hothouse melodrama Maugham emphasizes the betrayal of friendship, the curse of secrets from the past, the corruption of the English by the East. The hazards of intermarriage seem to reinforce his prejudice against any kind of marriage. Two speeches are striking. The lover, George Conway, expresses the idea, which Maugham would later repeat in *Don Fernando* and *The Summing Up,* that the truth about ourselves, if revealed, would be repellent: "there are few of us that wouldn't turn away from ourselves in horror if the innermost thoughts of our heart, the thoughts we're only conscious of to hate, were laid bare." And the corrupt Eurasian wife, Daisy, gives an ecstatic description of opium:

> After you've smoked a pipe or two your mind grows extraordinarily clear. You have a strange facility of speech and yet no desire to speak. . . . Your soul is gently released from the bondage of your body. . . . Death cannot frighten you, and want and misery are like blue mountains far away. You feel a heavenly power possess you and you can venture all things because suffering cannot touch you. . . . You hold space and time in the hollow of your hand. Then you come upon the dawn, all pearly and grey and silent, and there in the distance, like a dreamless sleep, is the sea.[13]

Maugham himself had found opium not only freed him from his stammer, but gave him the consoling illusion of transcending time and death.

10

Dangerous Journeys,
Dangerous Friends

1921–1925

IN MARCH–APRIL 1921, a year after their journey to China, Maugham and Haxton traveled up some dangerous rivers in Sarawak, British North Borneo. An engineer in Borneo recalled that a quarrel had broken up the regular bridge game between the resident, the doctor, the policeman and the factory manager. When Maugham and Haxton arrived the bridge game was "resumed, with the visitors playing in turn each of the two couples who were not on speaking terms." One can easily imagine Maugham transforming this set of isolated and irritable officials into a sinister story, where antagonism led to adultery, hatred, murder and suicide.

On April 25, 1921, in one of his longest and most interesting letters, Maugham told Bert Alanson about his Conradian voyage into the depths of that still wild and largely unexplored island:

> We have just returned from a very pleasant journey to Sarawak, during which we went up a river by launch, paddle boat and then poling till we got to something which we can flatter ourselves was the heart of Borneo. We slept in the dyak houses among the head-hunters, whom we found exceedingly polite and hospitable folk. . . .
>
> It was extraordinarily interesting to go day after day up the winding

river with the jungle thick and green on both sides of it. We saw monkeys taking the sun towards the end of the day, but though we were warned not to bathe far from the bank because the river was infested with crocodiles we never saw a single one.

Maugham then abandoned the romantic mode and described the most dangerous episode of his life:

On the way down river we had a most unlucky experience. They have on some of these Borneo rivers what is called a bore, a tidal wave several feet high that comes roaring up with the change of the tide. It is well known to be very dangerous and great precautions are taken to avoid it. But by some mischance we met it at the most dangerous part of the river and three days after the new moon which is the most dangerous time. It was a wall of seething roaring water eight feet high that burst upon us and before we knew where we were, we were all struggling in the water. We had a crew of prisoners who were paddling us down and they shouted to us to cling to the boat. This we fortunately did because we have heard since that with the undercurrent in that stormy sea of waves it would have been impossible to reach the shore. The boat began to turn over and over, and we struggled like squirrels in a cage to cling on until at last we got absolutely exhausted. I don't know what we should have done if it had not been for the two malay prisoners who managed to get a wet mattress to us when we were just about all in. Fortunately by then we had drifted a little nearer the shore and so with their help were able to reach it. I cannot tell you how good it felt to feel that slithering mud under one's feet. We lay on the bank for about half an hour absolutely exhausted until a paddle boat came along and took us off. We were all as near drowning as anyone could be and when we got back to Kuching, the capital of Sarawak, found our escape looked upon as almost miraculous.[1]

Maugham did not mention that Haxton—eighteen years younger, apparently much stronger, but weakened by his year as a German prisoner—had a heart attack when they reached the shore. They recovered from their ordeal by spending three months in a sanatorium at a hill station in Java.

Maugham recorded this near fatal incident in *A Writer's Notebook* and used it in "The Yellow Streak." The story centers on the tortured psychol-

ogy of Izzart, an ex–public school Englishman who speaks two native languages and is sent to escort a visiting engineer on a trip to the interior of
Borneo. Izzart's mother is a half-caste Malay and, fearful that "everyone
knew you couldn't rely on Eurasians," he lives in an agony of self-
consciousness and tries to hide his mixed blood. The two men are caught
in a tidal wave, and when the engineer calls for help, Izzart panics, ignores
him and struggles to the shore. Later on, the engineer turns up safely, and
the mortified Izzart blames his failure of nerve on "that wretched drop of
native blood in him." Both men, it turns out, are afraid of being cowards.
Just as Maugham and Haxton had been saved by Malays, so in the story
two Dyaks, disproving Izzart's racial theory, risk their lives to save the
engineer.

This adventure did nothing to deter Maugham from travel. In November 1922, approaching fifty, he boldly told Sinclair Lewis that he was
beginning a sixty-day march to the frontiers of China. He and Haxton
began in Rangoon, sailed up the Irrawaddy River to Pagan and Mandalay,
took a train and car to Thazi and Taunggyi in the Shan states, then trekked
east through five hundred miles of jungle to Keng Tung (near the Chinese
border) and Hwang Luk. Riding on ponies, with a baggage train of mules
following behind, they followed a circuitous route to avoid awkward
encounters with headhunting tribesmen. They crossed rivers and mountains, stayed at monasteries and rest houses, subsisting on fruit and tinned
food. They then took a car down to Lopburi and a train to Bangkok, in
Siam, where Maugham had a severe attack of malaria. "My temperature
soared," he wrote, "to those vertiginous heights that are common in
malaria, and neither wet sheets nor ice packs brought it down. I lay there,
panting and sleepless, and shapes of monstrous pagodas thronged my
brain." His fever hit 105°, and the hotel owner thought he was going to
die. After he recovered, they continued southeast by boat to Kep, north by
car to Phnom Penh, and by steamer and sampan to Angkor, in Cambodia.
Finally, they went southeast to Saigon, and took a ship up the coast to
Danang, Hue, Hanoi and Haiphong.

The Gentleman in the Parlour (1930), an account of this arduous but
admittedly uneventful journey, is (unlike his book on China) a consecutive
travelogue that actually describes the atmosphere of the places he visits.
He took his title from William Hazlitt's essay "On Going on a Journey."
Maugham agreed with Hazlitt's view that "we go on a journey chiefly to be
free of all impediments and inconveniences; to leave ourselves behind,

much more to get rid of others. . . . With change of place we change our ideas; nay, our opinions and feelings."[2]

Maugham was characteristically but frankly disillusioned by what he saw. The jungles were monotonous, the cities without history or traditions, the streets sordid. The temples were wet and smelly, empty and dead, without spiritual significance. But the tropics sometimes made all the hardships seem worthwhile. In an unusually lyrical description he praised "The depth of colour, the hot touch of the air on one's cheek, the dazzling yet strangely veiled light, the different walk of the people, the lazy breadth of their gestures, the silence, the solemnity, the dust—this was the real thing, and my jaded spirits rose." Indifferent to monuments, temples, citadels and forts, he was primarily interested in people and found the "peasant with his immemorial usages" most memorable.

Always an efficient recycler of his work, Maugham included several chapters from *The Gentleman in the Parlour* in his *Complete Stories*. In "Masterson," Maugham observes that "often in some lonely post in the jungle or in a stiff grand house, solitary in the midst of a teeming Chinese city, a man has told me stories about himself that I was sure he had never told to a living soul." Over scotch and soda the lonely Masterson confides that his beautiful and capable Burmese mistress, mother of his children, has left him. After they'd lived together for five years, she feared he would abandon her and insisted on a legal marriage. Unwilling to sacrifice his freedom and doubting that she really loved him, Masterson refused and was surprised when she left. In "A Marriage of Convenience," originally written as early as 1906, a retired French official tells the story of how, in middle age, he'd been offered a colonial governorship if he agreed to get married. He advertised for a wife and was overwhelmed by applications, but chose his friend's sensible cousin and took up his post in the East. A marriage, Maugham suggests, was much more likely to succeed if based solidly on common interests rather than passion. "Mirage" is narrated by an English opium addict. He claims to have been at St. Thomas's Hospital with Maugham, but was sent to jail for fraud. After twenty years with the Chinese Customs Service, he married a girl in French Indochina. He once tried going back to England, but it had "been like a mirage in the desert." He now dreams of returning to China, but remains in Haiphong with his memories: "He had China, and so long as he never saw it again he kept it."[3] For weak people illusion is more powerful, more sustaining, than reality.

11

BY NOW MAUGHAM, in his late forties, was an international literary celebrity, photographed and interviewed wherever he went. In 1923 the American journalist Burton Rascoe gave an accurate, if slightly grotesque, description of Maugham, who tended (like Mussolini) to emphasize his jutting jaw. He had a "high, slightly serrated forehead. His skin is a yellowish-olive; his nose is long, straight, high-bridged, and his nostrils curve upward. His mouth is wide, thin-lipped, severe in line, and he has a protruding, cleft chin which he mostly thrusts out with his head back." Maugham lived up to his role as a serious public man. He rarely smiled (his efforts to do so look forced), had formal manners and a severe, almost frozen expression.

Maugham's natural milieu was theatrical, literary and upper-class London, but traveling widened his range and he enjoyed meeting all kinds of people. In 1924 he pitched up in Mexico City, where he clashed with another wandering novelist, D. H. Lawrence. Like Maugham, Lawrence was a restless traveler who roamed the world in search of settings and characters to stimulate his imagination. He wanted to write about all five continents, but died before he could do Asia and Africa. He also suffered from tuberculosis, and was heading for his first near fatal hemorrhage in Oaxaca. Both lived for long periods in Spain, Germany, Italy, America and France, and always itched to travel as soon as they'd settled down. Maugham would have subscribed to Lawrence's motto: "When in doubt, move."

But Lawrence's travel was a desperate search for a warm climate to restore his health and peace of mind, and he asked a friend: "Where does one want to live? tell me if you can!" Maugham always returned to his permanent home; Lawrence never had one. Frequently pressed for money, Lawrence traveled simply; Maugham usually journeyed in luxury. Lawrence loathed Capri, where Maugham felt entirely at home. Always in delicate health, Lawrence had to be more cautious, and died young. Maugham was much tougher. He'd risked his life as a spy in Switzerland and Russia, survived tuberculosis, traveled in remote and dangerous places.

Lawrence thought Maugham was a superficial, commercial scribbler who catered to the establishment that had suppressed his own novel, *The Rainbow,* in 1915. A far greater writer, but living from hand to mouth, he

Maugham at Frederic Maugham's country house
in Gloucestershire, c. 1923

bitterly resented Maugham's popularity, financial success and self-indulgent way of life. He later told Aldous Huxley: "I hear Wells and Maugham and Co. were rolling their incomes round Nice for Xmas, rich as pigs." He knew Maugham was traveling with Haxton. If he'd heard from local gossip that Maugham brought boys to the hotel for sex, he would have been horrified. Lawrence himself had repressed homosexual feelings, but found such behavior repulsive.

For his part Maugham considered Lawrence "a pathological case." Like a character in his story, "Lord Montdrago," he could have called Lawrence "that half-baked, conceited intellectual, with inadequate knowledge, ill-considered ideas and impracticable plans, that compulsory education has brought forth from the working-classes."[4] He disliked, even feared the modernists, and felt superior to Lawrence, whose Midlands working-class background was quite alien to him.

Frieda Lawrence recorded in her autobiography, *Not I, But the Wind* (1934), how her husband made the first overture: "One day William Somerset Maugham was expected in Mexico City; so Lawrence wrote to him if they could meet." At the same time an American archeologist, Zelia Nuttall, who lived in the rather distant suburb of Coyoacán, invited them all to lunch. Haxton wrote back to Lawrence on Maugham's behalf, proposing (at Nuttall's suggestion) that they share a taxi. "Lawrence was angry," said Frieda, "that Maugham had answered through his secretary and wrote back: 'No, I won't share a car.'" Lawrence felt insulted. But he didn't realize that Maugham had used Haxton as an intermediary because his stammer was especially bad with strangers and on the telephone. Unreasonably irritable, Lawrence refused Maugham's offer. He and Frieda took the long ride out to the suburbs in a dirty and uncomfortable tram.

The ill-fated luncheon party (which Lawrence described in the third chapter of *The Plumed Serpent*) was ghastly. Maugham had a weakness for aristocrats, but didn't know that Frieda was a German baroness. She sat next to him and, to make conversation, asked how he liked Mexico. Piqued by Lawrence's rude refusal and in a dyspeptic mood, he abandoned his customary good manners and (according to Frieda) "answered crossly: 'Do you want me to admire men in big hats?' I said, 'I don't care what you admire.' And then the lunch was drowned in acidity all round. But after lunch I felt sorry for Maugham: he seemed to me an unhappy and acid man, who got no fun out of living."

Predictably enough, Lawrence disliked Maugham and described him as joyless, opportunistic and repressed: "Somerset Maugham . . . is no loss. Disagreeable, with no fun left in him, and terrified for fear he won't be able to do his next great book, with a vivid Mexican background, before Christmas.—A narrow-gutted 'artist' with a stutter." (Ironically, Maugham abandoned the idea of a Mexican novel, and Lawrence wrote *The Plumed Serpent*.) When Lawrence reviewed Maugham's *Ashenden,* he rancorously criticized it as superficial and bogus: "These stories, being 'serious,' are faked. Mr. Maugham is a splendid observer. He can bring before us persons and places most excellently. But as soon as the excellently observed characters have to move, it is a fake. Mr. Maugham gives them a humorous shake or two. We find they are nothing but puppets, instruments of the author's pet prejudice. The author's pet prejudice being 'humour,' it would be hard to find a bunch of more ill-humoured stories, in which the humour has gone more rancid."

Stung by this review, Maugham later paid him back in kind. Though they'd met only once and had no real connection, he admitted that

Lawrence disliked him. In 1955, twenty-five years after Lawrence's death, he described the luncheon to Richard Aldington, who had once been Lawrence's friend but had written a hostile book about him. Now distant from the event, Maugham said he'd found Lawrence lively, amiable and amusing, and did not realize until much later that the invitation to share a taxi had gravely offended him. He added that he liked *Sons and Lovers* and parts of *The Rainbow*, but was repelled by Lawrence's ranting tone and sloppy style. In his anthology of modern literature, he included two of Lawrence's letters but none of his fiction. Unable to separate his impression of the man from his art, he ran down Lawrence's work. "I never thought Lawrence's short stories very good," he wrote. "I find them formless and verbose . . . lush and airless. . . . [He had] the view of a sick man of abnormal irritability, whose nature was warped by poverty and cankered with a rankling envy."

Lawrence would have been furious, but not entirely surprised, to find that in *A Writer's Notebook* Maugham based his character sketch of the dying poet "Francesco" (Lawrence was called "Lorenzo") on a passage in Frieda's autobiography. In 1929, when Lawrence was ill in Florence, Frieda had attended the opening of an exhibition of his paintings (which was immediately closed down by the police) at the Warren Gallery in London. When an Italian friend asked Lawrence, "what will Frieda say when she arrives?" he replied: "Do you see those peaches in the bowl? She will say, 'What lovely peaches,' and she will devour them." And she did.[5]

III

MAUGHAM'S MOST INTIMATE friendships were with homosexual writers. Beverley Nichols and Noël Coward, two younger men, were close to him. The handsome, Oxford-educated Nichols, born in 1898, was a popular (and now forgotten) journalist, novelist and playwright. He met Maugham in the early 1920s, and astonished the older and more cautious man (as he did Noël Coward) with lurid tales of "male brothels and rough trade pick-ups, and where to go to pick up sailors, marines and guardsmen." Nichols boasted that he'd slept with Maugham, whom he flatteringly called "the most sexually voracious man I've ever known." Maugham repaid his sexual favors by reviewing his youthful autobiography in the *Sunday Times*.

In *A Case of Human Bondage* (1966), a bitchy and scandalous attack on

Maugham that attempted to cash in on his fame, Nichols described a truly horrible week at Syrie's new white-on-white house at Le Touquet, a resort on the Normandy coast, in 1925. "Teetering on the verge of a breakdown," Syrie made a hopeless and humiliating attempt to win Maugham back from Gerald Haxton, whom she and Nichols (Gerald's sexual rival at the villa) both hated. Maugham tried to impose an uneasy truce on his wife and his lover, but they fought like two angry cats. Syrie still wanted him and believed that "you must always be ready for love." She always hoped Maugham would return to her, but of course he never did.

Jealous of the relationship between Nichols and Haxton, Maugham "behaved like an hysterical old queer." While gambling at the casino, Gerald had ostentatiously shouted to Nichols: "Come over here, you pretty boy, and bring me luck." In the most shocking scene, Nichols, responding to "the most ghastly noise next door, like somebody being throttled," described Gerald, "on floor, stark naked, *covered* with thousand-franc notes. Never seen so much money in my life. On the bed, over his legs, practically in his hair. Gerald trying to be sick and sometimes succeeding."[6] Nichols did not explain that the drunk and sick Gerald was simply showing off, in his own fashion, his night's winnings at the tables.

Maugham's relations with the more self-assured Noël Coward, a year younger than Nichols, were more complicated. In 1935 Maugham, the literary link between the comedies of Wilde and Coward, gave Coward credit for inventing theatrical characters that influenced speech, style and manners for many years: "Mr. Coward not only portrayed the querulous frivolity of the decade that followed the Great War, but created a generation of querulously frivolous people." In his introduction to Coward's *Bittersweet and Other Plays,* he paid him a great compliment by predicting: "the future of the English drama is in the hands of Mr. Noël Coward." A witty lyricist and playwright, Coward was also a conventional composer of light music, patriotic songs and romantic musicals. His gay sensibility was akin to Cole Porter's, but he was sentimental and lacked that deep vein of sadness that makes Porter's wit so enduring.

Nichols wanted to be Maugham's pet; Coward, who admired yet disliked Maugham, was critical of his character and appalled by his coldness and selfishness. Unlike most people, Coward (though much younger) wasn't afraid of him and called him "the lizard of Oz." He dedicated his first serious play, *Point Valaine* (1935), to Maugham and used him as the model for Mortimer Quinn, a writer with a sardonic literary persona.

Frederic Maugham as lord chancellor, 1938

Quinn says: "I always affect to despise human nature. Cynical, detached, unscrupulous, an ironic observer and recorder of other people's passions. It is a nice façade to sit behind, but a trifle bleak. Perhaps I am misunderstood. I often toy with that idea. Perhaps I have suffered a great deal and am really a very lonely, loving spirit."

Three years later, in his story "Nature Study," Coward, more severe and satiric, based the character of Ellsworth Ponsonby on Maugham. The homosexual Ponsonby marries but is unable to have sex with his wife. Instead, he becomes what Coward euphemistically calls "a hundred percent rip-snorting beauty lover. Oh, dear, how can one reconcile being a beauty lover with being mean, prurient, sulky and pettishly tyrannical almost to the point of mania?" When he's blackmailed with compromising letters that threaten to expose his sexual life, his wife runs off with the chauffeur, and he's devastated. "The trouble with Ellsworth," the victimized wife remarks at the end of the story, "was that he had no love in his heart for any living soul except himself."

There are also hints of Maugham in John Blair-Kennedy, a cynical "novelist of some repute," visiting a tropical island based on Jamaica, in

Coward's *South Sea Bubble* (1956). Like Maugham, he complains about his stammer: "I can't even say a brief speech of thanks without stammering and stuttering and making a cracking fool of myself." He's on the island to find material, "to collect data and make notes for a satirical novel about British Colonial Administration." By acknowledging that he's "constantly having to crush down the most appalling urges," he admits to repressed homosexual desires.[7]

IV

LIKE COWARD, MAUGHAM was fond of portraying real people in his work. He based the character of Dr. Walter Fane in his Chinese novel, *The Painted Veil* (1925), on his brother Frederic. He described Walter as a "restrained, cold, and self-possessed man. . . . He thought himself so much better than anyone else, it was laughable; he had no sense of humour; [his wife] hated his supercilious air, his coldness, and his self-control." Maugham always had prickly relations with the older and taller Frederic, who was gaunt and acerbic, cold and forbidding, difficult and self-righteous. As Frederic's son, Robin, wrote, the tragedy of his father's life was that "a seemingly ill-suited marriage, almost constant worries about money, and a neurotically violent jealousy . . . did in the end sour his whole existence." His daughter Diana described him more sympathetically as clever, severe and distant, but with a great sense of humor. He always worked with manic energy; and when she came home from dances at two in the morning, she'd find him hard at it in his study. Frederic, who said he'd take an interest in his children when they reached the age of reason, once looked rather sadly at Diana and remarked (without intending to wound her): "I hoped you'd be a beauty, like my mother."

Frederic and Willie admired each other's prowess and were proud of each other's achievements. They enjoyed joking with, sniping at and making satirical remarks to one another. Willie said that poor Frederic loved good-looking blondes who consulted him about the law, but that he never had the guts to sin. Frederic, revolted by Willie's sexual life and relationship with Haxton, was horrified that his own brother was "queer" and thought he had a corrupting influence on his son. Robin added that "my father disapproved of everything in general, and of Willie's life in particular."[8]

Willie despised many aspects of his brother's character, but always sought—and rarely got—his approval. He complained to one friend that

"I've always sent him tickets for my first nights, and first editions of my b-b-b-books, but he's never even acknowledged one of them or let it be known, even by mistake, that he'd seen the play or read the book. Isn't he a sh-sh-sh-shameful fellow!" He told another friend that Frederic would rather perish than allow one word of appreciation to pass his stern lips. After Frederic's death at the age of ninety-two in 1958, Willie unleashed his lifelong resentment, and told Robin: "He was an odious man. I have met many detestable men in my life, but your father was easily the mer-most detestable. . . . Ever since I can remember, during all the years of my life until I was eighty, your father was beastly to me." Willie might have severed relations with his strange and difficult brother if he hadn't been very fond of his sister-in-law, Helen. Referring to her irrepressibly cheerful nature, which balanced Frederic's habitual gloom, Maugham told her: "My dear, you are a sort of woman whose idea of happiness is to eat cold mutton in a howling gale."[9]

Willie undoubtedly consulted Frederic when he ran into legal difficulties with the serialized version of *The Painted Veil.* He usually chose the names of his fictional characters from the towns in Bradshaw's railway guide, the telephone book or the obituaries of the *Times.* But when he called his hero Lane and set the novel in Hong Kong, he was threatened with a libel suit. He settled out of court for £250, but when the novel came out he was forced to change Lane to Fane and the colony to Tching-Yen (restored to Hong Kong in later editions). In a letter to his American agent Charles Towne, he raged that it was "a pure damnable and unfortunate coincidence that this man Lane should have the same surname as my hero and have lived in the same part of Hong Kong, but since he is not dead but alive . . . I do not quite see how he can say that I meant him." Gerald Kelly recalled Maugham declaring: "these people behave as if they'd invented adultery."[10]

In his preface to *The Painted Veil,* Maugham wrote that the novel was inspired by a passage in Dante's *Purgatorio* (5: 133–136) that he'd read with his landlady's daughter, Ersilia, in Florence in 1894. The lines, in Laurence Binyon's translation, were:

> Remember me, who am La Pia then.
> Siena made me and Maremma unmade:
> He knows who had ringed me with his jewel, when
> The vows of marriage we together said.

Ersilia told the young Maugham that Pia, a gentlewoman of Siena, was suspected by her jealous husband of adultery. Afraid of her family's vengeance if he murdered her, he took her to his castle in the marshy Tuscan region of Maremma, where, he hoped, the mephitic vapors would kill her. When that plan failed, he lost patience and had her thrown from a high window. But there's nothing in Dante about sending Pia to a marshy place to die. Paolo Milano merely says that "Pia de' Tolomei was wedded to Nello della Pietra, who, wishing to marry another woman, murdered her in his castle in the Tuscan Maremma." Charles Singleton states, more specifically, that she was "by Nello's orders thrown out of a window of his castle in the Maremma."[11] Either Ersilia made up a part of the story or Maugham attributed it to her. In the novel, Dr. Fane forces his adulterous wife, Kitty, to risk her life by accompanying him to a region infected with cholera.

The Painted Veil, one of Maugham's best novels, opens brilliantly. The adulterous lovers, Charlie and Kitty, are interrupted by her husband while having sex in Kitty's bed. He tries the door to show his presence, but doesn't attempt to enter the room.[12] Walter's discovery, Charlie's attempt to escape and Kitty's effort to brazen it out precipitate the crisis that forces Kitty into the cholera-stricken region. Like all Maugham's wretched wives, Kitty has more than a touch of Syrie. As Walter bitterly tells her: "I knew you were silly and frivolous and empty-headed. . . . I knew your aims and ideals were vulgar and commonplace. . . . I knew that you were second-rate. . . . I knew how frightened you were of intelligence." In two striking contrapuntal chapters Kitty talks first with her husband and then with her lover about what they should do. Walter, who knows more than she does about Charlie's shallow and selfish character, is sure that Charlie, anxious to avoid a scandal, won't divorce his wife and marry Kitty. When Charlie urges her to accompany Walter, so he can get rid of her in both senses, she agrees to Walter's potentially fatal demand and bitterly asks him: "I suppose I needn't take more than a few summer things and a shroud, need I?"

In Mei-tan-fu Kitty befriends Waddington, a Customs officer who has stayed behind to help with the epidemic. Maugham describes the cholera in allegorical terms—"the great city lay in terror; and death, sudden and ruthless, hurried through its tortuous streets"—and misses a great opportunity to strengthen the novel (as Mann does in "Death in Venice" and Camus in *The Plague*) by describing the progress of the disease. At first Kitty remains in her bungalow and doesn't offer to help. But Waddington reinforces Walter's condemnation of Charlie, and teaches her to appreciate Chinese culture and sympathize with the people. In the words of Shelley's "Sonnet" (which provides the title and epigraph of the novel), she lifts "the painted veil which those who live call Life" and helps the devoted nuns care for the Chinese orphans. Waddington illuminates the meaning of Tao, the Oriental way to fatalistic renunciation of desire: "Some of us look for the Way in opium and some in God, some of us in whisky and some in love."[13]

Walter's more interested in changing than in killing Kitty. Instead of being stricken by cholera, she's "cured" of her love for Charlie. In the midst of the epidemic, she realizes she's pregnant and truthfully tells Walter that she doesn't know who's the real father. Walter, an arrogant prig, is also a self-sacrificial and heroic martyr to science (a tribute to the positive side of Frederic's character). As Walter's plan misfires, he dies instead of Kitty, quoting Goldsmith's "Elegy on the Death of a Mad Dog": "The dog, to gain some private ends, / Went mad, and bit the man. . . . / The man recovered of the bite, / The dog it was that died."

The first two parts of the novel, in Hong Kong and Mei-tan-fu, vividly reveal the dissolution of Walter's humiliating passion for Kitty, the way that love can quickly change to hatred and the strange mixture of both in Walter and Kitty. When she returns to Hong Kong to complete the circle, she tells Charlie that she despises him. But in a complex twist of feeling she's again overcome by sexual passion, sleeps with him and hates herself for doing so. Kitty expresses Maugham's cynical view of marriage as a cash-for-sex transaction: "a man may want to sleep with [a woman] so much that he's willing to provide her with board and lodging for the rest of her life." The novel should have ended on this authentically bitter note. But Kitty then examines her life and wonders which path to follow. Rejecting the way of Tao, she reassuringly concludes that she should pursue "the path those dear nuns at the convent followed so humbly, the path that led to peace." Kitty must atone for her deceit and begin life anew, but her pious path seems improbable and forced.

This neat tying up of ends, which took the edge off Maugham's deep scepticism about the possibility of human love, pleased his readers and assured him of worldly success. After the novel was published, Maugham wrote his American agent Charlie Towne, a model for Charlie Townsend: "I am not so anxious to make a large sum of money out of a book as to have it as widely read as possible. I seek distinction rather than lucre."[14] But the great literary reputation continued to elude him.

11

Villa Mauresque

1926–1928

MAUGHAM HAD RETAINED close ties with the government since his days as a secret agent, and in May 1926 he became involved, in some mysterious way, with the General Strike in England. First the coal miners were locked out, and they were soon joined by workers in printing, transport, iron and steel, gas, electricity and building, until two and a half million workers were involved. Called off after only nine days, the strike failed because the Conservative government was able to deliver essential supplies and services, and won the propaganda battle. As the strike divided on class lines, many people, hostile to the power of the unions, helped to break it. Schoolboys from Eton, for example, came into London to run the tramcars.

On May 13 Arnold Bennett, who'd kept in touch with him since their Bohemian days in Paris, recorded that Maugham had high-level, Sherlock Holmesian duties with the London police: he "was what he called a 'sleuth' at Scotland Yard. A police car was sent for him always. The first night he worked all night from 11 p.m. to 8.30 a.m. He said the last few hours, after the dawn, were simply terrible, and he couldn't see how he would ever be able to get through them. I don't know what a 'sleuth' is." He may have been hired by his friend Winston Churchill who, as Chancellor of the Exchequer, helped break the strike. Maugham loved secrecy and working behind the scenes, and may have been trying to head off Communist agitators in the unions.

Maugham couldn't understand why anyone ever left London, which was the most agreeable place in the world. But virtually homeless for many years, as Syrie changed houses and appropriated his study, and forever in search of new material, he was always on the move. In a revealing passage in *The Summing Up,* he wrote that though he was attached to England, he never felt completely at home there. The characteristic English reticence seemed to intensify his own shyness, and the laws against homosexuality were severe and inhibiting. Referring to his burdensome and exasperating marriage, he added: "To me England has been a country where I had obligations that I did not want to fulfil and responsibilities that irked me. I never felt entirely myself till I had put at least the Channel between my native country and me."

In the decade since Haxton's acquittal, Maugham had hired the best lawyers and spent a great deal of money, but had not been able to rescind his banishment. With his marriage a shambles, he needed a place where he could live with Haxton, lead a freer homosexual life and—as the money began to pour in from stage and film adaptations—avoid high British taxes. He felt most at home in France, his real native country. Though Maugham could not write French as well as English and rarely used French expressions in his letters or works, he'd been fluent in the language since childhood. He thought it was easier than English, for the vocabulary was smaller, the structure relatively simple, the grammatical rules clear. If you followed them, you could write good French.

Maugham was even more prosperous than his most successful contemporaries: Shaw, Kipling, Wells, Galsworthy and Wodehouse. In October 1926 he bought the grand, two-story Villa Mauresque, with twelve acres of land, in Cap Ferrat, between Nice and Monte Carlo, for $48,500. It had central heating, seven bedrooms and four bathrooms, and separate apartments for the servants, and cost another $20,000 a year to maintain its luxurious standards. The villa was only a few hundred yards up the hill from the elegant Hôtel du Cap, whose landscaped gardens and prayer rug of a beach Scott Fitzgerald would describe in the opening paragraph of *Tender Is the Night* (1934). In the 1920s Fitzgerald's sun-worshipping friends Gerald and Sara Murphy helped make the Riviera a fashionable summer resort.

All the land on Cap Ferrat had originally been the property of King

Leopold II of Belgium, the brutal owner of the Congo, who'd constructed a palace for himself as well as separate houses for his three mistresses. In 1906 the great fornicator, afraid of dying without absolution,
had built the nearby Villa Mauresque for his personal confessor, a former
bishop of Algeria. The cupola on the roof, the colonnade in the patio, the
archway in the living room and the windows in the walls were also built (as
its name suggests) in an oppressively Moorish style, and a Renaissance
portico was incongruously tacked on to the wide terrace that overlooked
the Mediterranean. Maugham tore down this hideous lath-and-plaster
Hollywood-style stage set, leaving a plain, square, flat-roofed house that
perfectly suited his taste. He whitewashed the inside and outside walls, set
up his library, and filled the house with the paintings he'd bought (and
continued to buy) and the Oriental art he'd collected on his travels.

On the outside wall he painted the occult sign that his father had
brought back from his travels in Morocco. The rather shy Maugham
adopted this fearful and aggressive symbol as his own, and had had it
stamped on all his books since *The Hero,* in 1901, and on many of his personal possessions. This curious emblem looks like a shield and spear, or
the prow and mast of a ship seen from above, or two curved five-hackled
swords over the double-barred Cross of Lorraine. In fact, it's a stylized
image of a human hand, a symbolic protection against the evil eye. In
Morocco the defiant thrust of a hand—directed against an enemy—is
accompanied by the phrase "five fingers in your eye." In Islam the number
five has mystical significance: "there are five religious duties, five keys to
secret knowledge, five daily prayers and a solemn oath is repeated five
times."[1]

Invitations to Maugham's villa were highly prized, and a visit, always
memorable, conferred considerable prestige. Guests could later dine out
in London on the goings-on at the Mauresque. As the visitors' car climbed
the steep hill up to the house the noise of the motor and the wheels on the
gravel alerted the white-gloved butler, who silently opened the tall green
doors. "After crossing a marble entrance hall," one guest recalled, "I was
shown into a long bright salon. It had a wide open fireplace of Arles
stone. The room was furnished in a modern style with fine rugs. Books
filled gothic alcoves, all the colours being bright." The flamboyant Cecil
Beaton appraised the grandeur with a decorator's eye and recalled that the
thirty-nine-by-eighteen-foot "salon, with french windows opening out on
to a terrace, was impressively decorated with a huge sunburst of gilt carv-

ing, much golden gesso, huge sofas, and eighteenth-century paintings in carved frames." Another designer, fashionable on the Riviera (and mentioning two paintings Maugham acquired later on), suggested that Maugham's magnificent creation had far surpassed anything done by Syrie: "Generous, austere stairs mounted from the hall, which rose the height of the house. White and yellow were the colours, and I remember an over life-sized female figure in monochrome greys dating from Picasso's classical period, a highly-coloured Matisse, Chinese carpets on a black slate floor, and dolphin tables flanked by Spanish chairs. On the left, as one came in, sat a Kuan-Yin, the goddess of mercy found in Peking. Handsome twelfth- and thirteenth-century Siamese bronze heads decorated the landings."[2]

The house was equaled by the lush, semitropical gardens that rose in terraces behind it. They were filled with tangerine and lemon trees, oleanders, bougainvilleas and camellias, hibiscus and yellow mimosa; the scent of orange blossoms, arum lilies and verbena; and the sweet song of nightingales. Maugham planted avocado trees (then unknown in Europe) from California and had his cook transform their fruit into ice cream spiked with rum. The view over the pines of the sea and the Mediterranean coast was breathtaking. Maugham built a huge fifty-four-by-eighteen-foot swimming pool, following an eighteenth-century model, above the highest terrace. At one end water flowed from a marble faun, which he'd found in Florence, carved by Bernini.

A narrow passage, a small wooden staircase and a few steps across the flat roof led to a large oblong room, Maugham's study, ivory tower and sanctum sanctorum. Inspired by Gauguin's painting on glass panels and by the beautiful surroundings, he worked each morning, facing away from the view, for three concentrated hours. As he emerged from his study at precisely 12:45, guests would gather for drinks, as they did once again before dinner. They drank white Jura wine; Bacardi cocktails; a delicious mixture of gin, cream and raspberry juice; or Gerald's famous martini: gin, Noilly Prat and a dash of absinthe.

The discreet, well-trained staff consisted of the Italian cook, Annette Chiaramello, who remained with Maugham for forty years, never served the same meal twice during a guest's stay and was reputed to be the best cook on the Riviera; the chauffeur, butler and valet; the housemaid and kitchen maid; and the cadre of seven gardeners (reduced, in times of austerity, to only four). When Annette protested that she was overworked,

Maugham replied: "I cannot bring myself to be very sorry for you because you work for three months and then we go away for three months and all the time you are paid full wages." "But, monsieur," she replied, invoking a custom sacred to servants, "for the months while you are away I lose my commissions on everything I buy."

George "Dadie" Rylands, a handsome, theater-loving, well-connected don at Cambridge, emphasized Maugham's generosity and defended his acquisition of worldly goods, which less successful writers bitterly resented. "Why shouldn't one care about money," asked the grateful Rylands, "if one spends it well and buys pictures and entertains one's friends and has good food and is altogether a delightful, friendly host and benefactor? . . . He was a rich man and got richer and richer, but I think he used his wealth well."[3]

II

ALLUDING, IN *The Razor's Edge,* to the social milieu of the villa, Maugham wrote, in an elegant passage: "The shores of the Mediterranean were littered with royalties from all parts of Europe: some lured there on account of the climate, some in exile, and some [like Kitty and Hughie in *The Circle*] because a scandalous past or an unsuitable marriage made it more convenient for them to inhabit a foreign country." But he also complained to Barbara Back that his neighbors were so aged and decrepit that all the scandalous behavior had disappeared. Nobody seemed to fall in love anymore, and the Riviera had become (like Monte Carlo today) appallingly respectable.

He frequently dined with two titled neighbors. The sharp-tongued Cecil Beaton wrote that Lady Bateman, "a wealthy widow with little brain under a magnificent head of snow-white hair, was pretty, snobbish and spoilt." Lady Kenmare, according to the French artist Edouard MacAvoy (who most unusually called Maugham by his middle name) was more colorful: "Somerset tells me that she has successively married four Lords each one richer than the other. 'But the most admirable thing,' he adds, 'is that they all died a perfectly natural death.' "

Maugham described the local villagers at the other end of the social scale in a nicely balanced epigram: "They're Communists because they're poor and want to be rich; they're promiscuous because they are highly sexed; they're Catholics because they don't want to go to hell."[4] Maugham lived in France for forty years, had a French staff and a French doctor, knew Prince Rainier and the exiled queen of Romania, the irrepressible Jean Cocteau as well as some of the artists whose work he collected: Matisse, Marie Laurencin and Edouard MacAvoy. But he had no close French friends and socialized almost exclusively with the English residents and visitors.

No wonder, then, that Maugham, cut off from England and eager for gossip, counted on guests to earn their keep by amusing him, distracting him from the quiet and (if truth be told) sometimes boring routine in his paradisaical villa. His guests were suddenly transported from an ordinary existence under the drab skies of England into a magical, cloistered world of Mediterranean food and wine, bright colors and sparkling sea. For a guest the day began as his mosquito net, which had cocooned him during the night, was rolled back and breakfast was served on a tray in bed. The villa, glittering under the Riviera sunshine and Maugham's benign seigneurial rule, offered a tennis court and a swimming pool, stimulating conversation, superb food, fine wines, attentive servants, exotic gardens and spectacular views. Outside the house one could take walks in the hills, motor along the *corniche* and sail in the bay, dine in the local three-star restaurants, gamble at Monte—and enjoy all this splendor in the pristine days before tourists jammed the roads and packed the beaches.

Maugham's ideal guests were charming and clever, witty and entertaining. They played a good game of tennis and bridge and, most important, were gossipy, good-looking and gay. When Barbara Back tried to secure a charitable invitation for a moribund friend, Maugham categorically refused to turn the villa into a nursing home. He felt it was difficult to find a perfect or even tolerably good guest. Since life on the Riviera depended on sunshine, visitors could become a tiresome burden during the rain or mistral, when there was nothing much to do but mope about indoors. Though he greatly looked forward to visitors, he was sometimes fed up with them by the time they departed.

Maugham complained to Francis King that egoistic guests expected him to abandon his own work schedule and devote himself entirely to their comfort and amusement. Other visitors—demanding, inconsiderate, impossible—treated his domain like an occupied country which they had the right to pillage. But, as the cheerful, good-natured Arthur Marshall observed, Maugham was both cynical and tolerant: "He liked people to behave badly. It was what he expected, and when they did—they seldom let him down—he was amused." The most boorish and ungrateful guests sponged on and then criticized Maugham, carried back malicious gossip and even more tangible contraband. The critic John Weightman, in an apt phrase, called it a "Garden of Eden filled with the hissing of snakes." Exasperated after years of bountiful hospitality, Maugham confessed: "One can't run a Grand Hotel forever."[5]

The bad behavior Maugham anticipated yet dreaded was ingeniously varied. He had a long catalogue of complaints: guests who never shut doors and never turned out lights, dirtied beds with muddy boots and burned cigarette holes in the sheets, demanded special diets and wasted vintage wines, lapsed into silence or talked like maniacs, never put back a book or broke up a set by taking a volume away with them, borrowed money when leaving and failed to pay it back.

The sympathetic critic Raymond Mortimer, a regular guest, agreed with Beaton about Maugham's sudden rages and recalled the ultimate punishment—just short of calling the police: "he was a man of very violent temper, which on the whole he controlled, but sometimes he would simply let fly. Two men whom I know were staying with him were turned out of the house at a moment's notice and told to pack their bags." The hedonistic writer Cyril Connolly, a notorious offender who stole inscribed first editions from the houses of his friends, was caught green-handed. When staying with Maugham he "picked two avocadoes which his host was specially cultivating, was rightly suspected of the deed, and obliged to unpack his suitcase in order to hand the avocadoes back." On another occasion, larceny was foiled by what the butler saw. As a young guest was saying goodbye, "the butler appeared on the stairs with his luggage. Reaching the last step, he gave the largest of the cases a smart tap against the iron banisters thus forcing the lock, and out tumbled a first edition of Willie's collected works. The young man had apparently packed his own bag, and the butler, suspicious by nature, had given it the once-over."[6]

Despite these unfortunate incidents, embarrassing to both victim and felon, Maugham—who adored Gerald—had a soft spot for rascals. Soon after he moved into the villa he sent an angry letter firing his careless American agent Charlie Towne: "I will not conceal from you that I am extremely vexed at your having signed an agreement with [George] Doran which gives me nothing that I wanted but on the contrary takes away what I value most dearly, my freedom of action." Nevertheless, Maugham wrote, "though I consider you too arbitrary to be an agent, I continue to

Kenneth Clark

think you a charming and amiable companion." He offered Towne an 1868 brandy and a 1911 Pol Roget champagne to entice him to visit the villa.

Desmond MacCarthy, an old friend from Red Cross days, who in 1934 would write an appreciative pamphlet on "the English Maupassant," was an exemplary guest—both appreciative and amusing. In a lyrical letter to frozen friends in England, he extolled the glories of the Mediterranean and the perfection of the villa:

> I am sitting in bright warm sunshine on a paved terrace with orange and lemon trees, laden with fruit, growing out of it; with my back to a blue, blue sea, and looking up at a milk-white house, with very long windows, which makes the sky above it look even bluer than the sea. . . . My bedroom is high and small, with a sumptuous bathroom attached. It contains every object one wants, down to a row of perfectly pointed pencils. When I am in my bed, with its muslin curtains and white silk coverlet, I feel like a bride.[7]

The wealthy Kenneth Clark—who advised Maugham on his art collection, became director of the National Gallery in London and later bought his own private castle—found being a guest and following Maugham's strict regimen more stressful than relaxing: "he was exacting company in so far as he liked to be amused and was fairly easily bored and as neither my wife nor I played bridge we had to keep him amused by conversation, and every evening I used to think to myself, dear me, what would happen if I dry up?" Three years later, in his autobiography, Clark was more severe. He complained that Maugham liked to dominate the conversation, became impatient with the animated talk of others and (as in his work) liked to cut down his rivals:

> Staying there was rather a strain. He expected to be entertained, but not too much, as he enjoyed talking himself. More than once he spoke ironically of my flow of conversation. He told his stories with all the skill and economy that distinguish his writings, but sometimes digressed to express his contempt for the Bloomsburies, and his low opinion of Max Beerbohm and E. M. Forster. When Jean Cocteau (who called him "Somerset") came to call on him, and talked, as I thought, brilliantly, but non-stop, Mr. Maugham became extremely restive, and after a time showed him politely to the door.

Clark saw that Maugham was more than an impatient host. "He was very vulnerable," he added, "and his well-known cynicism was largely defensive."

III

MAUGHAM'S CHARACTER HAD evolved from the shy, shabby guest at country weekends, when he was struggling for recognition, to the domineering, apparently self-assured disciplinarian and adviser, when success had enabled him to acquire his own domain. Aware of his instinctive shrinking from physical contact and his resistance to easy familiarity, Maugham admitted he did not like to be touched (except when he was in sexual control) and tended to draw away if someone was emboldened to take his arm or grasp his shoulder. A Riviera neighbor observed a revealing inability to reach out to others: "He had great charm and a certain kindly warmth for those he liked, and as one approached would spring up, come forward, arms outstretched. The arms would drop back again to the sides without contact, but it was meant as a welcoming gesture."[8]

Rigidly disciplined in his work, Maugham hated to waste a second of his life. Always on time himself, he expected others to be equally punctual and ran the villa with the clockwork precision he had first observed in the house of Augustus Hare. He liked to hold court and, as guests wisely deferred to him, tended to win all the arguments. Sybil Colefax liked his paradoxical combination of "affable cynicism and petulant friendliness." But his childhood wounds remained (as did the soothing photograph of his mother on his bedside table), and he was, as he said of Flaubert, an "irascible, pessimistic, morbid and self-centred personality." Roderick Cameron noted that "Maugham was not one to suffer fools or bores gladly, and could at times be very caustic, but this for the onlooker gave a certain spice to the gathering—providing, of course, that one was not on the receiving end." C. P. Snow, grateful as a young writer for Maugham's useful advice, wrote that his "was a very astringent sort of friendliness, no nonsense about it and no sentimentality about it, but just hard, rather like visiting one's family lawyer."[9] But Maugham also had a well-disguised sentimental side, and wrote hundreds of letters profusely thanking people for remembering his birthday or sending gifts.

Even when young, Maugham always seemed old. His Edwardian manner was distant, formal and reserved, and his sallow skin and deeply etched wrinkles were accentuated by prolonged exposure to the Mediterranean sun. (He used special French soap for his wrinkles, but it seemed to do little good.) The "Old Party" emphasized his senescence from middle age onwards, and his greatest popularity and fame came with *The Razor's Edge* when he was seventy. The famous portrait by Graham Sutherland and the photograph by Yousuf Karsh were made in old age. His writing career lasted for sixty-five years, and he lived to be nearly ninety-two.

It's quite surprising to discover that the frail, timorous youth, who had no facility for games, was in fact extremely athletic. Somerset Maugham was a jock! He had taken arduous journeys on horseback in Spain and Siam, and continued to ride in his seventies on his estate in South Carolina. A prewar letter described his energetic participation in a stag hunt near Minehead, Somerset. He was terrified at first when cantering down the steep inclines, across riverbeds and over rough territory, but with an experienced pony he soon got the hang of it, forgot the danger and found it jolly good fun.

He went to boxing matches in Nice and to Davis Cup tournaments in Paris. He swam and dived in his pool, skated and skied in St. Moritz, played squash and golf on the Riviera. As an icy wind cut into his back on the golf course, he thought how foolish it was to do unpleasant things while pretending to amuse himself. He also surprised George Doran by waterskiing off Cap Ferrat: "Seated on a high chair on top of his aquaplane, tethered to his speedy launch, he skips over the Mediterranean at a speed of fifteen to twenty knots an hour, exhibiting a daring unsuspected of the artist and the student. He is not exactly a star tennis-player but he is a valorous contender and partner."

Maugham had his own tennis court, and was indeed a keen, vigorous and longtime player. Tennis, he said, needed "skill and judgement, a good eye and a cool head." He recalled how customs had changed from the gentlemanly time when ladies had worn long white skirts at country-house parties: "In the old days . . . we lobbed the ball gently over the net so the lady we were playing could hobble over gracefully and lob it back. Now . . . we stand at back center court and fight for our lives!"[10] He recognized the social advantages of sports, and in an early story wrote that for a new vicar athletic skills were more important than spiritual qualifications: "as long as he can play tennis and behave decently at a dinner party, our souls can take care of themselves."

When the fleet was in, he told Barbara Back, he not only pursued handsome sailors, but also played tennis with shy Polish officers who addressed him as "sir." Dadie Rylands remembered that Maugham played tennis "well in earlier days, very keenly." The writer Godfrey Winn, a champion in England who gave Maugham lessons at the villa, reported that he "played very much better than I had anticipated. He really did possess a forehand drive, though with it, little knowledge of court craft, or how to deal with a smash at the net."[11]

IV

EXCEPT FOR FIVE years' interruption during World War II, the Villa Mauresque remained Maugham's permanent home from 1926 until his death in 1965, though he continued to travel in search of new locales and new material. He also read a great deal about Malaya and was familiar with the country from his close study of Conrad. His journey to Malaya in 1921 made a deep impression, and its bored, isolated and disillusioned Englishmen became a favorite subject. Some of these men, like Charles Strickland in *The Moon and Sixpence,* wanted to escape the constraints and obligations of European civilization, and live a freer and more dissolute life in exotic places. Some were forced into exile by incompetence, scandal or crime; others banished themselves after personal failure or tragedy. As Kipling wrote of this appealing, immoral world: "The wildest dreams of Kew are the facts of Khatmandhu, / And the crimes of Clapham chaste in Marta-ban." Others, who interested Maugham the most, were unexceptional middle-class men and women sent to govern or ply their trade in a tropical climate and alien culture.

Maugham was severely criticized by colonial civil servants for abusing their "hospitality by ferreting out the family skeletons of his hosts and putting them into his books." More than one outraged host threatened to thrash him if he ever returned to Malaya or Borneo. He was, as he said of the Goncourt brothers, attacked for his indiscretion, lack of charity, coarseness and presumption. But the charge was unfair. Everyone he met knew he was a writer, and he never forced anyone to talk. In fact, as he wrote in "The Book-Bag," during these visits to remote outstations he played the salutary role of psychiatrist and father-confessor, whose willing ear relieved their pent-up guilt: "People who live so desperately alone, in the remote places of the earth, find it a relief to tell someone whom in all probability they will never meet again the story that had burdened perhaps for years their waking thoughts and their dreams at night."[12] The charac-ters who provided the raw material of Maugham's stories were themselves subject to intense scrutiny and endless gossip. His achievement was to transform these lives and immortalize their world.

The powerful stories in *The Casuarina Tree* (1926), set in the jungles of Malaya and Borneo, equaled the vivid and penetrating South Sea tales in *The Trembling of a Leaf.* Maugham was fascinated by the particular social code that governed life in a colonial settlement. His characters try to set an example to the natives, replicate suburban life in England, and deal with their own loneliness and inadequacies. Maugham liked to read detective fiction, and several of his finest stories have some elements of the genre: a closed community, with its special geography and climate, vocabulary and routine; people with guilty secrets, and others with partial knowledge of the truth; a violent crime, a plausible cover-up and a passionate confes-sion.

The situation at the beginning of Maugham's "Before the Party"

(December 1922) parallels Katherine Mansfield's "The Garden-Party" (published the previous February). Mansfield's Mrs. Sheridan, guilty of hypocrisy and insensitivity, callously goes ahead with her elaborate garden party despite the accidental death of her working-class neighbor. Maugham's Skinner family, though infinitely worse, are also worried about what people will think. The story is set in England, but centers on events in Borneo, where their son-in-law, Harold, a Resident in a remote outstation, has died of a fever. His young widow, Millicent, pale and strange, is dressed in mourning. Just as they're about to leave for a garden party, her sister confronts her with the revelation, from a chance visitor, that Harold had in fact committed suicide. Millicent's family are angry that she has lied to them, but she coldly and acidly tells them the real story: her alcoholic husband had been sent to England to find a bride as a condition of keeping his job; she'd been hastily married off to a desperate drunkard; she'd tried in vain to help him; and had finally cut his throat and disguised his death as suicide.

Millicent has got away with murder, but no one in the story escapes blame: Harold himself; the members of the club at Kuala Solor, who failed to warn the new bride about his drinking; and her family, who think the entire episode is terribly bad form. The story is melodramatic, but Maugham, like Mansfield, exposes middle-class hypocrisy. While Mansfield's story is all gradation of feeling, Maugham's vividly sketches two distinct social settings, and finely balances our revulsion and sympathy for the murderess.

Unlike Kipling and Conrad, his predecessors in colonial fiction, Maugham frequently focuses on women. They are often victims of their situation, and capable of cruel, irrational behavior. "P. & O." (1923) takes place on a ship (of the Peninsula & Oriental line) sailing from Malaya to England and contains several motifs common to other stories. It opens, like "The Letter," with a description of Singapore; contains, like "Honolulu," a black-magic spell; and, like the characters in "Before the Party," the passengers decide to proceed with their fancy-dress Christmas celebration after one of their number dies at sea. Mrs. Hamlyn, a woman of forty, is sailing from Yokohama to England to get a divorce after discovering that her husband has been having an affair with an older married woman. Her husband has appealed to her to wait out his autumnal adventure which, everyone knows, will not last. But she doesn't love her husband and, though she could tolerate a fling with a young thing, she's hurt by his love for an older woman. On the ship she meets Gallagher, an Irish planter, eager to retire to Galway. Cursed and bewitched by his abandoned Malay mistress, he suffers from uncontrollable hiccoughs, can't eat or sleep and gradually dies. Mrs. Hamlyn, also cursed by love, is moved by his agony, and his death puts her own problems in perspective. She decides to forgive her husband and, though she won't go back to him, hopes that he'll be happy.

"The Force of Circumstance" (1924), another story of a marriage in a remote outstation, opens with a sentence that sets the scene both physically and emotionally: "She was sitting on the verandah waiting for her husband to come in for luncheon." Doris, the young wife, briefly courted on Guy's last leave, has been in Borneo only for a short time. Like Maugham, she has read brooding, somber, Conradian novels about the Malay Archipelago, but she's happy with Guy and finds everything enchanting: the river, the native *kampong,* the servants, the routine and design of the house. She questions her husband about a local woman, carrying a baby and lingering near the house, and the two pale-skinned little boys she's seen in the village. The core of the story, the husband's sad and shameful confession, engages our sympathies. Ten years before, a young man just out of school and unbearably lonely, he'd bought a fifteen-year-old native girl from her parents, but had always planned to marry an English girl. Rationally, Doris forgives him, but she cannot overcome her physical revulsion, stops sleeping with her husband and (like Mrs. Hamlyn) returns to England. Guy, desperately lonely once again, takes back his obstinate native mistress.

In "The Outstation" (1924), Maugham once again took up the Conradian situation, in "Outpost of Progress," of two white men isolated in the tropics. Maugham's story begins with an ominous arrival. Warburton, the middle-aged Resident, needs an assistant, but he's been alone so long that he dislikes company and dreads the new man. Though he's a good administrator, speaks the local language and deals sensitively with the Malays and Dyaks, he lives a fantastically rigid life. He dresses elaborately for the exquisitely cooked and served dinner, takes a ritualistic walk, unwraps the daily *Times* in strict rotation, each copy six weeks late, and combs the society columns for details of the people he knew when he was a moneyed young man about town. The new assistant, Cooper, a boorish young man from Barbados who has served in the ranks during the war, offends him on the first night by coming to dinner in dirty clothes.

Maugham gives a masterly account of a hideous and monotonous hatred, inflamed by class consciousness. Cooper is competent but treats the natives harshly, bullies his servants until no one will work for him and refuses to heed Warburton's warnings. When Warburton complains about Cooper to the sultan's assistant, he's urged (as if he were at fault) to be tolerant of his rough edges. Warburton sees this rebuke as the death knell for the standards and dignity of the service, as Cooper, unable to ask for help, writhes in agonies of loneliness and resentment. The impasse ends in a trivial but crucial way, when Cooper appropriates Warburton's newspaper while he's away on tour. The older man is so outraged that he doesn't intervene when Cooper mistreats his servant. He's gratified when the servant takes revenge by stabbing the young man to death, and plans to bring him into his own house when he completes his term in prison. The colonial service has thrown together two socially antagonistic men—Warburton the snob and Cooper the fool—with tragic results. In "Mackintosh" and "The Outstation," both more subtle than Conrad's early story, the deaths occur through a sin of omission.

"The Letter" (1924) is, after "Rain," Maugham's most famous story. It's based on an actual case of an Englishwoman, Ethel Proudlock, the wife of a teacher in Kuala Lumpur, who supposedly shot William Steward when he attempted to rape her. Her trial for murder "was the sensation of the day, and it was discussed in all the clubs, at all the dinner tables, up and down the peninsula from Singapore to Penang." Found guilty and sentenced to death by hanging, she was pardoned by the sultan of Selangor, but went mad in prison, was sent back to England and died in an insane asylum.[13] Ten years later Maugham heard the real story from Ethel's lawyer. It had an adulterous triangle and murder, a Eurasian woman who hid her origins and a treacherous Chinese. The dust wrapper of *The Painted Veil*—with a remorseful white woman dressed in an Oriental robe, stared at by a Chinese woman hiding behind a curtain—would also have been appropriate for "The Letter."

Maugham told the story, as he heard it, from the point of view of the defense lawyer, Mr. Joyce. He intensified the drama by eliminating Mrs. Proudlock's Eurasian background and adding the incriminating letter. In Maugham's version Leslie Crosbie also claims that she shot Geoffrey Hammond, the manager of a neighboring rubber estate, when he tried to rape her. Cool and refined, fragile and delicate, she greets Joyce in prison as if he were coming to tea. Her husband, Robert, believes her story, calls her a plucky woman and reminds Joyce that everyone agrees she did the right thing. While Joyce is wondering why she fired six shots into Hammond, the victim's Chinese mistress sends him a copy of a letter which reveals that Leslie had invited Hammond to her house. Joyce realizes that Leslie, furious that her lover had left her for the Chinese woman, has murdered him in a jealous rage. Robert loyally agrees to buy back the letter. She's acquitted, but confesses to Joyce her adultery, jealousy and revenge. Joyce observes that "you can never tell what hidden possibilities of savagery there are in the most respectable of women. . . . You would never have thought that this quiet, refined woman was capable of such a fiendish passion." Leslie escapes punishment and implicates both husband and lawyer in her crime.

This female Jekyll-and-Hyde character was a natural for the stage, and Maugham turned the story into a play in 1927. Eugene O'Neill, who liked Maugham personally and admired his work, criticized the play when Katharine Cornell opened in the American production: "It didn't do her reputation so much good. No one thought anything of the play except as a cheap melodrama but it will probably make money." But the English version, with Gladys Cooper and Nigel Bruce, got great reviews. The *Sunday Times* critic wrote that "of the play itself, considered in its own plane, it would be impossible to speak too highly. It is perfect theatre. . . . The evening was sensationally successful, and the audience delighted almost to hysteria."[14]

"The Letter" was also turned into films in 1929 and 1940. The second movie—starring Bette Davis and Herbert Marshall, and directed by William Wyler—had many dramatic revelations: the heroine's adultery and motive for murder, the victim's marriage to a Eurasian woman and the lawyer's previous involvement with the murderess. But the Hollywood Production Code forced Warner Bros. to tack on a ludicrous moralistic ending. Both transgressors are punished when the blackmailing Eurasian rival stabs Davis to death and is arrested by the police. Nevertheless, the English critic James Agate wrote that in *The Letter,* still the best film based on Maugham's work, "the writing is taut and spare throughout . . . the unraveling of Maugham's story is masterful and the presentation visual and cinematic. . . . The audience at the trade show did not move a finger." Maugham rightly felt that the film was effective when it faithfully followed his story and failed when it didn't. When Christopher Isherwood asked what he liked about the film, he replied: "I liked all the p-parts I wrote."[15]

V

THE ACQUISITION OF the Villa Mauresque in France represented not only a commitment to Gerald, but a rejection of Syrie. It was clear well before Maugham bought the villa, and even before he dutifully married Syrie, that his attempt to share a life with her, however irregular, was doomed. His caustic portrait of Syrie in *Our Betters,* written when he was actually living with her, and the disastrous week at her house in Le Touquet hammered the final nails into their matrimonial coffin. When Willie Ashenden, in *Cakes and Ale,* remarks that authors' wives are odious, he is surely speaking for Maugham. In 1925 he mentioned Syrie's all-too-frequent complaints and his offer to let her divorce him—though he would not, despite his extreme unhappiness, initiate the suit: "I hope during my absence she will cease her complaining about me to all her friends (which must be tedious for them). . . . She has only to say the word and I am willing to let myself be divorced. I cannot change and she must either live with me as I am, or take her courage in both hands and make the break."

In his plays Maugham expressed his intense dissatisfaction with the chains of marriage and the process of divorce, with lawyers sniffing out scandal and prying into his private life. The heroine of *The Constant Wife* (1926), speaking for Maugham with bitter irony, rejects the idea that just because her husband "has married her he must provide for her wants and her luxuries, sacrifice his pleasures and comfort and convenience, and . . . be her slave and bondman." In *Home and Beauty* (1919) the lawyer Raham condemns the humiliating need to expose one's adultery in public to obtain a divorce (a practice also satirized in Evelyn Waugh's *A Handful of Dust,* 1934), and gives Maugham's views on how the hypocritical law should be reformed. He believed that "when two married persons agreed to separate it was nobody's business but their own. I think if they announced their determination before a justice of the peace, and were given six months to think the matter over, so that they might be certain they knew their minds, the marriage might then be dissolved without further trouble. Many lies would never be told, much dirty linen would never be washed in public."[16]

When their divorce, initiated in 1928, was finally granted by a court in Nice the following year, the long-suffering (but perhaps still guilt-ridden)

Maugham accepted a greatly disadvantageous settlement. Though both had been unfaithful and Syrie had built up an extremely lucrative decorating business, he "agreed to a lump sum payment of £12,000, £2,400 a year in alimony until Syrie remarried [which she never did], and £600 annual support payments for Liza. As well, Syrie was given the house in the King's Road, fully furnished, and a Rolls Royce." Glad to be rid of her at last, Maugham threw in the chauffeur with the Rolls. Wellcome had settled £2,400 a year on her in 1910; Maugham, with much less money, maintained her market value and paid the same price. In April 1929, a month before the divorce became final, he heard that Syrie was still spreading the vindictive rumors about his sexual life with Haxton that she'd first used to blackmail him into marriage in 1917. Though he pretended to be indifferent to the slander and told his niece that "no one attaches the smallest importance to anything said by that abandoned liar," he was deeply hurt.

Like many divorced couples, they continued their battles until death. In the early 1930s Maugham exposed Syrie's fraudulent attempt to force him to pay her income tax. She'd told Inland Revenue officials that between 1926 and 1930, when Maugham was living in France, they were actually living together in England and that *he* was responsible for £2,000 of her tax. After a French lover had jilted her, she made a second suicide attempt, jumped out of a mezzanine window in Cannes and broke both wrists. In December 1940, when Maugham, Syrie and Liza were all living in America, Maugham said that Syrie, who'd always tried to dominate Liza, had become completely hysterical and had a disastrous effect on their grown daughter: "Syrie has been making a terrible nuisance of herself and leading Liza a hell of a life. She has been making dreadful scenes and threatening to commit suicide: in fact the whole bag of tricks. Liza has only stood firm on one thing and that is a refusal to live with her." Before sailing for America Syrie had panicked about the thought of being torpedoed and asked Maugham what she should do if the ship went down. "Swallow, just swallow," he advised her. "I am assured that when you find yourself in the water, if you open your m-m-mouth wide, it's all over much more quickly."[17]

12

"Stately Homo"

IF MAUGHAM WAS the reigning monarch of the Villa Mauresque, Gerald was the crown prince. He typed the manuscripts, handled the correspondence, made the travel arrangements, helped run the household, enlivened the parties and pimped for Willie. Their entirely different personalities were in some ways well matched. Maugham provided an even keel for Gerald's rudderless existence, while Gerald, a reckless *bon viveur,* offered an animated alternative to Willie's forbidding formality and reserve. Maugham liked to stay home at night and retire early; Gerald tore up and down the Riviera, giving guests all the gaiety they wanted—or could bear. Idealizing their romance and ignoring all the problems that threatened and nearly wrecked their friendship, Glenway Wescott called it "the first completely beautiful, completely appropriate love affair [Maugham] had ever had."

Robin described Gerald as "well-dressed, attractive and slim, very European though he was American by nationality," and said he "exuded vitality and charm and money." Gerald Kelly's wife, Jane, adored Haxton, but he was disliked, even hated, by most of Maugham's family and friends. "He was a delightful creature," Jane gushed, "and he was the most proficient man I've ever met. There was nothing that he did, that he didn't do marvellously. He played marvellous tennis, he played marvellous bridge, he made marvellous models, he could swim, he could dive.... You couldn't help loving him. He was so delightful, gay company, terribly tact-ful. With his parties, he was just gaiety."[1]

Arthur Marshall, a homosexual schoolmaster and writer who impressed everyone with his "sense of the ludicrous as well as by his all-pervading niceness," observed Maugham's fondness for Gerald and will-ingness to put up with his faults. Gerald, for whom charm was a useful commodity, "charmed the birds from the trees. No matter how badly he behaved, Willie was always enraptured by him. I remember once we were waiting to play tennis, and Gerald hadn't turned up, and he was seen com-ing through the trees towards the court, and Willie said—very rare for him to be sentimental—'Oh look, good, here comes Master Hacky.' It was said with love, you know, and deep affection."

Thanks to Maugham, Gerald lived a hedonistic, luxurious and adven-turous life beyond his wildest dreams. As majordomo and factotum, he vacillated between gratitude and ill-concealed resentment of his humiliat-ing position. He liked to demonstrate his power by making Willie walk across the room to fetch him a drink and would even insult him in front of guests. When, to make conversation, Willie once genially said, "I've just had a h-h-hot bath," the drunken Gerald provocatively asked: "And did you masturbate?"—to which Willie, used to his antics but stammering more than usual, coolly replied: "As it h-h-h-happens, n-n-n-n-no."[2]

While Maugham kept Gerald, Gerald kept a tall, thin, pale-faced young French boy, Louis (Lulu) Legrand. The obliging Lulu slept with some of Maugham's homosexual friends, like Harold Nicolson and per-haps his nephew, Robin. Later, hustling in Paris, he used Maugham's flat to service his clients. Gerald, a self-destructive drunkard and reckless gambler, expected Maugham—and sometimes even Bert Alanson—to subsidize his considerable losses. Beverley Nichols reported that "Gerald was a fanatical gambler, and a sizeable proportion of [Maugham's] royal-ties . . . was destined to be absorbed by the green baize tables of Cannes and Monte Carlo." In 1928 Gerald confessed to Alanson: "I had the most awful winter in the various casinos along the coast, never getting a win at all. Fortunately this summer has smiled upon me, and I have made nearly ten thousand dollars. I have decided that that is enough and will gamble no more till winter"—though it's doubtful he kept his resolve.

In the summer of 1930 Gerald, a marvelous diver, surpassed himself with a drunken dive into an empty pool. He cut open his head, broke a vertebra in his neck and dislocated his spine. As Maugham ironically reported to Charlie Towne: "Gerald broke his neck two or three years ago, and if he had been a decent and respectable person he would certainly have been killed, but being neither he made a wonderful recovery and is now as well as ever. The only thing is that perhaps he cannot turn his head in the street to look back on someone who has caught his fancy as spryly as his wont."

In the early 1930s Maugham complained that Gerald "liked the bottle better than he liked me," and told Barbara Back that he refused to spend the rest of his life as keeper and nursemaid of a hopeless drunk. Liza once saw Gerald in a seizure of delirium tremens. After issuing a severe warning, Maugham said he hadn't seen much of Gerald, who spent most of his time playing bridge in Nice with crooks and cads. Though Gerald didn't do much secretarial work, Maugham was grateful that he was (for the moment) staying sober and keeping out of mischief. But Gerald, whom Maugham's niece Diana called "an evil man," could suddenly reveal the dark side of his character. When driving back to the villa with little Liza, he became either jealous of the child or annoyed by her dog. In a drunken rage, he grabbed her beloved pet, threw it out of the window and killed it.[3]

II

GERALD HELPED TO create and sustain the homosexual ambience at the villa. Here alone Maugham could relax and be relatively uninhibited, let his guard down and act with complete freedom. He could camp it up, flirt and even sleep with the handsome young guests. All his closest male friends, except Gerald Kelly and Bert Alanson, were homosexual. Many of them were writers, and all but Ellingham Brooks, E. F. Benson, Reggie Turner and Edward Marsh were considerably younger.[4] In the privacy and security of the villa he could finally allow himself to be, in Quentin Crisp's phrase, "one of the stately homos of England."

The unbuttoned, carnivalesque atmosphere, a striking contrast to Maugham's often forbidding formality, shocked both liberated women and straight men. The men swam naked, even in mixed company; and Rebecca West (mistress of H. G. Wells, and apparently forgiven for her severe review) reported that Haxton "taunted me with the sight of his nudity in the swimming tank." The bisexual poet Edna Millay, visiting the villa when Coward and Beaton were also guests, cried out: " 'Oh, Mr. Maugham, it's fairy land here!' ... Noël and Cecil were just a bit taken aback." The writer Frank Swinnerton, a great friend of Arnold Bennett, was invited with his wife to lunch at the villa. When they got there, they felt they were interrupting (or at least impeding) the sexual activities: "There was the celebrated Haxton and there were two other very precious looking gentlemen, one was very big bosomed and the other was very delicate, and my wife and I both had the extraordinary sensation that we should be better away. It was as though they were all willing us to go and so we went. My wife said, 'wasn't that strange, they didn't want us there any more.' "[5]

With the ladies banished, Maugham felt more at ease and inclined to jest. Asked why a Cambridge don wore a beard, he replied that they had to do *something* at King's. The college had been a notorious nest of homosexuals since the late-Victorian days of Oscar Browning. Dismissed from Eton, Browning was made a fellow of King's, where, as the *Dictionary of National Biography* would have it, he devoted himself to leading "young Englishmen toward the openings they desired." When Dadie Rylands returned to King's after a visit to the villa, Maugham was flattered and slightly surprised to hear from him. He always assumed that brilliant and beautiful young men would forget him as soon as they left the Mauresque and went back to their lawful vocations.

There was also a serious side to these visits. Maugham received about two hundred books a year from unknown writers, and loved to give paternal advice and encouragement to young authors. He invited the shallow but promising Godfrey Winn—an excellent bridge and tennis player—to the villa, sent him a first-class ticket on the Blue Train and guaranteed his losses at high-stakes bridge. He read every word of Winn's early novel, "though not a masochist by nature," and forced Winn to work in the mornings by threatening to ban him from lunch. His generosity was not entirely disinterested, and he also slept with Winn. Sexual life was a bit riskier outside the sacred precincts. During a picnic with some handsome young men in Rome, the American writer Frederic Prokosch heard a menacing *carabiniere* say that Maugham was corrupting the innocents. "He is p-perfectly right," said Maugham. "I *am* c-corrupting the innocents."

Haxton both tied Maugham to the villa and, as an intrepid traveler, freed him from it. After all the Baudelairean *luxe* and *volupté,* they needed an annual "cure" at their favorite spas, baths, *termi* and *Kurort*s: Vichy, in central France, the most boring place he ever stayed in; Abano, near Padua, in northeast Italy; Badgastein, south of Salzburg, in the Austrian Tyrol; and Brides-les-Bains, between Geneva and Turin, in the French

Barbara Back

Alps. Immersed in hydrotherapy, they drank the mineral waters, were vigorously massaged and enveloped in hot black mud, took radioactive baths and even endured high-pressure hosings. In a letter to Alanson of July 1925 Maugham described the sportive and rejuvenating regimen that appealed to his love of discipline and order: "We get up at half past seven and go down to the well, like Jacob . . . to drink a glass of hot medicated water. Then a medicated bath, and after that a cup of coffee and a rusk for breakfast; eighteen holes of golf follow, another drink of water and then a frugal luncheon. A short rest, tennis till six, more water, and a still more frugal dinner. A little bridge and bed."[6] Taking the sulphuric waters didn't do a bit of good. But the strict diet with no drink, moderate exercise and long walks in the romantic mountain scenery as well as the quiet life and mummified clientele were always good for the liver. Though Maugham was supposed to be the primary beneficiary, the cure also gave the alcoholic Haxton a welcome opportunity to dry out. A week in Vichy transformed the frequently intolerable Master Hacky into a reasonable, delightful and easy-to-get-on-with companion.

III

MAUGHAM'S CLOSEST LADY friend and most frequent correspondent was Barbara Back, whom he met in 1926. About ten years younger than Maugham, she was married to the eminent surgeon and accomplished mountaineer Ivor Back, who'd been a friend of Gerald Kelly and Aleister Crowley at Cambridge. "Solid and dark, with the air of being well-nourished," Ivor "had very bright and disrespectful eyes. He was also a racy talker without illusions or moral refinement." Barbara, a prominent society hostess, had a superb cook, a grand house and a Rolls-Royce. Tall, thin and beautiful, chic, elegant and intense, she was famous for her common sense, sparkling conversation and earthy wit. She danced well, and played a good game of golf and bridge, and Maugham liked to have her as a partner. She was a great gossip, and loved to reveal indiscretions and make up stories to amuse her friends. Her punningly titled book *Back Chat,* based on a gossip column she wrote for a popular newspaper and published by Heinemann in 1935, was dedicated to Maugham. Barbara got on well with Gerald, and hated Syrie as much as Maugham did. This long friendship with his ideal woman had a rare liveliness and spontaneity.

The tone of Maugham's letters to Barbara (he destroyed the ones she wrote to him) break through his characteristic reticence and are unusually witty, playful and lighthearted. He congratulated her when a friend committed suicide and left her all his money. He reported (perhaps in jest) that on the Riviera a certain Jan, a "fishy" guest or servant, was about to be arrested for stealing toilet paper from the house of Lady Guernsey. The former obstetrician even ventured a risqué medical joke. After a woman had triplets, a friend visiting her in the hospital said how wonderful it was. "Yes, the doctor tells me it only happens once in 167,000 times." "Goodness," her friend replied, "how did you ever find time to do your housework?" He also urged Barbara to reveal her most intimate feelings, and when she confessed she was in love with the poet Humbert Wolfe, asked what made her sexually excited. Though fond of Barbara, he could also be catty about her. When she was approaching sixty, he predicted that she'd try to look young until she turned into a figure of fun.[7]

Following his usual practice of putting friends into his work, Maugham used certain aspects of Barbara's character to describe Janet Marsh in "Virtue." Janet was "tall and fair and good to look at. . . . There was nothing that thrilled her more than the misfortunes of her friends. She . . . wanted to be in the thick of their difficulties. . . . You could not enter upon a love affair without finding her somehow your confidante, nor be mixed up in a divorce case without discovering that she too had a finger in the pie." Nobody seems to have noticed that Barbara was clearly the model for one of his most sympathetic women characters, Constance Middleton in *The Constant Wife.* Like Barbara, Constance is married to a famous surgeon; and in the play Maugham takes a few cracks at the medical profession. Dr. Middleton makes love to patients in his consulting room, keeps nervous patients waiting so they'll agree to expensive operations and, once he starts cutting, doesn't know when to stop. Like Barbara and Ivor, Maugham's husband and wife take separate holidays with their lovers. Maugham took an interest in Barbara's affairs and pressed her for details. On one occasion he suggested: "you might do worse than fly over to Copenhagen for a few days when you want to take a little jaunt with a new lover."

The title of *The Constant Wife* (1927), inspired by Restoration comedy, hints at Vanbrugh's *The Provok'd Wife* and Wycherley's *The Country Wife.* (It also echoed the titles of his own play *Caesar's Wife,* 1918, and of Margaret Kennedy's popular novel *The Constant Nymph,* 1924.) Constance was effectively played by Ethel Barrymore in America and in London by the beautiful Fay Compton, sister of the novelist Compton Mackenzie. According to Maugham Fay was a slut by nature, but a fine actress with a considerable following among the theatergoing public.

Constance, well aware that her husband John is deceiving her with her best friend, tries to maintain the precarious status quo by preventing her sister and friends from telling her the truth. The first act contrasts Constance's idealistic with her mother's more pragmatic view of marriage. But as the play progresses Constance becomes a liberated, modern woman, defiantly claiming the same rights as John. He first tries to defend his behavior by maintaining that "if a man's unfaithful to his wife she's an object of sympathy, whereas if a woman's unfaithful to her husband he's merely an object of ridicule." Constance, who's gone into business with a woman friend and achieved economic independence, is now in a position to tell him, "with calm courtesy, but with determination—to go to hell." Her lyrical and romantic speech at the end of the play, quite unusual in Maugham, undercuts her disillusioned attitude to love and enlightens her husband about what's missing in their marriage: "I want to feel about me the arms of a man who adores the ground I walk on. I want to see his face light up when I enter the room. . . . I want to let my hand fall on his shoulder and feel his lips softly touch my hair." Finally, she takes a long holiday with an old admirer and forces her husband to accept her shockingly egalitarian views. Though John first refuses to allow her to return after her sexual holiday, he quickly changes his mind. Just before the final curtain, he exclaims (in Maugham's private pun on Barbara's surname): "You are the most maddening, wilful, capricious, wrong-headed, delightful and enchanting woman man was ever cursed with having for a wife. Yes, damn you, come back."[8] Maugham believed that marriage could be sustained, as his was for ten years, only by periods of separation and adultery.

Maugham later felt that changing manners and mores had deprived *The Constant Wife* of its immediacy and that Constance's demand for equality had become commonplace. But he underestimated his own work. His play raised many issues that remain vital today: Is a wife responsible for, and should she condone, her husband's infidelity? Should different standards of morality apply to a husband and wife, and does she have the right to be unfaithful if her husband is? Do women take pleasure in dissimulation? Is it wrong for men to use their position to obtain sexual favors? Is marriage essentially a financial transaction and modern woman merely a parasite? Does a woman have the right to her own career? All these questions were hotly debated during the feminist (Maugham actually uses this word in the play) movement of the 1960s and still seemed relevant in the London and San Francisco productions of the play in 2002–03.

IV

ASHENDEN: OR THE BRITISH AGENT (1928) is Maugham's most subtle and influential book. It also reveals, though more indirectly than in *Of Human Bondage,* a great deal about his life. He rather elusively said that he chose the name of the eponymous narrator because "it is a common surname in the neighbourhood of Canterbury, where I spent many years of my youth. The first syllable had to me a peculiar consolation which I found suggestive." Ashenden suggests Ashford, a Kentish town near Canterbury as well as *Beauty from Ashes* (from Isaiah 61:3), the original title of *Of Human Bondage.* (In *Ashenden* His Excellency describes his own successful but emotional empty life as "all ashes.") A boy called Leonard Ashenden, Maugham's "form-friend for several years" at King's School, had once inspired his romantic feelings.

Like Maugham, Ashenden (who uses the code name "Somerville," close to "Somerset") studied at Heidelberg and once saw Ibsen, lived on Chesterfield Street in London, speaks fluent French and German, knows some Russian, constantly travels but is always anxious about missing his train, took the Trans-Siberian Railroad, was helped by the Czechs in Russia and had an affair with a Russian woman, Anastasia (modeled on Sasha Kropotkin). The book is dedicated to Gerald Kelly, who appears as the loquacious Irish painter O'Malley and has an extraordinary ability to capture the distinction of his sitters.

Like a doctor faced with pain he cannot cure, Ashenden maintains a clinically detached attitude and a tolerance for human weakness. He has the urgency (but not the lassitude) of Sherlock Holmes. After learning that a burglary is about to take place, he thinks "there was not a moment to lose"; after discovering a new plot, he says "the very greatest affairs were afoot." A professional writer and amateur spy, he's recruited by old friends. Though a minor player, he participates in great historical events and witnesses the deaths of victims caught in the crossfire of great powers. Like Conrad in *The Secret Agent* (1907), he believes the police and criminals have the same mentality. Like the English traitor Caypor, whom he captures and hands over for execution, he prefers devious to direct methods and takes exquisite pleasure in deceiving his rivals. He plays a subversive role and experiences the thrill of deceit: "He was travelling with a brand-new passport in his pocket, under a borrowed name, and this gave him an agreeable sense of owning a new personality." As writer and spy, Maugham impersonated his own characters.

In striking contrast to Ashenden, the shifty spy chief R. (known only by his initial) takes no risks and trusts no one, uses operatives for his own unscrupulous purposes and considers them all expendable. In a crucial passage Maugham condemns the self-serving immorality of such men, who achieve murderous ends without taking on the responsibility of murderous means: "Though ready enough to profit by the activities of obscure agents of whom they had never heard, they shut their eyes to dirty work so that they could put their clean hands on their hearts and congratulate themselves that they had never done anything that was unbecoming to men of honour."[9]

The best writers of the Great War needed an entire decade to absorb and portray their traumatic experiences. Hemingway's *A Farewell to Arms*, Graves' *Goodbye to All That*, Aldington's *Death of a Hero* and Remarque's *All Quiet on the Western Front* did not appear until 1929. *Ashenden*, published the previous year, was also (Maugham wrote) "a very truthful account of my experiences during the war when I was in the Secret Service. I venture to think that, at all counts in England, it is the first time anyone has written of this business who knew anything about it." "Mr. Harrington's Washing" was based on an actual incident, and so was the capture of Chandra Lal, who agitated against British rule in India.

The sixteen cosmopolitan stories, unified by the eye and voice of the narrator, are set mainly in Geneva and in Russia. Maugham was forced to destroy fourteen other stories which, according to Winston Churchill, contravened the Official Secrets Act. The most revealing and incriminating spy stories had to be replaced by several others in the Russian section that are more about love than espionage. "Behind the Scenes" concerns Maugham's attempt to improve the poor relations between the British and American ambassadors in Petrograd: Sir George Buchanan, who served in Russia from 1910 to 1918, and the notoriously ill-informed David Rowland Francis. Bruce Lockhart described the sixty-three-year-old Buchanan as "a frail-looking man with a tired, sad expression in his eyes. . . . His monocle, his finely-chiselled features, and his beautiful silver-grey hair gave him something of the appearance of a stage diplomat."[10]

In "His Excellency," the British ambassador tells Ashenden a long story about how he mistakenly renounced his great passion for a sluttish but vital acrobat in order to marry a wellborn lady and have a distinguished but essentially meaningless career. W. H. Auden, greatly taken by Maugham's portrayal of the conflict between passion and renunciation, wrote twice about this tale. In *Letters from Iceland* he noted that he and Louis MacNeice "read the short stories of Somerset Maugham aloud to each other / And the best one was called *His Excellency*." John Fuller writes that in Auden's poem "His Excellency" (1936), "When nothing was enough / But love, but love," "elegant and uncompromising ruthlessness is held in balance with a sense of lightly accomplished betrayal—a perfect match for the tone of bitter comedy in Maugham."[11]

"The Hairless Mexican," whose title may have come from Huxley's story "Little Mexican" (1924), is a brilliant portrait of a sinister character. Ordering Ashenden to accompany an agent to steal vitally important papers in Italy, R. dryly announces, in laconic dialogue that has reverberated through hardboiled fiction and films:

"He's known as the Hairless Mexican."
"Why?"
"Because he's hairless and because he's a Mexican."

The Mexican murderer claims that anyone can pull a trigger, and prefers a knife to a gun. Flamboyant and garrulous, repulsive yet fascinating, he doesn't quite play the game in the English way and, through an oversight, murders the wrong man. The Mexican, at the bottom of the social scale, is contrasted to R., a gentleman who draws the line at killing a king, but doesn't much mind if his agents do it. R. in turn is contrasted to Professor Z. (based on Thomas Masaryk), a nationalist fighting to liberate the Czechs from Austrian domination. Masaryk refused to do anything that outraged his conscience and was, like Kerensky himself, hopelessly ineffective against ruthless leaders like Lenin.

Maugham's realistic portrayal of a bloodthirsty Russia—very different from the idealized, prerevolutionary idea of Russian novelists, composers and dancers, of Diaghilev, Nijinsky and Pavlova—forced English readers to revise their naive view of the country. As a result, he had the dubious honor of being attacked by the Bolsheviks, who condemned his plays, as well as by the Nazis. According to Maugham, Joseph Goebbels, the Nazi minister of propaganda, believed the events in *Ashenden* were literally true, and in a radio broadcast of 1939 or 1940 "gave it as an example of British cynicism and brutality." There's no reference to *Ashenden* in Goebbels' wartime speeches, but he mentions Maugham several times in his *Diaries* and in conversations with friends. Goebbels was familiar with Maugham's novel *Theatre* and other unnamed works, urged Wilfred von Oven to read him and used the name of "Constance" from *The Constant Wife* (then playing in Berlin) to make a satirical point in a hostile article. On December 26, 1939, three months after the outbreak of the war, he noted: "Through Maugham you can get to know the profound depravity of English society."[12]

Julian Symons, thriller writer and literary critic, has said that "the modern spy story began with Somerset Maugham's *Ashenden* (1928). . . . Almost all later writers in the genre owe something to Maugham, including the first and in many ways the finest of them, Eric Ambler." Raymond Chandler, praising its menacing ambience, declared that "*Ashenden* is far ahead of any other spy story ever written. . . . [It reads] as though there were always something vague and sinister just behind the curtain. In most of the others you are just afraid of the man with the gun."[13] Ian Fleming's spy chief M. in the James Bond novels is clearly based on Maugham's R. Fleming's biographer said that in boyhood he was a "great addict of *Ashenden*." Ian Fleming later wrote to Maugham saying that "we are the only two writers who write about what people are really interested in: cards, money, gold and things like that."

Graham Greene, another novelist recruited as a spy, worked as an agent in West Africa during World War II. In his penetrating review of the film version of *Ashenden—The Secret Agent* (1936), whose title was lifted from Conrad—Greene condemned Hitchcock's absurd lack of realism: "[from] the secret agent who loudly discusses his instructions in front of the hall porter of a Swiss hotel and who brandishes his only clue to a murder [a cuff button] in a crowded casino, [to the] representation of a Secret Service which so arranges things that its agent's photograph appears in every paper." In the film, Greene concluded, "nothing is left of that witty and realistic fiction."

Greene's clever send-up of espionage in *Our Man in Havana* was inspired by Maugham's amateur agent who does his country's dirty work. In *The Quiet American* a French soldier expresses the theme of *Ashenden* when he declares: "We are fighting all of your wars, but you leave us the guilt." John le Carré, a spy who became a novelist, acknowledged that "the *Ashenden* stories were certainly an influence in my work. I suppose that Maugham was the first person to write about espionage in a mood of disenchantment and almost prosaic reality."[14] Maugham's Ashenden is the archetypal secret agent, a lonely hero whose double life gives him a special insight into the society he tries to protect.

13

Reputations: *Cakes and Ale*

1930–1933

IN THE EARLY 1930s Maugham, in his late fifties and at the height of his powers, wrote his best novel, his most powerful play and many of his finest stories. *Of Human Bondage* had been his most ambitious book and *Ashenden* his most influential, but *Cakes and Ale: or The Skeleton in the Cupboard* (1930), a satire on the writing of biography and the creation of a literary reputation, was his masterpiece. Like James' *The Aspern Papers* (1888), Nabokov's *The Real Life of Sebastian Knight* (1941) and Mann's *Doctor Faustus* (1947), *Cakes and Ale* is a fictional portrait of a biographer's quest. A deeply retrospective work, full of acute commentary on the present, it contains some of Maugham's wittiest and most poignant writing.

In his preface to the novel, Maugham explained how the idea first came to him. He imagined he'd been asked to record his boyhood memories of a famous novelist who'd lived nearby with his beautiful and promiscuous wife. It begins when Willie Ashenden, a serious, cold-eyed and successful writer in his fifties, is approached by Alroy Kear, a popular novelist and determined careerist, for information about Edward Driffield. Kear has been asked to write the biography by Amy, once the great man's secretary and second wife, now a widow and guardian of his reputation. Kear's questions seem simple: what was Driffield like in his obscure early days in Blackstable, and what was the influence of his first wife, Rosie? In Ashenden's cool, appraising and mocking narrative, Kear is savagely satirized as a biographer who industriously gathers material to please the widow, to create a commercially profitable work—and to betray the writer whose true genius he cannot understand.

Willie Ashenden, unlike the bereaved and wretched Philip Carey in *Of Human Bondage,* looks back at his awkward boyhood in Blackstable with some tenderness. The novel progresses by a series of contrasts: the snobbery of his uncle and aunt and the earthy kindness and humor of Edward and Rosie Driffield; Willie's disdain for and then love for Rosie; Willie's ignorance and Ashenden's worldliness. Ashenden also contrasts Driffield's shady past and his later respectability, his early openheartedness and later secrecy; and his two wives: the uneducated and loving Rosie, and the plain, pretentious Amy, bent on transforming the living writer into a mummified museum.

Amy's hypocrisy cannot suppress Rosie's gaiety and vitality, and she's the disreputable but inspiring skeleton in the closet. Amy is the self-appointed guardian of the flame; Rosie, the artist's muse. The novel focuses on how we perceive Rosie. Willie sees her as morally flawed, but honest and good; Kear and Amy denigrate her as vulgar, destructive and unfaithful. Maugham took the title from Sir Toby Belch's speech in *Twelfth Night* to Olivia's puritanical steward Malvolio—"Dost thou think, because thou art virtuous, there shall be no more cakes and ale?"—to suggest that Rosie's amoral vitality will triumph over Amy's disapproving "virtue."

Looking at photographs of Driffield, Ashenden observes that "the real man, to his death unknown and lonely, was a wraith that went a silent way unseen between the writer of his books and the man who led his life." Choosing an idea that perfectly illustrated the contrasts in his novel, Maugham borrowed this distinction between art and life from T. S. Eliot's influential essay "Tradition and the Individual Talent" (1917), where he observed: "the more perfect the artist, the more completely separate in him will be the man who suffers and the mind which creates."[1]

In the preface Maugham denied that he'd based his story on Thomas Hardy, who'd died in January 1928, but the parallels were overwhelming and his readers were not fooled. Both writers were small and thin, came from a humble background, liked to talk and drink with ordinary men, and had a keen interest in architecture. In *Jude the Obscure,* a disturbing novel condemned as obscene and banned by the libraries, Hardy described the heartrending deaths of the hero's children; Driffield's shocking *The Cup of Life* describes the death of his child. After the death of Emma, Hardy's

attractive first wife, he married the much younger Florence; in the novel
Rosie leaves Driffield, who is taken up by London literati and marries the
secretarial Amy. In real life, as in Maugham's novel, the great man was
awarded the Order of Merit and continued to write major works well into
his eighties.

At the turn of the century Hardy, father figure to the Georgians, was
the most notorious writer in England, but his reputation continued to rise
throughout the modern age. He was praised by Ford Madox Ford, D. H.
Lawrence and Ezra Pound; and hero-worshipped by Robert Graves,
Siegfried Sassoon and T. E. Lawrence, who saw the Old Master as the living link to the tradition of English poetry. The last of the great Victorians,
he was the only one to span the Edwardian and Georgian eras and make a
substantial contribution to postwar literature—a modern without being
modernist. He'd attacked conventional religion and sexual morality, and
after the fierce polemics aroused by *Tess of the D'Urbervilles* and *Jude the
Obscure* had stopped writing novels in 1897. But his work was still subversive and startling, and he published two volumes of poetry, after *The Waste
Land* had appeared, in his mid-eighties. When the great pessimist and
sceptic was buried in Westminster Abbey, T. E. Lawrence and Sassoon
were furious about the inappropriate religious funeral and the exploitation
of Hardy's death by the press. Maugham drew on this well-known situation when Ashenden calls Driffield a man "of strong feeling and extreme
callousness," and Kear responds with the bland formula: "he was the
kindest man I've ever met."

After Hardy's death, the manuscript of his autobiography was published under his wife's name as her biography. Robert Gittings wrote that
the first volume of the "so-called *Life* of Hardy was produced with suspicious speed on 2 November of that year. Florence had only time to
remove firmly nearly every complimentary reference to Emma, to her
courage, her decision, her encouragement, her successful London lunch-
parties, above all, any suggestion that she and Florence had been friends."[2]
Like other contemporary books—Graves' *Lawrence and the Arabs* (1927)
and Herbert Gorman's *James Joyce* (1939)—*The Life of Thomas Hardy* was
actually a veiled autobiography, substantially written by the subject. Sir
James Barrie, whom Maugham disliked, and the art critic Sir Sidney
Colvin, whom Maugham satirized as Barton Trafford in *Cakes and Ale,*
assisted Florence and were co-conspirators. Hardy's authorship of the
biography was not made public until 1940, three years after Florence's

death. But Maugham, a literary insider and keen observer, certainly saw through the fraud of Hardy's attempt to erect a literary monument to equal the one in Westminster Abbey, and his awareness of the fraud gives the novel additional bite. (It's wonderfully ironic that T. S. Eliot, who succeeded Hardy as the most prominent poet in England, also married his much younger secretary, who devoted the rest of *her* life to covering up the discreditable aspects of his first marriage.)

Rosie Driffield, modeled on Maugham's great love, Sue Jones, is his most complex and appealing female character. A common barmaid, consistently unfaithful to her husband, she has a disarming frankness, an eager zest for life and an irresistibly charming smile. Unlike Ashenden's family, who hide behind a mask of respectability, Rosie is openly and freely unconventional. She feels no shame when she and Driffield bolt from Blackstable without paying their bills. Sexually amoral, she indulges her natural affections and goes to bed with any man she chooses (including the ecstatic Ashenden, when they meet again in London). Her sexual adventures have no effect on her ingenuous character, and—though called a common strumpet—she remains "sincere, unspoiled, and artless." When her young daughter dies of meningitis, she assuages her grief by going out to supper with an actor friend and spending the night with him—a triumph, in her view, of life over death. Finally, she runs off to America with the married "Lord" George Kemp, the only man she ever really loved. Rosie remains a life force, even when Ashenden finally tracks her down in Yonkers, her once-golden hair now stiffly permed and dyed. Looking over the old photographs of Rosie, Kear calls her "a hefty wench" and Amy Driffield remarks that she looked like "a white nigger." Ashenden feels a pang of love; to him she was "virginal like the dawn . . . a tea rose."

Church records, when his uncle was vicar, reveal that the names Maugham used for his fictional characters belonged to real people who lived in Whitstable. In the church, as in Rosie's love life, one man displaced the other: "At the vestry meeting, the vicar, the Reverend H.M. Maugham in the chair, Mr. F. Kemp was chosen in place of Mr. C.M. Driffield, who'd become disqualified by reason of non-attendance to his duties." In *Cakes and Ale* "Lord" George Kemp, Rosie's most prominent and ultimately victorious lover, is a coal merchant known for his grand manner as well as for his cordial and breezy personality. When he goes bankrupt and, like the Driffields, shoots the moon and disappears with all the cash, the whole town is indignant: "They could not forgive him because he had always been so noisy and boisterous, because he had chaffed them and stood them drinks and given them garden parties, because he had driven such a smart trap and wore his brown billycock hat at such a rakish angle."[3]

Maugham conflated two Whitstable models to create his own George Kemp. According to a local informant, one of the prototypes for "Lord" George had a bland personality and led a boring existence—until he stole a great deal of money and ran off to America: "The real George Kemp led an unexciting kind of life, keeping a draper's shop & as side lines acting as Secretary to the Oyster Company, & as Registrar of Births & Deaths. . . . He was a fussy little man, busy in public affairs. . . . He owned a magic lantern & periodically would entertain the boys at the Board School. . . . He, to the great surprise & horror of the townspeople, mistook the Company's money for his own & fled the country. . . . His defalcations were probably due to his large & expensive family." But the model for "Lord" George's flamboyant personality and exuberant way of life was the architect and surveyor Arthur Albert Kemp (1865–1937):

> He moved to Whitstable in 1890 with his wife Fanny and children, and was appointed to run the Tankerton Estates. Right from the start he gained the reputation as one who lived life to the fullest. He always wore a rose in his button hole and his trouser pocket seemed to be a bottomless pit of half crowns. He would go missing for a few days at a time and would be down town with his cronies taking part in oyster eating competitions and boozing sessions . . . and [dallying] in the arms of a string of women. He took his female secretary with him on business trips to Belgium, and was considered something of a rake and lovable rogue.[4]

II

IN LATE MIDDLE age Maugham grew increasingly concerned with the whole issue of literary reputations, especially his own. The main character and satiric target in *Cakes and Ale* is the writer Alroy Kear, whose bogus reputation provides a striking contrast to Driffield's real one. The novel has some of Maugham's most epigrammatic prose on this subject, and some wicked portraits of London lionizers. In his discussions with Kear and in meditating on his own career, Ashenden rejects the idea, cherished by highbrow critics, that popularity is proof of mediocrity, and notes that Driffield was considered a genius by virtue of his longevity. In the final pages he concludes that the writer's life is filled with tribulation: poverty and indifference, a fickle public and the hazards of success, tedious interviews and photographs, the ceaseless demands of editors and tax-gatherers, wives and gushing society ladies, earnest youths and maidens, managers and agents, publishers and critics, admirers and bores. But the author has one great advantage: if troubled by "any emotion or any perplexing thought, he has only to put it down in black and white, using it as a theme of a story . . . to forget all about it. He is the only free man." Like Rosie, Maugham seemed to proclaim his freedom to think and say what he liked, regardless of public opinion. In reality, of course, he cared deeply about his reputation, and *Cakes and Ale* is an extended meditation on the relation of literary value to literary fame.

Willie Ashenden and Roy Kear form the great comic contrast in the novel. Ashenden becomes an investigator of his own past as well as Driffield's, energetically uncovering the truth as Kear desperately tries to cover it up. (His landlady in Half-Moon Street is Mrs. Hudson, a sly allusion to Sherlock Holmes.) He could, if he wished, throw a bombshell into Kear's whole story, and laughs at the ignorance and arrogance of the biographer. Chiefly because it won't pay, Kear is particularly keen to omit anything about Driffield's low-class habits and background. "I shall do much better," he says, "to be allusive and charming and rather subtle, you know the sort of thing, and tender."

Maugham had satirized ecclesiastical careerism in *The Bishop's Apron*, and now attacked literary careerism in *Cakes and Ale*. Repelled by Kear's coarse mind, Ashenden is fascinated by how he's achieved, with so little talent, such an important position in the literary world. Kear makes strenuous efforts to achieve popularity and advance his career by assiduous flattery while less fortunate writers fade into darkest obscurity. He courts influential authors, even defangs hostile critics by inviting them to lunch and humbly soliciting their advice. He butters up the naive young Americans who drop in at Mrs. Driffield's house (he may one day need hospitality or lecture fees at their university), but brutally drops anyone who can no longer be exploited. He is, in short, a snob and a fraud, a time-server and bum-sucker.

In fact, Maugham shared some significant traits with his victim, the

Hugh Walpole

now forgotten Hugh Walpole. Both were born abroad (Walpole in New Zealand) and came to England as young boys. They grew up in churchy families; and Walpole's father, a bishop, was also named Somerset. Both attended King's School (though Walpole was ten years younger) and had served in Russia during the war—Walpole as a war correspondent and in a Red Cross unit attached to the Russian army. Most importantly, both were homosexuals, and this common bond sharpened the sting of Maugham's portrait. Maugham enjoyed poking fun at him, "telling his friends of an alleged attempt by Hugh Walpole to violate the Master, and of [Henry] James' passionate recoil—'I can't, I can't!'" In the novel Maugham says that Kear "must be forever denied the joys of domesticity and the satisfaction of parenthood" (which of course Maugham himself had had), and ironically reports that the American professors comment on the "virility" of his books.

In contrast to Maugham, Walpole was tall and fair. Kear, tall and well built, with wide shoulders and a confident bearing, looks honest, clean and healthy. Alec Waugh described Walpole as "tall, broad with a bulldog chin. Incipient baldness accentuated his high-domed forehead. He was fresh complexioned. . . . He had a boyish eagerness: he looked thoroughly wholesome . . . had an easy forthcoming manner." Frank Swinnerton—emphasizing, as Maugham did, Walpole's negative qualities—called him "boisterous, laughing, copious, vain, and—not schemingly, almost naively—ambitious."[5] Walpole, recognizing in the text the same digs Maugham had made in conversation, reluctantly admitted his likeness to Kear yet tried to blame Maugham for having the same defects: "There were countless little points that were known especially between us, that he had chaffed me on in the past. . . . Was there real justification for that point of view? After real examination, I could clear myself on most of the criticism, although I can quite clearly see that I might appear just such a figure to a cynic and an uneasy unhappy man like Willie. It is his nature to be deeply sentimental and to be revolted by his sentimentality, so he turns on anyone he thinks sentimental."

Walpole confided his misery to Virginia Woolf, a keen observer of London literary life. In her diary of November 5, 1930, she took malicious pleasure in Maugham's barbs:

> Hugh & his piteous, writhing & wincing & ridiculous & flaying alive story of Willie Maugham's portrait. Indeed it was a clever piece of torture; Hugh palpably exposed as the hypocritical booming thick skinned popular novelist, who lectures on young novelists & makes his own books sell: who is thick fingered & insensitive in every department. . . . "That's not what I mind so much. What I mind are a few little things—little things Willie & I had together—only he & I knew—those he has put into print. That's what I can't get over. . . . I can't tell you all the meanings there are to me in his saying I was like a man in love with a duchess"—(the meaning is that Hugh is in love with a male opera singer) [the Danish-American tenor Lauritz Melchior].

Three days later, unable to contain her delight in Walpole's torment, Woolf improved the story and told her sister of his public ridicule and ruined reputation:

> Poor Hugh is most cruelly and maliciously at the same time unmistakably and amusingly caricatured. He was sitting on his bed with only one sock on when he opened it. There he sat with only one sock on till 11 the next morning reading it. Also, we gathered, in tears. . . . "There are little things

that make me shudder. And that man has been my dearest friend for 20 years. And now I'm the laughing stock of London. And he writes to say he didn't mean it for me."

Commenting on the effect of Maugham's mockery, Alec Waugh later noted that Walpole made a lot of money and was knighted in 1937. But when his "name appeared in the Honours List, people said, 'Ah, it's a consolation prize for *Cakes and Ale.*'" Walpole "had lost the respect of the only people whose respect he valued. He had become a joke to the intelligentsia."[6]

In 1919, ten years before his novel was published, Maugham acknowledged his affection for and attraction to the young and handsome Walpole. With the characteristically arch tone he used to express personal feelings, he said he'd blessed Walpole by metaphorically placing a shaking hand on his youthful locks. *Cakes and Ale* revealed how Walpole's methods of self-promotion had angered him over the next decade. But when the novel appeared, Maugham, for tactical and legal reasons, tried to mollify his victim by asserting that Kear was based on himself: "I certainly never intended Alroy Kear to be a portrait of you," he wrote to Walpole. "He is made up of a dozen people and the greater part of him is myself. There is more of me in him than of any other writer I know. I suggest that if there is anything in him that you recognize it is because to a greater or less extent we are all the same. Certain characteristics we all have and I gave them to Alroy Kear because I found them in myself. They do not seem to me less absurd because I have them." In a sense, this was true. Maugham craved critical recognition as much as Walpole, but he did not do what Walpole did to get it. In a second preface, to the 1950 Modern Library edition of *Cakes and Ale* (nine years after Walpole's death), Maugham again condemned Walpole's opportunism and hypocrisy, and finally admitted that he was the model for Alroy Kear. He described his old rival as a genial fellow whose friends laughed at him but found him appealing.

The true subject of *Cakes and Ale,* then, is literary reputations—not only of Hardy and Walpole, but also of Maugham himself. In 1934 Edmund Wilson, who would savage one of Maugham's late novels and do more than anyone else to hurt his reputation, recorded how competitive Maugham was about his writing life. He'd goaded Compton Mackenzie to keep up with Walpole, his close contemporary, and the angry Mackenzie had threatened to retaliate: "Maugham, in his malicious way, had once said to him years ago, when C. M. was just making his reputation, 'You'd better hurry up. Walpole is getting ahead of you!' Mackenzie had replied, 'Look here, Maugham: if you're going to be rude, I can be ruder than you—and when I'm rude, my rudeness is unforgivable.' "[7] Maugham liked to depict himself as aloof from the struggle, but he actually viewed writing as a fierce competition.

Instead of mellowing toward Walpole as he grew older, Maugham seemed to become even more furious and unforgiving. Sam Behrman reported that Maugham "detested Walpole. . . . If *Cakes and Ale* had helped to dispatch him, the book had succeeded beyond Willie's hopes." In 1949 Maugham told an American reporter that Walpole "was not angry because his feelings were hurt, but because, being a careerist, he feared his career might suffer from the satire." "I don't think I was cruel at all," he added, using one of his favorite similes. "I thought Walpole was an awful creature: he was as mean as cat's meat, and I hated the way he advertised and pushed himself."[8] Generous himself, Maugham loathed meanness in others, and felt Walpole deserved everything he got.

Maugham's satire provoked a counterattack as well as two novels by Walpole with nasty little portraits of Maugham. Evelyn Wiebe (1872–1942), a friend of Florence Hardy, had written (under the pseudonym of Elinor Mordaunt) many travel books on Asia, which had been eclipsed by Maugham's superior works. In 1931, under the name of "A. Riposte," she published *Gin and Bitters,* which rather feebly portrayed Maugham as Leverson Hurle, "a small dark man, proud of his smallness; rather sallow; showing, even then, yellow pouches under his dark eyes; eyes as sad and disillusioned as those of a sick monkey."

Maugham claimed to be indifferent to *Gin and Bitters.* He sent a telegram to Walpole signed "Alroy Maugham" and, alluding to Walpole's novel of 1913, assured him that he was ready to endure all personal attacks with "FORTITUDE." Though deeply wounded, Walpole good-naturedly assured Maugham that he had nothing to do with *Gin and Bitters* and urged him to suppress the damp squib that had damaged Maugham's reputation as well as his own:

> I do most earnestly beg you to injunct its publication in England. It is a *foul* book (I have no idea who wrote it save that it's a woman). If there were any doubt for whom it is intended that would be different, but already there have been paragraphs in the press here making it quite clear.

It will undoubtedly make a sensation and although you may not care what anyone says, it is a disgrace that people who don't know you should have that impression of you. . . . I'm not writing this from hysteria or any motive but one of real and true affection for yourself.

A contemporary cartoon showed Walpole punching the author of *Gin and Bitters* to prove he was *not* the satiric victim of *Cakes and Ale.*

Though Mordaunt's attempt to discredit Maugham would have fizzled out on its own, Heinemann persuaded him to issue a writ for libel. The English edition was called *Full Circle,* which alluded to one of Maugham's best-known plays and suggested some kind of retribution. Its publisher, Martin Secker, wrote that it was "a very readable book, containing an unkind but not I think entirely untrue portrait of Somerset Maugham. I had to withdraw the book very soon after it appeared, following terrible threats of libel proceedings and heavy damages from his solicitors. I had to destroy the rest of the edition, so that copies are quite scarce."[9]

Though not nearly as cutting as Maugham, Walpole could be equally duplicitous. In his novel *Captain Nicholas,* 1934 (whose title alludes to Maugham's fictional Captain Nichols in *The Moon and Sixpence* and *The Narrow Corner*), the novelist Somerset Ball is mocked by younger writers for his falseness. Suggesting (perhaps more than he intended) both the Villa Mauresque and homosexual baths, Walpole wrote of Ball: "his work is all iridescent, false in colour, brittle like those awful Moorish rooms you see in Turkish baths. It's even more glittering than the real thing and *all* sham from ceiling to floor." Three years later Maugham reappeared in Walpole's *John Cornelius* as Archie Bertrand, a clear-eyed realist with a straightforward style who tells the truth as he sees it:

His long bony body, the pale cadaverous countenance on top of it, does not speak for cheerfulness. He is, both in his outward self and in his books, a cynic, a pessimist. . . . Bertrand succeeded, beyond any man of his time, in one of the arts that for ever eluded Cornelius—the theatre. Then Bertrand's constantly expressed disbelief in men's virtues, their love, loyalty, sincerity, disturbed and distressed Cornelius, who wanted before everything to believe in his fellow men.[10]

In the end, the controversy with Mordaunt and Walpole merely fueled sales of *Cakes and Ale,* which quickly buried its rivals.

The critic Leslie Marchand, reviewing the novel in 1930, noted how Maugham's perfectly honed clinical prose exposed Walpole's pathological falsity: "It is a style that serves his general purpose of stripping life to the bone with a thin, sharp knife that lays open to view the normal flesh and the healthy flow of blood as well as the cancerous sore beneath." Evelyn Waugh, who learned a great deal from Maugham's satiric style, also admired his narrative skill. "The real interest and value of *Cakes and Ale,*" he wrote,

> depend upon the manner and method of its construction, rather than upon its subject. Mr. Maugham works with supreme adroitness and ease; he has in literature that quality which Americans, in social life, describe as "poise." I do not know of any living writer who seems to have his work so much *under control.* . . . This simple story is transformed into a novel by Mr. Maugham's brilliant technical dexterity. He is a master for creating the appetite for information, of withholding it until the right moment, and then providing it surprisingly.

Noël Coward reread the book in 1962. Ignoring the tender portrait of Rosie and the nostalgic scenes of boyhood, he felt the novel reflected the radical defects in Maugham's personality: "A brilliant novel but, oh, how poor Willie's unfortunate character shines through it. There is neither kindness nor compassion in it, wit, narrative quality, diamond-sharp observation, one or two streaks of profound vulgarity, much malice and no heart." The novel, however, gave Maugham the chance to revisit his childhood in Whitstable with humor, rather than bitterness, to express his own literary and moral values and blast those of his enemies. He liked it the best of all his books and, when looking for something good to read one evening, remarked: "What a pity that I wrote *Cakes and Ale.* It would be the very thing."[11]

III

IN 1931 MAUGHAM brought out *Six Stories Written in the First Person Singular.* The title emphasizes the importance of the narrator; and in "Virtue," "The Human Element" and "Alien Corn," "Maugham," the sophisticated traveler and writer, who lives abroad and revisits his upper-class friends in London, comments on and participates in the stories. People confide in him and ask his opinion, and they don't always like what they hear. "Virtue" displays his impatience with English attitudes about sex and love. A middle-aged wife's romantic yet platonic affair with a young Borneo planter on holiday in London leads to tragedy when her suspicious husband goes to pieces and commits suicide. In the meantime the young man has returned to Borneo and written to her to end the affair. Maugham and his meddlesome friend Janet Marsh, who has abetted the woman in her romantic fantasies, debate the issues of the story. Maugham argues that if the couple had gone to bed together the affair would have run its course and the husband would be none the wiser. His wife's virtue and honesty were irresponsible and cruel. Janet accuses him of cynicism, yet he maintains: "I prefer a loose woman to a selfish one and a wanton to a fool."

In "The Human Element" Maugham meets Carruthers, a diplomat and author, staying in an empty Rome hotel. He confides the story of his long-cherished but unrequited love for an aristocratic Englishwoman. Once married, now divorced, she lives in Rhodes—an unusual setting for a Maugham story. Carruthers has been to Greece to propose to her again, but discovered—through a series of scandalous revelations—that her handsome, low-class English chauffeur is her longtime lover. Carruthers is devastated, and cannot understand why she again refuses him. The worldly Maugham understands her perfectly. She is a serious writer, and her lover, taking care of her in every way, gives her the freedom to think and work that's more important than social status or money. The commitment to writing is a crucial issue throughout the story, and Maugham the professional looks down on the dilettante diplomat, who pretends it's merely a hobby. Repeating an idea from *Cakes and Ale,* Maugham consoles the diplomat and urges him to relieve his misery by writing a story about it.

The title of "The Alien Corn," the most substantial story in the volume, comes from Keats' "Ode to a Nightingale" and alludes to the biblical Ruth, who chooses a foreign God and foreign people as her own: "Perhaps the selfsame song that found a path / Through the sad heart of Ruth, when, sick for home, / She stood in tears amid the alien corn." Ruth's religion and "song" suggest the Jewish and musical themes of a story that portrays the conflicts and passions in a family who attempt to graft themselves onto an alien culture. George is the son of a wealthy German-Jewish family who've so completely transformed themselves, so carefully constructed their way of life, that they actually believe they belong to the English gentry. He disappoints them by leaving Oxford, refusing to join the army or enter Parliament, and going to Munich to study piano. His father gives him two years to prove he's first-rate; if he fails, he promises to abandon his musical ambitions. When his time is up, he plays before a famous pianist and (like Philip with his art teacher in *Of Human Bondage*) is frankly told he has no talent. Though he already knows the truth about his artistic limitations, he shoots himself.

The struggle between George and his family is only ostensibly about his choice of a career. It's really about social and cultural conflicts. Music, "in the blood of all of them," is a metaphor for the cosmopolitan Jewish culture the Rabensteins have buried under their new name, Bland.[12] George dreads becoming a fake Englishman and feels at home in Munich as he never does in his father's fake English house. His inability to resolve these conflicts drives him to suicide. Like Lawrence's "The Rocking-Horse Winner," the story also has a deeper, more universal theme: the cruel sacrifice of a child for his parents' worldly ambitions.

The best stories in *Ah King* (1933), named after a devoted Chinese servant, are set in Malaya and come close to the high standard of the earlier Eastern tales. A minor story, "The Vessel of Wrath," is named after the biblical proverb, "a woman scorned is a vessel of wrath," and set in the Dutch East Indies. Like "Rain," the story portrays a missionary and a sinner. But it's a lively and amusing tale about a prim spinster who reforms a drunkard and finally marries him, and probably inspired C. S. Forester's *The African Queen* (1935). In the film of 1938 Charles Laughton and Elsa Lanchester played it as broad comedy.

Two of the Malayan stories are exceptionally dark and sexually morbid. In "The Book-Bag" Maugham's host tells the story, suggested by Byron's relationship with his half-sister, Augusta Leigh, of two siblings who live isolated, self-contained lives on a Malayan plantation. When the brother goes to England, marries and returns with his bride, the jealous sister shoots herself and the shocked young wife flees back to England. This hothouse story was rejected by Maugham's favorite editor at *Cosmopolitan,* who drew the line at incest. "Neil MacAdam" pits a prim, innocent and somewhat androgynous Scot against the notoriously promiscuous Russian wife of his boss. On an expedition into the jungle, she declares her love and desperately tries to seduce him; when he resists, she threatens to accuse him of rape. Appalled by her advances, he leaves her in the jungle, where she gets lost and dies. These stories exploit the jungle setting to heighten a perverse sexuality.

The more successful "The Door of Opportunity," "Footprints in the Jungle" and "The Back of Beyond" are perceptive portraits of ordinary marriages gone wrong. Like "The Yellow Streak," "The Door of Opportunity" describes an act of cowardice in a dangerous situation. The district officer, unaware of and indifferent to the hostility he arouses, regards himself as intellectually superior to the planters. When Chinese coolies riot and kill the manager of a nearby rubber estate, he refuses to help, despite his wife's urging, and waits for reinforcements. When he goes upriver with the police, they find that three Dutch planters have captured the ringleaders and suppressed the rebellion. Mocked throughout the colony, the officer is summoned by the governor and fired, but still insists that he acted sensibly by refusing to risk his life for nothing. His wife is mortified and, when they return to London, leaves him. He's hidden his cowardice under intellectual swagger, but his blind self-righteousness finally cracks.

"Footprints in the Jungle" is a detective story with a violent love triangle. As in Hemingway's "The Short Happy Life of Francis Macomber" (1936), the wife sleeps with her husband's friend, the husband is shot when he discovers her adultery, and the guilty lovers successfully cover up the crime. The murder in the jungle is made to look like a robbery. The policeman discovers the truth a year later when a coolie finds the victim's watch, but he hasn't enough evidence to convict the criminal. Like the wife who'd slashed her alcoholic husband's throat in "Before the Party," the murderous couple, now a cheerful pair of middle-aged bridge players, continue to lead an apparently normal, decent life.

In "The Back of Beyond" George Moon, the Resident, known for his cold efficiency, is about to retire. On the day of his farewell party Tom, a young planter, comes to say goodbye and confides in him. A few days before he'd received news that his closest friend, a fellow planter, has died unexpectedly on board a ship to England. Upon hearing this news Tom's wife expresses such overwhelming grief that he realizes, and she admits, that they'd been lovers. Tom beats her, and now feels his marriage is over. Moon tells him that he'd made a great mistake when, long ago, he divorced his own unfaithful wife. This shocks the idealistic Tom, who says that Moon must be cynical; but Moon, as if speaking for Maugham, defends himself. If to "take human nature as you find it," he tells the planter, "smiling when it's absurd and grieved without exaggeration when it's piti-ful, is to be cynical, then I suppose I'm a cynic. Mostly human nature is both absurd and pitiful, but if life has taught you tolerance you find in it more to smile at than to weep."

Unlike Kipling's and Conrad's idealistic, self-sacrificial and dedicated heroes, Maugham's Englishmen rarely find redemption in their work. If they restrict themselves to the other Englishmen in the club, they become as narrow and provincial as commuters in the London suburbs; if they become entangled with native women, they come to disaster. Citing Maugham's considerable strengths in a favorable review of *Ah King,* the novelist William Plomer wrote: "To be a man of the world, to be acquainted with all sorts of different people, to be tolerant, to be curious, to have a capacity for enjoyment, to be the master of a clear and unaf-fected prose style—these are great advantages."[13]

IV

The Narrow Corner (1932) is Maugham's most elusive and underrated novel. The ominous title comes from Marcus Aurelius' *Meditations* (III: 10)—"Short, therefore, is man's life, and narrow is the corner of the earth wherein he dwells"—and suggests a remote place, a tight spot and the grave. Maugham's characters are Conradian white men, lured by the mirage of the East or running away from the West. Once there, they dis-integrate. As a Dutch official remarks: "It's a mistake to live alone in a place like this. They brood. They get homesick. The heat is killing. And then one day they can't stand it any more, and they just put a bullet through their heads."

Maugham took his inspiration from Conrad's *Victory* (1915). In both novels three strangers, suddenly arriving on a remote volcanic island in the Dutch East Indies, come into violent conflict with a pair of European lovers. In *Victory,* Jones, Ricardo and Pedro are criminals on the run. In *The Narrow Corner,* all three outcasts of the islands also have a shady past and a secret guilt. Fred Blake has fled Australia after murdering his mistress' husband; Captain Nichols has lost his certificate after trouble with an insurance company; and Dr. Saunders has been removed from the medical register for unethical practices. Most important, Maugham also adopts the covert theme in Conrad's novel. The homosexual connection between Dr.

Saunders and his Chinese servant Ah Kay, between Blake and Erik Christessen, echoes that of Jones and Ricardo as well as of Jones and the tragic hero Axel Heyst.[14]

Maugham first evokes the homosexual theme in his rapturous description of the androgynous Ah Kay: "He was a slim, comely youth with large black eyes and a skin as smooth as a girl's." He had exquisite white teeth, a slender ivory beauty and "a languorous elegance that was strangely touching." Saunders felt, or hoped, that Ah Kay regarded him with affection. In a similar fashion, both Saunders and the physically unattractive Nichols admire the astonishing manly beauty of Fred Blake. Like Melville's handsome sailor Billy Budd, Blake is cursed by his own sexual attractiveness, which leads to his untimely death. Blake had exquisite white teeth as well as "tousled hair, clear skin and blue eyes" and a springtime radiance. A fictional embodiment of Maugham's ideal man, he was broad-chested and tall, "with square shoulders, a small waist and slender hips; his arms and neck were tanned, but the rest of his body was very white."

On the tiny island of Kanda Meira (actually, Bandanaira, in the Indonesian Moluccas, northeast of Timor) the intruders find George Frith, a widower who lives on a nutmeg plantation with his beautiful young daughter Louise, and devotes his life to translating Camoëns' epic poem *The Lusiads*. Louise is informally engaged to a tall, powerfully built Dane, Erik Christessen, who works for a Danish company and had once been deeply in love with Louise's late mother. Blake is immediately attracted to the charming sincerity of the huge Dane, who brought out his own youthfulness and "loosened his constraint so that he seemed to flower with a new adolescence." He trusts, admires and even wants to care for Erik: "what had excited his embarrassed admiration . . . was the plain, simple goodness that shone in him with so clear and steadfast a light."

Despite—or perhaps because of—this intense admiration, Blake is also attracted to Louise, who, like Ah Kay, is seductively androgynous, "very slim, with the narrow hips of a boy." She's also drawn to Blake, and they soon become lovers. Like Maugham and Walter Payne in real life, Philip Carey and Henry Griffiths in *Of Human Bondage,* Blake forms a vicarious sexual bond with Erik by sharing the same woman with him. Just as Erik displaced his love for her mother onto Louise, so Blake displaces his love for Erik onto her. The love that dare not speak its name whispers suggestively through many of Maugham's works.

When the idealistic, almost saintly Christessen discovers that Louise and Blake have betrayed him, he shoots himself. Louise tells Saunders that "Erik killed himself because I'd fallen short of the ideal he'd made of me." But Blake is closer to the truth when he hints that Erik cared more for him than for Louise. He tells Saunders that "I seem to bring misfortune wherever I go," and the doctor caustically replies: "You should put a little vitriol on your handsome face. . . . You are certainly a public danger." Both Blake and Erik had loved older women. Blake was, he admits, responsible for the deaths of his Australian mistress and her husband— she was suspected of murdering him and hanged herself—as well as for Erik's suicide. Unable to forgive *Louise* for Erik's death, Blake now finds her repulsive and never wants to see her again.

At the end of the novel Blake, appalled by Saunders' cynical loss of faith and hope, is completely disillusioned: "If life means that virtue is trampled on and honesty is mocked and beauty is fouled, then to hell with life. . . . It fills me with horror."[15] The theme of illusion is evoked in the last paragraph and last word of the novel, and all the characters remain absorbed in their own unreality. Saunders' illusions are sustained by opium; Nichols believes he can escape from his predatory wife; Frith thinks his obscure translation will achieve success and secure Louise's future; Erik idealizes both the island and Louise; Louise hopes she can have both Erik and Blake; Blake thinks he can have both Erik and Louise. Finally, Saunders' homosexual longings for Ah Kay and Blake, and Blake's for Erik, are even more illusory, though more powerful, than heterosexual love. According to Robin, Maugham called *The Narrow Corner* his "queer" novel and was grateful that no one had noticed the real subject. Despite its covert theme, the book was a great success in America and Maugham earned a 20% royalty on sixty-seven thousand copies.

v

For Services Rendered (1932), Maugham's *Heartbreak House,* is his most serious and moving play. Despite the superb London cast—including Cedric Hardwicke, Ralph Richardson and Flora Robson—Maugham knew the subject was dark and unpalatable and did not expect it to be successful. In his preface he recalled conceiving and then rejecting strategies that would make the play more appealing: "During the rehearsals of this piece I amused myself by devising the way in which it might have been written to achieve popularity. Any dramatist will see how easily the changes could have been made. The characters have only to be sentimentalised a little to affect their behaviour at the crucial moments of the play and everything might have ended happily."

Like Lawrence's *Women in Love* (1920), the play portrays the effects of war and the psychological wounds on noncombatants. The Ardsley family and their circle of friends have all been injured by the war and have made terrible sacrifices. The blind son has no future; the mother has a fatal disease; the oldest daughter is unhappily married to a drunkard; the younger sisters must either become spinsters or kept women. The former naval commander, forcibly demobilized, commits suicide to avoid bankruptcy and jail. The rich man's wife is deceived and then abandoned. Everyone was happier before the war and has lost all hope after it. At the end, the crazed sister, believing the dead commander has proposed to her, comes down the steps in her best frock and in a cracked voice sings "God Save the King." Such patriotic sentiments had helped lead England into a victorious, but ultimately disastrous, war.

Frederic Raphael called *For Services Rendered* "a savage and brilliant attack on the illusions of the post-war world; it exposed once again the futility of heroism and the self-deception of those who uttered pious sentiments while others fought their battles." Maugham's play, like the savage poetry of Sassoon, Graves and Owen, brought home the truth—along with the mutilated bodies—that all the sacrifices had been meaningless. As Sassoon wrote, with bitter irony:

> Does it matter?—losing your sight? . . .
> There's such splendid work for the blind;
> And people will always be kind,
> As you sit on the terrace remembering
> And turning your face to the light.[16]

Maugham had praised Hemingway as the "most versatile and powerful contemporary writer of fiction in the English-speaking countries." The style and theme of his play were similar to Hemingway's *A Farewell to Arms*. Both writers achieved an incisive prose by deleting every word that was not absolutely necessary. "I try to say what I have to say with the greatest possible economy of language," Maugham noted. "I write as

though I were writing telegrams. And when I have finished, I go over it all
again to see what can be deleted."

In a famous passage in *A Farewell to Arms,* published three years before
For Services Rendered, Frederic Henry exclaims: "I was always embarrassed
by the words sacred, glorious, and sacrifice and the expression in vain. . . .
Abstract words such as glory, honor, courage, or hallow were obscene
beside the concrete names of villages, the numbers of roads, the names of
rivers, the numbers of regiments and the dates." The abstractions were
lies. Only the actual places where men had fought had any dignity and
meaning. Maugham's blind hero, Simon Ardsley, expresses exactly the
same idea: "I know that we were the dupes of the incompetent fools who
ruled the nations. I know that we were sacrificed to their vanity, their greed
and their stupidity. . . . It's all bunk what they're saying to you, about honour and patriotism and glory."[17]

Sheppey (1933), Maugham's farewell to his dramatic art, is named after
an island near Whitstable, off the north coast of Kent. The strange mixture of styles—comic, didactic, fantastic—and the allegorical figure of
death made it a theatrical disaster. A humble barber and good man, like
Dirk Stroeve and Erik Christessen, Sheppey wins a fortune in the Irish
sweepstakes and wants to give away all his money. He also wants to live
like Jesus and quotes Matthew 19:21: "If thou wilt be perfect, go and sell
that thou hast, and give to the poor, and thou shalt have treasure in
heaven." Sheppey is considered crazy by his family, friends and doctors,
who tell him that Christian principles have no validity in the modern
world. Preserving his illusions, he dies in his sleep before they can put him
in an insane asylum.

Though most of Maugham's plays had appealed to popular taste, he'd
now written two serious dramas to please himself. But neither had been a
success and, always obsessed by the "pattern" of his life and the need to
control the phases of his career, he decided to abandon the stage. Ratio-
nalizing his decision, he told one interviewer: " 'The theatre is a young
person's game.' He thought a play should be instinct with the latest modes
of thinking, feeling about the problems of life, and turns of speech.
Young writers are more sensitive to the niceties and flexibilities of such
matters." He also explained to Godfrey Winn that he left the stage before
he became completely out of touch with current thought and language:
"No author should continue to write plays after he is fifty. He is inviting
derision if he does. Fashions change in the theatre much more radically

and swiftly than they do in other forms of art. You try to adapt yourself to the new mood, and only succeed in seeming old-fashioned. I had two fail- ures running, and so packed up."

The stage director Richard Eyre summarized the daring and innova- tion, the provocation and poignancy of Maugham's best plays:

> *Our Betters* was banned and if you ever see it you'll understand why—in what other play is a whole act so graphically constructed around off-stage sexual intercourse? *The Constant Wife* is a lively feminist vehicle: if your husband plays around, boot him out and get a sex-life. . . . *For Services Ren- dered* is a dark, sharp, cynical inquest into the death of First World War illusions. *The Circle* is . . . a celebration of the death of youthful sexual attraction which really does leave you wanting to cut your throat.

John Russell Taylor, surveying Maugham's career, called him "one of the greatest comic dramatists in the history of the British stage."[18]

14

India and Eternal Youth

1934—1938

AFTER HIS DIVING accident Gerald moderated his frenetic, reckless behavior. He was rewarded in 1936 with a new toy: a large and luxurious sailboat. The forty-five-ton, two-masted former fishing vessel, with an auxiliary diesel engine, was named *Sara,* after his mother. It had every convenience, as well as a sexually obliging crew, and was perfect when Maugham and his torrent of guests wanted to swim, lunch or cruise along the glittering coast.

The rigid routine of the Villa Mauresque was slightly enlivened by visits from the duke and duchess of Windsor, who had gone into exile and were drifting around the Riviera. The former King Edward VIII gave up the English throne in 1936 to marry the twice-divorced American socialite Wallis Simpson. The duke and duchess conveyed great prestige on their host and inspired the kind of upmarket gossip his English friends longed to hear. Maugham knew that the duke was a complete philistine, with no interest in literature, music or art, and he maintained an ironic distance from the dull, uprooted pair, the archetypal scandalous couple from one of his comedies. When Barbara Back's son wished to escape from his family, Maugham drily remarked that he didn't *have* to follow the duke's example and flee to Paris.

Raymond Mortimer, present on one occasion, found the exiled ex-king miserable, bored and out of touch: "We drank pink champagne. I called her Ma'am. I found her physically attractive [since she looked like a man in drag]—*un morceau de roi*. He looked so wretched and sad. He wanted to talk to me alone because I was a journalist, he wanted to know what was going on in England." During a bridge game with the duchess, Maugham had put down his hand and remarked: " 'I am afraid I am not a very good partner. I've only got a couple of k-k-kings.' Never able to resist a wisecrack, [she] flashed back: 'What's the use of them? They only abdi-cate.' " To which he loyally remarked: "I d-d-don't think that's in v-v-very good t-t-t-taste."[1]

Despite his hermetic luxury and exalted company, Maugham was often bored, eager for guests and gossip, keen to travel and find new stories. The villa "is a bad writing location," he told Garson Kanin, because, like the duke, "it is out of touch with the stream of life, with people, with happen-ings of import.... The best imaginations want constant stimulation. Sights and sounds." In late 1935 Maugham, who in the course of his life traveled everywhere in the world except sub-Saharan Africa, made his only journey to South America. He restricted his visit to the remote penal colony of Saint-Laurent du Maroni, on the coast of French Guiana, about eighty miles west of Devil's Island. The governor offered him and Gerald a house with two convicted murderers as their servants. Convicts had saved him from the tidal wave in Borneo, and Maugham got on equally well with these men. He told a friend that "I went over miles of the prison camp and think I saw everything there was to see. I was able to talk to a great many of the prisoners." He used this unusual experience in his novel *Christmas Holiday* and in the minor story "A Man with a Conscience" (both 1939), in which he ignored the brutal punishments and painted a pleasant picture of the infamous colony: "St. Laurent du Maroni is the centre of the French penal settlements of Guiana, and a hundred yards from the quay at which you land is the great gateway of the prison camp. These pretty little houses in their tropical gardens are the residences of the prison officials, and if the streets are neat and clean it is because there is no lack of convicts to keep them so."[2]

Maugham also returned to Spain, his favorite country, and in 1935 pub-lished *Don Fernando, or Variations on Some Spanish Themes*. Unlike *Land of the Blessed Virgin, Don Fernando* is not a travel book but a cultural history, a study of the leading figures, as well as the manners and customs, of the sixteenth-century Spanish Golden Age. The most revealing chapter is the strange, speculative account of El Greco. Maugham had devoted several pages to El Greco in *Of Human Bondage,* but never disclosed the secret that Philip Carey "felt the mysterious painter held for him." If he'd wanted to write about a homosexual artist, Maugham could have chosen the well-documented examples of Leonardo and Michelangelo, Sodoma and Caravaggio. El Greco had a common-law wife and son, but very little is known about his personal and sexual life. The absence of evidence allowed Maugham to speculate that El Greco's eccentric, antinaturalistic style, his sublimated passion, manic ecstasy and rapturous transfiguration of the flesh, his "tortured fantasy and sinister strangeness," derived from his homosexual "idiosyncrasy and abnormality."

Maugham's interpretation was probably based on his response to the writhing, full-frontal, naked male bodies in El Greco's *Laocoön* (1610) and his portrayal of ecstatic penetration in *St. Sebastian* (1578). He had also read two influential works: Carl Justi's "The Novice El Greco" (1908), which crudely asserted, "Launched on his career by a pathological problem, pushed by fortune to follow an ever rockier road, El Greco represents the most monumental example of artistic degeneration"; and Max Dvorak's "El Greco and Mannerism" (1921), which took a psychological approach and emphasized his neuroticism. Dvorak saw El Greco as a mystical Mannerist who would show the way to a world ruled by the spirit. He called El Greco "a great artist and a prophetic soul" and compared his emotional exaltation to Michelangelo's. In *Death in the Afternoon* (1932) Hemingway also argued that El Greco was homosexual: "Do you make him a maricón? ... Did you ever see more classic examples anywhere than he painted? Do you think that was all accident or do you think all those citizens were queer? The only saint I know who is universally represented as built that way is San Sebastian. Greco made them all that way. Look at the pictures. Don't take my word for it." Maugham strongly identified with El Greco and took his neurosis and degeneracy as evidence of his homosexuality.

In his most extensive and direct discussion of a subject he usually avoided, Maugham described El Greco's homosexuality in entirely negative terms—narrow, unnatural and emotionally deprived; frivolous, embittered, detached and self-righteous:

It cannot be denied that the homosexual has a narrower outlook on the world than the normal man. In certain respects the natural responses of the species are denied him. Some at least of the broad and typical human emotions he can never experience. . . .

A distinctive trait of the homosexual is a lack of deep seriousness over certain things that normal men take seriously. This ranges from an inane flippancy to a sardonic humour. . . .

He stands on the bank, aloof and ironical, and watches the river of life flow on. He is persuaded that opinion is no more than prejudice.

Disregarding many great writers from Plato and Sappho to Gide and Proust, Maugham concluded: "the homosexual can never reach the supreme heights of genius."[3] All this had very little to do with El Greco, but revealed a great deal about Maugham's own guilt and fear that homosexuality was an artistic handicap. Though a supporter and admirer of many homosexual writers, Maugham believed that great art needed to be grounded in "typical human emotions" and the "natural responses of the species." He was intensely ambitious, and may even have married Syrie and had a child to experience a wider range of human feelings and become a greater artist.

Maugham returned to this biographical theorizing in his equally intuitive but more convincing discussion of Herman Melville in *Great Novelists and Their Novels* (1954). He didn't mention the striking homosexual theme and the hero's thematically significant stammer in *Billy Budd*—though he'd heard Benjamin Britten's operatic version of the novella, with a libretto by E. M. Forster, in 1951. But speaking of the androgynous Harry Bolton in *Redburn*—whose complexion (Melville wrote) was "feminine as a girl's . . . his eyes were large, black and womanly"—he noted that it's "odd that so manly a fellow as [Melville] should have invented a character who was so obviously homosexual."

Maugham then moved (as he was unable to do with El Greco) from Melville's work to his life. He observed that "Melville had an eye for masculine beauty . . . [and] remarks more than once on the physical perfection of the young men with whom he consorted." Speculating that Melville (like himself) may have married to fight dismaying inclinations, he asked (in a rhetorical sentence, full of self-consciously Jamesian hesitations and indirections) how forbidden desires, repressed in life, affected a writer's work: "who can tell what instincts, perhaps even unrecognized and if recognized angrily repressed and never, except perhaps in imagination, indulged in, who can tell, I say, what instincts may dwell in a man's being which, though never yielded to, may yet have an overwhelming effect on his disposition?"

Graham Greene, Maugham's qualified admirer, favorably reviewed *Don Fernando*. He praised Maugham's portrayal of "the fierce asceticisms of Loyola and St. Peter of Alcantara, the conceits of Lope de Vega, the ribaldry of the picaresque novelists, the food and the architecture and the painters of Spain, the grim bright goaty land," and concluded that it was "Maugham's best book."[4] This is a surprising judgment, considering the longueurs of *Don Fernando* and the excellence of *Cakes and Ale* and *The Narrow Corner*. But Greene seems to have admired the book's mixture of personal revelation and enthusiasm for another culture.

Maugham had a pervasive influence on Greene's work. The title of Maugham's play *The Tenth Man* was echoed in Greene's novel *The Tenth Man* (1985). The Baudelairean idea expressed in Maugham's "The Fall of Edward Barnard" (with its theological title)—"Perhaps even the best of us are sinners and the worst of us are saints"—is crucial to the paradoxical mixture of good and evil of the whiskey priest in *The Power and the Glory* (1940) and Scobie in *The Heart of the Matter* (1948). Maugham's sharply drawn alien landscapes and disillusioned mood influenced the menacing descriptions in Greene's spy novel *The Human Factor* (1978). In *The End of the Affair* (1951), a critic calls the autobiographical writer Bendrix "a skilled craftsman whose work has greater sympathy perhaps than Mr. Maugham's."[5]

Their personal relations could be hostile. Ten years after *Don Fernando*, Greene criticized Maugham for compromising his gifts as a novelist by repeating the kind of formulaic stories that had achieved such popular acclaim: "There is such an immense talent, couldn't he, we feel, have tried for something a little more difficult, couldn't he sometimes take a few risks?" When told that "Greene said that *The Sacred Flame* was the worst play ever written, [Maugham] replied that he made that remark before writing *The Living Room*." He also said that Greene's *The End of the Affair* "s-s-shows what a really n-n-nasty man he is. I've known him for years and n-n-never thought that before." Yet they met occasionally, and could be friendly and relaxed together. One of Greene's friends recalled that "in 1956 [Greene] spent an evening with Somerset Maugham, who for once threw off his shyness and reminisced fascinatingly about writers and others whom he had known in the 1890s. Greene sat entranced, drinking steadily, and next morning had a fearful hangover and could not remember a word that Maugham had said."[6]

Maugham took pride in writing clearly and intelligibly. His editor was Alexander Frere, who'd joined Heinemann in 1923. Like Max Perkins, Hemingway's editor at Scribner's, Frere was afraid of offending the firm's most lucrative author and usually sent his typescripts directly to the printer. Maugham was, nevertheless, willing to accept criticism. According to Kenneth Clark he "was a very very very conscientious craftsman and he was prepared to do anything to get it right." Beginning with *Don Fernando* in 1935 and continuing through fourteen books to *The Vagrant Mood* in 1953, all his work was scrupulously edited by Edward Marsh (who was knighted in 1937). Two years older than Maugham, Marsh was an eminent civil servant, friend of Rupert Brooke and influential editor of *Georgian Poetry* from 1912 until 1922. As Winston Churchill's private secretary he not only corrected but also *wrote* some of Churchill's work. A devoted friend, he produced hundreds of pages of corrections and criticism— some of it quite severe—of Maugham's work and saved him from many mistakes. Maugham, humbly grateful, was delighted when at last he spotted a rare grammatical error in one of Marsh's books.[7]

Maugham took every opportunity to profit from constructive criticism. After reading Raymond Mortimer's review of *Don Fernando,* he wisely cut many pages of sixteenth-century dialogue from later editions. When the London *Times* reviewed the stories in *Cosmopolitans* (1936) under the condescending headline "The Mixture as Before," he was happy to adopt the phrase that doctors used to reorder a prescription and used it as the title of his next volume of stories. During what he called "supervisions" with the Cambridge don Dadie Rylands, Maugham gave him his latest work and said: "Now criticize it as you would one of your undergraduates' essays."[8] As late as 1956, three years after Marsh's death and in Maugham's sixtieth year as a writer, he asked the novelist Richard Aldington for frank comments, insisting that he could take strong criticism if it came from someone whose judgment he respected. Though Maugham was often called arrogant, he was extraordinarily modest about his craft.

II

IN 1931 OSBERT and Sacheverell Sitwell invited Maugham to meet T. S. Eliot, but the distinguished guests remained silently on guard during the dinner, and the evening, despite copious libations, remained a frost. Maugham painfully recalled: "Not a soul would talk. The time dragged; alcohol did nothing to us. We began to look surreptitiously at our watches; longing for a time when we might leave without rudeness." Eliot's obscure and difficult work—the antithesis of Maugham's—was greatly admired by highbrow critics; but Maugham disliked both his mandarin literary persona and his avant-garde art. In 1942 he told Glenway Wescott that he got very little out of Eliot's pompous and dry-as-dust essays.

Maugham criticized Eliot, but borrowed his images and ideas. In addition to the allusion to "Prufrock" in the title of *On a Chinese Screen* and the reference to Eliot's "the man who suffers and the mind which creates" in *Cakes and Ale,* he echoed (again without acknowledgment) a famous passage in "The Metaphysical Poets" (1921) in *The Summing Up.* Eliot wrote: "Donne looked into a great deal more than the heart. One must look into the cerebral cortex, and nervous system, and the digestive tracts." Adopting Eliot's medical metaphor, Maugham described artists' creativity as "an organic thing that develops, not of course only in their brains, but in their heart, their nerves, and their viscera."[9]

Maugham's long weekend in November 1936 at Renishaw, the Sitwells' family home in Derbyshire, was much more successful than the dinner with Eliot. The ancient pile, built in 1625, had a splendid view of the formal garden and yew hedge, of the lake and the park that stretched into the distance. There was no central heating and the corridors were icy, but plentiful coal from the family mines fueled the blazing fires in every room. Osbert, a charming if precious host, served food and drink that perfectly suited his guest. He loved to meditate on the long history of the Sitwells while surrounded by possessions that had belonged to the family since the reign of Charles II.

In August 1935 Maugham was shocked by the death, at the age of seventy, of his older brother Charles, which brought back a surge of memories about his own youth and family. He told Gerald Kelly that Charles was kind, unenvious and unselfish, and cryptically added that he'd had a rotten life. Maugham's annual visits to London to attend the theater, visit friends and catch up on the gossip also gave him the chance to see his daughter. Tiny, elegant and without much formal education, Liza was conventional, reserved and rather severe. Dominated by Syrie, she led the emptyheaded life of a celebrity debutante, and had become emotionally as well as physically distant from her father. Trying to idealize their relations, especially during her childhood, she later recalled: "Whenever he was home he used to read to me—Kipling and his other favourites—before I went to sleep. I treasured those moments. After the divorce . . . whenever he came to London, he took me to lunch at Claridge's, or to the theatre." In reality, as Liza admitted in a more candid moment: "I really didn't know him at all."

In *On a Chinese Screen* a character, speaking for Maugham, expressed resentment and jealousy of his son-in-law and emotional rival: "It's a bit thick to bring a child into the world and to educate her and be fond of her and all that sort of thing just for some man you've never even seen." In July 1937 Liza married Vincent Paravicini, the tall, handsome son of the Swiss minister to England. Nicolas Somerset, the son of this golden couple, was born the following October. Moved by the birth of his grandson but unwilling to show his emotions, Maugham retreated behind a theatrical mask and archly quoted Shakespeare's *As You Like It*. He was delighted to be a grandfather, but couldn't decide how to dress for the role. Should he grow a distinguished white beard and show a gentle benevolence or adopt a cadaverous and acidulous demeanor, "lean but not slippered"?

Between 1923 and 1929 Maugham published twenty-nine stories of 1,200–1,500 words in *Cosmopolitan* and *International Magazine,* which paid several thousand dollars each, and collected them in *Cosmopolitans: Very Short Stories* (1936). This volume, much inferior to his previous ones, contained only one outstanding tale, "Mr. Know-All" (1924). The vulgar hero, like the musician in "The Alien Corn," is Jewish. Max Kelada comes from the Levant, has an Oriental smile, curly black hair, dark skin, lustrous eyes and a hooked nose. A self-proclaimed expert on every subject, he's mocked by the other passengers (en route from San Francisco to Yokohama) as a know-it-all. When a woman who's spent a year apart from her husband claims her string of pearls are worth only $18, Kelada, a jewelry expert, confidently bets her husband they're worth at least $15,000. But after seeing the terrified look in the wife's eyes, he admits he's wrong, and, truly a gentleman, saves her reputation while sacrificing his own. "If I had a pretty little wife," he tells the exasperated narrator who shares his cabin, "I shouldn't let her spend a year in New York while I stayed at Kobe."[10]

In this story Maugham treats the theme of infidelity in a light and sophisticated manner. The unexpected ending, based on the uncertain value of the necklace, recalls de Maupassant's "The Necklace" (1884), a tragic and ironic tale of a young woman who borrows a diamond necklace from a wealthy friend to wear at a ball and loses it on the way home. She buys a necklace to replace it, spends years working to pay for it and finally learns she has ruined her life for an imitation. After Maugham's story was made into one of the films in *Trio* (1950), he said it was based on a real woman. Left alone for a year, she had an affair with a rich admirer who gave her an expensive necklace as a farewell present.

Maugham had sympathetic insight into Jewish characters in "The Alien Corn" and "Mr. Know-All," and close friendships with Bert Alanson and many Jewish writers. But some of the Jews he met on his travels offended his English sense of decorum, and he penned some caustic portraits. In *A Writer's Notebook* in 1916, he described an American Jew named Elfenbein, traveling from Honolulu to Sydney. He shouts all the time, is shrewd about money and is defensively self-conscious about his race. Though sensitive and kind, he can also be noisy and vulgar. He turns up again in *The Gentleman in the Parlour,* traveling on a ship from Haiphong to Hong Kong. In this more substantial portrait, he has few redeeming qualities: "He was aggressive and irascible. . . . Everyone seemed in conspiracy to slight or injure him. . . . He was odious. . . . It never occurred to him that you might not want his company. . . . He was the kind of Jew that made you understand the pogrom." Nevertheless, he ends the book with Elfenbein's definition of the human race: "their heart's in the right place, but their head's a thoroughly inefficient organ." When Maugham sailed from New York to France in June 1946, the passengers were mostly prosperous Jews who'd spent the war in America and were returning home. The worst ones, he remarked, inspired the Gentiles with rabid anti-Semitism.

Two years after *Cosmopolitans* appeared, the Spanish-born Harvard philosopher George Santayana wrote a scathing letter about the book. Like many highbrow writers, he accused Maugham of superficiality and of selling out for cash. Santayana "wondered at anybody wishing to write such stories. . . . They are not pleasing, they are not pertinent to one's real interests, they are not true: they are simply graphic or plausible, like a bit of a dream that one might drop into in an afternoon nap. Why record it? I suppose to make money, because writing stories is a profession." In the early 1940s, more than a decade before this letter was published, Maugham wrote an equally unflattering account of Santayana's work. Attributing Santayana's reputation to the American propensity to overvalue foreigners, he justly attacked the overwrought prose that obscured rather than clarified his meaning: "I have never much liked Santayana's style. It is too florid for my taste, and in the luxuriant garden of his jew-elled, cadenced phrases, I find myself frequently unable to seize upon his meaning."[11] Writers and critics may have been exasperated by Maugham's productivity, but his popular style has outlasted Santayana's precious prose.

III

THEATRE (1937), a cynical minor novel with an insider's view of the stage, reprises two of Maugham's favorite themes: disillusionment and sexual revulsion in marriage, and an older man's hopeless love for a mar-ried woman. Like other novels about theater people—Henry James' *The Tragic Muse* (1890), Klaus Mann's *Mephisto* (1936) and Margaret Drabble's *The Garrick Year* (1964)—it describes the temptations of acting and the double-edged power of the art of pretence. This brittle comedy of man-ners would have been more successful as a play, where Maugham could maintain the light tone despite the characters' bad behavior.

Like Syrie, the heroine, Julia Lambert, is vain, ignorant of art and cul-ture, manipulative and domineering. One of the greatest actresses of her time, she never stops acting and gradually loses her sense of reality. Instead of descending into madness, she realizes that for her, at least, the world of "make-believe *is* the only reality." The promiscuous Julia is a sex-ual magnet for all the other characters in the novel: her handsome and ineffectual husband, Michael; her old admirer, Charles; her young lover, Tom; the unnamed Spaniard whom she impulsively sleeps with on a train; and her lesbian patron Dolly de Vries. Julia is all ego, but has no fixed iden-tity. She is a sort of witch, capable of merging into every character she plays, satisfying a different need for each lover, keeping everyone in thrall and in play, yet incapable of loving anyone.

A current of perversity runs through the novel. Julia's own son Roger arouses her sexual jealousy and becomes her rival with Tom. Her longing for Tom suggests Maugham's homosexual feelings. She remembers "Tom's slim, youthful body against hers, his warm nakedness and the peculiar feel of his lips, his smile, at once shy and roguish, and the smell of his curly hair." The homosexual theme surfaces when Tom and Roger become attracted to each other, and when Charles timidly declines Julia's sexual advances and she's forced to "draw one of two conclusions: one is that he is homosexual and the other is that he is impotent. . . . She asked

herself if Charles had used his devotion to her as a cover to distract attention from his real inclinations."

Julia's selfishness reaches its peak at the end of the novel, when she
uses all her dramatic skills to destroy a young rival's career. Secure in her
self-love and her talent for deception, she's not at all concerned about the
harm she has done. Maugham's chilling portrait of Julia is not balanced by
any sympathetic characters; the others are either vapid or vicious. In a
nasty but enjoyable book, he depicts the theater as a social jungle where
actors must be ruthless as well as talented to achieve success.

In a shrewd review of *Theatre* Elizabeth Bowen, noting Maugham's
fatal inability to describe sexual passion convincingly, concluded that it
was "an astringent tragi-comedy, with twin subjects, love and art. Mr.
Maugham anatomises emotion without emotion; he handles without pity
a world where he finds no pity. His disabused clearness and hardness do, it
is true, diminish any subject a little. If great art has to have an inherent
kindness, his is not great art. But what a writer he is!"[12]

The autobiographical *The Summing Up,* 1938 (whose title borrows a
term from the legal profession), was more incisive and engaging. By now
Maugham had become a monument, and the book sold more than
100,000 copies in America. Instead of offering personal revelations (not at
all his cup of tea), he discussed the subjects that interest him most: literature, art, drama, ethics, religion and philosophy. He began, however, with
his irascible grandfather, beloved parents, and early life in Paris and on the
coast of Normandy. He described the evolution of his prose style from
mannered to chaste; his reserved and reticent personality; and his reputation as a cynic. He touched briefly on the King's School, friendship with
Brooks at Heidelberg and training at St. Thomas's Hospital; and confessed
that he'd never experienced fulfillment in love. After mentioning his alien-
ation from England and years in Seville, he devoted many pages to his
career as a dramatist and novelist, and described his stammer and his difficulty in achieving success. He discussed philosophy and his loss of belief,
and concluded that life has no meaning. In the absence of God, he put his
humanistic faith in Truth, Beauty and Goodness.

In the Victorian period the great writers—Dickens and Thackeray,
Tennyson and Browning—were also the most popular. But the great
modernists—Conrad and Joyce, Yeats and Eliot—were obscure and difficult, elitist and alienated from the general reading public. Maugham strad-
dled these periods and mediated between highbrow and popular culture.

Lytton Strachey, denigrating as always, had put down *The Painted Veil,* as if he were marking an exam, as "class II, division I." But no critic could explain why, with all his unevenness and imperfections, Maugham had been able to maintain a vast and faithful public for more than forty years.

No other writer (not even Norman Mailer) has been so obsessed with his own critical reputation. *The Summing Up* fired the opening shots of Maugham's running battle with the critics, who (he complained) did not expect perfection from their cook or their friends but demanded it from writers. Referring to the first five stages of his career—when he wrote *Liza of Lambeth,* his early comedies, *The Moon and Sixpence,* his exotic stories and masterpieces like *Cakes and Ale*—he justly complained: "In my twenties the critics said I was brutal, in my thirties they said I was flippant, in my forties they said I was cynical, in my fifties they said I was competent, and now in my sixties they say I am superficial." He maintained, with some bitterness: "I have no illusions about my literary position. There are but two important critics [Desmond MacCarthy and Raymond Mortimer] in my own country who have troubled to take me seriously, and when clever young men write essays about contemporary fiction they never think of considering me. . . . I look upon it as very natural then that the world of letters should have attached no great importance to my work."[13]

Despite the self-pitying tone and the public lament that helped to undermine his reputation, *The Summing Up was* praised by influential highbrow critics. Strachey's Bloomsbury friend, the eminent bluestocking Virginia Woolf, greatly admired the book: "She liked the clarity of his style, and also the honesty with which he tried to get at the truth. She liked the analysis of his own methods of writing." Stephen Vincent Benét, then a respected poet, called it "an autobiography of extreme intellectual honesty, by a man who wished to make a certain thing out of his life and has worked it out to that pattern. It is honest, in the field of its lens. And for consistent clarity and consistent ease, it is hard to match in contemporary writing."

Maugham gave comfort to the enemy in two ways. He maintained that he traveled only to get fictional material and was merely an entertainer; and he crudely abridged and even attacked (as with James and Chekhov) writers far greater than himself. Beginning with his preface to *Creatures of Circumstance* (1947), Maugham took up a Russian word that had crept into English after the Revolution, disparaged his impressive achievement and fatally conceded: "I have never pretended to be anything but a story teller. . . . It is a misfortune for me that the telling of a story just for the sake of a story is not an activity that is in favour with the intelligentsia."[14] In his heavy-handed abridgment, *The World's Ten Greatest Novels* (1948), he ranted: "how stupid it is of a certain class of critics, and unhappily also of a portion of the public that regards itself as belonging to the intelligentsia, to condemn a book because it is a bestseller. It is inept to suppose that a book that vast numbers of people want to read, and so buy, is necessarily worse than a book that very few people want to read, and so don't buy." Four years later, in *The Vagrant Mood,* he again voiced this tedious complaint: "my literary friends do not, I am sorry to say, look upon me as a member of the intelligentsia." And in 1956, after writing for sixty years, he continued to complain, to an increasingly unsympathetic audience, that "I was accepted as a member of the intelligentsia . . . which, some years later, when I became a popular writer of light comedies, I lost; and have never since regained."[15]

IV

IN JANUARY 1938, accompanied by Haxton, Maugham traveled to India. He had never been there before, partly because he didn't want to compete with his old rival, Rudyard Kipling, who was born in India. Maugham didn't care about Indian art, was prejudiced against the English colonial officials and thought he wouldn't like the country. Armed with introductions from his Riviera neighbor the Aga Khan, he completed a huge circle during his three-month journey on the subcontinent. He began in Bombay, went down the west coast to the Portuguese colony of Goa and continued south to Madras, near the bottom of the Indian triangle. The main attraction in Maduri—"a huge, continuous bazaar crammed with shops, street markets and temples," with pilgrims' hostels and home industries—was the enormous Sri Meenakshi Temple, "a riotously baroque example of Dravidian architecture" that drew thousands of people from all over the country.

He then went on to Tiruvannamalai, southwest of Madras, with its towering gateways and hundred temples. Turning north, he visited Hyderabad, and its fierce Golconda Fort, in the center of India; and Bidar, northwest of Hyderabad, a walled town with dazzling Islamic mosaics and tombs of ancient kings. He pressed on to Nagpur, an orange-growing region that had once been the home of aboriginal tribesmen. He then followed the traditional route to the Moghul cities along the Ganges, moving northwest from teeming Calcutta to Benares, with its naked holy men and burning bodies on the banks of the sacred river; to Agra and the Taj Mahal; to Delhi, the imperial capital; and back to Bombay for the ship home.

In his preface to *The Razor's Edge,* his novel about Indian mysticism, Maugham said he was more interested in Indian thought than in big-game hunting or the great tourist sites: "When I got to India and the Indians to whom I had letters of introduction found that I neither wanted to shoot a tiger, nor sell anything, but was desirous to meet philosophers, writers and holy men, they were interested and did everything in the world to meet my wishes." With a serious purpose and as guests of various maharajahs, Maugham and Gerald were on their best behavior. There were no sexual "larks," and both were terribly good.

He did, of course, see some extraordinary and quite horrifying things, including a fakir who took a blunt dagger and gouged out his own eye. In a disgusting spectacle that baffled Dr. Maugham, the fakir then walked about with the eyeball hanging out of the socket, put it back, rubbed it a bit and seemed perfectly all right. Just before his visit to the Hindu "saint" in Tiruvannamalai, Maugham fainted. Some pilgrims were pleased to believe he was overcome with awe at the prospect of an audience with the holy man, but he suffered from recurrent fainting spells, caused when his solar plexus pressed his diaphragm against his heart. "Darkness descends upon me," he wrote, "and I know nothing more till I regain consciousness."[16] He feared that one day the pressure would continue too long and finish him off. But these episodes, though frightening, were never fatal.

In his essay on "The Saint," Maugham seems to accept the holy man's mystical beliefs, but his description seems to parody the mumbo jumbo that had been served up to English audiences in the 1870s by Madame Blavatsky: "Often [the saint] did not pray at all, but let the deep within himself flow on and into the deep without. . . . By referring to himself as *this,* by writing dashes instead of his name as a signature, he meant to indicate that he was no longer a person, but a spirit absorbed in the Infinite." The fatal flaw in this essay and in *The Razor's Edge* is that Maugham, whose profound scepticism had led him to reject Christianity, didn't have a mystical bone in his body. He thought religious faith was accidental and subjective, that belief to one man was superstition to another. If the Christian "had been born in Morocco, he would have been a Mahometan, if in Cey-

Christopher Isherwood, early 1950s

lon a Buddhist; and in that case Christianity would have seemed to him as absurd and obviously untrue as those religions seem to the Christian."[17]

In Hyderabad, halfway through his journey, Maugham's concerns were more material than spiritual. He wondered, after being treated like a prince, whether he could ever readjust to paying for his own car and his own expenses. He'd had misgivings about the trip and expected to be disappointed, but he met a lot of strange people, found much to interest him and was fascinated by the experience.

Maugham shared an interest in Indian mysticism with Christopher Isherwood, who was converted to Vedanta and became a disciple of Swami Prabhavananda after moving to Los Angeles in 1939. He first met the short, ruddy and vivacious Isherwood in November 1938—shortly after he'd returned from India and Isherwood had published his Berlin stories—at a dinner party in London that included Max Beerbohm and Virginia Woolf. Maugham and Isherwood in fact had much in common. Isherwood had had a brief career as a medical student and had even watched an amputation at St. Thomas's Hospital. They were both homosexuals who lived abroad, wrote in a clear prose style intended to amuse and entertain their readers, and made a lot of money from the movies. They had traveled to India and China, and would adopt their young lovers as their sons. Both Maugham and Isherwood were puzzled and intrigued by the other's elusive character. Maugham called Isherwood "that delightful, strange man whom you could never really know." Isherwood, observing Maugham on an American lecture tour in 1941 and alluding to his Victorian origins and endless travels, told E. M. Forster: "He reminds me of an old Gladstone bag covered with labels. God only knows what is inside."

Isherwood's autobiography and recently published *Diaries* contain (along with Glenway Wescott's more uninhibited *Journals*) the most vivid and perceptive accounts of Maugham's character. In *Christopher and His Kind,* which made him a pioneer of Gay Liberation, Isherwood described himself in the third person. Piercing Maugham's forbidding persona, he wrote that "his dark watchful bridge player's eyes intimidated Christopher; also his stammer, which somehow made you feel that you were stammering, not he. But, behind the grim, vigorously lined mask of the face, Christopher was aware of a shy warmth, to which he was eager to respond. He would be honored to adopt Maugham as Uncle Willie, if only Maugham would let him."[18] Though Maugham never quite warmed to the avuncular role, he did become a generous, hospitable and intimate friend.

They continued to meet when Maugham worked in Hollywood during the war. In Isherwood's *Prater Violet,* the producer Chatsworth exclaims, in a backhanded compliment: " 'For years I've had one great ambition. . . . Tosca. With Garbo. . . . And do you know who I want to write it?' Chatsworth's tone prepared us for the biggest shock of all. Silence. 'Somerset Maugham.' . . . If I can't get Maugham, I won't do it at all.' " In January 1941 Isherwood noted Maugham's profound hostility to Indian mysticism and to Gerald Heard (Isherwood's English guru) as well as his homosexual guilt and his bad temper: "I was so pleased to see Willie again—that old, old parrot, with his flat black eyes, blinking and attentive, his courtly politeness and his hypnotic stammer. . . . Willie had made fun of Gerald [Heard], albeit quite affectionately, at a cocktail party next day, and had deplored my wasting my time with mysticism when I ought to be writing novels. But then he's like that: a mass of guilt and contradictions. I doubt if anybody really understands him."

When he visited the Villa Mauresque, Isherwood was surprised by the extraordinary vitality of his aged host and by the luxury of his establishment:

Willie himself shows immense energy—today he walked up to the abandoned chapel at the top of the hill and all along the ridge, over a trail of
broken stones. . . .

I want to say ssh!—as if we were in Mecca in disguise, and might give
ourselves away and be instantly strangled. . . . This place is truly a palace.
Ice water, Vichy and cookies in glass caskets by the beds. Your clothes
unpacked by the faultless menservants—I think there are only two, but
there seem to be about twenty. And they unpacked *everything*—including
Don [Bachardy's] movie magazines, our powder to kill crab lice and our
K.Y. [a sexual lubricant].

Maugham called Isherwood a contrary creature who hadn't yet fully
understood himself. Cautious and circumspect, the canny ex-spy who'd
never been caught in a homosexual act gave him some good advice:
"You'd b-better warn your friend Denham [Fouts] that his apartment is
b-being watched by the p-police."[19] Fond of vatic pronouncements, and
thinking of the impressive and influential tradition that included Wilde,
Gide, Proust, Mann, Forster and Lawrence, Maugham told Rylands that
"the future of literature belongs to homosexuality." He'd already predicted that "the future of English drama is in the hands of Noël Coward."
Now, like a king dividing his realm and handing over his scepter (but keeping it, as it were, in the family), he paid Isherwood a tremendous compliment by telling Virginia Woolf: "That young man holds the future of the
English novel in his hands." In 1954, when Isherwood published *The World
in the Evening* (whose heroine was partly based on Virginia Woolf),
Maugham retracted this prediction and blamed Gerald Heard for seducing Isherwood into Vedantism: "Perhaps I shouldn't have felt so let down
if I had not so greatly admired and cherished the Christopher of twenty
years ago. What damage Gerald Heard did to our English literature when
he induced . . . these talented writers to desert their native country for
America!"[20]

V

IN SEPTEMBER 1938, between returning from India and meeting the
youthful Isherwood, Maugham for the first time entered the slightly sinister clinic of Dr. Paul Niehans in Vevey, Switzerland, a country where,

Scott Fitzgerald wrote, "very few things begin, but many things end." The son of a doctor and of a mother who was the illegitimate daughter of King Frederick III of Prussia, the tall, handsome and athletic Niehans was "a top student, a sure marksman, an agile and inveterate equestrian, a champion mountain climber" and a swordsman who fought duels with romantic rivals. After earning a doctorate in theology and a medical degree, Niehans helped combat a typhus epidemic in the Balkans and, as a Swiss medical officer in the Great War, led two hundred Austrians in a battle against the Italians. His rejuvenation clinic, started in 1931, is still run by his descendants in the Hôtel Trois Couronnes in Vevey. Its hopeful if spurious treatment soon became quite fashionable among Maugham's rich and famous friends: Winston Churchill, the duke of Windsor, Noël Coward and Rebecca West; aging political leaders: Pope Pius XII, Konrad Adenauer, Charles de Gaulle and Bernard Baruch; and entertainers equally desperate to retain their youth: Charlie Chaplin, Marlene Dietrich, Gloria Swanson and Hedda Hopper.[21]

Niehans, author of *La Sénéscence et le rajeunissement* (*Old Age and Rejuvenation*), scraped cells from the still-warm flesh of lamb fetuses to revitalize human organs. After the slaughter and the silence of the lambs, he floated the cells in a serum and injected them into his patients with a huge hypodermic syringe. Though Maugham never went so far as to keep a flock of sheep and his own butcher on the grounds of his villa, he thought his revitalization was worth more than a few lamb chops. He repeated the Cellular Therapy in his eighties, in 1958 and again in 1962.

There is no medical evidence that Niehans' treatment, any more than Yeats' Steinach operation, actually worked. But the psychological impact was strong. Niehans' apparent success depended on a typical upper-class fraud: his royal blood and distinguished appearance, his persuasive manner and luxurious surroundings, his illustrious clientele, formidable reputation and secret formula. His exorbitant fees made his gullible customers believe that it *had* to be worth it. After the therapy, they were forced to give up drinking and smoking for three months, which probably accounted for any improvement that followed.

According to Maugham's Riviera doctor Georges Rosanoff, who "remained convinced that such therapy was harmful," the massive injections of fetal cells caused such a severe physical reaction that patients needed several weeks to recover. Coward, overwhelmed by the fad, wrote of Niehans: "I have a profound respect for the old boy. He has, I believe, a streak of genius. Everyone I know who has been treated by him swears that he is marvellous. . . . They can't *all* be idiotic!" The more sceptical Dr. Maugham confessed: "I don't know that it's worth a damn, and there's always the risk that something as violent as this may kill one. But, at my advanced years, it seems a worthwhile risk, a good gamble." Maugham remained exceptionally agile and lively into advanced old age. His postwar companion, Alan Searle, confided to Harold Acton that in gerontophilic Egypt "the lubricious natives had been magnetized by Mr. Maugham—whereas nobody deigned to glance at his junior."[22]

15

War Propaganda and Hollywood

1939–1941

MAUGHAM LIKED KNOWING members of the aristocracy, and was particularly delighted when his own family ascended from *Who's Who* to *Burke's Peerage*. In 1938 Frederic Maugham became lord chancellor, the highest legal position in England, and retired with a peerage the following year. Ten years later Liza married the son of a marquess and became Lady John Hope. After Frederic's death in 1958 his son, Robin, became the second Viscount Maugham.

Immensely proud of his brother's achievement, Maugham (no doubt referring to himself as well) told Bert Alanson: "It's very wonderful . . . that an obscure young man, without money or influence to help him, should by sheer merit in his profession achieve [such] a position." When Frederic's cheeky daughter Honor had lunch with Willie at the Savoy, someone mentioned a man who'd been kind to his wife. Honor cuttingly remarked, "no one could accuse the Maugham brothers of that." Though Willie referred to Helen Maugham, martyred by her marriage to the icy Frederic, as "your sainted mother," he was still loyal to Frederic and furious at the insult to both of them.

Disgusted by Willie's homosexuality and unwilling to acknowledge his literary achievement, Frederic was nevertheless proud of his brother's success. Evelyn Waugh recorded that during tea at the House of Lords in August 1946, "an old lord whose name I didn't hear sat with us. Frank [Pakenham] said I was a writer. 'My younger brother wrote a book the other day which sold a million copies.' It was Lord Maugham"—and the book was *The Razor's Edge*. The brothers were politically as well as temperamentally opposed. Bruce Lockhart reported that Frederic supported Neville Chamberlain's policy of appeasing Hitler and sacrificing Czechoslovakia: "Lord Maugham was so devoted to Mr. Chamberlain that, with little or no first-hand knowledge, he wrote a violent attack on the Czechoslovaks. In his *Strictly Personal* Mr. Somerset Maugham describes Mr. Chamberlain as 'a man, sincere no doubt and honest, but muddled with self-conceit, who put his party before his country and by his ineptitude and stubbornness brought it to the verge of ruin.' "[1] Both brothers—one in the cabinet, the other living on the Continent—had their fingers on the pulse of Europe. But Frederic predicted there would be no war, and Willie believed a war against Nazi Germany was inevitable.

Maugham published *Christmas Holiday* in February 1939, seven months before the war broke out. The title sounds banal, but points to an ironic contrast, which runs throughout the novel, between the traditional English Christmas and Charley Mason's trip to Paris (a gift from his parents) during the last week of 1937; between the "holiday" Charley inadvertently bestows on Lydia, the Russian prostitute who stays with him in his hotel, and the sordid life she normally lives; and between the holiday his parents have in mind for him and his actual experiences.

In his preface Maugham later gave an interesting account of how he got the idea for the novel. He had attended the Paris trial of Guy Davin (married to a Russian woman), who was convicted of murdering a rich homosexual friend and sent to Devil's Island. He made the creation of the book sound easy: "I only had to make [Charley] the sort of sensitive, ingenuous youth I wanted, invent plausible reasons for bringing him to Paris and devise the circumstances that would bring him into contact with one or other of the persons connected with the sordid crime."

In Paris the idealistic, naive Charley looks up his school friend Simon, a cynical, ambitious journalist who's given up Communism and preaches Fascist power-worship. Attracted to Charley but envious of his well-off artistic family and cheerful temperament, Simon suppresses his homosexual longings. When asked to take Charley to a brothel, he deliberately introduces him to Lydia, the Russian wife of Robert Berger, a convicted and transported murderer. In a Dostoyevskian self-abasement, the soulful Lydia works as a prostitute to atone for Berger's sin, hoping, somehow, that "my humiliation, my degradation, my bitter, ceaseless pain, will wash his soul clean."

Maugham based Lydia, known professionally as Princess Olga, on his friend and lover Princess Sasha Kropotkin, who'd once told Bernard Shaw, emphasizing Russia's spirituality, that her country "would give the world back its lost soul." Lydia's "high cheek-bones, fleshy little nose and eyes not set deep in their sockets" resemble the fine eyes, high cheek-bones and snub nose of Anastasia Leonidov in *Ashenden*. Like Sasha, Lydia had been poor, hungry and lonely, exiled and outcast; had lived in England for many years; and had intense conversations with the English hero about the Russian spirit in Tolstoy, Dostoyevsky and Turgenev.

Maugham uses the conventional comic situation of the young man in search of sex to frame the novel. Everyone—Simon, Charley's father, even the hotel clerk and the maid—assume he's having a sexual adventure. Charley plans to spend his five days looking at art, listening to music and getting some sexual experience, but instead becomes absorbed in the story of Lydia's passionate love for Robert, and how he committed the crime and was caught. He sees very few paintings; the music he hears leaves him cold; and though Lydia shares his room, he gets no sex at all. He hears Robert's story in three different ways: first from Lydia, then from Simon and finally by reading Simon's newspaper articles on the trial. The amoral Robert had used his good looks to entrap an English bookmaker and minor drug dealer and, as the hunter became the prey, had murdered him purely for sport. Charley gets perverse insights into love: the lesbian madam in the brothel, dressed in suit and tie; Simon's repressed sexuality; Lydia's mindless physical passion; Robert's ambiguous, criminal charm; and the homosexual low-life world of the bookie, whom the police assume "had been killed by some rough who wanted more money than he was prepared to give."[2]

Maugham's layered narrative teases out all the ironies of the story and shows Charley gradually discovering "that perhaps men were more complicated than he had imagined." Evelyn Waugh said the novel was the "work of a highly experienced writer, and one reads it with a feeling of increasing respect for his mastery of his trade. . . . It is brilliantly done and needs studying closely in detail; the transitions from direct speech to stylized narrative, the change of narrator as Simon takes up part of the story, the suspense that is created even though the reader already knows what the climax will be, are models of technique."

Glenway Wescott admired Maugham's political perception as much as Waugh valued his artistic skill. He argued that though the impending war is never mentioned, Maugham "explains more of the human basis of Fascism and Nazism and Communism than anyone else has done: the self-fascinated, intoxicated, insensible character of all that new leadership in Europe [Simon]; the womanish passivity of the unhappy masses dependent on it and devoted to it [Lydia]; the Anglo-Saxon bewilderment in the matter, which still generally prevails [Charley]; and the seeds of historic evil yet to come." Charley smiles at Simon's ominous predictions of war and social upheaval, and at the end of the novel, essentially unchanged by his Christmas holiday, resumes his ordinary English life. Charley doesn't realize that "the bottom had fallen out of his world." He embodies the good nature and complacency of the English who, "like children building castles on the sea sand . . . might at any moment be swept away by a tidal wave."[3] Living at a distance from England, Maugham was always perceptive about the way the world was changing.

II

When the war broke out in September 1939, Maugham said: "I was left without a staff, some were mobilized and some fled home to Italy, so there was nothing for me to do but to leave the house myself." He and Gerald took refuge on the *Sara,* which was docked in Villefranche. When the naval commander ordered them to leave, they set sail with a crew of three, passed Toulon and continued west to Marseilles, got caught in a storm and spent a month in the seaside town of Bandol. As Gerald swept, cooked and tidied up, Maugham established his regular routine: "At twelve there was wireless news from Marseilles. Then luncheon and a nap. In the afternoon I walked for exercise up and down the front or stood watching the boys and old men" playing *boules*. After scanning the afternoon papers, and waiting for the evening news, he amused himself by reading, and got through two detective stories a day. At sunset they had to shut themselves into the boat. Finally, thinking they'd be stranded there forever, they boldly hired an old taxi, told the astonished driver to take them the 110 miles to Cap Ferrat and reached home without hindrance by nightfall.

During the static "phony war" in the last six weeks of 1939, the British

Ministry of Information asked Maugham to write a short, propagandistic book for an English audience. He was instructed to find out "what conditions were in the army, how the peasants were taking the war that was being waged in their midst, and how the German propaganda was affecting the troops."[4] Kipling had published a patriotic pamphlet called *France at War* in 1915 just as Conan Doyle had brought out *A Visit to Three Fronts* in 1916. Maugham's equally effective *France at War* (1940) praised the French military effort and the high morale of the country, and sold eighty-seven thousand copies in the first two weeks.

Maugham took his task seriously. He interviewed a bishop and a country priest, and went to Strasbourg, which had evacuated its civilian population and was awaiting destruction. He toured munitions factories, the headquarters of the Fourteenth Division at Nancy and naval bases at Toulon; sailed on a torpedo boat and on a heavy cruiser. The commander of the Maginot Line, along the eastern border of France from Luxembourg to the Swiss frontier, assured him that they could hold out for six months. (When the attack came, they surrendered in four days.)

Like the Renaissance ambassador paid to lie abroad for his country, Maugham revved up the rhetoric and tried to give a plausibly positive account of French morale: "How intense the French effort is and with what determination the whole country has applied its energies to the prosecution of the struggle! Nor do I think we yet realize the spirit that has enabled the nation to accept with fortitude and resignation the sacrifices they have been called upon to make. . . . I have never known them more calm, more resolute, more single-minded. They have a sufficient confidence in their leaders and a whole-hearted trust in the generals who command their great armies."

There was a striking contrast between the entirely optimistic *France at War,* when he was merely doing his duty (and advocating the patriotic views he'd savaged in *For Services Rendered*), and his more candid account of the same events the following year. In *Strictly Personal* Maugham admitted that he'd been deeply shocked by the sudden collapse of France after the German onslaught in June 1940, which made his propaganda seem absurd, and frankly summarized the reasons for the military disaster: "The General Staff was incompetent; the officers were vain, ill-instructed in modern warfare and insufficiently determined; the men were dissatisfied and halfhearted." When Wescott asked what France would be like after the war, Maugham exclaimed: "By that time they will have eaten so much shit that they will stink of it." He thought they would never forgive the English for their shame.[5]

On Goebbels' blacklist for describing his espionage in *Ashenden,* Maugham had to get out of the country as quickly as possible. At Cannes the authorities had requisitioned a coal ship, the best they could get, to rescue British residents. Maugham was told to be on the quay the next morning with a small suitcase, a blanket and food for three days. For reading he took Plato's *Trial of Socrates,* Thackeray's *Henry Esmond* and Charlotte Brontë's *Villette.* Italian submarines were patrolling the Mediterranean, and the voyage would be quite dangerous. Since his narrow escape in Borneo he'd been terrified of drowning, but preferred the risky journey to internment in a Fascist prison camp. Gerald's American citizenship, a liability in the past, now became an advantage. As a citizen of a neutral country he could stay behind, close up the villa and make sure all the precious possessions were safely hidden away.

On the harsh voyage, vividly described in *Strictly Personal,* five hundred people were crammed into a filthy ship meant for a crew of thirty-eight. A few people went mad. Many others died en route, and the ship had to stop for a minute so the corpses thrown overboard wouldn't foul the propeller. The ship docked only briefly in Gibraltar, and the passengers were unable to change their clothes. Despite the dirt, chaos and danger, a Jeeves-like butler hovered solicitously and contrived to uphold the immutable class system: "Because I was a friend of his mistress," Maugham wrote, "he saw fit to give me the sort of attention he would have done if I had been a visitor in her house; at the crack of dawn he brought me a cup of tea, he brushed my grimy clothes and, though I was entirely indifferent to it, shined my shoes." Despite the butler's devotion, Maugham foresaw the crumbling of the old order in England. He shrewdly predicted, as early as 1941, that the next general election—which took place in July 1945, swept Churchill out of office and surprised most politicians—"will see a great Labour majority in the House of Commons."

Back in England, Maugham resumed his literary acquaintance with Cyril Connolly, E. M. Forster and Virginia Woolf. Connolly had just started *Horizon* which, after the demise of Eliot's *Criterion* in 1939, had become the leading literary magazine in England. In response, no doubt, to Connolly's invitation, Maugham sent him a lively essay on "The Decline and Fall of the Detective Story." He analyzed the classic elements invented by Poe and his disciple Conan Doyle, discussed E. C. Bentley's

Trent's Last Case and the work of Dorothy Sayers, and ended by praising Dashiell Hammett and Raymond Chandler, whose hardboiled novels had swamped the traditional English genre. Though publication in *Horizon* would have been a coup for both author and editor, Connolly rejected the piece on the spurious grounds that "it would do nothing to add to its author's reputation." Taking the highbrow's revenge on the all-too-successful Maugham, Connolly paradoxically told another contributor: "I don't say this is a *bad* article. It's good enough to be accepted for *Horizon* but not quite good enough for me to publish."[6] It finally appeared in *The Vagrant Mood* (1952).

Four years later, in October 1944, Connolly published "Raffles and Miss Blandish," by his old school chum George Orwell, on the very same subject. Maugham had stated: "It is a fault of the American authors of crime stories that they are seldom satisfied with one, or even two murders; they shoot, stab, poison or blackjack *en masse*." Orwell had been reading Maugham since boyhood, and Connolly may have shown him the essay. In any case, there's a striking similarity of ideas in Maugham's essay and Orwell's more famous piece. Orwell argued that there was an "immense difference in moral atmosphere" between E. W. Hornung's *Raffles* (1900), which had an almost schoolboy attitude, and James Hadley Chase's *No Orchids for Miss Blandish* (1949), which, filled with cruelty and corruption, was "a header into the cesspool."[7] Orwell blamed Chase's horrors on the American obsession with violence—though the author was (like Raymond Chandler) English. Though often accused of being spiteful and vindictive, Maugham did not resent Connolly's rejection. In 1946 he told Monroe Wheeler, Wescott's companion and a curator at the Museum of Modern Art, that though Connolly had a porcine appearance he was amusing and kind, and urged Wheeler to meet him.

While Maugham's masterpieces, like *Of Human Bondage, Ashenden* and *Cakes and Ale,* failed to establish his literary status, the reputation of Forster, who had not published a novel since *A Passage to India* in 1924, paradoxically continued to grow. In 1932 Forster had invited the young South African novelist William Plomer to meet Maugham and the art critic Herbert Read. The occasion was a disaster. Read, extremely hostile and aggressive toward Maugham, attacked "contemptible people who write for money, like you." Maugham, with his stammer and Edwardian manners, did not respond to such boorish behavior. The Left-wing Read went on to make his own career: he earned as much money as he could, became an establishment figure and eventually accepted a knighthood.

Forster, not immune to the lure of celebrity, took care to maintain relations with Maugham. Great figures always like to know and be seen with each other. A few years later Forster ran into the critic Walter Allen and told him: " 'I'm walking across the Park to lunch with Willie Maugham. I do so whenever he's in London.' Then it was as though he were assailed by a sudden doubt. He thought and then he said: 'I can't think why.' " Maugham was a sharp critic of Forster and wrote to Isherwood about the fatal weakness in Forster's characters. Forster was a gifted novelist, he said, with sensitivity, style, keen powers of observation and the ability to create living people. But, citing the melodramatic ending of *Howards End* and the behavior of Adela and Mrs. Moore in the Indian caves, he concluded that Forster could not make his characters behave in a convincing way.

In November 1938 Virginia Woolf, forgetting that Maugham's stammer made it very difficult for him to speak, wrote a vitriolic description of his morbid appearance and disconcerting silence:

Willie Maugham came in: like a dead man whose beard or moustache had grown a little grisly bristle after death. And his lips are drawn back like a dead man's. He has small ferret eyes. A look of suffering & malignity & meanness & suspicion. A mechanical voice as if he had to raise a lever at each word—stiffens talk into something hard cut & measured. . . . Sat like an animal in a trap: or like a steel trap. And I could not say anything that loosed his dead man's jaw.

Maugham, by contrast, gave a brilliantly sympathetic and solicitous account of Woolf exhibiting, like Lear on the heath, her crazed and suicidal impulses in the midst of the London Blitz:

We were dining out together in Westminster—rather bravely it seems to me now because the raids were at their height. She was enchanting and we all stayed late. I and a friend said we would take her home but she utterly refused to let anyone accompany her, so there was nothing for it but for us to follow her at some distance—there were no taxis—and see that she came to no harm. We reached Whitehall and all was well, but just past the Admiralty two planes came over and the barrage began. We shouted to her to take cover but in the noise she couldn't hear us. She made no attempt to take cover but stood in the middle of the road and threw her arms in the air. She appeared to be worshipping the flashing sky. It was a most weird sight to watch her there, lit up now and then by the flashes of the guns. Then the planes passed by and she moved on, with us still behind.[8]

III

IN OCTOBER 1940 Maugham traveled to the United States, where he spent the rest of the war. He was reunited with Haxton, came to know a number of writers and made many speeches urging isolationist America to support Britain in the struggle against Fascism. Met by his publishers, the Doubledays, at La Guardia Airport, "his first remark was a request for an old-fashioned. In the airport bar he pulled out an ampule of poison and broke it into little pieces, saying, 'I won't need this now, Nelson.' " The writer Paul Horgan, who met the sixty-seven-year-old Maugham in New York the following year, recorded his striking appearance and world-weary manner:

> His face was pale, with deep wrinkles coursing down beside his wide mouth, which was permanently turned down. His eyes were startling. . . . His fixed gaze seemed to enter, diagnose, and judge person or object, all without emotion. If his manner was diffident, still, his effect was subduing. Weariness underlay a polite air. . . . His thin, dark hair was brushed straight flat backward above his high white forehead and seemed to draw his dark eyebrows up in angles of discomfort, as though from a chronic headache.[9]

Maugham was pleased by his enormous success in America as well as exhausted and exasperated by his celebrity. "I am tired," he wrote. "I have been interviewed too much, photographed too much and had too many parties given for me." It was difficult to find something to say to all the well-meaning but tedious flatterers, and a strain to have to live up to their unrealistic expectations. As he told Godfrey Winn: "when people chatter and chatter to me, saying all the flattering things that they imagine I want them to say, I know what they are really thinking underneath—what a dis-

Glenway Wescott, Bill Miller and Maugham, early 1940s

agreeable old party, and how dull he is in real life! How can he ever write all those clever books and amusing plays?" On one occasion a stranger rang up, crudely flattered him and would not accept his polite but firm refusal to meet. Finally, in desperation, Maugham said: " 'But I don't want to hear your poem, sir.' There was a dreadful pause; then the voice said, 'Oh, go to hell.' "[10]

Maugham's closest American friend (after Bert Alanson) was Glenway Wescott, with whom he was unusually frank and uninhibited. Like Isherwood, Wescott was a young, handsome, homosexual writer. He "had been raised on a Wisconsin farm and his early life had been soured by the hostility of a father who despised his effeminate, artistic son. The conflict between them caused him to leave home at an early age and lead a wandering, unsettled life with various relatives. Finally he entered the University of Chicago on a scholarship. There he met Monroe Wheeler and the two began a friendship which, although not without its own bitterness and turmoil, was very durable." Katherine Anne Porter, who married Wescott's brother, was "put off by [Wheeler's] constant name dropping and his preoccupation with famous and titled acquaintances"—of whom

Maugham was preeminent. She called Wescott "a completely, boldly, successfully, genuinely wicked person [who] . . . made an art out of making mischief and keeping it at a boil with . . . constant intrigue."

Wescott's *Journals* offer some rich examples of his duplicity. In 1930, before he met Maugham, Wescott adopted a fashionably condescending attitude toward his work: "At least I *have* found *one* worthwhile book by Maugham—*The Gentleman in the Parlour*—rich with the reward of literary virtue, beautifully written in the hard way, but not, I am amused to observe, ever exactly beautiful. His lack of talent is so basic; it must be in the very cerebral tissue, like ophthalmic migraine. There is something minutely wrong not only with every sentence but with every idea." Later on, when he got to know Maugham and derived substantial prestige and benefits from his friendship, Wescott became considerably more tolerant of his "faults" and tended to overpraise the Master.

Maugham thought Wescott—more than twenty-five years younger than himself—amiable, charming and pleasantly loquacious. When he said that Wescott never seemed to get much fun out of sex, Wescott replied that he remained silent when things went well and complained only when frustrated. When Wescott became blocked as a writer, Maugham offered some professional advice. The important thing was to get the words down on paper; once this was done, he could always revise at his leisure. When his disciple finally gave up fiction in 1951, Maugham thought Wescott would be much happier without straining to do something he could never do well. He had, Maugham felt, every gift that the novelist needs except the one that was absolutely essential: invention.

In England Maugham had often been helped by Jewish friends: the publisher William Heinemann, the producer Charles Frohman, the novelists Reggie Turner, Ada Leverson and G. B. Stern. His wife had also been half Jewish. In both New York and California, where many of the people associated with the arts were Jews, his friends included not only the faithful Bert Alanson, to whom he owed a great deal, but also the American Cellular-Therapy doctor Max Wolf, the film director George Cukor, and the warm and witty writers Garson Kanin, Dorothy Parker, S. J. Perelman and Jerome Weidman. The playwright S. N. Behrman, a rabbi's son who admired Maugham but was also aware of his faults, noted that his expression "conveyed a kind of primitive resignation, as if he expected very little from life, but that he meant to make up for that little by distributing petty revenges. . . . I have never met anyone who had greater will-power, greater self-control than W. S. Maugham."[11]

Maugham's most unusual American friend was the flamboyant Jerome Zipkin (1915–95)—graduate of the Hun School and Princeton, real estate heir, bon viveur and social butterfly. Called the "First Fop," he later gained a modicum of fame as the intimate friend and "walker" of Nancy Reagan. When a waiter once asked if he could do anything for him, Zipkin, famous for his sharp wit, replied: "You can remove the lady on my right." Truman Capote, retaliating for some insult, cruelly exclaimed that his "face was the shape of a bidet." When visiting the villa, Zipkin loved to cruise the homosexual haunts with Haxton, and flattered Maugham with a flood of expensive gifts. After Zipkin had increased the rents of the poor Puerto Ricans living in his cold-water flats, Maugham caustically remarked that he could afford to be generous. He once told Zipkin, who was very good company: "it's no good asking you to write to me because I know you can't write anything but cheques: all the same you might tell one of your twenty-seven secretaries to let me know how you are and when you are coming to Europe."

Though Maugham was an extremely profitable client, he had a great deal of trouble with his literary agents. He dismissed William Morris Colles (who'd represented him from 1897 to 1905) for failing to press Heinemann to promote *The Merry-Go-Round,* and was successfully sued by Colles for a commission on the stage version of *The Explorer.* Maugham retained J. B. Pinker from 1905 until Pinker's death in 1922. He sacked Charlie Towne (1923–27) for signing a disadvantageous contract, but they remained on good terms. Another rascal, his wartime agent Jacques Chambrun (1941–47), was a charlatan and so-called count. He "had a bald head and the well-fleshed features of a gourmand. It was an ugly face, pendulous and lumpy . . . but the ugliness had a certain charm and elegance to it. . . . Everything about him gave off an aura of prosperity and good-natured joie de vivre."[12] Chambrun not only charged Maugham exorbitant commissions of 20 to 30%, but also kept more than $30,000 of his royalties. Maugham finally replaced Chambrun with Pinker's old rival, the stodgy A. P. Watt agency, which represented him for the rest of his life.

The British government asked Maugham to use his prestige in the United States and give speeches in support of the war, and he did this repeatedly despite his agonizing stammer. He had sought treatment of his impediment, brought on by stress in his childhood, though his visits to a psychoanalyst had (he joked) merely increased his sexual desires. Dr. Leahy, a Harley Street specialist, had taught him to keep his stammer under control, but it still prevented him from speaking or broke his train of thought. Maugham hated to have his stammer interrupted, and friends learned to be patient as he snapped his fingers or punched his fist into his hand in order to release the blocked consonant.

Don Bachardy, who visited the villa with Isherwood after the war, was surprised at the extent of Maugham's disability, which even after treatment led to long, dramatic silences when he was stuck on a word. Bachardy could barely control his laughter when the great man lost his dignity and was reduced to the level of an ordinary chap: "That's when he seems oldest—his mouth opens and shuts with rasping attempts at words, his hands tremble, and finally his whole body shakes with convulsions. Sometimes Alan [Searle] prompts him, and sometimes Willie manages to finish alone. But he always recovers and immediately regains perfect composure as though nothing embarrassing has happened." Maugham's conversation with the French artist Marie Laurencin, who asked him for an English translation of *je m'en fous,* revealed how he used his stammer for dramatic effect: " 'Wee . . . ell,' he stuttered, clicking his fingers trying to get the word out, 'I told her if she really wanted to know, i i i . . . t meant I dooo . . . n't give a fuck.' "

Maugham nevertheless became an effective public lecturer and used his glacial geniality to cultivate goodwill in America. Cecil Roberts, in New York during the war, noted the contrast between his public and private speech: "I was astonished to find that on the platform his stammer wholly disappeared. He was fluent and easy as a public speaker."[13] Sometimes—when nervous, tired or ill—Maugham would forget, in the midst of a witty and moving speech, what he was supposed to say. He then stared at the respectfully puzzled audience until the words came back to him. Lecturing at Yale in November 1942 and leading up to the dramatic curtain line, he started to say "the price of liberty is . . ." But he couldn't remember what the hell it was and had to leave his eager listeners in the dark. In a postwar speech at the Garrick Club in London, he gave the dinner guests an impressive display of courage and self-control. Breezing along and telling them " 'anything I may yet have to learn about life will be learned, not from the dusty highways and byways which I frequented in my youth, but from a comparatively secure and certainly more comfortable refuge . . . the v——.' He stalled at the *v*. . . . 'I'm just thinking of what I shall say next. . . . I'm sorry to keep you waiting. . . .' Then suddenly . . . he came out with it: 'the veranda of a luxury hotel.' "

In America Maugham not only made speeches, but also worked for British Intelligence as a secret agent. In a brilliant memo of December 8, 1940, to Lord Beaverbrook, minister of aircraft production in Churchill's cabinet, Maugham—a keen observer but not an expert in the field— summed up a difficult problem and offered a practical solution. He felt the British had wasted a lot of money when buying urgently needed American planes because they did not know enough about the methods of production and signed disadvantageous contracts. They could improve the situation by having British experts supervise the production of their planes, scrutinize the contracts, investigate the costs and study the price of modifications. He also kept a close watch on British subjects in America who "kept bad company, or expressed pro-German sentiments, or spent large sums of money of mysterious provenance. . . . 'Do you realize,' he told Wescott, 'that there isn't a week that passes that I don't get one of my poor wretched countrymen sent back to England?' "[14]

IV

FOUR OF THE ten stories in *The Mixture as Before* (1940), though not Maugham's best, are worth noting. The hero of "The Lotus Eater" (an echo of Homer and Tennyson)—like those in *The Moon and Sixpence* and "The Fall of Edward Bernard"—abandons his office job in a city and takes up an idyllic life in an exotic locale. Thomas Wilson, based on Ellingham Brooks on Capri, plans to kill himself when his money runs out. But when that time comes he hasn't the willpower to do so. Having wasted his life, he puts off death, as he'd put off his writing, from day to day.

"Lord Montdrago" is one of Maugham's rare supernatural stories. The proud and snobbish hero, the Conservative secretary for foreign affairs, is tormented by nightmares about his Welsh political rival Owen Griffiths (based on Lloyd George), whose career he has ridiculed and ruined. A psychoanalyst advises him to apologize and clear his conscience, but he cannot bring himself to do so. Driven to the edge of sanity, he commits suicide. When Griffiths dies on the very same day, he seems to be seeking revenge after death: "the enemy he had so cruelly wronged, unappeased, escaping from his own mortality, had pursued him to some other sphere, there to torment him still." In *Three Cases of Murder* (1954), a rather absurd film of crime and punishment, Orson Welles is melodramatically effective as the guilt-ridden Lord Montdrago.

Lionel Trilling defined the theme of "The Treasure" as the "high value of natural impulse and the absurdity of social convention." In this story, an English gentleman hires the perfect parlormaid and considers her a treasure. On an impulse he invites her to the cinema, supper and dancing, and takes her to bed. Appalled and embarrassed by his own behavior, he feels he has to dismiss her. But, knowing her proper station and wanting to keep her job, she behaves perfectly and acts as if nothing has happened: "Nothing in Pritchard's demeanour suggested that she had the smallest recollection of the night before. He gave a sigh of relief. It was going to be all right. She need not go." For the English, Maugham suggests, any behavior is possible as long as the social pretences are observed and the lower orders collude with their masters to maintain the status quo.

In "The Facts of Life"—a moral fable partly based on Liza's husband Vincent Paravicini, who played in tennis tournaments in Monte Carlo—a young Englishman (as in *Christmas Holiday*) is treated by his parents to a tennis jaunt in France. The boy's father, telling the story to three cronies (as Marlow did in Conrad's *Heart of Darkness*), warns his son not to gamble, lend money or get involved with women. Studiously ignoring this pompous advice, the boy wins at the tables, gets back his loan, sleeps with a woman and—in a Jamesian triumph of English innocence over European corruption—makes six thousand francs while doing so. V. S. Pritchett called the story a "brilliant comedy of extraordinary ingenuity and narrative skill . . . [that] exposed the fatal weakness of the moralist position."[15]

Maugham greatly improved the titles of his works when he stopped using the names or professions of his main characters—*Liza of Lambeth, The Hero, Mrs. Craddock, The Explorer* and *The Magician*—and adopted more resonant and suggestive titles from literary sources: *Of Human Bondage* (Spinoza), *The Moon and Sixpence* (a parable), *East of Suez* (Kipling), *The Sacred Flame* (Coleridge), *The Gentleman in the Parlour* (Hazlitt), *Cakes and Ale* (Shakespeare), *The Narrow Corner* (Marcus Aurelius) and *Up at the Villa* (Browning). *The Trembling of a Leaf* (Sainte-Beuve), *The Painted Veil* (Shelley), and *The Razor's Edge* (the *Upanishads*) all suggest the dangerously fine line between the extremes of experience.

Up at the Villa (1941), a slight, improbable novella, is still quite readable. In this work, as in "The Human Element" (1930), a wealthy widow refuses a proposal by her older, longtime admirer, and has an impulsive affair with a much younger and socially unacceptable lover. In the novella Mary Panton picks up and sleeps with Karl, an impoverished Austrian exile whom she scarcely knows, out of pity rather than lust or love. The sexually sacrificial heroine had told Rowley Flint, a charming waster and rotter (based on Gerald Haxton) who's also proposed to her: "if I ever ran across someone who was poor, alone and unhappy, who'd never had any pleasure in life, who'd never known any of the good things money can buy—and if I could give him a unique experience, an hour of absolute happiness . . . then I'd give him gladly everything I had to give."

Besides this absurdly generous impulse, there are several other disturbing improbabilities. Edgar, Mary's would-be husband, worries about her dining alone at night, but insists she carry a revolver she doesn't know how to use. When she wants to end their brief affair, Karl operatically exclaims: " 'But I must see you again. Once more, only once more. Or else I shall die.' 'My dear, don't be unreasonable. I tell you it's impossible. When we part now we part forever.' " Humiliated by her pity, Karl—in another operatic gesture—shoots himself with her gun. After Rowley helps her dispose of the corpse, he wittily remarks: "Now you can cry if you want to."

Mary confesses the affair and suicide to Edgar, whom she respects but doesn't love, so he won't feel obliged to marry her. In an interesting twist of the plot, he agrees to marry her despite her appalling behavior and to renounce the high office he's been offered in Bengal. But Mary, eager to be the wife of a governor, changes her mind and again refuses his offer. Rowley then blackmails her into marrying him. Maugham, for all his worldly experience, had a limited understanding of the emotional relations of men and women.

In the *Nation* of May 3, 1941, Morton Zabel, a first-rate critic and professor at the University of Chicago, savaged *Up at the Villa* by calling it "as unmitigated a specimen of fictional drivel as has appeared under respectable authorship within living memory." In his retrospective demolition of Maugham's character and works, Zabel, without a word of praise, condemned him for artistic timidity, lack of high seriousness and selling out to commercial interests:

> Since *Cakes and Ale* in 1930, he has turned out a succession of luxurious pot-boilers, *Cosmopolitan* thrillers, and Hollywood slick-jobs, equaled only by the similar procession of banalities that followed *Of Human Bondage* in

1915.... He lapsed into the perfect model of the literary journeyman, hostile to artistic risk or innovation, invulnerable to the serious claims of his profession, and apparently without conscience when it comes to lending his remarkable equipment to the highest sales values that tawdry smartness and banality command.

Zabel's rage was fueled by Maugham's *Books and You* (1940), a reading list with superficial comments on English, American and European literature. Maugham emphasized reading for pleasure and rashly criticized writers—James, Yeats and Joyce—far greater than himself.

The novella also had its defenders. Anthony West (son of H. G. Wells and Rebecca West), writing in the highbrow *New Statesman,* said that Maugham had brilliantly represented "three completely different types of male pride . . . exposed to a particularly deadly type of feminine sexual ethics."[16] The operatic quality of the love and death themes in the novella aroused interest in Hollywood, and Warner Bros. paid $30,000 for film rights. Isherwood (who would also work on the screenplay of *The Hour Before the Dawn*) wrote what he called "a bad script from a bad story." The studio could never satisfy the censor, and the film did not appear until 2000. The scene in which Rowley helps Mary dispose of the corpse was well done; but the movie, with Kristin Scott-Thomas, the badly miscast Sean Penn and Jeremy Davies, was a great bore.

Maugham spent the spring and summer of 1941 in Hollywood, where Haxton had an affair with Isherwood's future lover Bill Caskey. Though Maugham liked America, he was not impressed by what he saw there. After lunching with John Barrymore, who was sodden with drink and would die the following year, he exclaimed: "What a ham! He now wears his hair dark red with a white *mèche* [lock] sweeping up from the forehead, but he still has a perfect nose." Maugham had received help with *Of Human Bondage* from Sinclair Lewis and Theodore Dreiser, and had great admiration for Hemingway. But his condescending attitude toward Scott Fitzgerald, who'd died in 1940 after a disastrous career in Hollywood, reflected Fitzgerald's abysmal reputation in the decade after his death. Maugham dismissed *The Great Gatsby* and *Tender Is the Night* as disappointing and wondered if they could still be read.

Maugham was naturally drawn to the émigré English novelists, Isherwood and Huxley, who gathered round their forceful but muddled guru, Gerald Heard. Maugham called Huxley "perhaps the most learned *novelist* who ever lived," but remarked that "he is living in a colony not remarkable for its erudition." "They're all very busy with their soul's welfare," he regretfully noted, "and can't spare much time for social intercourse."[17] When Huxley's *Time Must Have a Stop*—about the conflict between spiritual and profane pleasure—appeared three years later, Maugham again lamented the pernicious influence of the Vedantic mystics. He called the novel well written and intelligent, but regretted that natural human feelings seemed to arouse Huxley's contempt. The book had hate, anger and a sickly self-consciousness, but no tolerance, charity or kindness.

When the syndrome that had caused Maugham to faint in India recurred in Hollywood, the stage director Harold Clurman maliciously *blamed* him—as if he were drunk rather than ill. He described Maugham "literally falling on his face in Romanoff's restaurant in Beverly Hills" and being rescued by Haxton: "A tall, burly companion (secretary or attendant?) lifted him from the floor and bore his body to the men's room." When living on Chesterfield Street with Syrie, Maugham had complained of coming down from his study and not knowing any of the guests in the house. In Hollywood he asked the host of a large party if he knew any of the guests and was told: "No. Do you?" Maugham praised the hospitality, cordiality and kindness he found in Hollywood, but concluded that life there was mindless and horrible.

Maugham kept in touch with Liza, who also spent the war years in America. He once told her that he'd always wanted a son and confessed that "it took me nineteen years to get over the fact that you weren't a boy." He rather defensively described their relationship by saying: "I think I was as good a father as she and the circumstances permitted me to be. I've always provided for her and for her children when that was necessary. I haven't demanded any loyalty or duty. I care for her." After her daughter Camilla was born in New York in 1941, Liza's relations with her handsome husband Vincent became strained. He drank heavily, gambled and lost a lot of money, and had many love affairs. When American women went mad about him, she became jealous and possessive, but, now more sensible and more aware of the value of money, she realized that he was weak and malleable, and she wanted a stronger man. Finally, their marriage collapsed. Reaffirming his fatalistic attitude to marriage, Maugham accepted the inevitable and said: "Obviously it is hard when two young things are separated for three years, one mustn't expect too much from human nature."[18]

16

Yemassee and
Haxton's Death

1942–1944

AFTER THE JAPANESE attacked Pearl Harbor in December 1941 and
America entered the war, there was no longer a need for Maugham's propagandistic speeches. Cut off from his villa and drifting around America,
he wanted a home and a place to write his new novel, *The Razor's Edge*.
Nelson Doubleday had offered to build a house for him on his South Carolina plantation, and at the end of the year Maugham moved to Yemassee
where, apart from summers on Martha's Vineyard, he spent the next four
years. Haxton, bored in that isolated spot, soon left to take a clerical job
with the Office of Strategic Services, an espionage agency in Washington.

The three-bedroom, three-bathroom, white clapboard house had a
fireplace and built-in bookcases. There were also two separate cottages—
one to write in, the other for the three black servants: a cook, a maid and
a gardener. Remote and lonely, two miles from the main house where
the Doubledays spent their holidays, Yemassee was forty miles north of
Beaufort and sixty miles west of Charleston. Impressed by his jungly
surroundings—with its dense briars and mossy cypress trees, treacherous
bogs and quicksands, wild animals and venomous snakes—Maugham said:
"I face a great marsh, 1,000 acres of it, and on the side I have the river
Combahee; and behind a great row of magnificent pines. It is a lovely spot,

but it is far from everywhere . . . thirteen miles in fine weather . . . twenty miles in wet . . . from the nearest village."

Wescott, who visited Maugham and went riding with him, described the miasmic setting: "the river is backed up all around it, coiled like a serpent in a nest of banks and islets. . . . [One rides] some miles through the swamp, where everything is a little broken or rotten, posting through mud and water, ducking one's head down under the loose branches, unable to see where one is headed." Ellen Doubleday recorded the daily routine that increased Maugham's efficiency, provided a bit of social life and assuaged his loneliness:

> An early morning cup of Nescafé, made by himself, breakfast at eight in his own room where he remained reading "serious" books until 10 a.m., at which time he went to his writing room and was not seen again until exactly five minutes to one, when gimlets were served, followed by luncheon. Then a nap, the mail, a ride or a walk, and tea. At five he would appear at our house, ready for a game of bridge or gin rummy. At six, we had a drink and when the dinner gong sounded at seven, he usually went home for dinner. To bed around ten, when he tried to put himself to sleep with thrillers. There were occasional social, literary, and shopping jaunts to Charleston.[1]

Maugham settled in; and when a friend sent some saffron he planned to make one of his favorite dishes, *arroz a la valenciana,* as soon as he had guests to eat it.

While Maugham was far away in South Carolina, Heinemann tried to organize a tribute to him. The English usually celebrated the birthdays of eminent literary figures, like Shaw, Wells and the Webbs, but many people refused to write about Maugham and others never sent in their essays. After only two articles had been received, the project was canceled. Maugham's icy reserve and waspish attitude kept most people at a distance and—unlike Hardy and James—he was not revered or even well liked. His seventieth birthday passed without notice. Apart from a few exchanges with the maids he didn't speak to anyone all day, and spent the evening playing patience and listening to the news. Though many people would have been honored to spend time with Maugham, he was usually all alone.

Maugham's summer regimen at the Colonial Inn at Edgartown on Martha's Vineyard, off the south coast of Cape Cod, was also as regular as

Immanuel Kant's. He wrote in the morning, lunched alone in the hotel dining room, then took a short ferry ride to Chappaquiddick, where he got a healthy-looking suntan. The American social critic Max Eastman described meeting him "reclining in nothing but a blue bathrobe on a curved beach of wave-washed gray rock." After putting on slacks, a blue blazer and a foulard, he played bridge. He changed for dinner at the Yacht Club and went to the movies (no matter what was playing) every night. "I bathed a great deal, ate the most delicious clams in the world," he wrote, and (always attracted to Russians) "met some agreeable people, including Max Eastman, a charmer—with a crazy, gay Russian wife who cooked me delicious Russian food."

During his lonely but productive years at Yemassee, Willie invited his nephew Robin to visit. Willie never had a son, Robin was alienated from his forbidding father, and the two became close friends and confidants. A vivid incident, described in Robin's autobiography, seemed to symbolize his lifelong estrangement from Frederic. One evening, in a rare and alarming appearance in young Robin's nursery, Frederic brought him a bar of chocolate. Granted permission to eat it (after consuming a large dinner), Robin wolfed it all down. Then, while incorrectly reciting his multiplication tables, he threw up—to his father's horror—all over the floor.

Well educated at Eton and Cambridge and trained as a barrister, Robin seemed destined for a career in politics. But he chose to be a writer and lived in the homosexual world of theater and films, both in Brighton and in Ibiza. Willie's letters to Robin were paternal, tolerant and generous as well as ironic and witty. Old-fashioned, serious and correct in his outward life, he thought Robin should marry, have children and perpetuate the family name and title. While Frederic severely disapproved of Willie, Willie affectionately disapproved of Robin, criticizing his heavy drinking and dissolute friends.

Willie gave Robin avuncular advice about his writing and warned him of a tendency toward sentimentality that ill-became a Maugham. He also took an anxious interest in the military career of the last male Maugham, whose death would mean the end of their name. Willie boasted that during heavy fighting in North Africa Robin had a few of his tanks shot to pieces, but had destroyed five belonging to the enemy. After being wounded in the summer of 1942 by a piece of shrapnel in the chest, he was machine-gunned by a German plane while waiting to be evacuated.

Maugham and Robin Maugham, 1945

Finally, he was severely hurt when a piece of metal entered his brain—and never fully recovered from that wound.

Willie was as uninhibited with Robin as he was with Isherwood and Wescott. Frederic believed the Villa Mauresque would corrupt Robin's morals and weaken his character (if that were possible). But Willie, abandoning his attempt to reform Robin and striking back at Frederic, had urged him to visit the Riviera "with a boy friend, for I could not cope with you alone." After the war, when Robin went to Morocco, he slyly warned him: "Don't let an angry sheik catch you in his harem and cruelly castrate you. It would cramp your style."

By 1952, as disappointed as Frederic was with Robin, Willie called him as immature, scattered and frivolous as a child. His friends were disreputable, his spending reckless. "He has made a mess of pretty well everything he has tried to do," Willie told Alanson, "but remains convinced that he's a wonderful fellow. I don't see how he can fail to come to a sticky end. . . . It's all a terrible pity; he was a nice lad, with high spirits and great vivacity." After writing many novels and travel books, Robin finally achieved critical and financial success in 1963, when Joseph Losey made his novel *The Servant* into an excellent film with a screenplay by Harold Pinter. After Willie's death, Robin revealed his jealousy of Maugham in three increasingly unreliable and malicious memoirs.

An episode of mutual exploitation—a great contrast to his relations with Robin—took place on one of Maugham's visits to New York in the spring of 1943. David Posner, a teenage student at Lawrenceville School, wrote a fan letter to Maugham, was invited to meet the old man—and seduced him. "I was starry-eyed," Posner wrote. "I was hoping it would happen. I thought that the way to intimacy and to an understanding of his work was through his body. . . . He wasn't particularly virile, but he was full of lust. He was rather businesslike about sex, but it's equally true that there were occasions when we would spend a long time just fondling."[2] In return for sexual favors, Maugham paid Posner's way through Harvard.

II

MAUGHAM DISLIKED HIS propagandistic novel, *The Hour Before the Dawn* (1942), a story about the fortunes of an English family in war. At the request of the Ministry of Information, the author of the antiwar *For Services Rendered* felt obliged to crank out some convoluted patriotic speeches. The bereaved mother says that "we must try to find in our hearts the strength to look upon his death as a sacrifice we make willingly for the sake of the land we love and all we hold dear in this England to which we owe everything we are." He complained that he wrote the book "first as a movie, then as a serial, and now as a full length novel, and as you can imag-

ine got heartily sick of it. . . . It was hateful work and I found it very hard
to do because that sort of thing isn't really in my line. . . . The worst of it is
that I know very well it isn't a good novel and now that America is in the
war I need not have written it at all."

Though written to order, the novel is skillfully done, better than most
of his early fiction and still quite readable. The plot is unnecessarily complicated, and Maugham, like a Russian novelist, introduces far too many
characters at the beginning: the retired General and Mrs. Henderson; their
children: Roger (a daring intelligence officer) and his wife, May (torn
between loyalty and passion); Jim (a much abused conscientious objector)
and Dora (an Austrian émigré living with the family); the comically
affected Jane (who goes back into a burning house to fetch her makeup)
and Ian (her hopelessly inept husband); and Tommy (their youngest boy,
killed in a bombing raid on a nearby airfield). Maugham arouses our interest in the fate of the two pairs of lovers. May, in love with the Hendersons'
estate agent Dick Murray, leaves her husband and commits herself to Dick
after he's blinded in the war. Maugham had already foreshadowed the
fifth-column subplot of the novel in *Strictly Personal:* "there is an airdrome
somewhere in England which since the war has been repeatedly
bombed. . . . The airmen could not make out how the Germans had ever
discovered it, for it was in a secluded place and so well camouflaged that it
was practically invisible from the air." The delightfully ingratiating Dora
turns out to be a spy, and Jim strangles her after she lights a fire that guides
the German planes to the secret target.

In this novel Maugham alludes to the plot of Lawrence's *Lady Chatterley's Lover* (1928). Mrs. Henderson, trying to account for the eccentricity of
her daughter Jane, ironically tells her: "You're so vulgar, the neighbours
can't help thinking there must have been a little nonsense between me and
one of the gamekeepers." Later on May, like Connie Chatterley, would
stand "stark naked, and look at herself in the glass and revel in the beauty
of her slim figure, her breasts small and virginal." Fearful about Dick's fate
in the war and incessantly praying for him, May "conceived the notion that
if she promised God to give him up, God would spare him."[3] Greene borrowed this "bargain with God" scene and used it with great effect in *The
End of the Affair* (1951).

Maugham never published *The Hour Before the Dawn* in England, but it
reached a fourth American printing by October 1942 and was translated

into four languages. He sold serial rights to *Redbook* for $25,000 and film rights to Paramount (Isherwood revised the screenplay) for $65,000. Not bad, he boasted, for two months' work.

Alone in Yemassee, reflecting on his own traumatic experiences in World War I as World War II raged in Europe, Maugham revisited France and India in his imagination. In *The Razor's Edge* he returned to the theme of a young man who disappoints his family and friends while trying to find his way in the world. The novel begins as Larry Darrell, after aerial combat in the Great War, is welcomed back to Chicago by his bourgeois fiancée, Isabel, but realizes that nothing can ever be the same for him again. He leaves on a journey of self-discovery, and Isabel eventually marries his wealthy friend Gray Maturin. Maugham, who appears under his own name as narrator, describes the settings that range from America to Europe and India, and shares the confidences of the characters.

Larry's nagging fear that he was responsible for the death of a comrade, his searing guilt that made life seem cruel and meaningless, reprise the traumatic guilt of the main characters in *The Hero* and *The Explorer* as well as the bitterness of the blinded hero in *For Services Rendered*. One of the great lines of the novel—"The dead look so terribly dead when they're dead"—comes straight out of Maugham's experiences as a medical orderly and could have been spoken by Hemingway's wounded warrior Jake Barnes.

Maugham's most vivid characters had always been based on real people: Crowley in *The Magician;* Brooks, Kelly and O'Conor in *Of Human Bondage;* Syrie and Haxton in *Our Betters;* Sadie Thompson in "Rain"; Frederic Maugham in *The Painted Veil;* Barbara Back in *The Constant Wife;* Sasha Kropotkin in *Ashenden* and *Christmas Holiday;* Sue Jones, Thomas Hardy and Hugh Walpole in *Cakes and Ale;* Haxton in *Up at the Villa*. The same is true of the characters in *The Razor's Edge* (1944). Gray Maturin is modeled on Nelson Doubleday, Larry Darrell on Christopher Isherwood and Elliott Templeton on Henry "Chips" Channon. In his affectionate portrait of his publisher Maugham wrote that the impressively virile Maturin, a millionaire who owns a plantation in South Carolina, "was so kindly, so unselfish, so upright, so reliable, so unassuming that it was impossible not to like him."

Larry doesn't look like Isherwood, but both men have a boyish charm and natural grace; a modest, friendly and gentle manner; a curious self-possession and ingenuous smile. Like Larry, Isherwood had for a time renounced the world to study Indian mysticism and follow a holy master. In 1945 *Time* magazine stated, with some exaggeration, that Isherwood "lives monastically with three other men and eight women in a small house adjoining the alabaster temple of the Vedanta Society of Southern California. He shares his income and the housework with his fellow students, and daily ponders the teaching of his master, Swami Prabhavananda."

The connection with Maugham's fictional character troubled and irritated Isherwood, who felt that his identity had somehow been stolen. Responding to the *Time* article, he insisted: "I am not, as you have twice stated in your columns, the original, or part-original, of Larry in Maugham's *Razor's Edge*. I can stand a good deal of kidding from my friends, but this rumor [started by *Time*] has poisoned my life for the past six months and I wish it would die as quickly as possible." The fictional portrait, Isherwood felt, seemed to denigrate Vedanta and diminish the seriousness of his quest for oneness with God. Larry drops out of the novel for considerable periods of time, and the narrator actually encourages the reader to skip the tedious chapter on Indian mysticism that rather crudely interrupts the narrative. The novel, Isherwood wrote, gives "the impression that becoming a saint is just no trouble at all." Recognizing the difficulty of describing mystical experience, he added that "Maugham is greatly to be admired for his more ambitious attempt—even if . . . it is not altogether successful."[4] He was as critical of the novel as Maugham was of Isherwood's mystical volume, *Vedanta for the Western World* (1945).

The precious snob Elliott Templeton, based on "Chips" Channon and played in high-camp fashion by Clifton Webb in the film, is a worldly contrast to Larry. Channon, a wealthy Chicago-born homosexual and London socialite, was short, red-haired and thoroughly anglicized. After serving with the American Red Cross in World War I, he attended Christchurch, Oxford, and converted to Catholicism. He married the brewery heiress Lady Honor Guinness in 1933 and divorced her twelve years later. Pro-Chamberlain, anti-Churchill and anti-Semitic, he was Conservative M.P. for Southend from 1935 to 1958, undersecretary of foreign affairs from 1938 to 1941 and knighted in 1957. Unlike Isherwood, Channon loved publicity and in 1944 eagerly acknowledged his role in the novel: "I saw much of Somerset Maugham, who never before was a friend. He has put me into a book, *The Razor's Edge,* and when I dined with him, I asked him why he had done it, and he explained with some embarrassment, that he had split me into three characters, and then written a book about all three. So I am Elliott Templeton, Larry, himself the hero of the book, and another: however, I am flattered, and the book is a masterpiece."

The literary (as opposed to the personal) model for Templeton was Proust's magnificent Baron de Charlus. The description of Charlus' inverse snobbery in *The Past Recaptured* influenced Templeton's account of the social hierarchy in heaven. Proust wrote: "No doubt the snobbery of the gutter may be understood as easily as snobbery of the other kind. The two had in fact long been united, alternating one with the other, in M. de Charlus, who thought no one was smart enough to be numbered among his social acquaintances, no one sufficiently a ruffian to be worth knowing in other ways." Applying this idea to the celestial sphere, Templeton states: "I have always moved in the best society in Europe and I have no doubt that I shall move in the best society in heaven. . . . It would be highly unsuitable to lodge the *hoi polloi* in a way to which they're entirely unaccustomed."

Templeton's mandarin diction ("in the particular position I shall occupy I *feel* that a pearl is indicated"), his gorgeous silk dressing gown and startlingly chromatic dress, his extensive collection of richly bound pornography and residence in France, where "every facility is afforded to sexual irregularity," make him Maugham's most flamboyant and sympathetic homosexual character. Maugham's description of El Greco, his prototypical homosexual, applies perfectly to Templeton: "He has a lively sense of beauty, but is apt to see beauty especially in decoration. He loves luxury and attaches peculiar value to elegance. He is emotional, but fantastic. He is vain, loquacious, witty and theatrical." Innately frivolous, he "stands on the bank, aloof and ironical, and watches the river of life flow on."[5]

Maugham's important female characters, like Isabel Bradley, are the Lady Macbeths of society, willing to do anything and manipulate anyone to get what they want. Skilled liars and monstrous dissimulators, they dominate the stage and easily eclipse all the men. Isabel's revealing catalogue of narcissistic desires

> I want to have fun. I want to do all the things that people do. I want to go
> to parties, I want to go to dances, I want to play golf and ride horseback.
> I want to wear nice clothes.

is lifted directly from Hemingway's "Cat in the Rain" (1925):

> I want to eat at a table with my own silver and I want candles. And I want
> it to be spring and I want to brush my hair out in front of a mirror and I
> want a kitty and I want some new clothes.

Both "want" lists, which repeat the verb six times, are, like the characters themselves, childish, egoistic and trivial.

Maugham's story "The Buried Talent" (an allusion to Matthew 26:25), published in the *International Magazine* in February 1934 and never reprinted in his collected stories, clearly anticipates the death of Sophie Macdonald in the novel. A tragic drunkard, drug addict and nymphomaniac, she plans to marry Larry but is murdered and thrown into the sea. In the story, as in the novel, "she sold herself to coarse and vulgar men for a hundred francs. Any money she could get hold of she spent on drink and drugs. . . . She was fished out one morning from the harbour at Toulon with a knife thrust in her back."[6]

The narrator "Maugham" reveals a great deal about himself: his life as a young scholar in Heidelberg, as a medical student, as an admirer of El Greco in Seville, as a Bohemian in Paris, as a friend of Savinkov in Russia, as the owner of a villa in Cap Ferrat, as a collector of Pissarro and Monet, Renoir and Gauguin. Maugham gives himself some of his wittiest lines. He paradoxically states that the French mortuary was not doing a "lively business" and epigrammatically observes that "American women expect to find in their husbands a perfection that English women only hope to find in their butlers." His women also make clever remarks. Isabel warns him not to "bet much on my virginity," and Sophie tells him that opium dens have a "nice homey feeling."[7]

The epigraph of the novel, from the third *valli* of the *Katha Upanishad*, a basic text of Hinduism, announces the quest for salvation: "The sharp edge of a razor is difficult to pass over [or "difficult to tread"]; thus the wise say the path to Salvation is hard." (The Christian equivalent is Matthew 7:14: "Strait is the gate, and narrow is the way, which leadeth unto life, and few there be that find it.") Like the hero of *The Moon and Sixpence* who escapes from Europe to become an artist in the South Seas, Larry Darrell flees Chicago in search of knowledge. He's tutored by two mentors, the Polish coal miner Kosti and the Benedictine monk Father

Ensheim, before finding his guru in India. But the holy man Shri Ganesha turns out to be a coffee-colored, toga-wrapped version of the all-wise, goody-goody Mother Superior in *The Painted Veil.*

Many modern writers—Yeats, Graves, Huxley, Koestler, Auden and Isherwood—had plunged into the mists of the supernatural, the paranormal and the crankish, and by doing so had damaged their reputations. Maugham, by contrast, had concluded that "life has no meaning" and treated Ignatius Loyola's mysticism with detached amusement. He'd criticized Huxley and Isherwood's infatuation with Vedanta and mocked "the swamis swarming in America."[8] He called Indian mysticism "an impressive fantasy" and couldn't give a credible account of his hero's conversion. When the swami vaguely explains, "By meditation on the formless one, I found rest in the Absolute," Larry "didn't know what to think"—and neither do we. Larry's flying during the war is meant to make him feel "at home with the infinite" and to suggest a search for God. After finding enlightenment, he states: "I had a sense that a knowledge more than human possessed me, so that everything that had been confused was clear." But his transcendent state, which clarifies nothing, merely leads to his ludicrous desire to become a taxi driver. Maugham would have written a much more penetrating and persuasive (though less popular) novel if he'd followed his natural impulse to satirize rather than exalt Vedanta.

Cyril Connolly called Maugham "the worldliest of our novelists, and yet fascinated by those who renounce the world." He noted his weak attempt to portray mystical experience, but made a strong case for *The Razor's Edge:* "He handles his four or five characters to perfection and includes himself—not as a fictional character, but as the flesh-and-blood Willie Maugham of real life—with complete mastery. . . . Here at last is a great writer, on the threshold of old age, determined to tell the truth in a form which releases all the possibilities of his art." Raymond Chandler also defined his artistic strengths and explained why (unlike Connolly) most highbrow critics refused to recognize his merits. Maugham has "that neat and inexorable perception of character and motive which belongs to the great judge or the great diplomat. . . . His plots are cool and deadly and his timing is absolutely flawless. . . . The highbrows find it hard enough to forgive popularity . . . but popularity plus pretensions to any kind of literary distinction—that is too, too much. How they must have suffered over Maugham!"[9]

World War I had almost buried *Of Human Bondage,* but World War II gained readers for *The Razor's Edge*. Millions of people, appalled by the massive destruction and slaughter, were searching for a religious alternative to materialism. Maugham's book suggested that it was possible to discover the meaning of human existence, achieve enlightenment and become a saint. His novel shrewdly anticipated the ideas of Allen Ginsberg and the Beatles, who in the 1960s encouraged their followers to study Eastern religions and log in some time in the ashrams.

Of Human Bondage was still selling 30,000 copies a year, *The Summing Up* had sold more than 100,000 and even *Christmas Holiday* reached 44,750. *The Razor's Edge,* for which Maugham received an advance of $100,000, had a first English edition of 50,000 and a first American of 375,000. His bibliographer noted that he'd first achieved recognition in America "through the serialisation of his short stories in the Hearst magazines *Cosmopolitan* and *Nash's*. For these contributions he was paid a dollar a word up to 6,000 words. In a letter to Eddie Marsh . . . Maugham writes: 'Since you toiled over the proof it may slightly interest you to know that by the end of its first month *The Razor's Edge* had sold 507,000 copies. I will not pretend that I am not staggered.' " By his eightieth birthday in 1954, the novel (as Frederic boasted to Evelyn Waugh) had sold 1,400,000. No wonder that Nelson Doubleday was willing to do anything to please his most successful author.

Maugham also sold screen rights of *The Razor's Edge* for $250,000 against a 20% share of the net profits. George Cukor, stage manager of the 1926 American production of *The Constant Wife,* was supposed to direct the film, based on the screenplay that Maugham had offered to write free of charge. Cukor described how Maugham masterfully manipulated a Hollywood tycoon and finally extracted a very handsome payment:

> Mr. Zanuck, a dynamic little man, began to give his notions of exactly how the story should be treated. Mr. Maugham listened for a bit, then said, "Look here—I'll start from the beginning and do my best. If you don't like what I've done you can chuck the whole thing into the waste paper basket." After we'd left Mr. Zanuck's office Mr. Maugham's only comment was, "He speaks very loud, doesn't he? I don't like people who shout." . . .
>
> [Mr. Zanuck] asked "Would you please give me a list of your expenses?" Mr. Maugham said, "One dollar for a hair cut. I can't think of anything else." The next day Mr. Zanuck took me aside and told me that he'd like to give Mr. Maugham a present to show his appreciation. "Would

Maugham, c. 1944

he like a beautiful gold cigarette case from Cartier?" I said, "I'm sure he has a great many cigarette cases." "Then some very grand cufflinks?" I didn't think that was such a good idea either. I then suggested that Mr. Maugham might like a painting. Zanuck, very taken with the idea, said, "Maybe Mr. Maugham would go and select any painting he liked [up to $15,000]." It was then that W.S.M., clever fellow that he is, acquired a Pissarro.

Maugham later explained how he managed to get the painting he really wanted: "I bought a snow scene by Matisse. But I could not get the Pissarro out of my mind; I thought I should always regret it if I did not have it, so I exchanged the Matisse" for Pissarro's harbor scene in Rouen.[10]

When he completed the script, Maugham told Zanuck that it should be acted like a play onstage: "It was a comedy and should be played lightly. 'The actors should pick up one another's cues as smartly as possible, and there's no harm if they cut in on one another as people do in ordinary life.' Maugham was 'against pauses and silences' in favor of 'speed, speed, speed.' " In the end Zanuck rejected Maugham's script as too sophisticated and chose one by Lamar Trotti. Cukor said it "had what the studio called entertainment, which means dancing and country clubs and all that crap. Nothing to indicate you were supposed to sit down and listen to what was being said." Crudely comparing *The Razor's Edge* with the immensely popular *Going My Way* (1944), Zanuck said: "[Bing] Crosby wore a collar and talked baseball. Larry doesn't wear a collar and he talks religion."

Apart from Clifton Webb's brilliant performance, the movie, directed by Edmund Goulding instead of the more talented Cukor, was a complete dud. Pauline Kael called it "almost as irresistibly funny and terrible as *The Fountainhead*."[11] The Himalayan scenes were shot near Denver, and if Larry had looked westward he could have found his mystical answer among the swamis of Hollywood.

III

IN 1944 MAUGHAM's literary triumph coincided with personal tragedy. Though he loved him dearly, he'd been having serious difficulties with Gerald, the only one with "the power to unlock a door inside his shut-away secret wall." Godfrey Winn, a close but unsympathetic observer of Gerald's startling disintegration, reported that "Haxton, becoming more and more blurred in his speech, would insist on staying up all night . . . visiting a succession of squalid bars or bordels about which he would drop lurid hints subsequently in a bout of alcoholic confidences." His physical appearance, Winn noted, had decayed as his hostility to Maugham increased: "Already the signs of dissipation that was ultimately to destroy him were beginning to show on his face, and in his increasingly bloodshot eyes. . . . Haxton was grey beneath his tan, and his hand shook holding the cards at the bridge table, when he would speak to my host in a voice that was hardly that of an employee, let alone a privileged companion."

Since Maugham was paying a great deal for Gerald's gambling expenses and alcoholic adventures, Winn suspected that he was blackmailing his master. "You do not know what it is like," Maugham lamented, "and I hope you never will, to be married to someone who is married to drink." The move to Yemassee, far from the bars and casinos Gerald had haunted on the Riviera, created the impetus for him to move to Washington, and Maugham paid him off with $35,000. He'd become a tremendous liability, and Maugham was immensely relieved that he was no longer responsible for him.

When Gerald became seriously ill in April 1944 Maugham was inexorably drawn back into his life. Gerald had no one else to care for him, and Maugham could not bear the thought of him dying alone. Gerald suffered from Addison's disease and had also neglected his pleurisy, which turned into tuberculosis. During his ten weeks in Doctors Hospital in New York, it seemed as if he might die at any moment. Desperately seeking a cure, Maugham took him by ambulance to a tuberculosis sanatorium in Saranac Lake, a famous health resort in upstate New York, where he got worse and worse. When the doctors gave up hope, the increasingly frantic Maugham brought him to the Leahy Clinic in Boston, and then completed the circle by returning to the hospital in New York. Despite heavy doses of morphine, Gerald was racked by an agonizing cough. Instead of becoming strong enough for an operation, he continued to waste away.

On August 1 Gerald signed a will leaving his personal possessions to Maugham and his money to Robin, with whom he'd shared many sexual escapades. Two weeks later, attempting to be brave and cheerful in a letter to Barbara Back, Gerald revealed that he didn't know his lung disease was fatal:

> Babs, my sweet, I am in Boston at the moment and it is 101 in the shade, not very good for my T.B. but that is getting along fairly well. My trouble is that after every meal or even half a glass of warm milk I blow up as though I was going to have quintuplets. I am here to see specialists and so far, beyond deciding that the trouble is *not* tubercular, they've found nothing but ounces of morphia to relieve the very bad pain. It's the pain which tires me so much that writing is difficult and even getting washed is a burden.

In late August Maugham warned a friend to keep up Gerald's morale by remaining optimistic when visiting the hospital.

The following month Maugham admitted that Gerald "twice has been on the point of dying. The doctors hold out very little hope of recovery." But in October (only a month before the end) Gerald, still deluded, told Barbara Back: "I had what is now called an acute case but used to be called galloping, so it will be at least six months before they can start a thoracoplasty"—an operation that would collapse the diseased lung and allow it to rest.[12] When Maugham visited his emaciated friend, lying on his back and staring into space, he saw death on his face. On November 7, 1944, at Doctors Hospital in New York, Gerald died.

Maugham reported that, though inevitably depressed, Gerald in his last days had finally learned patience and resignation. But this was not quite true. For thirty years Gerald had given him pleasure, if not happiness, but he'd come to resent Maugham's love and secretly hated him. He now openly expressed this hatred and made their last hours together sheer torture. Friends reported that "while sitting by Gerald's bed, [Maugham] had been forced to listen to a violent denunciation of himself spat out by Gerald in a delirium, a wild forecast of the fun Gerald would have after Willie's death." Full of anger about his humiliating role, "hour by hour he screamed and railed against the only real friend he had ever had, the friend who had been so incredibly generous to him. Appalling, venomous obscenities poured forth from his subconsciousness."

This torrent of bitterness in the midst of his grief deeply wounded Maugham and made it impossible to maintain his clinical detachment. Usually too guarded and reserved to be a spontaneous and revealing letter writer, he finally shattered his secret wall and poured out his heart. In a December letter to Barbara Back he described Gerald's death wish: "What pains me more than the rest is the thought that the whole thing was so futile. I warned him, all the doctors he went to warned him that he was killing himself. He did not want to die, but he would not do what they told him; it looked as though he was rushing to death." He told Charlie Towne that he was too old to cope with such grief, and wrote Isherwood that he would never get over Gerald's death and didn't know what to do with the remaining years of his life. Six months later his loneliness and grief were as painful as ever. As the first anniversary approached, he wrote Gerald Kelly that though Haxton had been very irritating, he'd also been vital and devoted. Though he had a new companion waiting in the wings, Maugham claimed that he could never again hope to replace such a friend. His grief was certainly genuine and a part of him seemed to be dying with Gerald; but he also showed his old self-control and resilience, his belief that life must go on. When Cecil Roberts called on him at the Ritz just after Gerald's death, he dramatically exclaimed: "I don't want to see you! I don't want to see anyone! I want to die!" But when Roberts went back to the room a few hours later, he'd regained his customary composure and said: "Let's go down and lunch."[13]

Wondering if he'd helped extinguish the youthful idealism that once had inspired Gerald to join the Red Cross, serve at the front and risk his life, Maugham was consumed by guilt as well as grief. It seemed that by buying Gerald's devotion he had unmanned him. In their long years together Gerald had grown accustomed to live on a grand scale, but never had enough to do, and always resented his inferior and sometimes humiliating position. Maugham, who'd been tubercular himself, feared that he might have infected Gerald. For some time he'd dreaded, yet secretly wished for, Gerald's death. He now felt guilty about wanting to get rid of him (as he'd once wished to get rid of Syrie) and replace him with Alan Searle.

17

Alan Searle and Art

1945–1946

MAUGHAM'S AMERICAN FRIENDS made much of him, but he was often sad and depressed during the war years. The political and social landscape of Europe had been changed forever. Gerald's deterioration and death, the despoliation of his villa and the ravages of France and England, the two countries closest to his heart, all signaled the end of an era. His writing routine at Yemassee and trips to New York for social life had kept him occupied and consoled, but now at seventy he had to start over again: to set up house and find someone new to share his life. Negative reviews of his latest book would threaten his reputation and put him on the defensive but, ever resourceful and with formidable inner strength, Maugham took refuge in restoring his home and building his art collection.

In September 1945, a few weeks after the end of the war, Maugham and Liza met the Alansons at Yosemite National Park, east of San Francisco. He complained that the hotel was uncomfortable and the food vile, but a photograph shows the old friends standing contentedly in the summer sunshine beneath the towering Sierra Nevadas. The dapper Alanson and his attractive wife, Mabel, gaze fondly at each other. Liza, hand on hip, looks elegant in a smart suit and blouse. Maugham, dressed formally in a double-breasted suit and tie, velour hat in hand, forces a rather grim smile. A few months later, back in France, Maugham told Alanson that he'd read

Maugham with Bert Alanson, and Liza and Mabel Alanson,
Yosemite National Park, 1945

about a riot at Alcatraz, the island prison near Alanson's house, and was amazed that Alanson had actually heard the gunfire. Maugham fondly and gratefully recalled their lucky first meeting, en route to Honolulu in 1916. He'd earned a good income from his writing, but Alanson's immensely profitable investments on his behalf had made a fortune. With Bert's help he bought and maintained the villa, collected his paintings and gave away large sums of money for charitable purposes.

Maugham, like his contemporary Bertrand Russell, thought no one born after the Edwardian age could have known true happiness. "We, who were in the full vigour of our youth before the First World War," he said, "may not unreasonably claim that we knew the sweetness of life." Despite his great wealth and his understandable nostalgia for a more pleasant and orderly past, Maugham's politics were surprisingly progressive and Left-wing. He'd predicted a postwar Labour victory as early as 1941, and six weeks before the July 1945 election, he hoped Labour would win, clear out the Tories' dead wood and implement a policy of social reform. When

Churchill was unexpectedly swept out of office, Maugham wrote Robin (who would one day take his father's seat in the House of Lords) that old and successful men were usually surrounded by people who told them only what they wanted to hear. Churchill had been unaware of postwar realities; close advisers, like Beaverbrook and Brendan Bracken, had failed to warn him of the danger of defeat and had dug his political grave. Maugham thought it "monstrous that women are still unable to earn equal pay when they do work equal to men's work" and welcomed the "excellent measures" of the Labour Party's welfare state, which greatly improved the life of the working class.[1]

After the war, with Haxton gone and his villa wrecked and looted, Maugham could have moved back to England. He told the diplomat Harold Nicolson that "France is dead. She may revive, but today she is dead. She has lost *'la fierté qui faisait croire à son génie' *"—the pride that makes one believe in her genius. Nevertheless, in June 1946, he decided to resume his life in France with his new companion, Alan Searle.

The villa had first been occupied by the Italians, who took Maugham's cars; then by the Germans, who ripped up his furniture, emptied his wine cellar and stole his boat. British ships, trying to hit the semaphore on top of a nearby hill, had bombed the house. The French had stolen everything that was left; and he particularly regretted the loss of the Chinese statue that stood in the hall and the two gold and black Negro figures that he preferred to the real blacks in South Carolina. His beloved Pekinese dogs had disappeared in 1940 and, his staff regretfully informed him, had been "eaten long ago."

He was shocked when he first saw the ruined villa, and was afraid of being blown to bits by a mine. All the windows were shattered, and many trees, destroyed by shell fire, would have to be cut down. Some of the damage had already been repaired, but the walls were pocked with shell and bullet holes. Gradually, he replaced the windowpanes, repaired and repainted the walls, replanted the garden and restocked the cellar. The French government was supposed to pay for the war damage, but he never expected to collect.

He cut the prewar staff of thirteen down to five. When his butler, who'd been with him for a very long time, received an offer to work in Brazil, Maugham refused to raise his wages and "told him to take it. The fact is, that for twenty-six years I never really liked him." The embittered butler took revenge by destroying Maugham's precious list of addresses and telephone numbers. Some of his servants and friends wound up in prison. The maid Nina, arrested as a Gestapo agent, was jailed for three years. His Riviera neighbor Horace de Carbuccia, a corrupt politician and editor of the pro-Fascist and anti-Semitic *Gringoire,* got five years hard labor for collaborating with the Germans.

Maugham had now become the subject of academic dissertations and would-be biographers. During and after the war he got back in touch with Karl Pfeiffer, one of his young bridge partners in New York, who'd served in the American army and become a college professor. In 1941 Pfeiffer had sent him Richard Cordell's pioneering biographical and critical study, first published in 1937. After refusing to help Cordell verify the facts, Maugham complained of his mistakes. Haxton, writing on Maugham's behalf, had told Pfeiffer: "I beseech you to throw it in the waste basket as he seems to have got every fact wrong, including the name of Willie's grandfather." Cautiously recommending Pfeiffer to Alanson, who generously entertained Maugham's friends when they passed through San Francisco, Maugham called him an intelligent man who knew his works better than anyone else, but might bore Alanson by endlessly talking about them.

During the war, when Maugham said that Haxton was unhappy and useless at Yemassee, Pfeiffer had offered to come to South Carolina and replace him as secretary. But Maugham was wary. Pfeiffer had his own literary ambitions, and his exploitative schemes and obsessive note taking exhausted Maugham's patience. Maugham chose Searle and then severed relations with Pfeiffer, who retaliated with a hostile book that called Maugham a "short, ugly" man who could "be caustic and cruel without warning or provocation."[2] When the book appeared in 1959, Maugham was angered by its mean-spirited vulgarity.

II

MAUGHAM WAS ALWAYS aware of the pattern of his life: he'd had three mistresses and now needed a third secretary-companion. Alan Searle had understudied the role for years and was ready for his long-delayed entrance on Maugham's stage. Maugham had first met Alan in London in the spring of 1928; and when he made his annual trips to England he'd ask him to make reservations at the Dorchester and invite him to stay in his suite. He liked to escape from life with Gerald and enjoy Alan's more sub-

Alan Searle with Maugham, early 1950s

dued and restful company, and his letters to Alan (while living with Gerald) were paternal and affectionate.

Born in 1905, the son of a tailor, Searle grew up in Bermondsey, a London suburb. He'd been the lover of Lytton Strachey, who called him "my Bronzino boy." Like Gerald, Alan had an absent father and had been coddled by an irritating and emotionally demanding mother, but they had little else in common. A shy social worker from a working-class background, with a pronounced cockney accent, Alan was meek and colorless, conscientious and caring. He had worked for years as a prison visitor at Wormwood Scrubs in west London. His job was to go "regularly to the prison and see a number of inmates, talk to them about their day-to-day routines, listen to their problems and longer-term worries they may wish to confide, pass on to the prison authorities and their probation officers any requests or complaints they might have, sample the food and note conditions and morale in the prison generally." When prisoners were released, he tried to persuade employers to give them jobs and a chance to lead a normal life. A few acquaintances thought Alan himself might actually have been "an inmate of Wandsworth, a gaol for first-time offenders, about which [he] was particularly well-informed."

Writing from New York during the war and using a nautical metaphor,

Maugham had told Alan that Gerald's job in Washington had left him high
and dry. He felt he could just about manage on his own at the moment,
but asked if Alan could think of anyone who might replace Gerald. He
confessed that he was difficult to get on with, but mentioned the considerable perks of the job: decent salary, luxurious board and lodging, and
first-class travel up and down the world. If Alan (then thirty-eight years
old) knew of a suitable candidate between thirty-five and forty, Maugham
would be glad to have his name. This enticingly composed letter obliquely
offered Searle the position without actually promising to hire him. Alan
finally came to America in December 1945, and while still in New York
Maugham told friends how useful and comforting it was to have him
around.

"The nanny of Maugham's second childhood," Searle was as suitable a
companion for his old age as Gerald had been for his younger years. He
lacked Gerald's fire, vitality and energy, but was sober, efficient, honest and
gentle: "deferential, glad to be of use, / politic, cautious and meticulous."
Maugham, enjoying the calm that replaced Gerald's emotional turbulence,
was grateful that he no longer had to man the battle stations. Sam Behrman,
contrasting the two men, wrote that Searle, who had neat features and dark
wavy hair, helped maintain an aura of respectability: "Thin, almost cadaverous, mercurial, Gerald was sardonic, at the ready with any word on any
subject. Alan was plump and shy. He dressed soberly, in double-breasted,
dark suits; there was something aldermanic about him."[3]

By 1941 the portly, chipmunk-cheeked Alan had lost his Bronzino-boy
good looks. He admitted that "as a young man he had been quite a dish,
but now he was quite a tureen." Wescott described him as "such a funny
creature: a lovely cockney cameo face filled out now so that it is more than
a bit woodchucky. Kindness personified; very capable; dapper through
and through; antique-loving." David Posner, more perceptive about his
sexual rival, called him "sweet and kind on the surface but unctuous and
moneygrubbing inside." Maugham's niece added that Searle was
absolutely charming, a good host and wonderful with Willie. But he ruthlessly looked out for his own interests. He kept away all friends who might
benefit from Maugham's will and, during a long-standing feud, alienated
him from his family. Expressing his implacable hostility to his mercenary
rival, Liza, he told Alanson: "you are the only person in the world he has
any deep feelings about. He is starved for affection; he gets none from his
family—they've only one idea."[4]

Alan felt inadequate and uneasy with the grand writers, artists, politicians and aristocrats who visited the villa. Most visitors barely tolerated and often patronized him. Intensely aware of social gradations but trying to reassure him, Maugham wrote: "My dear child. Do not be silly. As if anyone cared what your parenting was." Alan was not convinced and, like a cad in a Graham Greene novel, wore an old Etonian tie to bolster his ego. But he dealt efficiently with many tedious yet essential tasks. After they returned to France, Alan made the travel arrangements and answered the voluminous fan mail, writing as many as four hundred letters a week. He had to protect his master from the public. "A lot of people pursue Willie that he doesn't want to be mixed up with," he complained to Alanson, "so I take them on, and behave like a disagreeable old spinster, and I *do* protect him, but, by God!, they do give me hell, and I don't like it very much." Alan took care to ingratiate himself with Maugham's rich friends, like Alanson and Zipkin, complaining of his lot, yet declaring his devotion.

Searle's obsessive mother had made him a sickly and miserable adolescent, and he became a great valetudinarian. (Later on, Maugham wickedly said that Alan, on one of their visits to England, was going to have "great fun" spending a fortnight with his old mum in Brighton.) Alan provided sex, companionship and, later on, nursing, to a physically unattractive and demanding man thirty-one years older than himself. He was secretary and majordomo, in charge of supervising servants, booking in guests and, as hostess, arranging for their comfort. Alan had exchanged an obscure existence in a London bedsit to a splendid life of luxurious surroundings, glamorous travel and hobnobbing with celebrities, but he inevitably suffered the loss of personal freedom and self-esteem.

In Haxton the psychological strain showed up in heavy drinking and gambling; in Searle it resulted in hypochondria and endless illnesses: psoriasis all over his body, lumbago, jaundice, scarred lung tissue, rheumatism of the spinal cord, kidney stones, liver disease and (after Maugham's death) chronic depression, obesity, asthma, bronchitis, influenza and Parkinson's disease. Alan carefully cultivated his whining, sickly persona to arouse Maugham's sympathy and paternal feelings. Though they'd been lovers since the late 1920s, they also had a father-son relationship. If Gerald had been the beloved scapegrace son, Alan was the delicate little boy who needed cherishing.

When he escaped from Maugham's forbidding shadow, Alan could abandon his aldermanic exterior and be campy, vain and sexually adventurous. When the exiled queen of Spain was invited to lunch, he told his gossipy confidant Jerry Zipkin, he'd spent the morning practicing his curtsy. Something of a voyeur, he used a powerful telescope to spy on small vessels in the harbor and exclaimed: "You have no idea what some people will do on boats."[5] Relieved that the pornographic photographs he'd ordered had passed safely through French customs, Alan used them to excite himself and jokingly lamented that they'd "utterly ruined my health and strength." In 1950 he returned from Morocco, where boys had been readily available, and told Zipkin, with some exaggeration: "I have come back a changed man: nothing over eleven for me from now on." Six years later, once again in North Africa, he himself became the love object: "all Egyptians, in addition to being beautiful, were also Gerontophiles. I haven't had such success since I was twelve."[6] He loved to read muscle magazines and was ecstatic when his photo appeared in the April 1960 issue of *Physique Pictorial.*

Alan's first loyalty was to Maugham, who remained sexually active until his late eighties, and he assured friends that Maugham was "the most marvelous lover I ever had." But he suffered from an occupational hazard, bleeding piles, "a most exhausting and humiliating complaint" that suggested he was the passive partner. Like Gerald, he was not monogamous. He'd pick up sailors in Villefranche and slip them into the villa for champagne, a midnight dip and sex. His affair with an American sailor lasted for two years.

Arthur Marshall, who was very fond of Maugham, believed Searle had a positive influence. He noted that on one of his visits to the villa, Maugham "was even kinder and more benign and gentle and also affectionate, and the reason for that, of course, was that Gerald had been exchanged for Alan, and his life with Alan was much happier than with Gerald." A photograph shows them dining elegantly and alone under the high white arcades of the marble patio, surrounded by Oriental treasures, formally dressed in dinner jackets, seated at a candlelit table. But they seem to be onstage rather than in real life, and they look agonizingly bored. Another photograph shows Maugham feeding his dachshund tidbits from the table (a high point of the day) as Alan looks wearily on.

Isolated by fame, wealth and luxury, Maugham sometimes seemed as lonely with Alan at the villa as he'd been at Yemassee. In May 1948 he reported that they hadn't talked to anyone else for more than a week. Alan fussed and pottered around the house from morning till night while Maugham occupied himself with writing, an afternoon walk, listening to the radio, playing patience and reading detective stories before going early to bed. He rather wistfully told Osbert Sitwell's lover that Alan was sweet but terribly unexciting, calming but soporific. There was, alas, nobody for Maugham to be funny with or about. Alan, an entrenched complainer, occasionally grew vexed and quarrelsome. After a nasty exchange with Maugham he threatened: " 'I'm going to leave you and marry a rich wife.' The writer gave him a cold look, then said bluntly: 'Living with a rich wife is hard work, and you simply don't know how to do it.' "[7]

Maugham sometimes thought of moving to London or Switzerland. He told one of his nieces that the Riviera "is dead and dull. I have good servants, good food, a beautiful house and a nice garden. But that does not prevent me from being bored." In *The Summing Up* he mentioned the great emotional tragedy of his life. He'd squandered his feelings on people who cared nothing about him, and neither wife nor mistresses nor paid companions had ever returned his deepest affection: "Though I have been in love a good many times I have never experienced the bliss of requited love. . . . I have most loved people who cared little or nothing for me, and when people have loved me I have been embarrassed."[8]

III

MAUGHAM'S *Then and Now*, published in May 1946, damaged his literary reputation as much as the war had damaged his villa. He'd based *The Making of a Saint* (1898) on an episode in Machiavelli's *History of Florence*. *Then and Now*, a historical novel about Machiavelli's love intrigues in Renaissance Italy, was inspired by his comedy *La Mandragola* (*The Mandrake Root*, 1518). Maugham said the title of his novel, written when Hitler was still alive and the Nazis were in power, was meant to emphasize the political parallels between the sixteenth century and the modern age. One sympathetic critic saw the book as "a study both of the man who wrote *The Prince* and of the man [Cesare Borgia] who was his model. . . . It is all as exciting as any gangster story of modern politics." But Diana Trilling, who'd attacked *The Razor's Edge* in 1944, now savaged this quite unreadable novel. She wrote that it "alternates between a textbook dryness of historical pedagogy and an embarrassingly primitive effort to liven things up. . . . Not every page of *Then and Now* is [equally vulgar] but few of them fail to proclaim, by their deadness or coyness, its lamentable inadequacy to the historical subject it purports to fictionalize."

Edmund Wilson's attack on this wooden historical novel was based on a misguided grudge against Maugham. Despite his hostility to the intelligentsia, Maugham had always admired Wilson. In "Why D'You Dislike Us?," an article published in the *Saturday Evening Post* on April 11, 1942, four years before Wilson's onslaught, Maugham attempted to explain America's hostility to England. He called Wilson "the most acute critic now writing in America," but noted that "when you read between the lines of his intelligent books you can hardly fail to notice his general attitude of exasperated contempt for the English." Wilson certainly detested the monarchy, the House of Lords and the established Church. The rigid hierarchies, class distinctions and studied reticence of the English, their arrogance, rudeness and cutting remarks grated against his democratic beliefs and provoked him to bait them in person and in print. When Wilson attacked Huxley's mystical novel, *Time Must Have a Stop* (1944), which Maugham disliked but found brilliant, he condemned the review as patronizing and impertinent, stupid and unfair.

In 1945 Nelson Doubleday had sent Maugham the typescript of Wilson's most ambitious and controversial work of fiction, *Memoirs of Hecate County,* and asked his advice about whether to publish it. Maugham liked the satiric, misogynistic book, and Doubleday brought it out in March 1946. Unaware of this crucial recommendation, Wilson mistakenly believed that when Maugham donated the original manuscript of *Of Human Bondage* to the Library of Congress, he "revenged himself for my criticism with the most scarifying cliché in his armory, saying that *Hecate County* was 'execrably bad.' "[9] In fact, Maugham never mentioned Wilson's book in his presentation speech, which took place in April 1946—two months *before* Wilson's review. Wilson was furious and resentful that *Hecate County* had been vilified by the critics and eventually suppressed for obscenity, while Maugham's trashy novel was taken up by the book clubs, became a bestseller and eventually sold 750,000 copies in America.

Wilson believed that serious literature should be self-consciously experimental, original in technique and difficult in content. When Maugham raised his head above the literary parapet, Wilson picked him off. In the *New Yorker* of June 8, 1946, he angrily (and awkwardly) wrote that Maugham's "language is such a tissue of clichés that one's wonder is finally aroused at the writer's ability to assemble so many and at his unfailing ability to put anything in an original way." He concluded that Maugham was "a half-trashy novelist, who writes badly, but is patronized by half-serious readers, who do not care much about writing." Nursing an ill-founded grudge, focusing on one of his weakest novels and ignoring his first-rate works—which he admitted he'd never read—Wilson wrote a devastating but extremely unfair review.

Defending his style against Wilson's attack, Maugham later said that his deliberately plain style had pleased readers for more than half a century: "The critic I am waiting for is the one who will explain why, with all my faults, I have been read for so many years by so many people. . . . Edmund Wilson reproaches me because I haven't what he calls a personal style so that when you read a page you know at once who the author is. That surely means he has acquired a mannerism (Henry James, Meredith, and others). But that is just what I have tried to avoid." In November 1952, when an editor at W. H. Allen suggested that Wilson collaborate with Behrman on Maugham's biography, Maugham told Behrman: "There is no race in the world as stupid as publishers."[10] Wilson's attack expressed the desire of young modernists to follow a different literary path and must have seemed like another postwar nail in Maugham's coffin. His fame, once again, made him a convenient target and exemplar of a discredited past. Maugham never became hardened to such abuse. He might feign indifference, but he was deeply hurt.

IV

MAUGHAM'S LIFE LACKED passion, and his work was attacked. But he'd made a million dollars on *The Razor's Edge* and soothed his wounded feelings by spending it on his impressive art collection, which he seriously began to acquire after the war. His list of the greatest works of art in the world included the Taj Mahal in Agra, Michelangelo's Medici tombs and the fresco of Adam with his outstretched arm in the Sistine Chapel in Rome, Velázquez's *Pope Innocent X* in Rome, Titian's *Entombment of Christ* in the Louvre and *The Martyrdom of St. Maurice,* by Titian's disciple El Greco, in El Escorial. But he never tried to buy an El Greco or works by other Old Masters. His art collecting resembled that of Charley Mason's family in *Christmas Holiday:* "they really liked pictures and if they did not buy any before the cultured opinion of the day had agreed on their merits this was due partly to a modest lack of confidence in their own judgment and partly to a fear that they might be making a bad bargain."

Though he was a connoisseur in his own right, Maugham was prepared to pay for the taste and sound judgment of his principal dealers in Paris and New York: Paul Rosenberg, Georges Wildenstein and Paul Durand-Ruel. He was also advised by two leading authorities: Monroe Wheeler, curator at the Museum of Modern Art in New York, and Kenneth Clark, director of the National Gallery in London. Clark praised Maugham's "remarkable responsiveness to what was best in absolutely contemporary or even abstract art."

In addition to the major work by Gauguin, acquired in Tahiti in 1917, Maugham owned eighteen important French paintings completed between 1870 and 1940. They included Lautrec's male nude; Renoir's nude and walking women; Matisse's standing and reclining women; Utrillo's Breton village; Pissarro's Rouen harbor and winter landscape; Monet's Dutch canal; Renoir and Sisley's French river scenes; Vuillard's still life; Bonnard's domestic interior; Rouault's crucifixion; Léger's abstract work; Picasso's woman seated in a garden, his death of a harlequin and his monumental classical figure—heavily draped, large-eyed and staring into space with an almost divine detachment. This imposing woman had a strange affinity with Kelly's portrait of Sue Jones.[11]

Renoir's ample red-haired nude, *Andrée* (1915), is seated with her back to the viewer and her face in profile. After she'd posed in the morning, Renoir would order the model, who was also his cook, to get dressed, return to her main occupation and prepare lunch. Maugham wrote Wheeler that he hung this sensual painting in the bedroom and it was the first thing he saw when he woke up in the morning.

Lautrec's *Le Polisseur* (1887), which Beverley Nichols (stretching a point) claimed had an "uncanny resemblance" to Gerald, was an early, atypical work. It portrayed a young man on his hands and knees—like a runner about to start a race—who'd stripped off his clothes while polishing a floor. Maugham, who used it to test the knowledge of his guests, wrote: "I often asked the experts who came to see my pictures whether they could guess who painted it. Only one of them could. My old friend, Sir Kenneth Clark, looked at it for two minutes and then said, 'No one could have painted that head or that foot but Toulouse-Lautrec,' and of course he was right."

The most appealing and perhaps the greatest painting in his collection was Matisse's *Woman Seated in an Armchair* (1940), now in the National Gallery in Washington. In the foreground of the picture a bosomy woman in a patterned white blouse and green skirt reclines on a padded yellow armchair and footstool. Her hair is brown, her eyes slit, her lips smudged; her features are indistinct and her hands disappear on the arms of the chair. A white door is closed behind her; and there are paintings on the walls, fruit in bowls and flowers in a large vase resting on a red table. The diagonal white stripes on the dark blue floor converge on the chair and sharpen the perspective. In about 1950, after buying the painting, Maugham came to know Matisse. When Maugham visited him, "he lay on a great old-fashioned double brass bed, with big brass knobs at the four corners. . . . Matisse liked me to come and see him so that he could ask me how they were getting on with the chapel at Vence, for which he had designed the decoration, and each time I left him he begged me to go to Vence again and tell him exactly what the workmen were doing."

Maugham, the subject of more than fifty portraits, was probably painted, drawn and sculpted more than any other writer in history. He gave some thought to the emotional dynamics between artist and subject, and wrote that portraits are "to some extent a collaboration between the painter and his sitter; the sitter must give something; there must be something in him which excites the painter's sensibility."[12] His old friend Gerald Kelly painted him at least thirty times between 1906 and 1963. In 1951 Kelly told Alanson that he still had a great many portraits of Maugham. Since nobody wanted them, he offered to ship them to San Francisco. That year Jacob Epstein sculpted a bronze head, with beaky nose and jutting chin. He noted how easily Maugham established rapport with his artists: "he reminded me strongly of some old Roman patrician. In spite of his fastidious and aloof expression he proved a model sitter, was most genial whilst posing and discoursed on contemporary letters most entertainingly."

The handsome French painter Edouard MacAvoy (1905–91) left a verbal as well as visual portrait of Maugham. Born in Bordeaux, a pupil of Pierre Bonnard, he was a professor at the Académie Julian and did penetrating portraits of Pope John XXIII, Picasso, André Gide, Jean Cocteau and many other literary figures. In his autobiography, MacAvoy emphasized Maugham's Oriental detachment: "a mysterious Asiatic influence pervades the face of this Anglo-Saxon grand seigneur. Today he wears a

*Gerald Kelly
painting Maugham*

*Portrait of Maugham
by Gerald Kelly, 1949*

Jacob Epstein sculpting Maugham, 1951

pure Buddhist mask. He has wisdom, renunciation, profound peace born of complete disillusionment, a sceptical gaiety." In 1947 MacAvoy portrayed Maugham seated in front of an olive screen. He wears a white shirt and loose tan and brown robe decorated with a maze of green and blue lines. One skeletal hand rests on his knee, the other hangs down from the arm of his chair. His face seems both tranquil and powerful, and he stares off into space with a disenchanted expression.

MacAvoy told André Gide that he was greatly impressed by the villa as well as by the astonishing youthfulness of the seventy-five-year-old writer, whose face had evoked exotic imagery—Roman, Buddhist and now Indian: "In La Mauresque Somerset receives like a maharajah: with comfort, luxury, beauty, rare pictures, gardens and blue swimming pool. Maugham was completely naked, at his sovereign ease, diving like a young man." MacAvoy also explained why Maugham was irritated by his Riviera neighbor Jean Cocteau. When Isherwood and Bachardy, who admired Cocteau, asked to meet him, Maugham had dismissed the nonstop talker as "a bothersome man." Cocteau, fantasizing about Maugham's taste, told MacAvoy that "Maugham has an extraordinary need for duchesses and extraordinary need for murderers.... Then he mixes them up and his ladies become like the thieves."[13] The homosexual Cocteau was probably referring not only to Maugham's predilection for titles, but also to the

Graham Sutherland, portrait of
Maugham, 1949

rough trade of the past, picked up on the docks and brought home by Haxton.

Graham Sutherland's great painting established his reputation as a portrait artist and led to many important commissions. The contrast to Kelly's *Jester* (1911) reveals Maugham's evolution from young dandy to aged saurian. The Oriental motifs in the painting indicate his lifelong interest in the art and thought of Japan, China and Southeast Asia. Sutherland portrayed him seated on a low bamboo stool, with crossed arms and legs, against a lemon background with lightly sketched palm fronds. He wears a red scarf, and chocolate-colored socks and smoking jacket. His eyes are hooded and pouched, his forehead and cheeks deeply grooved, his mouth is turned down, his chin prominent. His disdainful yet defiant expression suggests a lifetime of intense but disillusioned scrutiny.

Maugham loved Sutherland's penetrating portrait as much as Churchill hated his. Churchill said Sutherland's portrait "makes me look like a half-wit," and his family brutally destroyed it. After this bitter experience, Sutherland noted how extraordinary it was for Maugham to like, or even accept, his portrait: "only those totally without physical vanity, educated in painting, or with exceptionally good manners, can disguise their feelings of shock or even revulsion when they are confronted for the first time with a reasonably truthful image of themselves."

Maugham, remarkably free of egoism, found it "gay and pleasing." " 'The first time I saw it I was shocked,' he said. 'I was really stunned. Could this face really be mine? And then I began to realize that here was far more of me than I ever saw myself.' He saw himself as a sardonic, aloof and quietly amused observer of human frailty." He then added: "There is no doubt that Graham has painted me with an expression I sometimes have, even without being aware of it." Though Maugham liked the portrait, he disputed the fee, which reinforced his reputation of being mean with money. When Sutherland suggested £500, Searle, who often had to take the flak, "came around with £300 and said that as it was in cash [and not taxable], it really represented £500, and anyway, Mr. Maugham couldn't afford more. Graham was not pleased with the arrangement, and some minor altercation with Searle ensued."[14] The portrait was not universally admired. Max Beerbohm thought Maugham "looks as if he'd been tortured." Gerald Kelly, who'd studied his face for half a century, exclaimed: "To think that I have known Willie since 1902 and have only just recognized that, disguised as an old madame, he kept a brothel in Shanghai!" Kenneth Clark called it "undoubtedly the greatest portrait of the twentieth century."[15]

18

The Lizard of Oz

1947–1950

THE POSTWAR YEARS in England were austere, and almost every-thing—housing, fuel, clothing, food—was in short supply. There had been more to eat during the war than after it; and in 1946, when wheat destined for Britain was sent to feed the defeated Germans, bread was rationed for the first time. Severe currency restrictions made it difficult to take money out of the country. In 1947 Maugham took advantage of his foreign residence and ample funds to found the Somerset Maugham Prize, which gave £500 to young British writers to travel abroad for six months. The judges were the historian Veronica Wedgwood, the poet Cecil Day-Lewis and the short-story writer V. S. Pritchett. Their choices were excellent and included many authors who went on to establish major reputations: V. S. Naipaul, Kingsley Amis, Doris Lessing, Seamus Heaney, Ted Hughes, Thom Gunn, Francis King, John le Carré and John Wain.

Evelyn Waugh, now in his forties, told their mutual friend Ann Fleming: "Please explain to Dr. Maugham that what is required is not encouragement to young writers but consolation to the old." In a witty letter to the *Times* in April 1947, Waugh wondered what deceits he might employ to win the prize:

Does Mr. Maugham realize what a huge temptation he is putting before elderly writers? To have £500 of our own—let alone of Mr. Maugham's—

to spend abroad is beyond our dreams. We may not even spend the royalties on our translations in the countries where they are earned. What will we not do to qualify for Mr. Maugham's munificence? What forging of birth certificates, dyeing of whiskers, and lifting of faces! To what parodies of experimental styles will we not push our experienced pens![1]

In July 1947 Maugham published his last book of stories, *Creatures of Circumstance,* whose deterministic title recalled Hardy's *Satires of Circumstance* (1914). In "Flotsam and Jetsam" the setting is Conradian: an impoverished plantation in a remote jungle outpost; the plot another variant of Hemingway's "The Short Happy Life of Francis Macomber" (1936): the husband has killed his wife's lover and gotten away with the crime. An anthropologist, stricken by malaria, is forced to take refuge with the planter and his wife. The wife is afflicted with hideous tics that symbolize her mental, moral and spiritual disintegration; the husband is brutally indifferent. The visitor finally manages to escape, but the couple must remain in a marital hell of exile and abandonment. "How would you like to see no one," the wife asks, "week in and week out, day after day for sixteen years, except the man you hate most in the world?"

"Unconquered," a tale of infanticide, passionate hatred and self-destructive revenge, is a political allegory of the German occupation of France. A French couple collaborate, but their daughter desperately resists. A German soldier rapes her and returns three months later to find her pregnant. She loves a French soldier (who dies in a prison camp), and hates the German for what he's done to her and to her country. Her parents grow fond of the German soldier, who brings them urgently needed food and clothes, and invite him to work on the farm after the war. He wants to marry the daughter and care for their child, but when the baby, who looks like the father, is born, she drowns it in a nearby brook.

The two most subtle stories, "Episode" and "The Kite" (in which Alan Searle appears as Ned Preston), were inspired by Searle's experience as a prison visitor. The homosexual theme that's merely suggested in the first story is fully developed in the second. In "Episode" Ned seductively tells a prisoner: "I shouldn't be surprised if you had had friends who . . . were caught in a compromising situation in one of the parks." And (as in "Red") Maugham rapturously describes the troubling sexuality of the handsome red-haired postman who's been sent to jail for stealing money: "It was really a great beauty. Perhaps it was this that gave him so sensual a look. . . . His eyes were bold, and when he smiled or laughed, which in the healthy vitality of his youth he did constantly, his expression was wonderfully alluring."[2] His girl, opposing her family, has promised to marry him after he gets out. He thinks about her constantly for eighteen months, but when he's released he loses interest in her—and perhaps all women—and she kills herself.

Over the years Maugham had found oblique ways to write about homosexual themes and characters. He exalted male beauty in *Mrs. Craddock,* disguised Harry Philips as Mildred in *Of Human Bondage,* described the mutual attraction of Blake and Christessen in *The Narrow Corner,* discussed homosexuality in El Greco and Melville, portrayed a homosexual hustler in *Christmas Holiday* and created the flagrantly campy Elliott Templeton in *The Razor's Edge.* In one of his last stories, "The Kite," ostensibly a domestic comedy about a young husband's obsessive kite flying, he used sexual language to reveal his hidden theme.

The insanely jealous, kite-smashing wife feels her husband loves the kite more than her. "Contemptible I call it. . . . I won't have it," she says. "I'm not going to have you make a fool of yourself." Her husband sometimes "panted . . . [and] couldn't get it up." But when things went well he became almost orgasmic: "He just couldn't keep away from it. He doted on it. . . . He had never had such a thrill in his life. . . . It was grand to see that little thing soaring so sweetly, but even as he watched it, he thought of the great big one. . . . In some queer way . . . it represents an ideal of freedom and adventure." Clearly the absurd and childish pastime, which destroys his marriage and sends him to jail, represents more than flying a kite. As the narrator suggestively asks: "What d'you suppose there is in kite-flying that makes the damn fool so mad about it?" Maugham had experienced the same excitement when he escaped from Syrie to Gerald. The soaring kite stands for the unfettered pursuit of his own sexual destiny.

V. S. Pritchett, reviewing the book in the *New Statesman,* called Maugham "half-hermit, half man of the world," and said "his real subject is stoicism. . . . How much can a human being endure?"[3] Maugham felt his books continued to rivet his audience because his heroes (like the husband in "The Kite") were caricatures, and readers could have the pleasure of recognizing themselves and still feel superior to his characters.

II

LIZA AND VINCENT Paravicini were divorced in 1947, and in July 1948 she married Lord John Hope. He was the son of the marquess of Linlithgow, one of the largest landowners in Scotland, director of the Midland Bank and viceroy of India from 1936 to 1943. For moral reasons Linlithgow had refused to receive Haxton when he'd traveled to India with Maugham in 1938. Maharajahs might entertain Gerald; the viceroy would not. John Hope, educated at Eton and Christchurch, Oxford, had served with the Scots Guards in Italy during the war and in 1945 became a Conservative M.P. for North Midlothian. From 1959 to 1962 he was minister of works in Harold Macmillan's government.

Maugham had not forgotten the offense to Gerald and himself. He now felt intensely hostile to both father and son, which put Liza in a sticky situation. Ann Fleming wrote Waugh that "Willie loathes Lord John Hope, and poor Liza is ill at case but a cautious, discreet, ambitious girl." Maugham harshly exclaimed: "I liked Liza's first husband very much. Her present one I cannot endure. He is useless." And he cynically added: "He married her for my money and she married him for his title."[4] His longstanding grudge against John Hope, which began in 1947, finally erupted in the family feud of 1962.

Maugham also complained about the editorial assault on his books that were no longer protected by copyright: "they may cut my work, emend it, edit, mutilate—change an ending if they like—and I have no recourse whatever. Do you call that *fair?*" Nevertheless, and without realizing the contradiction, in 1948 he embarked on a lucrative but ill-fated project, *Great Novelists and Their Novels.* In that work he ruthlessly abridged what he called the irritating, tedious and absurd "digressions and irrelevances that interrupted the narration."[5]

Maugham's choice of the ten greatest novels—nine from the nineteenth century and none from the twentieth—was sound. There were one American, two Russian, three French and four English novels: *Tom Jones, Pride and Prejudice, The Red and the Black, Old Man Goriot, Wuthering Heights, David Copperfield, Moby-Dick, Madame Bovary, War and Peace* and *The Brothers Karamazov.* The most notable absences were *Robinson Crusoe,* works by George Eliot and by Henry James, and Mann's *Buddenbrooks.* Though Maugham did not want his own biography to be written, he took a dis-

Maugham seated on a sofa, with Mediterranean in background, 1947

tinctly biographical approach in his criticism, and even suggested parallels between his own life and those of the writers he considered. Like Tolstoy, Maugham lost his parents when he was a child. Like Stendhal, he harbored old resentments. Like Emily Brontë, he disliked children. Like Melville, he married to combat homosexual desires.

He had very little to say about the novels and, when introducing another anthology, frankly admitted: "I am more interested in an author's personality than in the book he writes." "Even though an author's books mean nothing very much to me I like to know what sort of life he led, what he looked like and how he talked." He declared that Balzac was "the greatest novelist who ever lived," but his tactless abridgment of his betters, potted biographies and banal comments—Tolstoy "was an old man. He was eighty. A year passed and another. He was eighty-two"[6]—merely confirmed the critics' view of him as hopelessly middlebrow.

In 1948 the infinitely versatile Maugham began a new phase of his film work. Eager to acquire new readers and earn more money, but sceptical about the whole business, he wondered if movies were worth all the trouble. Jean Cocteau—who'd made highly innovative and intensely personal art films, like *Blood of the Poet* and *Beauty and the Beast*—reported their conversation on this subject: "Somerset Maugham in great form, very lively, with gold rings on his green ascot. He asks me if I don't frequently regret the effort a film costs me. An art form so fragile and so fugitive. I answer that I do, but that everything is fragile and fugitive."

Maugham's overflowing invention supported a small army of minor writers, as well as established authors like R. C. Sherriff and Eric Ambler, who adapted his fiction for the stage and screen, radio and television. Sherriff—author of the impressive play *Journey's End*, about his combat experiences in the Great War—was intelligent enough to use most of Maugham's dialogue in his script of *Quartet* (1948). When Maugham introduced this film, the first of three fine compendiums of his stories, he was engagingly gentle and modest. Seated at his desk and fiddling with a letter opener, he spoke slowly and deliberately, with only a hint of a stammer. Repeating a famous passage from *The Summing Up*, he rather bitterly recounted how the critics had condemned his work in each decade of his life. They might carp, he complacently implied, but his books continued to sell and sell.

The film version of "The Kite," which portrays women as birds of prey, eliminates the homosexual theme just as "The Alien Corn" deletes the Jewish theme. Caught between his jealous mother and his jealous wife, the hero returns home from jail and exclaims: "I've had enough of marriage to last me a lifetime." In the story he remains obdurate and refuses to support his wife; in the film, which tacks on a happy ending, he goes back to his wife and she agrees to join him when he flies his kite. It's a charming film, but leaves out a crucial element of the story.

In his poem "The Ladies," Kipling wrote that "The colonel's lady an' Judy O'Grady / Are sisters under the skin." Maugham adopted Kipling's title, and in his "Colonel's Lady" the upper-class heroine feels the same passion as ordinary women. In the film a dowdy, middle-aged woman publishes a wildly successful book of love poems. Her stuffy husband, embarrassed by the personal revelations and by the hot stuff in the "lushest book since *Lady Chatterley*," hates being married to a notorious author. He can't believe that his mousy wife, who's made him look a perfect fool, could ever have experienced such lust. "What in the name of heaven," he asks, "did the fellow ever see in her?" The film has a better ending than the story. Though his feeling for his wife has died long ago, *he* was the lover who'd inspired her passion.

Maugham gave a brief introduction to each film in *Trio* (1950) as he lit a cigarette and sat in his villa, with the spectacular Mediterranean coast in the background. When he appeared as presenter for the third time, in *Encore* (1952), he expressed one of his cardinal beliefs—"A novelist must arrange the facts to entertain his readers"—and disarmingly told the audience: "You probably are beginning to think I fancy myself as a film star." These films paid off handsomely. Robin noted that Willie's books had sold eighty million copies and "about eighty [of his stories] had been performed on television. . . . Penguin have produced over one hundred thousand copies of nine or ten of his books. Plays of his are being performed all over the world."[7] Maugham believed he achieved greater fame from the film versions of his works than from the works themselves.[8]

III

CATALINA (1948), Maugham's last novel, seems more scholarly than imaginative. His heavyweight sources—in addition to histories of Spain, picaresque novels, and plays by Lope de Vega and Calderón—included contemporary autobiographies, accounts of the Inquisition and cultural studies. Set in seventeenth-century Spain, *Catalina* (like a crucial scene in *Of Human Bondage*) concerns a cripple's prayer to be cured of lameness—and, in this case, a miraculous remedy. Maugham's return to historical novels in old age showed the waning of his creative powers; and *Catalina,* like *Then and Now,* was a critical disaster. But, like its predecessor, it also had a first printing of fifty thousand, was a Book-of-the-Month Club selection and sold extremely well.

Maugham's dedications read like a *Who's Who* of his social circle. He dedicated thirteen of his books, about one-fifth of the total, to members of his family: Aunt Julia Maugham and Syrie; lovers: Violet Hunt, Harry

Philips and (after his death) Haxton; close friends: Walter Payne, Gerald Kelly and Bert Alanson; older hostesses: Mrs. Edward Johnston, wife of the British vice-consul in Seville in the late 1890s, and Mrs. George Steevens; an actress: Ethel Barrymore, who starred in the first American production of *The Constant Wife;* and three acquaintances: the composer Herbert Bunning and his wife, Marguerite, who attended first nights of his early plays, and Barbara Rothschild, married to the third baron. Notably absent from the dedicatees were his brothers Charles and Henry; Sasha Kropotkin, Sue Jones, Barbara Back and Ann Fleming; Robin Maugham, Christopher Isherwood, Glenway Wescott and Alan Searle.[9]

Maugham published his greatest stories—*The Trembling of a Leaf* and *Ashenden*—in the 1920s; two of his greatest novels—*Cakes and Ale* and *The Narrow Corner*—in the 1930s; then went into a decline with several minor works—*Theatre, Christmas Holiday, Up at the Villa* and *The Razor's Edge;* and hit bottom in the late 1940s with his last two historical novels. The best books of his later years were the perceptive and revealing autobiographies: *The Summing Up* (1938), *Strictly Personal* (1941) and *A Writer's Notebook* (1949). Maugham's orderly, disciplined habits enabled him to produce an enormous amount of work, and he scrupulously planned his literary career. His friend G. B. Stern noted that Maugham announced his intention "to stop writing plays when he was sixty, short stories when he was sixty-five, and novels after the half-dozen he had in mind were finished." Aware of his diminishing powers and fearful that his writing might deteriorate to the point of senility, he strictly adhered to his retirement plan.

Maugham said *Sheppey* (1933) would end his thirty-year career as a playwright. Declaring that the stories in *Ah King* (1933) were his last exotic ones, he abandoned the colonial scene and shifted his interest from Batavia to Belgravia. In *The Mixture as Before* (1940), he said he would not write any more stories. But when *Creatures of Circumstance* (1947) appeared, he slyly claimed that "any" had been a misprint for "many." He stated that *Catalina* would be his last novel, and that he would now devote himself to essays. The publisher announced that *Points of View* (1959) would be the last book by the eighty-five-year-old author, who formally took leave of the reading public he'd first attracted with *Liza of Lambeth* more than sixty years before. In the course of his long career Maugham had moved from recycling his early novels and plays into different genres, to ceasing to write in various literary forms, to a Prospero-like farewell to his art. Hemingway once said that authors are never allowed to retire, but in 1948

Maugham could afford to stop writing fiction and had earned the right to do so. He'd taken leave of his lovers, wife and country, and would finally complete the pattern by severing relations with Liza and her family.

Maugham did everything he could to stave off old age. He surrounded himself with comforts, secured a competent companion and endured Dr. Niehans' oversized needles and sacrificial lambs to retain his vigor. Though he had no illusions about continuing his literary career, he was keen to keep his mind active. One diversion that occupied his leisure time, from the Bath Club in London to the rubbers with royalty on the Riviera, was bridge, which he called "the most interesting game that the art of man has ever devised." Though he hated trivial games that "add so much horror to social intercourse" and had satirized the heartless bridge players in *Smith,* he extolled the virtues of his favorite pastime: "To have learnt to play a good game of bridge is the safest insurance against the tedium of old age. . . . What decision, what quickness of apprehension, what judgment, what knowledge of character, are required to play a difficult hand perfectly."[10]

Maugham described himself as a bridge player and as a writer in the same way: well up in the second class. In 1954 he agreed to write an introduction to Charles Goren's *Standard Book of Bidding* (published by Doubleday) if Goren would elevate him to the big leagues by playing bridge with him. "We had an excellent game, a *most* excellent," he exulted. "I won 25 bucks from Goren. Nothing in my life has ever pleased me more." Goren, for his part, vaguely remarked that "by expert standards [Maugham] was not to be feared as a player, yet he had the ability and the wisdom to bring something quite special to the game." Maugham defined this special quality when he said that a good bridge player had to be truthful, clearheaded, prudent and considerate. His own manners, however, were sometimes abrasive, and he liked to dominate the people around him. When a woman objected to his cigar at bridge, he imperiously replied: "I'm sorry you don't like it. . . . But I intend to smoke it anyway."[11]

After lecturing at Columbia University in November 1950, Maugham played bridge with another great figure. Softening his criticism for Bert Alanson's sake, he told him that Dwight Eisenhower (then president of Columbia) was nice, unpretentious and straightforward, and played a pleasant game. But, mistaking Eisenhower's geniality for dimness, he told Alexander Frere that he'd *lost* $12 to the man who "is probably a very great general, but he's a bloody bad bridge player and a very stupid man."

Maugham seated on floor in front of bookcase, 1950

Though Maugham's writing career was coming to an end, his publishing ventures were far from over. Just as Doubleday's predecessor George Doran had called Maugham a shrewd bargainer who knew his own worth, so his current editor observed: "He'll always begin by saying, 'Of course, I know nothing about business,' but before the conversation is over he will have got from Nelson everything he wants—which, incidentally, is plenty." He was grateful for Doubleday's hospitality at Yemassee and his success in selling his books in America, and liked having the Doubledays stay at the villa. When Nelson became terminally ill, Maugham sailed to New York to see him for the last time, and was deeply moved by his death in 1949. In the privately printed tribute to his old friend, he rose to the elegiac occasion and paid tribute to Nelson's good looks in his finest neoclassical sentence: "With his great height he was in his youth of a striking beauty, in middle age of an imposing and handsome presence, and even at the end, though worn by sickness, with death in his face and the awareness of death in his eyes, he bore a look of distinction."[12]

Maugham had reached an age when old friends began to die but, in his mid-seventies, he still had an intense interest in living. In 1947 Bruce Lockhart, who'd first met Maugham in Russia, gave a vivid account of his Oriental appearance (which Sutherland would soon capture in his great portrait), his intellectual liveliness and his Edwardian dandyism: "He has aged and his face has changed. The complexion is more sallow, more Chinese; the lines deeper and more sinister. But his mind was alert. He talked more than I have ever heard him before. He looked very neat and dapper and a monocle dangled on his waistcoat from a cord." The following year Chips Channon was struck by Maugham's sexual vigor and cosmopolitan tastes: "Willie has had a long amorous career, and now at 75 is still lusty. He has been everywhere, met everybody, tasted everything. His interest in the world and in Society and food and drink, is acute." In 1950 Frances Partridge, the sharp-tongued Bloomsbury camp follower, "sat next to Somerset Maugham at tea and was charmed by him. He belongs in a reptile house, a chameleon by choice, with his pale deep furrowed face, sunken glittering eyes and the mouth that opens deliberately and sometimes sticks there."[13] In old age, and with nearly twenty more years to live, he remained formidably impressive.

19

Royalty and Honors

1951–1955

KIPLING'S PURITANICAL WAY of life, conservative politics and glo-
rification of Empire (rather than emphasis on its seamy side) precluded
close friendship with Maugham. But Maugham always kept Kipling—who
was nine years older, had won the Nobel Prize and died in 1936—within
his sights. In the introduction to his *Choice of Kipling's Prose,* 1952 (which
complemented Eliot's *Choice of Kipling's Verse*), he praised his rival's wide
reading, "quick mind and wonderful power of observation," and concluded: "He is our greatest story writer. I can't believe he will ever be
equalled. I am sure he can never be excelled." In his essay "The Short
Story" in *Points of View* (1959), Maugham cut and slashed his way through
the work of James, Maupassant, Chekhov and Mansfield (retaliating for
her negative review of *The Moon and Sixpence*). But he spared Kipling and
noted how his fictional characters had influenced people's behavior: "He
had a fertile invention and to a supreme degree the gift of narrating incident in a surprising and dramatic fashion. . . . When one traveled in the
East, it was astonishing how often one came across men who had mod-
elled themselves on the creatures of his invention." In the radical 1960s,
when Kipling's reputation had declined, Maugham gallantly defended him
and regretted that "the stories of Rudyard Kipling, which once enjoyed so
amazing a popularity, now suffer an undeserved neglect."[1]

Maugham, "a pretty good likeness . . .
in his old age," c. 1951

Maugham continued to impress his younger contemporaries, who rejoiced in invitations to the villa. One of them paid tribute to his amazing youthfulness: "Maugham, though he is in his mid-seventies, has the appearance of a vigorous sixty. He plays a good game of tennis, his dives are daring and graceful, and after a twenty-minute swim he will emerge only slightly breathless." Glenway Wescott, observing him in June 1952 and emphasizing his otherworldly appearance,

> remembered him at the pool, naked except for a broad-brimmed straw hat, saying, "I must take my dive." He complained of a pain in the groin, but otherwise looked fit. His face was lined, but his body had the most lovely skin in the world. He was shapely but tiny and with his little pot-belly he looked like the king of the frogs in the fairy tale. With his satiny worn skin he looked as if he was bound in the best quality English calf, you know, the kind of glove leather that doesn't last very long.

He was proud of the etched-in corrugations that were cunningly captured in Sutherland's portrait. In 1954, when a photographer appealed to his vanity and asked if he should retouch his image, he replied: "Certainly not. It's taken me 80 years to get those lines. Why should I allow you to remove them in two minutes?"

Maugham encouraged friends to visit and liven up his rather stolid life with Searle. The diplomat Harold Nicolson, who owned a grand house in Kent, enjoyed the hedonism and alluded to the homosexual ambience: "It really is the perfect holiday. The heat is intense, the garden lovely, the chair long and cool, the lime-juice at hand, a bathing pool if one wishes to splash, scenery, books, gramophones, pretty people." Cecil Beaton also approved of the luxurious if slightly decadent regime: "Life at the Villa is ideal for the semi-invalid: breakfast in bed; the garden below the balcony a sea of magenta and blue cinerarias; no need to put in an appearance before midday.... On the terrace the lunch visitors assemble: maybe witty, delicious and slightly scatty."[2]

Maugham, with good reason, found the behavior of some of his guests a trial and a bore. When Waugh and Diana Cooper—the exceptionally beautiful daughter of the duke of Rutland, former actress and wife of the wartime ambassador to France—visited in April 1952, "Alan Searle, who was filling the role of hostess, offended Diana by giving Waugh the better of the two rooms and offering him rather than her a sprig of heliotrope. Waugh had vitamin tablets in his bathroom, while Diana merely had aspirins. Evelyn Waugh called Somerset Maugham 'Doctor' every other sentence and read his [own] new novel aloud for more than two hours after dinner." Admitting a worse social blunder, Waugh told their mutual friend Harold Acton: "I spent two nights at Cap Ferrat with Mr. Maugham (who has lost his fine cook) & made a great gaffe. The first evening he asked me what someone was like and I said: 'A pansy with a stammer.' All the Picassos on the walls blanched." Though lucky not to be sent down at once, Waugh was never invited back. Maugham's curt, final judgment was that Alec Waugh was "*far* nicer than his brother, who I think is quite odious."[3]

Maugham's relations with the flamboyant Ian and Ann Fleming were much warmer, if bizarre. Fleming's biographer noted that "the Hairless Mexican in Somerset Maugham's *Ashenden* had done something to install Le Chiffre [in Fleming's *Casino Royale*, 1953], just as R., the Intelligence colonel who recruits Ashenden, brings [Fleming's] M. to mind." When the first James Bond novel was published, Maugham wrote Fleming that he'd found it riveting and stayed up half the night reading it to the end: "It goes with a swing from the first page to the last and is really thrilling all through.

Ann Fleming

I particularly enjoyed the battle at the casino between your hero and M. Chiffre. You really managed to get the tension to the highest possible pitch."

In 1954 Fleming substantially increased Maugham's wealth and fame by arranging for his *Great Novelists and Their Novels* to be serialized in the London *Sunday Times*. The paper originally planned to publish four to six of the introductions and pay him £3,000. But the essays were so phenomenally successful that the series was extended to an unprecedented fifteen weeks. When Fleming's *Moonraker* (1955) continued the amazing sales of *Live and Let Die,* he told Fleming: "You have held the reader's interest with great skill from beginning to end, and there is less of your sadistic instincts to which you give expression in your previous two novels."[4]

Maugham was very fond of Ian's wife, Ann, granddaughter of the eleventh earl of Wemyss. Beautiful and well connected, a witty and charming hostess, she was also bold enough to chasten Waugh (Maugham merely gave him an icy stare) by banging a serving spoon on his offensively prominent ear trumpet. Maugham complimented Ann, a stylish purveyor of delicious gossip, by calling her "the Madame de Sévigné of our day." Ann's first husband was killed in the war. In 1952 she divorced the newspaper tycoon Lord Rothermere in order to marry Ian Fleming. Offering avuncular advice, Maugham contrasted the social customs of the Edwardian and postwar eras: "In my young days such a procedure would have shut all the doors of Mayfair against you, but I daresay in these degenerate times you may get away with it. But tolerant as people are now I don't think you ought to make a habit of it." After their marriage, Maugham, contrasting his sedate life with their sybaritic one, told Ian: "Give my love to Annie, and tell her I hope she is resisting your wish to give parties or go to parties every day of the week. The poor girl must have a little peace and quiet sometimes."

Ann, like most guests, enjoyed the self-indulgent luxury of the villa and, with the eye of an experienced hostess, itemized its many virtues: "the perfect martini served in a sunny garden, a high standard of cooking, a variety of menu, a choice of wonderful smells in the bathroom, soap, essences and shaving lotions." Ann's flurried arrival suggested, she confessed to Waugh, louche sexual assignations: "there were letters, postcards, telegrams awaiting me, so Willie suspected a plot to use his house as a hotel and angle an invitation for a lover."

Though the lover never materialized, Maugham had to put up with the unintentionally offensive behavior of the King's School Old Boy, war hero and travel writer Patrick Leigh Fermor. Unnerved, as Waugh was, by Maugham's constant stammer, the exuberantly drunk Fermor committed (according to Ann) a similar blunder: "The conversation turned to occupational diseases and Paddy shouted at length on the stuttering that typified the College of Heralds." He then compounded the felony by imitating a friend's response to Mantegna's *Assumption of the Virgin:* " 'that is a m-most un-un-w-warrantable assumption': Alan and I exchanged glances of despair and the evening was wrecked. . . . [Willie then] walked up to Paddy and said, 'G-Goodbye, you will have left before I am up in the morning.' He then vanished like a primeval crab, leaving a slime of silence; it was broken by Paddy who cried 'Oh what have I done?' and slammed his whisky glass on the table, it broke to pieces cutting his hand and showering the valuable carpet with blood and splinters. Alan and I were reduced to mad laughter."

Ann loved strife and had deliberately exaggerated the sad story— which she found hilarious and Fermor thought painful—in order to entertain Waugh. According to Fermor's more reliable account (based on a letter he wrote at the time), Maugham had asked Ann to bring him to lunch. When they met, Maugham invited him to stay on as his guest and write at the villa. After drinking too much Fermor quoted Diana Cooper's absurd belief that everyone in the College of Heralds had a stammer. Noting that day was the Feast of the Assumption, Fermor mentioned Correggio's painting in the Louvre and repeated his stammering friend's bon mot. He made a "classic Freudian error," but had no intention of mocking Maugham's stammer. No one was aware that anything was wrong until Maugham bid him a premature farewell. Fermor was mortified to learn that Maugham thought he'd deliberately tried to wound him.

There was no shattered glass or blood on the carpet. But the nervous Fermor made things even worse by catching a monogrammed sheet in the zipper of his suitcase and had to slip out of the villa with the shreds hanging out of his bag. A few days later, after friends had intervened on Fermor's behalf, Maugham felt that he had been sufficiently punished by the summary dismissal. Maugham invited him back for a reconciliation feast, but was not willing to forgive him. It was a very stiff occasion, and they never regained a friendly footing.[5]

Maugham also became an unwilling witness to the Flemings' quite horrifying sex life. Ian was a dominant personality and had often told Ann (who didn't at first take him literally): "I want to leave some kind of mark on you." Searle's claim that Ian beat Ann when they were guests at the villa and left the bloody towels as evidence was confirmed by Anthony Powell and by Fleming's biographer. Powell noted that "the towels so prodigally sent to the laundry were used to alleviate the smart when Ian Fleming whipped his wife during sexual encounters taking place during their visit." Ann shared her husband's predilections, provided the masochistic complement to his sadism and perversely confessed: "I long for you even if you whip me because I love being hurt by you."[6] Ann's bloody sheets made the villa sound like Churchill's description of life in the old British navy, "Rum, buggery and the lash."

With such grisly guests, it's scarcely surprising that by 1954 Maugham felt obliged to curtail his visitors. He found it increasingly difficult to put them up and put up with them, and complained that he no longer felt strong enough to cope with the English invaders. "All this entertaining has finally tired me," he said, "& I have made up my mind to give it up. . . . I am in better health & able to work better when I live a very quiet & regular life." The biographer and critic Peter Quennell, an uneasy if not ungrateful guest, explained that Maugham's social rigidity, oppressive formality and pessimistic gloom sometimes made nervous visitors behave in strange ways:

> Maugham was a severe host. He imposed a regime and demanded a standard of behaviour that his guests neglected at their peril; and a single ill-judged remark or minor mis-step might plunge them into permanent disgrace. . . . I was never wholly at ease in his company; and his sombre mask, with its deep, despondent furrows and its saurian folds and creases, had so strange an effect. . . . Planned for a life of well-earned ease, his house and gardens had a haunted air; I was perpetually conscious of their master's presence, and of the clouds he spread around him.[7]

Like many old people, Maugham believed that the years of his youth were superior to the decadent present, that the good times of the old days were better than contemporary pleasures. But when Robin innocently asked: "what is the happiest memory of your life?," Maugham—despite friends, villa, paintings, wealth and fame—sadly confessed: "I cer-can't think of a single moment." Anthony Powell, who occasionally lunched with Maugham in the 1950s, exaggerated (but did not attempt to explain) his fundamental sadness: "an undoubtedly tragic, if sometimes not very attractive figure, [his] immense popular success in one area of his life contrasted with ghastly interior misery at the other. The stutter . . . was in ordinary conversation far less in evidence than I had expected. . . . The slight hesitation had charm rather than the reverse."

Though Maugham had never suffered severe hardship, grinding poverty or lack of recognition, serious physical or mental illness, scandal or public disgrace, Quennell agreed with Powell that his life was essentially sad and tried to account for his misery: "The deep-rooted unhappiness that pervaded his life had had many different causes. The death, during his early childhood, of a mother he adored; his lonely youth; the loss of Gerald Haxton, the companion of his middle years and the only human being he had ever equally admired and loved; and, throughout his existence, the humiliating stutter that often throttled him and left him nearly speechless—each had contributed something to the shipwreck of his soul."[8] His worldview—compounded by the failure of his marriage, his repressed sexual life and his lack of love—was dark. Like Kafka's, it precluded happiness; and, like Kafka, he may have cultivated it to inspire his art.

II

ROYALTY AND HONORS undoubtedly cheered him up. In April 1954 the Aga Khan, the fabulously wealthy religious leader who'd provided useful introductions to Indian maharajahs in 1938, asked for a preface to his *Memoirs*. Though Maugham had refused to pay Graham Sutherland properly, he insisted on a proper fee. He told his agent: "If I had been commissioned to do it I would not have dreamt of undertaking it for less than $2,500. I leave you to make the best arrangement you can, but I expect you to refuse quite firmly an insignificant amount." Maugham would exact his fee or do the job for nothing; the Aga Khan had to pay the going price or lose face.

Maugham was bored by the duke and duchess of Windsor. But he was delighted when the king and queen of Greece, wanting him all to themselves, invited him to a private luncheon, and was pleased to tell a gossip columnist that he played bridge with the exiled queen of Spain. When he remarked, with a connoisseur's eye, that her pear-shaped pearl seemed familiar to him, the queen explained: "You saw it in a Velázquez portrait of Philip II."[9]

Having passed his seventieth birthday in the solitary woods of South Carolina, Maugham must have had richer hopes as his eightieth approached in 1954. His publishers planned a *Festschrift,* to be edited by the novelist Jocelyn Brooke, and invited thirty British and American writers to contribute. Max Beerbohm, Compton Mackenzie, Noël Coward, Evelyn Waugh, Peter Quennell, William Plomer, Cecil Day-Lewis, Rosamond Lehmann and Vita Sackville-West—many of whom were old friends and had eagerly accepted his hospitality—all made transparent excuses. Raymond Mortimer and Anthony Powell were the only ones who agreed to write (Powell the only one who actually delivered), and the project was regretfully abandoned. Willie, as usual, felt unloved; and his war against the intelligentsia continued for the rest of his life.

There were, however, consolations, which he perhaps too eagerly sought. Canon F. J. Shirley, the headmaster of King's School, had been courting him as a potential benefactor. Born in 1890, Shirley had read history at Oxford, fought in the Great War and trained as a barrister before finding his "true vocation as an ordained schoolmaster." In October 1952 Maugham wrote Shirley about his most ardent hopes:

> I will tell you my two secret wishes—I have never revealed them to any living person. I think I ought to have the O.M. I don't want anything else—I would refuse anything like a knighthood. But they gave Hardy the O.M. and I think I am the greatest living writer of English, and they ought to give it to me. My other secret is that I should like my ashes to be buried somewhere in the Precincts [of the cathedral and school].

The second wish, with Canon Shirley's help, was granted; the first eluded him. The Order of Merit was created in 1902 and limited to twenty-four members. Among Maugham's contemporaries the honor had been (or would be) awarded to J. M. Barrie, John Galsworthy, J. B. Priestley, E. M. Forster, T. S. Eliot, Graham Greene and Graham Sutherland, who'd built his reputation on Maugham's portrait. If Barrie, Galsworthy and Priestley, then why not Willie Maugham? The problem, he explained to Sam Behrman, was that it was also the "Order of Morals." As a homosexual living in self-imposed, tax-free exile, he simply didn't qualify.

Shifting his ground a bit and expanding his ambitions, though apparently resigned to disappointment, he remarked: "Three [very different] things and three things only I would have been grateful for"—a knighthood, the Nobel Prize and "a b-bit of true love." But getting his wish fulfilled might also, as in a fairy tale, be disappointing. "Life is long and s-sad and horrid and one takes refuge in unfulfillment. . . . I still revel in unfulfillment." The Nobel Prize was (or would be) awarded to several English-language writers whose work was inferior to his own: Galsworthy, Sinclair Lewis, Pearl Buck and John Steinbeck. But in 1957, when the Maugham enthusiast Klaus Jonas suggested him as a candidate, the Swedish critics adamantly replied that "Maugham's writing did not fall under the criteria for the prize and there was not the slightest chance that he would ever get it."[10]

Wyndham Lewis, who never achieved proper recognition for his art or his writing and died in poverty, caustically commented: "In England if you only live long enough you become a great painter." He also told a friend: "I am approaching the age when society usually says to itself: 'We might as well recognize the existence of that unpleasant person. He'll be dead soon.' " And so it was with Maugham. His old friend Gerald Kelly, who continued to crank out portraits of Maugham as well as of the royal family, had been knighted in 1945 and became president of the Royal Academy in 1949. He knew how the power structure worked, made the right connections and got Willie (almost) what he wanted.

The closest he'd come to royal recognition, Maugham revealed in a speech at Columbia University in November 1950, was when the queen (later the queen mother, whose taste ran to Barbara Cartland) graciously informed his brother that "though she had not read any of Mr. Maugham's works, she has looked at all of them." (This, oddly enough, was also Frederic's position.) Kelly, however, told Alanson how at a Royal Academy banquet in February 1953 he'd cunningly introduced Maugham to the young Queen Elizabeth:

> I had wanted the Queen to be amused, and I asked whether I could put Willie to sit next to her, and she said she would be too frightened, and I had to reassure her that he could, if he chose, be the nicest company. And she agreed to take the risk! As we walked into dinner she said to me: —"I thought Mr. Maugham lived in the south of France." And I said that he had come over in order to sit next to her, and she blushed like the girl that she is, and said: "That is the prettiest compliment I have ever been paid."[11]

The less distinguished but still impressive award, the Companion of Honour, was founded in 1917 and limited to sixty-five members. Kelly's royal introduction had worked magic; and Maugham's old friend Winston Churchill wrote a cordial personal letter announcing that the honor was on the way to the companion. In June 1954, dressed in a morning coat and a top hat hired for ten shillings from Moss Bros. (his own had been destroyed in the Blitz), he arrived for the simple ceremony at Buckingham Palace. He was led through many rooms and down many long corridors. Quite alone, he was presented to the queen at precisely 11:45. He bowed, stepped forward, shook hands and received the insignia in a small leather case. Like most of her doting subjects, he found the queen charming, pretty and well dressed, and admired her clear eyes and rosy skin. He was invited to sit down, and they chatted inconsequentially for fifteen minutes. Then, politely dismissed, he rose, shook hands again, bowed, retreated— and for once was pleased by the occasion. Eliot sent him a fan letter and a dozen roses, which made him feel like "an elderly t-t-tart." But the eupho-

*Maugham on his eightieth birthday, "in my study & with
all the books I have ever written," 1954*

ria quickly dissipated, and he told Arthur Marshall: " 'don't you realize
what the C.H. means? It means we-well done, but' . . . it wasn't the O.M."

Maugham was also slightly mollified by honorary degrees from the
universities of Toulouse and of Oxford (in 1952); by being made an honorary senator of Heidelberg, accompanied by endlessly boring speeches
and a diploma for "his impeccable portrayal of human character" (in
1960); and by being named—with Churchill, Forster, John Masefield and
G. M. Trevelyan—a newly created Companion of Literature by the Royal
Society of Literature (also in 1960).

In the spring of 1955 Syrie, whom he'd scarcely seen for thirty years,
became ill and took to her bed. But she was very tough, Maugham
thought, and didn't seem to get any worse. On July 28 a telegram from
Liza announced that her mother had died at the age of seventy-six. Still
bitter about the £2,400 alimony he'd been paying every year since 1929,
and anticipating the title ("Looking Back") of his last attack on Syrie, he
wrote: "It would be hypocrisy on my part to pretend that I am deeply
grieved at Syrie's death. She had me every which way from the beginning

Maugham at the villa, with Picasso's La Grecque *in the background, 1954*

and never ceased to give me hell. Her hope, for some years, I have been told, was that she would survive me. I wonder, when she looked back, if she ever did, whether it occurred to her what a mess she had made of her life." Syrie's dishonesty and lies, he felt, had led to her lonely and miserable death.[12]

Alan Searle found Maugham increasingly difficult. In a long series of whining letters to Alanson, he sought avuncular sympathy (if not money) for his own sad plight. He had to walk warily to maintain a modicum of freedom without offending his master, and lamented that "living with Willie has become a great nervous strain. His celebrity in Europe has reached its peak, and I am hard put to protect him from the Press and all and sundry. I get insulted most days by all the people I keep at bay, but it's all part of the job." In some respects he must have longed for Willie's death; at the same time he was terribly afraid of what would happen to him afterward. In his early fifties, he thought he was too old to make a fresh start; and he hated Liza and her family, who were dangerous rivals for Maugham's affection, loyalty and money. When Maugham was ill in 1958, Searle told Alanson: "His condition rather frightened me and I suddenly wondered what on earth would become of me if anything happened to him. Protecting him from people he hasn't wanted to see has made me a lot of enemies, and his family, of course, are longing to cut my throat, so I am afraid that when the dread day comes, I am in for a pretty rough time—I shall be homeless and jobless in a very few hours."

When Willie's illness provoked a crisis, Alan, to protect himself and alienate Willie from his daughter, circulated malicious stories about her rapacity, lack of feeling and indifference to his welfare: "It has been a great responsibility to have to make all the decisions. Willie was too ill to care very much, and none of his family or relations did a thing, though they would have been the first to blame me if anything had gone wrong. . . . The family are coming for Easter. That I dread. They did not come last year because they had something better to do."

In December 1955 Isherwood, who also lived with a much younger and dependent man, found Alan "a rather sad figure but not really a pitiful one, because he obviously cares for Willie and considers these years spent with him well worth while."[13] But when provoked, the imperious Willie could treat Alan like a servant, or worse. When Alan teased a frog in the garden with a twig and ignored an order to leave it alone, Willie brought him into line with a sharp and humiliating kick. Refusing to give Alan peace of mind, Maugham kept him anxiously uncertain to make sure he'd remain until the very end. Alan had taken the king's shilling, and he would not be paid off till the end of the voyage.

20

The Old Party

1956–1961

HAROLD ACTON, ANOTHER homosexual expatriate, observed that Maugham, despite his sexual life and liberal politics, followed to the end of his days the social customs of an old-fashioned gentleman: "He was very Edwardian, really, in his mannerisms and in his attitude, and extremely conventional. He would have loathed the permissiveness of [1974]. It really would have upset him." When the literary editor of the *Sunday Times* asked Maugham to name for his Christmas survey a book that had interested him during the year, he chose Kingsley Amis' *Lucky Jim* (1954). Admiring it for all the wrong reasons, he showed how out of touch he was with contemporary feelings and behavior.

Ignoring the comic exaggeration of Amis' wicked satire on academic life, Maugham let fly with an ill-natured and unfortunate mixture of snobbery and misreading. His attack on the fictional characters (not on Amis himself or the quality of the novel) made him look like a reactionary old Tory and gave quite the wrong impression of his basically progressive social views:

> Kingsley Amis is so talented, his observation is so keen, that you cannot fail to be convinced that the young men he so brilliantly describes truly represent the class with which his novel is concerned. They do not go to university to acquire culture, but to get a job and when they have one,

scamp it. They have no manners, and are woefully unable to deal with any social predicament. Their idea of a celebration is to go to a public house and drink six beers. They are mean, malicious and envious. They will write anonymous letters to harass a fellow undergraduate and listen in to a telephone conversation that is no business of theirs. Charity, kindliness, generosity are qualities which they hold in contempt. They are scum.

Maugham failed to see that Amis, in his anarchic assault on hypocritical academics and pretentious artists, actually admired the subversive hero that Maugham so heartily despised. When Amis thanked him for the £500 Travel Award that he'd won earlier that year, Maugham's "reply was very friendly and full of praise for *Lucky Jim* but it took Amis aback; it commended him as a man of like-minded cultivation (had not Amis been at Oxford?) who had performed a vital social service." Maugham, Amis said, "was fascinated by the portrayal I gave of a new wave of barbarians who were just then coming of age and entering universities, and how appalling it was that they were destroying all civilised standards."[1] Maugham's blast made him look foolish, but it was a great advertisement for the novel and helped define Amis' place among the Angry Young Men and The Movement.

Yet the younger writers of the 1950s still respected Maugham. Amis tolerantly called him "the only writer whose books you read to the end with interest, sympathy and enjoyment." He also said that Maugham helped "restore one's confidence in traditional forms of writing." Amis' third novel, *I Like It Here*, which the Travel Award had enabled him to write, uses "Zumzit-Mum" as a cosmopolitan contrast to the provincial hero, Garnet Bowen. A passport photo gave Bowen "a chance to behave like a Somerset Maugham character by comparing his new one with the one he had taken for his only previous civilian trip abroad." His room in the Portuguese Algarve "was Maugham-like, but of the Far East and not the Riviera sub-type." And a character he meets on a ship would provide "a marvelous story for someone, but not, unfortunately, for him. Only a rather worse or much older writer than himself could tackle it satisfactorily. W. Somerset Maugham (on grounds of age, not lack of merit) was the kind of chap."[2] After traveling abroad at Maugham's expense, Amis gave his novel a deliberately provincial title and made fun of everything foreign.

While the Amis controversy boiled up, another massive dose of sheep

Maugham with his dog Ching, on a staircase of the villa, c. 1959

cells from Dr. Niehans seemed to revive both Maugham and Alan and stimulate their sex life. Writing to Alexander Frere, who'd just had an operation, Alan alluded to a recent report advocating more tolerant laws for adult homosexuals and flippantly asked: "What did you have off or out? We had something in, or rather UP. I had no idea it was such a pleasant sensation; it's enough to make a feller change his views and cry 'Vive Wolfenden.' " Alan, livelier in his letters than in person (when he was usually subdued by Maugham), continued to parody his rejuvenation: "When I see little boys and girls in the street, I want to go and play with them (don't misunderstand me) and Mr. Maugham says I gave a silly little pout when he refused to buy me some toys this morning, so it looks as though the treatment has worked!"

When Diana Cooper heard about the treatments from Maugham she exaggerated the sacrificial slaughter as well as the role of randy Bedouin played by Alan (whom she seemed to despise):

> We had Willie Maugham and his catamite Searle to lunch yesterday—they both had the "cell" treatment in Switzerland—the cells and serums of flocks of muttons and beefs and goat still pulsating with life are pumped into you—with frightening success. Willie's past mending but Searle has become a garrulous Tom Cat—right out of his bed—I heard him say while waiting for Willie's much increased impediment—to allow a word out—in a cockney-pansy voice, "My dear you can't imagine what it's like—I wake up to find myself under a *tent*"—here an obscene gesture was made, denoting a fabulous erection—"it hasn't happened to me since I was in scouts!"[3]

Maugham, that engaging Gila monster, began to refer to himself as an Old Party with "sallow, wrinkled skin and tired eyes." The social butterfly was turning into a slothful caterpillar who preferred "to stay at home, bathe in my pool, read my books and play patience. Old age!" On their trip to Italy in 1956, however, Alan was amazed by his energy: "Willie is quite extraordinary; at the end of a day's arduous sightseeing, he would come back as flush as a daisy, while I was quite worn out." Alan boasted, as late as 1961, that his eighty-seven-year-old companion still had an active sex life: "Willie is in great form and has a permanently swallowed canary expression—I'm rather afraid with reason too—and I feel like an old retired sea captain about to return to sea."[4]

Maugham always lived in splendor, not only at the villa but also on his annual trips to London, where he was treated as an honored guest. One writer enviously reported that "he always has the same suite at the Dorchester on the fourth floor, overlooking the park, and the huge sitting room is furnished with his own books, pictures, Epstein's bust of him, etc.—all of which the hotel stores when he is away." Though frail, he had not lost his urge to travel and be on the move. Before being permanently confined to quarters, he wanted to have a final look at some of his favorite places.

In October 1959 he and Alan set out, on their last long voyage, for Japan. Maugham's main contact there was the young novelist Francis

Francis King, 1950s

King, who was working for the British Council in Kyoto. King had distinct affinities with Maugham: he was cosmopolitan (he'd been born in Switzerland, grown up in India and worked in Italy, Greece, Egypt and Finland) and wrote finely observed novels and stories. When he later won the Travel Award, Maugham told him: "I note for the last ten years or so you've been living abroad, and I think in this case I really should stipulate that you ought to go and live in Sheffield or Birmingham for three months."

A few years before they'd first met in Japan, Maugham had adopted an avuncular tone and advised King to leave Greece. He realized that King was leading a pleasant life, but felt he'd exhausted the country's fictional possibilities and was wasting his time as a writer. King had to choose, Maugham told him, between life and art. Allowing a rare insight into *both* sides of the correspondence—for Maugham always destroyed all letters after answering them—King recalled: "I had told him in a letter how, having written *The Widow* and *The Man on the Rock* simultaneously and then, in quick succession *The Firewalkers* and *The Dark Glasses,* I now found myself without a single idea for another book. Later, in Japan, he was to tell me how he had always found that travel ignited his creativity. I therefore think that his advice in the letter was derived from his own experience. In the event, it proved to be right. . . . The moment I reached Japan my mind was bursting with ideas. Three books—the first of them, *The Custom House,* one of my longest and best—followed."[5]

Maugham was received like royalty in Japan. The homosexual writer Yukio Mishima gave him a volume of *Five Modern No Plays* with a flattering inscription. Huge crowds turned out to see him wherever he went; and Alan followed dutifully behind, bearing the bouquets and gifts like a lady-in-waiting. Though pleased by the enthusiastic mob, Maugham sourly noted the marked contrast to England: "University professors queue up each morning in my hotel to get me to sign copies of my books. But when I stay in London, no one cares a damn that I'm there." King remembered that the professors clung to Maugham like the snakes to Laocoön, but that he was far more interested in hearing about the scandalous behavior of their friends. King recalled that "when we were having a meal or a drink after sightseeing—it was often difficult to shake off the Japanese professors, most of whom Maugham found terribly tedious, even though he was always courteous to them, taking pains with the most idiotic of their questions—we usually exchanged literary gossip, for which (as you will know) I have as ravenous an appetite as he had."

Escorting him around for a week, King was impressed by Maugham's penetrating insight and keen thirst for new experiences. He invited a Jewish sinologist to dinner with Maugham, who seemed utterly exhausted and hardly spoke a word. On the way back to the hotel Maugham remarked that the man was half Chinese, which King, who knew him well, had never realized. Maugham's "powers of observation were working even when he was very old and very tired and not feeling very well." What most impressed King "was his desire for information about Japanese life and culture even at that advanced age. He still felt he had something important to learn. . . . He was often almost dead from exhaustion but he was determined to see all that he could."[6]

While Maugham tried to understand life in Japan, Alan, thirty years younger, was out for seedy pleasures and a good time. "We arrived in Tokyo two days ago," he ecstatically told Zipkin, "and already I am an authority on buck teeth and bow legs . . . and I've grown two inches." Wishing to see a bit of low life, he rather archly told the Heinemann's agent that *Maugham* wanted "to attend a show, primarily sexual, where (for instance) women on stage used parts of their anatomy not intended for that purpose to smoke cigarettes, propel ping-pong balls into basket-ball type nets and so on." Though afraid that Maugham might be disgusted, they duly made the arrangements, which were finally canceled because of Maugham's "fatigue."

The real reason for the cancellation, King explained, was Maugham's desire to dominate, even enslave, his companion. Alan told King: " 'I want you to show me the queer bars and clubs. Willie will trot up to bed as soon as dinner is over.' . . . But when he heard that Alan, John [Haylock] and I were going out for a drink (that was how Alan put it to him) he at once objected: 'No, Alan, I'm not f-f-feeling at all well tonight! I'd like to have you n-n-near at hand in case I need a d-d-doctor.' Seeing us out, Alan exclaimed, 'Oh, how I long to be *free!*' " Alan occasionally managed to escape from Willie's clutches to go shopping. But he regretfully reported that he had not bought the outsized dildos that Zipkin had requested: "I didn't bring your sex-kit from Japan because we had such troubles at the shop over the size and shape. They recommended things I am sure would have put you into a nursing home!"[7]

On the way back to Europe they stopped at Maugham's old haunts in Singapore. His comparatively frosty reception (the old Malaya hands were still licking their wounds) made him go into hiding: "Many, many people wanted to meet the great man but he was old, not well and very tired and spent most of his time in his air-conditioned suite at the Raffles [Hotel]." In contrast to his exquisite politeness in Japan, he caustically punctured the social upstarts at the Singapore Club by announcing in a loud voice: "Observing these people, I am no longer surprised there is such a scarcity of domestic servants back home in England." As Orwell, echoing Maugham, wrote in *The Road to Wigan Pier*, lower-middle-class people could live like aristocrats in the East: "in India, with cheap horses, free shooting, and hordes of black servants, it was so easy to play at being a gentleman."[8]

II

THE FIVE LONG, readable essays in Maugham's last book, *Points of View* (1959)—like those in *The Vagrant Mood* (1952) and *Great Novelists and Their Novels* (1954)—emphasize the life of the subject. They are appreciative but rather superficial; long on plot summary and short on analysis of meaning. They offer conventional judgments, but surprisingly few insights about literary craft and technique. The essays are useful if you know very little about the subject; if not, not. "The Three Novels of a Poet" expressed his admiration for Goethe's *The Sorrows of Young Werther, Wilhelm Meister's Apprenticeship* and *The Elective Affinities*. "The Saint" described the Indian mystic whom he met in Tiruvannamalai in 1938 and who influenced *The Razor's Edge*. "Prose and Dr. Tillotson" was about the seventeenth-century archbishop of Canterbury whose prose style influenced Dryden. "The Short Story" defended the plot-driven fiction of Maupassant and Kipling, and attacked the more atmospheric but static tales of James, Chekhov and Mansfield. "Three Journalists" portrayed four keepers of journals: the Goncourt brothers and the obscure Jules Renard and Paul Léautaud. It's a great pity that he did not devote more than a few sentences to the cosmopolitan and contentious André Gide, who'd bravely defended homosexuality in *Corydon* (1924) and won the Nobel Prize in 1947. Maugham did mention, however, that Gide's *Journals* were "more consistently interesting than those of the other Journalists whom I propose here to deal with. He had more talent than they and a more catholic culture. For a Frenchman he was widely traveled and well read in the literature of countries other than his own. He loved music and was himself a fine pianist."

The most striking aspect of this book was Maugham's unremitting and unfair attack on his rival Katherine Mansfield, whose reputation began to rise rapidly in the 1950s. Maugham thought her impressionistic stories had no form. "They remind me of great jelly-fishes," he wrote in the *Travellers' Library* (1933), "iridescent and strangely lovely as they float aimlessly about the sea, but floppy and inert." Ten years later, in his *Introduction to Modern English and American Literature,* he ignored her achievement and was intolerably condescending: "She had a small and delicate talent and a sensitive feeling for visual things, but when she tried to write a story of any length, it broke to pieces in the middle because it was not supported by a structure of sufficient strength." Finally, in *Points of View*, he attributed her artistic failure to her personal defects: "Katherine Mansfield's stories are the outpourings of a lonely, sensitive, neurotic, sick woman who never felt quite at home in the Europe she had chosen to live in."[9] He had always disapproved of Mansfield's Chekhovian technique, but particularly resented the fact that highbrow magazines had published her stories but rejected his own.

Great writers like Samuel Johnson, Dickens, Hardy, James and Freud, hoping to obliterate the record of their most personal thoughts and intimate secrets, had methodically destroyed their private papers. At the end of *The Moon and Sixpence* Strickland's Tahitian mistress, following his orders, burns his house and all his remaining masterpieces. Maugham was also a destroyer. After making a minimal selection for his fascinating *Writer's Notebook* (1949), he'd burned fifteen precious volumes of his diaries. Wescott noted that his letters also went the way of all paper: "every afternoon when he has done his little stint of correspondence, he tears everything into small scraps with a kind of spiteful haste and energy; and now and then he calls our attention to the fact, and says that he trusts we all do likewise with whatever he may write to us. And yet I feel sure that he has never indited a line of any intimacy [except about Gerald's death]; not in the last fifty years at all events."

In 1966, a year after Maugham's death, Searle confirmed that he'd "destroyed most of his personal and private papers and letters a few years ago. Those that remained were given to me with the proviso that they should remain unseen—a wish that I intend to honour. The manuscript of Mr. Maugham's memoirs was also given to me, with an even more strong proviso. I intend to destroy it." Instead, he preserved and sold the memoir, which still exists. Maugham had revealed a great deal about himself in the autobiographical *Of Human Bondage, The Summing Up* and *A Writer's Notebook,* but was still reticent when writing about himself. He told a visiting Russian: "my doubts, torments, fears, my confusion belong to me alone."[10]

The mass of paper that Maugham gleefully destroyed was bountifully replenished every day. Books, both bound and in typescript, poured into the villa like a Niagara cascade: strangers asked for help; publishers requested quotes; cranks and ideologues attempted to convert him to their views; retired colonels and civil servants sent everlasting anecdotes of

Maugham and a fellow pupil, Charles Etheridge, King's School, 1958

tiger shoots in Malaya and what Bloggs had said to Blimp after the Indian Mutiny; poets inscribed slim, pathetic volumes published at their own expense. Maugham told Frederic Raphael that "his work was interrupted by, on the average, five manuscripts and some four hundred letters a week. They come mainly from young men and old ladies." He also complained to a demanding correspondent that every mail brought a flood of requests for donations. Though politely answered by the faithful Alan, the letters finally bewildered, harassed and exasperated him.

The villa, even with reduced servants, now cost £23,000 a year to maintain, but Maugham was earning as much as $5 a word and the money poured in along with the burdensome manuscripts. He tried to fend off strangers, but often helped young writers and was remarkably munificent with gifts to King's School. Knowing he couldn't last much longer, Canon Shirley began to court him seriously in the mid-1950s, and Maugham was determined to outdo Hugh Walpole's benefactions. After nostalgia for the past overcame the miserable reality of his childhood at King's, he gave a number of eighteenth-century mezzotints to enhance the masters' Common Room; £3,000 for a new boathouse; £5,000 to house a substantial part of his own library; and the valuable manuscripts of his first and last novels: *Liza of Lambeth* and *Catalina*.

As early as 1942 he'd condemned public schools as "the great breeding-ground of snobbery in England," though he recognized that they provided a superior education. In 1953 he donated £10,000 for a scholarship to offer talented working-class boys a chance to be educated at the school and go on to a university. A local lad, the first and only Maugham Scholar at King's, was admitted to Oxford. This idealistic project belied the apparent snobbery he'd expressed in his letter about *Lucky Jim,* yet his response to the boy's success was ambivalent. He told Shirley, with "a characteristic cold douche: 'I am glad to know that [the boy] has got a Scholarship, but sorry he is joining the white collar class—which means a starvation wage and poor prospects. But I know that this is your idea of earthly bliss.' "[11] The scholarship failed to take hold for lack of suitable applicants, and the money, with Maugham's permission, was used to complete a new physics building.

III

MAUGHAM—WHO'D ENTERTAINED dukes and dined with queens— now completed his royal flush by his friendship with the most attractive and romantic couple on the Riviera, Prince Rainier and Grace Kelly. After their horribly uncomfortable wedding ceremony in April 1956—several hours in formal dress in the icebox of a cathedral—he was rewarded by a banquet at the palace, replete with mountains of caviar and oceans of champagne. His wedding present, which had to compete with a Rolls-Royce from the grateful citizens of Monaco, was a three-volume set of his collected stories, handsomely bound in Morocco leather. Maugham, who'd probably heard gossip about Grace's notorious promiscuity, caustically insisted that he, rather than "the tottering firm of Heinemann,

Maugham and Winston Churchill, c. 1951

should pay for a wedding present for the prince and his presumably chaste bride." A few months after the wedding, he thrilled his granddaughter by taking her to a party in Monte Carlo where Grace looked enchanting and very much in love with the prince. Searle (who loved dropping names and was easily awed) later wrote, after dining with the royal couple, that Grace "really is lovely, and has a nice sense of humour and is very gay and amusing. She has improved the prince beyond all recognition."[12]

Loving contact with other celebrities, Maugham cultivated the friendship of three eminent contemporaries. In June 1956 he visited the art historian Bernard Berenson, nine years his senior. He lived in exquisite splendor near Florence in his villa, I Tatti, which was also filled with precious paintings. Berenson eyed his guest warily and liked what he saw. He described Maugham's "lined, wrinkled face, senile mouth, kindly expression (or is it mere resignation?). Stammered. Utterly unaffected." Maugham was simplicity itself, and there was no trace of playing up to his reputation. But when the visitor failed to respond to his Italian primitives, Berenson put down his aged rival by weirdly noting that he "showed a fantastic absence of feeling for visual art" and by concluding, even more absurdly, that Alan had better taste. Maugham also began to see a great deal of his Riviera neighbor, the Canadian-born newspaper tycoon Lord Beaverbrook, whom he'd advised about aircraft production in the early years of World War II, and used to call "dear Max." Annoyed that Alan had become Beaverbrook's great favorite, he now referred to him as "that mis-shapen old ape at Cap d'Ail."[13]

Partly through Beaverbrook, who often invited the francophile Churchill to his Villa Capponcina, Maugham renewed his friendship with the exact contemporary he'd known since before the Great War. Maugham once told Robert Boothby, who'd been Churchill's parliamentary private secretary, that he'd failed to act on inside information from the great man: "if I believed one word of what Churchill told me before the War, I'd be a very much richer man than I am today. But I didn't believe a word he said about what was going to happen." Edouard MacAvoy recalled that Churchill had actually asked Maugham's advice soon after Maugham's visit to India in 1938. " 'You who know the Indians so well, what would you do in our place?' asked Churchill. '*Shoot or clear out*,' answered Maugham. 'You know very well that we can do neither one nor the other,' " Churchill replied. In "Looking Back" Maugham sketched Churchill's sublimely egoistic character: "Winston was self-centred. . . . He had little consideration for others. . . . He had little patience with stupidity and was apt to think people stupid when they did not agree with him. . . . He could not bear to think that posterity should see him as Sutherland had seen him."[14]

In September 1957 Ann Fleming told Waugh that an amusing rivalry had developed between Maugham and Churchill: "Maugham delights in being a year older than Sir Winston, and triumphantly exhibits his nimble movements, good eyesight and hearing in comparison to Sir Winston's old rogue elephant's swaying and total lack of hearing." A bit later Maugham told Frere that the two men had reached a solipsistic standoff: "One of the advantages of dining with Winston was that he didn't hear a word I said and I never heard a word he said, so we were both very happy." In 1958, in a more somber spirit, Searle described Churchill's tragic deterioration: "Winston is coming to luncheon today. He is a very sad sight now. His mind has completely collapsed—I hate to see the end of a great man." Maugham, as usual, had the last word: "If you think I'm g-g-ga-ga, you should see W-W-Winston."[15]

21

Family Values

1962–1965

IN THE EARLY 1960s art thieves were at work on the French Riviera. The mayor of St. Jean–Cap Ferrat, concerned about the collection of his most famous resident, personally inspected the Villa Mauresque. He warned Maugham: " 'I have never seen a house that so obviously invites robbers to enter and steal. If you want to keep your pictures you must do something about it. You must build a strong room and keep your pictures in it.' " Maugham maintained that for many years the paintings "had given me great pleasure; now they were an anxiety." This was his explanation of why he auctioned off his art collection in London on April 10, 1962. But there clearly was more than one thing to do about it. He certainly didn't need the money from the sale, and could well afford to install the best security system and hire private guards. Instead, he sold his beloved paintings and left his vast walls depressingly bare.

Maugham's real reasons stemmed from his growing suspicions of Liza, exacerbated by his hatred of her mother and husband. When he began to collect paintings seriously after the war, he gave a number of works to Liza in order to avoid punitive death duties, but retained possession of them during his lifetime. In December 1949 he affectionately wrote her: "Dearest Liza. . . . It may interest you to know that you now own a very fine Sisley and a Renoir of a nude lady, rather buxom and light tomato color, not very big but very beautiful. We brought her down [from Paris] with us in the car and she already hangs in my bedroom. The Sisley is a large picture and will come by train. . . . My love to you all. Daddy."

In a letter of November 1961 Maugham, concerned about taxes, wrote to Lord Beaverbrook suggesting that he was tempted to move to Lausanne to be closer to Niehans and avoid death duties. But he felt his own well-being was more important than his family's and decided to stay in France. "I am too old to start a life here," he wrote, "and though on my death the taxes would be less than they would otherwise be, I do not see why I should care." Maugham did not love Liza deeply, but he was glad to be a father and grandfather, and proud of his wealth and his astute purchases. If Alan Searle had not stirred up Lear-like fears of being dispossessed by a wicked daughter, Maugham would have sent Liza, rather than Sotheby's, the paintings that he had bought for her.

According to one biographer, Sotheby's sent the handsome homosexual Bruce Chatwin to secure the prestigious collection, for which he later wrote the catalogue. Chatwin enjoyed mimicking "Searle issuing instructions: 'Bruce, do let Willie play with your hair.' But he found the atmosphere surrounding the author 'seedy,' 'grotesque,' 'murky.' "[1] The thirty-five pictures in the sale included the thirty-three that were handsomely illustrated in *Purely for My Pleasure* (also published in April 1962) and Graham Sutherland's *Thorn Forms* and *Datura Flowers in Glass*. It excluded three less important works by Barrable, Zoffany and de Wilde as well as a charming still life by Vuillard, promised to Searle.

Like most Impressionist art, Maugham's paintings were an excellent investment that made a tremendous profit in a short period of time. The Gauguin, bought for 400 francs in 1917, sold for $104,720. The Lautrec, bought for $10,000 in 1950, sold for $75,600 to the American millionaire Huntington Hartford, who outbid Lord Beaverbrook. The Matisse, also bought for $10,000 in 1950, sold for $106,400. The Monet, bought for $14,000 in 1949, sold for $112,000. The two Renoirs, bought in 1949–50 for $79,000, sold for $134,000. Picasso's Blue Period *Death of Harlequin,* with another painting of a woman in a garden on the verso, was the star of the sale and fetched $224,000. The phenomenally successful auction drew a crowd of 2,500 and made $1,466,000.

This ill-advised sale led to Maugham's permanent estrangement from his only child. Two old friends who kept in touch with him at the end of his life provided some insight into his character and motives. The politician Robert Boothby got on well with the stoical Maugham because, unlike Liza, he never asked for anything and wasn't afraid of him:

> It was a strange thing. Willie had a terrible stammer, but when we were alone it would just disappear. I think the reason was that I wanted nothing from him and he, thank God, wanted nothing from me. Sex, you see, never came into our relationship. I was always aware of who he was surrounded by, but I never gave a damn. He taught me to see life as he saw it. The senselessness of it, coupled with a determination to see the bloody thing through. He did frighten a lot of people. He was a formidable little man. His face was like a mask, rather like a tortoise. He never frightened me, nor tried to, because he knew he couldn't.

Like Axel Heyst, the tragically remote hero of Conrad's *Victory,* Maugham distrusted human emotions and intimate relations, and believed "he who forms a tie is lost. The germ of corruption has entered into his soul." Raymond Mortimer, reviewing *Purely for My Pleasure,* emphasized Maugham's chilling aloofness—a radical flaw in both his character and his art: "A distrust of life, presumably the sour fruit of a most miserable childhood, seems to have made him reluctant to care deeply for anyone or anything—even for pictures, even for the words that are the material of his art. I think that no great writer, not even Hume or Gibbon, has been so detached."[2] The sale was a deliberate farewell to cherished possessions—another stage of Maugham's detachment from life itself.

Glenway Wescott, always a close observer, explained how money, and Maugham's lifelong conflict about his sexuality, poisoned his relations with both Alan and Liza:

> As of a few years ago, W. S. Maugham, in ingratitude—and in divided mind about homosexuality, fundamental disbelief in it—had decided not to bequeath Alan enough to live on. (The superfluity all to go to his daughter, Lady John Hope.)
>
> But think what a happy, humorous life Alan could look forward to, with a sufficient income. How hard it will be for him to shift for himself, accustomed to luxury and sexuality, growing old, losing all his looks, and burning, burning! W.S.M. ought to be able to imagine all that.

Maugham *did* imagine all that—and so, even more intensely, did Alan. But as Maugham aged, grew weaker and increasingly dependent, he used Alan's anxiety about money to maintain his power and ensure his friend's devotion. Always the dramatist, he set the stage for the high-stakes battle and let the two adversaries fight it out.

Liza was connected to Maugham by blood, Alan by their intimate friendship and communal life in France. Forced to play a pocket-Iago and serpent in the garden, Alan spied on guests by opening their letters before posting them and was hostile to anyone who'd dared to be critical. When Maugham gave Alan the manuscript of *Great Novelists and Their Novels,* Liza suggested Alan leave it to her. Alan would rather destroy it than do that, and told Alanson he might give it to Stanford. In the end he disappointed everyone by selling it, and it's now at the University of Texas.

Alan dreaded Liza's visits. They took place in an atmosphere of palpable animosity (which Maugham may have provoked and enjoyed), but gave Liza and her children the opportunity to strengthen their bonds with Maugham. Alan wanted to leave when they came, but had to stay to protect his own interests. Never keen on small children, Maugham rarely invited other guests when Liza visited, yet didn't want to remain alone with her. The family, Alan complained to Zipkin, "made me feel so unwanted and like a stranger in the house. How lucky you are never to have known the humiliation of dependence." Maugham stoked the fires by warning Searle: "If I should die while we are traveling, you get back [to the villa] as soon as you can. You will be up against the most ruthless and predatory people in the world. Get your own things and get them away as fast as you can."[3]

In the end, convinced by Searle's accusations and fearful that Liza might have him declared incompetent, Maugham tried to disinherit her and she fought back. Their bitter struggle for money was worthy of Balzac. When he auctioned the paintings that (as his letters proved) legally belonged to her, she sued him for the proceeds of nine of them. The Renoir and Sisley as well as others by Monet, Lautrec, Bonnard, Matisse, Rouault and Utrillo had all been acquired after the war and were sold for $648,900. Maugham, who rightly felt he'd always been generous to Liza and her family, seemed genuinely surprised at being hauled into court. He'd already given Liza houses worth $112,000; paid for the education of her son Nicolas; given him and his sister, Camilla, a trust fund worth $400,000; and was planning to leave Liza the villa (worth $560,000) and a

Diana Marr-Johnson, Maugham's niece, May 2002

life interest on two million dollars. He told Robin that the pictures now claimed by Liza had always belonged to him: "I knew of course that John Hope and Liza wanted to get the money from the sale of my pictures, but as I had never given them to Liza, I did not take the matter very seriously. . . . I thought their attitude was merely a bluff."

Maugham now asserted that Liza "never cared a rap about me." He also claimed that she was not in fact his daughter and that her real father was Henry Wellcome. This shocking allegation branded her with the stigma of illegitimacy. At the same time, he tried to adopt Alan legally so he could leave everything to his "son." Liza, shocked and brokenhearted by his bizarre behavior, thought he considered Searle an employee and couldn't understand why he wanted to disinherit her. "I love him dearly," she maintained. "We have never had a row, not even a cross word." John Hope, searching for an explanation, thought Maugham hated the idea that *he* would inherit the villa. Making no effort to conceal his contempt, Maugham referred to his son-in-law as "Hopeless" and claimed "he would pick a brass farthing out of a dog's turd."[4]

Liza had previously agreed, at Maugham's request, that Alan would get all the book royalties after her father's death. But her generosity did little to calm Alan's fears that he'd be left out in the cold. She blamed him for provoking the suit after Maugham had lapsed into senility and told a reporter: "Without his awful influence my father would have been simply gaga. Instead, he became paranoid; he was convinced that I wanted to have him certified." As evidence, she said he'd vindictively screamed out in the night: "I will show them! I'll put them back into the gutter where they belong! I'll get even with them! Sons of bitches!" Maugham's niece Diana agreed that his disease contributed to the quarrel. It was terrible for Liza to be disowned and rejected. He had senile dementia and had become "quite dippy," yet in his lucid phases would express his old affection and tell Diana: "Do you know my daughter Liza? She bravely drives a bubble car in London and is a very good mother."[5]

Alan continued to whine about the brutal and beastly attacks in the English press, accompanied by satiric cartoons ("Nurse, he's just said da-da") about the ludicrous adoption. He condemned Liza—who'd merely tried to protect her legal rights—in many vitriolic but pitiful letters that showed both sides had suffered from his plot: "His vile so-called daughter has broken him and made his last years a misery. . . . It has nearly killed him and you would be shocked at the change in him. . . . When I see what that bitch has done to him it fills my heart with murder. *She* goes around saying 'I love my daddy and I want to be with him.' I wonder she doesn't drop dead."

In the end, despite Alan's lamentations, Liza won both cases. On June 12, 1963, a court in Nice declared that Maugham and Liza, as British subjects, were subject to British law, which stated that a child born out of wedlock becomes legitimate when the couple marry. The court also voided the adoption and ruled that Maugham, as a resident of France, was subject to French law, which prevented a parent from disinheriting a legitimate child.[6] Seven months later, on January 22, 1964, Liza's suit against Maugham was settled out of court. She got £229,500 for the pictures, the right to inherit the villa and her considerable court costs—all of which came close to one million dollars. Yet Liza's legal victory meant paradoxically that Alan had won. As a result she was now permanently estranged from Maugham, who left her no more than he had to, and Alan got a much greater share of the estate.

II

LIZA'S LAWSUIT REVIVED Maugham's bitter memories of her birth, his unfortunate marriage and his costly divorce. He retaliated by exposing Liza's illegitimacy and attacking Syrie in a three-part autobiographical essay, "Looking Back." Beaverbrook impetuously offered £75,000 for British Empire rights, but after considerable bargaining one of his editors beat Maugham down to £35,000. This was still an enormous sum, and Maugham delightedly told Frere: "I don't think any living writer has ever earned as much money per word as I have over this." The piece was serialized in Huntington Hartford's *Show* magazine (June–August 1962) as well as in the London *Sunday Express.* Two of the parts were unexceptionable: the first covered much the same ground as the first half of *Of Human Bondage* and the Rosie episodes of *Cakes and Ale;* the third described his lack of belief, friendship with Churchill, attitude toward Kipling and trip to French Guiana, and contained a moving eulogy of Haxton.

Though Maugham "cut all the best—or worst—bits out of it,"[7] the fascinating second part was the real bombshell. Maugham described meeting Syrie; her Jewish origins; her first marriage and child with Wellcome (not mentioning that the boy was mentally retarded); Selfridge's liaison with and financial support of Syrie; her love for Maugham; their adulterous sexual relations; his involvement in her scandalous divorce; his high-minded reasons for marrying her; their bizarre plan to give away their own child as soon as it was born; Liza's illegitimacy; his work as a secret agent in Russia; his convalescence in a Scottish sanatorium; his friendship with Haxton; his insistence on freedom to live and travel with Gerald; her slanderous accusations about his private life; her tedious "scenes"; her snobbery; her intellectual shallowness; her bitchy character; her unscrupulous business dealings; her constant interference with his work; her suicide attempts; and, finally, their divorce.

Frere, "shocked at what seemed to him the ramblings of a madman," felt that "Looking Back" would both wound Liza and damage Maugham's reputation. When both Heinemann and Doubleday refused to publish it as a book, Maugham was furious and dismissed Frere as his literary executor. Graham Greene, in a letter to the *Daily Telegraph,* called it "the sick Maugham's senile and scandalous work." And Robert Boothby (offering an amateur medical diagnosis) agreed that "the brain went gradually, slowly, gradually, but the last two years, when he wrote that final dreadful book, the brain had gone."[8]

Maugham's friends had frequently remarked that "he hated anything to be known about him, and was very, very cagey, and we never discussed certain subjects at all. . . . He is so restrained and so well disciplined that we may find ourselves wishing that he would sometimes let himself go." In *The Summing Up* he'd put a limit to intimacy and refused to lay bare his heart. But in "Looking Back" the impulse to express his most personal feelings overcame his notorious caution and reticence. He boldly and bravely dropped his mask, spoke out against hypocritical social conventions and finally told the truth. His critics and Syrie's friends, who never had to live with her, questioned the propriety and condemned the caddishness of the attacks on his dead wife and living daughter. But they could not refute Maugham's charges.

"Looking Back" may have violated the rules of decorum, but it is far from being the ramblings of a senile, brain-damaged madman. The memoir contained many poignant and penetrating revelations and showed Maugham in full command of his formidable satiric powers. Deeply wounded by Syrie, who he felt had ruined his life, he fought back with his pen. "It cost him great pain," Kenneth Clark observed, "but it was something he had to get off his chest."[9] Maugham's late masterpiece, which deserves to be published as a book, belongs with fiercely honest retrospective works like Hemingway's *A Moveable Feast* (1961); Anthony West's *Heritage* (1984), about Rebecca West and H. G. Wells, the parents who'd rejected him; and Paul Theroux's *Sir Vidia's Shadow* (1998).

Noël Coward's relations with Maugham, until the publication of "Looking Back," had always been wary but amicable. After visiting the villa in June 1958 he gratefully noted: "I spent lovely four days with Willie. It is an exquisitely comfortable house to stay in. Perfect valeting, delicious food, good conversation and peace." Four years later in Lausanne, Coward's firsthand account of Maugham's clear mind and sharp tongue contradicted the gloomy reports (circulated by Searle to elicit pity for himself) of his brain-damaged dementia: "Willie Maugham and Alan Searle came over for lunch. They are staying at the Beau Rivage. Willie looks wonderful, bright as a button. His stammer is a bit heavier and he is a trifle deaf but shows no other signs of being eighty-eight." On this occasion Willie had suddenly turned to him. "Yer-you know, Noël," he said, "it's very ker-kind of you to invite me to stay in your villa for three months." Noël gazed

*Maugham smoking cigarette in brocaded
dressing gown, c. 1963*

at him in astonishment. "Now whatever crossed your strange little Chinese mind to suppose that I should issue such an invitation?" . . . "Werwell it's going to take three months to teach me this patience," Willie said. "And I'd far rather learn it at *your* expense than at *mine*."[10]

Coward, Syrie's close friend, disliked "Looking Back" as much as Frere, Greene and Boothby. Though he condemned it on moral grounds, he also recognized its literary merit. Only four months after they'd met in Lausanne, he attributed the work to diabolical possession: "I have read Willie Maugham's final spate of venom in *Show Magazine*. It is well written and entirely contemptible. . . . Some evil spirit has entered his body. He is dangerous, a creature to be feared and shunned." Coward was haunted by the fear of what Maugham might publish about *his* sexual life.

Coward's line "Somerset and all the Maughams do it," added to Cole Porter's song "Let's Do It (Let's Fall in Love)," provided the title of Robin's

first memoir.[11] His last play, *A Song at Twilight,* recycled the themes of homosexuality and blackmail in his earlier story "Nature Study" (1938). Set in the
Hôtel Beau Rivage in Lausanne, the play is a savage and dishonest portrait
of Maugham. It opened in London in April 1966, only four months after
his death; and the main character, played by Coward himself with a prominent stammer, bore an unmistakable resemblance to Maugham.

In the play Carlotta, a former mistress, threatens to blackmail Sir Hugo
Latymer, an eminent married writer, with incriminating letters he'd once
written to his homosexual lover. The original version was even closer to
the personal life of Maugham, who was very eager to recover and burn his
personal and sometimes indiscreet letters: "the friend who [originally]
comes back is in fact a man, and it's a homosexual relationship. There is
the threat of letters. In fact the man doesn't appear in the [final version of]
the play, but the woman who brings the letters back brings with her the
terrible danger of this friendship being made public."

Though Coward had also subjected himself to cellular therapy, he
mocks the treatment when Carlotta (punning on Nancy Mitford's once-
famous social distinctions, U and Non-U) says: "Niehans injects living
cells from an unborn ewe, and as long as he doesn't pick a Non-U Ewe it
works like a charm." The main victim of Coward's caustic attack is
Latymer-Maugham. Carlotta, referring to his love letters, says: "They were
written in your earlier years remember, before your mind had become corrupted by fame and your heart by caution," and calls his autobiography
"the most superlative example of sustained camouflage that [I have] ever
read." She also condemns her passive victim for going "through life holding your fellow creatures in such bitter contempt."[12] Her most savage
onslaught zeroes in on his vicious behavior toward his former lover, the
alcoholic Perry Sheldon: "You discarded him ruthlessly, without a shred
of gratitude or compassion. Having corrupted his character, destroyed his
ambition and deprived him of hope. You wrote him off like a bad
check. . . . You [also] used me and betrayed me as you've always used and
betrayed every human being who has ever shown you the slightest sign of
true affection."

Several of Coward's satiric darts failed to hit the mark. He suggests
that Syrie had blackmailed Maugham with compromising letters, yet
defends her from the attack in "Looking Back." Coward was completely
mistaken when he accused Maugham of corrupting, destroying and dis-
carding Gerald Haxton (Perry Sheldon in the play). Haxton, corrupt long

before he met Maugham, was responsible for the defects of his own character. Maugham may have wished, in the end, to get rid of Haxton. But when his wish came true in an ironic way, he devotedly cared for Haxton during his illness, and was overcome by guilt and grief when he died. The letters he wrote after Gerald's death revealed Maugham's deep love.

Coward accused Maugham of being corrupt and deceitful by living a false life and disguising his homosexuality. But Coward himself remained securely in the closet and, like Maugham, was always cautious and secretive about his sex life. His witty comedies and musicals hinted at naughtiness, but never strayed beyond the confines of middlebrow good taste. One friend perceptively told him: " 'Noël, your plays are fine, they're first-class. But they're not nearly as good as what you could write.' . . . Even when he wrote his autobiographies, he never said anything about himself at all. . . . He was a brilliantly clever man, he had a fine mind—but he wasn't showing that to anybody." As Maugham told the more daring and reckless Robin: "Why do you think that Noël and I have never stuck our personal predilections down the public's throats? Because we know it would outrage them."

As an artist, Coward remained under Maugham's influence. In his "short stories there is a tremendous debt to Maugham in construction and style, in the use of the orient, in the use of characters met in bars, the use of storytellers." But Coward attacked Maugham personally for exactly the kind of subterfuge and dishonesty that he himself habitually practiced. Coward's biographer wrote that "at the end of his life and [in] his last play, he remains firmly behind the mask. 'One's real inside self is a private place,' he declared in 1969, 'and should always stay like that. It is no one else's business.' "[13] When Maugham finally and bravely revealed his own personal life, as Coward had never dared to do, Coward condemned him as a contemptible and dangerous creature.

III

IN HIS SEVENTIES Maugham, Niehans' devotee, said that the French doctors "advise me to let nature take its course. At my age that's the last thing one wants." He began to go deaf in his early seventies, and in old age found that it took a long time to recover from any illness. But in his eighties he remained in remarkably good health and in September 1960, when he still had five more years to go, wrote: "I can expect to live on for a while if I take care to do nothing whatever that I want to do." Old age had its compensations. Free from the torments of jealousy and the pain of unrequited love, he now felt a Sophoclean calm. "One is no longer buffeted by passions," he announced, with his usual detachment, "and the most welcome respite is that of sex. It is an extremely pleasant desire . . . but I am glad it is over."[14] The lifelong sceptic also faced death with surprising equanimity and resignation. Certain that he'd created works of lasting value, he was ready to go out like a spent candle. People "are shocked if you mention [death]," he told Godfrey Winn. "I wait for it now without rancour or surprise. Every morning my valet tiptoes into my room as though he expects to find me dead in my bed."

Writing about his eighty-four-year-old brother Frederic, Maugham expressed his own fears when he told Robin: "Sometimes he seemed almost childish. Oh dear, I do hope I don't go like that. I should hate to see people being tolerant to me because I was so old and rather foolish and [feeling] allowances must be made for me because of my past." But he was, like many very old people, egoistic, willful and cantankerous—filled with self-pity and indignation about his declining powers. After a short trip in December 1963, Searle exaggerated Maugham's desperate condition and prematurely announced: "Willie is glad to be home again, but is deteriorating rapidly. I wish for his sake that he could slip quietly away. It breaks my heart to watch him."[15] Six months later, after a difficult trip to northern Italy, Searle, eternally complaining and seeking sympathy, expressed haughty dissatisfaction with the lesser servants: "Venice was a failure and it has finally taught me that our travelling days are over. I took the valet and chauffeur to help me, but they proved useless." But George Cukor, who met them there, offered a far brighter picture of Maugham's lucidity: "the last time I saw him was in Venice, and his mind would come and go; he wouldn't remember you from lunch to dinner, but then again he was brilliant."

In his last years Maugham, whose face resembled the cracked glaze of an Oriental vase, claimed he needed (in addition to his afternoon nap) only six hours of sleep. He realized he was becoming increasingly deaf and losing his memory. But on January 25, 1964, his ninetieth birthday, he still led a calm, orderly and reasonably contented life:

He has coffee and rolls in bed at 8, strolls in the garden if it is fine; he also likes to read [Agatha Christie and Raymond Chandler] in the morning, but that is becoming increasingly difficult because he has cataracts. He has an eleven o'clock whisky and, before lunch, a martini; he enjoys his food. After lunch he sleeps. Then he takes Li and Ching [his Pekinese] . . . and George, his dachshund, for a walk down the road opposite, to the sea. He reads again until 6, when he has another whisky, plays patience with Alan Searle until dinner and by 8.30 is in bed.[16]

In his last year Maugham moved from the Miltonic "Calm of mind all passion spent" to "That last infirmity of noble mind," and followed with only slight fluctuations a steady downward course. His senile dementia seemed like a retributive disease on the old Swiftian Struldbrug. He'd wanted to live forever but, hanging on in a state of extreme decrepitude, now longed for the release of death. Harold Acton described their last meeting: "He got the Sitwells mixed up with Hitler . . . and Munich with Monaco. Everything got very mixed up, but he kept the most beautiful table. He was a non-stop smoker and he kept stubbing out the cigarettes on the lacquered table and drinking a cocktail and looking, I must say, a centenarian. He really looked extremely old. I thought of the wasted thousands for those treatments in Switzerland." Niehans had managed to keep "his body alive, but not his mind."

Maugham finally became unpredictable, paranoid and sometimes violent. He'd condemn himself as an evil and horrible old man, and sob that all his friends had wound up hating him. Pursued by the old demons, he'd mistake a visitor for his former wife and scream out: "Syrie, you bitch. You've ruined my whole life. How dare you come into my house? Get out of it at once." He'd take the arm of his niece Diana, speak affectionately to her and then suddenly cry out, as if she were another person: "Fuck you, fuck you, fuck you."[17]

Toward the end, Maugham was as demanding and impulsive as a small child. While dining at home he sometimes threw his food on the floor. In a restaurant with Frere, the Edwardian gentleman suddenly dropped his mask and shouted (as perhaps many people would like to do): "you've got to get me out of this fuckin' party." Ted Morgan reported an incident with the same lack of sympathy that Harold Clurman had shown when Maugham fainted in Hollywood. During a dinner at the villa with an M.P. and the art critic Douglas Cooper, Maugham "defecated on the rug, and scooped up a handful of feces like a guilty child." Cooper later published a letter in *Books and Bookmen* "denying all knowledge of the story and pointing out that he had never visited Maugham with Sir Malcolm Bullock who was, in any case, not a friend of his. He also said that he had no correspondence with Ted Morgan and had no idea where he had obtained this nonsensical story."[18]

Searle, bemoaning his fate and fearing for the future (all contributions were gratefully accepted), made the worst of a bad situation. "This isn't a life," he complained to Robin. "It's a nightmare I'm leading." Though sailors beckoned from Villefranche, he found it hard to escape for more than a half hour at a time. He said that Maugham was trapped in a strange and frightening existence, and exclaimed: "His memory has now gone completely and his mind wanders. He lives in some terrifying world of his own which must be grim if his screams and terror are anything to go by." Exaggerating as always and seeking sympathy for himself rather than for Maugham, he told Zipkin in April 1965: "I have been shut up with a madman now for nearly four years, and his beastliness is beyond endurance. If I had the courage I would commit suicide." But with Maugham's riches finally within his grasp, he somehow soldiered on. In September 1965, three months before Maugham's death, Noël Coward stopped by for a last careful look at the old friend he was about to crucify in *A Song at Twilight*: "I called on Willie Maugham and I am glad I did because he was wretchedly, pathetically grateful. He is living out his last days in a deep nightmare, poor beast. He barely makes sense and, of course he *knows* his mind has gone."[19]

On December 10, a month before his ninety-second birthday, Maugham fell a couple of times in the villa, cutting his face and head. After telling Alan—"I've been looking for you for two years and we have much to talk about. I want to thank you and say goodbye"—he suffered a stroke, lapsed into a coma and was rushed to the Anglo-American Hospital in Nice. His French doctor Georges Rosanoff loyally declared: "In his room, the old man agonized for more than a week. When the state of our dear patient became such that the imminence of his death was no longer in doubt, the dying Maugham was transported to the Mauresque, where the gates opened to let him pass, for the last time, alive." In fact, Maugham died in the hospital on December 15, 1965. Since French law required autopsies for patients who expired in hospitals, his body was spirited back to the villa by ambulance. The next day Alan announced that he'd died at home and in his own bed. The one-day delay had given him a slight head-start against Liza's "ruthless and predatory" family. But Alan was horrified

King's School garden, where Maugham's ashes are placed

to discover that while he was at the hospital with Maugham the servants had cleared out the valuable wine cellar and departed.

Searle was not invited to the private funeral, and there was (as Maugham wished) no memorial service. His body was cremated and his ashes were buried on the grounds of King's School, a place he'd once professed to hate. (If he couldn't have Westminster Abbey, then the sacred precincts of Canterbury Cathedral would have to do.) Though miserable in the junior school, he'd been happier in his last year. He dramatically exaggerated his torments in *Of Human Bondage* and portrayed his childhood more favorably in *Cakes and Ale*. As time distanced him from his childhood, his schooldays seemed more and more appealing. Maugham had always been attached to Kent. As he wrote in *The Explorer* in 1907: "It is only we who live away from England who really love it."[20] Self-exiled and with no close family ties, the county and the old school became his final resting place, his last home.

22

Afterlife

MAUGHAM WAS THE most highly paid writer of his time. By 1956, "according to a report from Doubleday, a total of 4,339,520 copies of the various editions of his novels had been sold. The best seller of them all was *The Razor's Edge,* published in 1944, which had then sold 1,367,283 copies. *Of Human Bondage* has never sold fewer than 30,000 copies in any of its last thirty years." His *Collected Stories* sold 300,000 copies the first year. His books throughout the world have sold close to forty million copies and he earned nearly forty million dollars in royalties. Carried away by these vertiginous figures, Maugham once claimed to have sold eighty million.

The poor, Maugham once wrote, always want something. In a single week the persistent demands of strangers for never-to-be-repaid "loans" amounted to £36,000 and, if answered, would have eaten up his earnings. Nevertheless, he anonymously provided funds for G. B. Stern, Richard Aldington and other serious but impoverished writers. He gave all his manuscripts to relatives and friends, libraries and institutions. He was always generous with advice and criticism, with gifts and money, with lunch and dinner invitations, and with paradisal hospitality to grateful and sometimes spiteful guests. He founded the Maugham Travel Award and was a munificent donor to King's School. He left all his royalties (after Searle's death) to the Royal Literary Fund, which in the 1980s received between $250,000 and $373,000 a year to assist needy authors. Though resented, envied and even hated by other writers, no author in history ever did more for his colleagues than Somerset Maugham. As Boswell said of Johnson, there was "genuine humanity and real kindness in this great man, who has been most unjustly represented as altogether harsh and destitute of tenderness."[1]

In his last years Maugham had tormented Liza and Alan about their prospective inheritance, but he made ample provision for them after his death. She received the trust funds established in 1929 and 1949, and inherited the Villa Mauresque. Bought by Maugham in 1926 for $48,500, it was sold in 1969 to Samuel Landau, a New York real estate developer. He lived in the villa, and sold most of the land to a French group that divided it into lots. Alan got the Vuillard still life; a legacy of $140,000; the contents of the villa, which he sold at auction for $76,000; and all the royalties during his lifetime.[2] He hired Maugham's butler to care for him and lived in Monte Carlo. Still complaining that he'd not yet been paid off by Maugham's estate, he traveled extensively—to Munich and a clinic in Hampshire, to New York and California—and tipped generously while staying at luxurious hotels. He became lonely, lost and bewildered, had several nervous breakdowns and never wrote a memoir of his life with Willie. He died of Parkinson's disease on August 25, 1985, at the age of eighty, and left everything to his boyfriends.

II

WHEN BALZAC'S VAUTRIN asked Rubempré, "what do you want from life?," he answered: "to be famous and to be loved." Maugham was witty, intelligent and famous. But why wasn't he loved? The *New York Times* obituary distilled the received opinion of his character: "no one liked him very much. . . . He was slow to buy a drink, he did not suffer fools gladly and his comments were wounding. . . . There was a vein of almost feminine maliciousness in his remarks about contemporaries." Maugham was egoistic and touchy, cold and forbidding. He erected a barrier between himself and the world and failed to inspire affection. Raymond Chandler, who understood his vulnerability, wrote that his "declared attitude about not caring much emotionally about people is a defence mechanism, [and] he lacks the kind of surface warmth that attracts people."

Maugham had repressed his natural impulse to homosexuality for the sake of respectability and social acceptance, and paid the price for this rigid self-control. A theatrical friend observed the cost of repression: "his demeanour was a queer amalgam of chilling sarcasm and pedantic harshness; beneath the metallic rhythm of his conversation I detected a hint of unexpected ribaldry in the close embrace of primness. . . . A profound melancholy seemed to lurk beneath the ironic crust, a profound and irritated grudge against his personal defeat by life." He confided in those close to him, like Isherwood and Wescott, and could, if he wished, be charming. In youth he knew love and never lacked friends, yet he revealed his real self to very few people and feared that no one really liked him. No matter how famous and sought after he became, he always expected to be ignored or rejected.

There were other reasons, apart from his chilling character, for Maugham's personal unpopularity. He lived abroad in considerable luxury and avoided high British taxes. Syrie's malicious rumors encouraged homophobic gossip. His honest if ungracious attack on his wife and bitter quarrel with his daughter left a bad impression on the public. He enjoyed writing and composed with great facility in an age when highly admired authors, like Joyce and Kafka, tortured themselves with creative agony. Writers resented his productivity and success. He frequently complained about lack of recognition from the intelligentsia and maladroitly attacked writers much greater than himself. Gore Vidal, Maugham's best critic, observed: "I have just been reading Somerset Maugham's book on the great novelists of the past. A fascinating exercise. He fits them into a private pantheon of his own—chopping off Hardy's wrist, lopping off Conrad's legs—in which, in a prominent central position, there is a *gap*, which can only be filled by a certain, well-known, wizened little figure."[3]

Two eminent modern critics, Leon Edel and Lionel Trilling, emphasized Maugham's limitations. In his review of Ted Morgan's biography, Edel wrote that Maugham failed to create profound characters: "Those searching eyes could see all the concrete things, but not the deeper emotions; he could describe man's human bondage, but not the bondage of the hidden psyche. For a long time this made him a dull subject for literary criticism—there seemed little to say about him except that he was competent, professional, and really 'slick.' " Trilling was also disappointed by the lack of complex meaning in his fiction: "[He] does not undertake to engage our deeper feelings or to communicate anything new about the nature of human existence. . . . Maugham does not sound our depths or invite us to sound his, and quite possibly he has no depths to be sounded."[4] Such critics attacked Maugham for not being a different sort of writer—a Dostoyevsky or a Henry James—instead of appreciating his extraordinary dramatic and narrative talents. With his practical, objective, atheistic turn of mind, Maugham did not struggle with existentialism or Freudian analysis, nor did he value complexity for its own sake. He was interested in listening to people's stories, in observing behavior and telling a tale. His canvas was colorful, his characters vivid, his plots excellent.

A century has passed since *Liza of Lambeth,* and Maugham remains extremely popular with writers as well as readers. Many distinguished authors, from Virginia Woolf and Evelyn Waugh to Anthony Burgess and Gore Vidal, have praised his work. Like Stevie Smith, who admired his "cool, controlled manner," they all learned about narrative from reading his fiction. Maugham's "faultless technique taught [Francis King] how to tell a story, to master the writer's craft." Frederic Raphael, the novelist and screenwriter, observed: "I am not alone in owing Willie a debt. . . . He was not, in truth, a great writer, but he combined urgency with durability, intelligence with professionalism. . . . He did what he set out to do: he did not compile a few precious volumes but a solid, enjoyable *oeuvre*."

Maugham was a literary force round the world. Like Kipling and Conrad, he made the East his own and helped establish the idea of the Orient in the minds of English readers. He left a deep impression on his public, and real people seemed to imitate his fictional characters. In 1933 Malcolm Lowry "found himself sharing a cabin with 'three Somerset Maugham colonels [homeward bound from India] who were dying of the hiccups' "—exactly as in the story "P. & O." (1923). Maugham also influenced the Orient's view of England. Since many of his works were used as school textbooks, "for quite a long time boys and girls throughout the East have been learning our language by means of his stories."[5]

III

MAUGHAM "DEVELOPED NO coterie and was sustained by no reliable faction," but he would have been gratified by the tremendous impact of his character and his work on other writers, especially on George Orwell, Anthony Burgess and V. S. Naipaul.[6] Orwell's bald statement—"the modern writer who has influenced me most is Somerset Maugham, whom I admire immensely for his power of telling a story straightforwardly and without frills"—has often been quoted. But the extent of Orwell's debt has never been fully explored. Both writers had been extremely miserable at school. One of Orwell's most famous passages echoed Maugham's catalogue of his formidable childhood disabilities. In *The Summing Up* Maugham stated: "I was small; I had endurance but little physical strength; I stammered; I was shy; I had poor health. I had no facility for games." In "Such, Such Were the Joys" Orwell repeated the series of short phrases beginning with "I": "I had no money, I was weak, I was ugly. I was unpopular, I had a chronic cough, I was cowardly, I smelt."[7]

Maugham and Orwell chose not to go to a university for precisely the same reasons: they were told that their families could not afford the expense and that there was no chance of getting a scholarship. In any case, after the freedom of Heidelberg Maugham "could not bear the thought of going to Cambridge and being subjected once more to restraint . . . [which] would be little better than a continuation of his life at school." Orwell also refused to prolong his schooldays in the womb of a university and went straight from Eton into the Burmese police. Though they strongly disapproved of their schools, Maugham was buried at King's and Orwell put his son down for Eton. Despite their lack of a university education, they became gifted linguists and mastered seven languages. In an odd coincidence, both came very close to drowning: Maugham in a tidal wave in Borneo and Orwell in a whirlpool in the Scottish Hebrides.

Both authors repudiated their early work and did not allow it to be reprinted in their lifetime. Maugham said of *The Explorer,* as he did of *The Bishop's Apron:* "I have a great dislike for it, and if it were possible would willingly suppress it. At one time it irked my conscience like the recollection of a discreditable action." Orwell felt exactly the same about his two inferior novels. *A Clergyman's Daughter,* he said, "was written simply as an exercise and I oughtn't to have published it, but I was desperate for money, ditto when I wrote *Keep the A[spidistra Flying]*. At that time I simply hadn't a book in me but I was half starved and had to turn out something to bring in £100 or so." Both complained about the drudgery and exploitation of book reviewing. Maugham said: "we know that [the critic] is paid less well than a skilled artisan in a factory. Of all the forms of literary activity this is the most miserably rewarded." Orwell agreed that "the prolonged, indiscriminate reviewing of books is a quite exceptionally thankless, irritating and exhausting job."[8]

Both were masters of lucid prose, and advocated direct language and unambiguous expression. They believed that the writer ought to communicate in the clearest possible way and employed a plain style that appealed to their readers' common sense. Maugham wrote that "good prose should be like the clothes of a well-dressed man, appropriate but unobtrusive"; Orwell echoed him in his famous simile: "Good prose is like a window pane." Both were also deeply moved when young by Milton's high style. Maugham noted: "I remember the exultation, the sense of freedom which came to me when first I read in my youth the first few books of *Paradise Lost*." Orwell also recalled that "when I was about sixteen I suddenly discovered the joy of mere words. . . . The lines from *Paradise Lost* . . . sent shivers down my backbone."[9]

When discussing in *The Road to Wigan Pier* the "impassible quality of class-distinctions in the West," Orwell declared that *On a Chinese Screen* was the only book that honestly discussed this subject. Maugham bluntly stated: "I do not blame the working man because he stinks, but stink he does"; Orwell confirmed: "That was what we were taught [in my childhood]—*the lower classes smell*."[10] Both were deeply concerned with the lives of the urban poor. In the *Manchester Evening News* of January 3, 1949 (the last year of his life), Orwell praised a reprint of *Liza of Lambeth*. In *Of Human Bondage* Philip Carey goes down and out in London, starving and sleeping rough in the parks, just as Orwell would do in *Down and Out in Paris and London*. In Maugham's Lambeth novel and in Orwell's *A Clergyman's Daughter* the characters escape from the squalor of the city to a rustic idyll of hop picking in Kent.

Though Orwell admired Kipling, he rejected his imperialist creed and was far more in tune with Maugham's view of the East. He was moved by Maugham's portrayal of cynical, disillusioned characters, by the "kind of stoical resignation, the stiff upper lip of the pukka sahib somewhere east of Suez, carrying on with his job [like Orwell in Burma] without believing in it." In *The Gentleman in the Parlour* Maugham observed of Southeast Asia: "I get sick of this hot sunshine and these garish colours"; in *The Road to Wigan Pier* Orwell recalled: "The landscapes of Burma, which, when I was among them, so appalled me as to assume the qualities of a nightmare, afterwards stayed hauntingly in my mind." Describing an execution in *On a Chinese Screen,* Maugham declared: "how terrible it was to make an end of life deliberately." In "A Hanging," one of his best essays, the ex-policeman Orwell also saw "the unspeakable wrongness, of cutting a life short."[11]

Orwell's *Burmese Days* most clearly shows Maugham's impact. *On a Chi-*

nese Screen described the East as a marriage market that offers an English-woman who "wished to be all things to all unmarried men" the last chance to find a mate. In Orwell's novel Elizabeth Lackersteen's uncle remarks that she'll "pick up a husband out here a damn sight easier than at home." In Maugham's story "The Force of Circumstance" the hero doesn't tell his new wife that he's had a Malayan mistress. When the mistress forces him to reveal the truth, the disgusted wife exclaims: "I think of those thin, black arms of hers round you and it fills me with a physical nausea" and can't bear to be with him any longer. In *Burmese Days* Elizabeth is equally horrified and breaks off relations with Flory when she discovers, after the humiliating revelation in church, that he has a Burmese mistress. Graham Greene noted that in "Rain" Maugham had stamped the idea of the hypocritical and sexually repressed (American) missionary on the popular imagination. In *The Road to Wigan Pier* Orwell remembers the humiliating condescension of an "ass of an American missionary, a teetotal cock-virgin from the Middle West," who pities his official complicity in the dirty work of empire in Burma.[12]

In *Cakes and Ale* Maugham described bicycling through the peaceful Kentish countryside of prewar England: "as you rode along in the warm, keen air, you had a sensation that the world was standing still and that life would last forever." Orwell evoked exactly the same feeling in "Boys' Weeklies": "Everything is safe, solid and unquestionable. Everything will be the same for ever and ever." When the narrator of Maugham's novel returns to his boyhood village, he's horrified by the pollution and urban development: "the garden was squalid and untidy, and the pond in which I used to fish for roach was choked up. The glebe fields had been cut up into building lots. There were rows of little brick houses with bumpy ill-made roads. . . . The old turnpike house was a trim tea shop." With this passage clearly in mind, Orwell wrote that when George Bowling returns to his childhood home in *Coming Up for Air,* he finds the river crowded and polluted, and the sacred pool of fish a drained cavern filled with tin cans: "where the water-meadows used to be [were] tea-houses, penny-in-the-slot machines, sweet kiosks. . . . The town was smothered under red brick, our house was full of Wendy and her junk, the Thames was poisoned with motor-oil and paper bags."[13]

When Maugham's hero returns to bucolic England in *The Explorer,* "he thought of the green hedgerows and the pompous elm trees; he thought of the lovely wayside cottages with their simple flowers and of the winding roads that were so good to walk on. He was breathing the English air now, and his spirit was uplifted." This passage influenced Orwell's nostalgic description of England, after returning from a long trip abroad, in the opening section of "England, Your England" and in the final paragraph of *Homage to Catalonia:* "Down here it was still the England I had known in my childhood: the railway-cuttings smothered in wild flowers, the deep meadows where the great shining horses browse and meditate, the slow moving streams bordered by willows, the green bosoms of the elms, the larkspurs in the cottage gardens."[14]

Most significantly, the deeply ingrained theme of guilt—Maugham's for homosexuality, Orwell's for imperialism—zigzagged through their lives and work. Both believed that a ruthlessly honest autobiography would inevitably reveal a truly horrible character. Maugham exclaimed: "I suppose there are few of us that wouldn't turn away from ourselves in horror if the innermost thoughts of our heart, the thoughts we're only conscious of to hate, were laid bare. . . . If I set down every action in my life and every thought that has crossed my mind the world would consider me a monster of depravity." Orwell developed this idea in "Without Benefit of Clergy," his essay on the bizarre character of Salvador Dalí, when he said that "Autobiography is only to be trusted when it reveals something disgraceful. A man who gives a good account of himself is probably lying, since any life when viewed from the inside is simply a series of defeats."[15]

Many of Orwell's passages are so close to—virtually interchangeable with—Maugham's that he must have absorbed his ideas and phrasing, or deliberately imitated them. For all their differences, Maugham and Orwell had a strikingly similar prose style and worldview. They had crucial experiences in common: unhappiness at school, refusal to go to university and rejection of their early novels. They disliked book reviewing; were committed to lucid prose and clear writing; had a sympathetic interest in the working class. They were disenchanted with the Orient, nostalgic for prewar England and horrified by modern pollution. Both felt profound guilt and self-hatred.

Anthony Burgess wrote that his novel *Time for a Tiger* (1956) "was sometimes compared unfavourably with the Eastern stories of Somerset Maugham, who was considered, and still is, the true fictional expert on Malaya." The hero of Burgess' *Earthly Powers* (1980), the greatest imaginative work based on Maugham, is an eighty-one-year-old "retired" novelist

and notorious homosexual who's outlived his contemporaries and survived into honored but bitter old age. When the novel opens and the archbishop is announced by a servant, Kenneth Toomey is in bed with his
young secretary and lover. Like Maugham, Toomey is immoral, agnostic
and rational, with "the famous ancient grimness of one who has experienced life very keenly." He owns a great collection of modern art that he
bought for very little and that is now fabulously valuable. He's the author
of many successful plays and three volumes of cosmopolitan *Collected Stories,* some of them filmed as *"Duet* or *Terzetto."* He was awarded the C.H.
but not the O.M., which he disdainfully calls the Order of Morals. He's
also professionally "involved in the making of a saint" (the title of
Maugham's second novel) and "assists in the canonization of the late
Pope."[16]

Maugham, the dramatic link between Wilde and Coward, was also the
fictional link between Conrad, Orwell and Naipaul. The young Naipaul
said he "wanted to be a 'sophisticated' writer, a world traveller, like Somerset Maugham, writing about exotic foreign places and the shocking ways
of the rich," and took the title of *A Bend in the River* (1979) from one of
Maugham's best exotic stories, "The Outstation" (1924). Naipaul also felt
that Maugham, like Hemingway and Isherwood, was one of those writers
who'd "invited an interest in what we might call their professional personalities." Paul Theroux reported that Naipaul "was fascinated by Somerset
Maugham. He wanted to write something about Proust's critical study,
'Contre Sainte-Beuve' and Maugham, contrasting the two writers' aesthet-
ics. . . . 'I'm not [primarily] interested in the work,' Naipaul said. 'I'm interested in the man.' "[17]

"Maugham even provides his own legend in every story," Naipaul
observed of the fascinating persona. "Maugham the traveller, the cynical
playwright, the sentimental teacher, the man who is not at all fazed by anything that human beings do." His lifelong interest in Maugham's enigmatic
character culminated in *Half a Life* (2001). In the opening chapter, "A Visit
from Somerset Maugham," the father of the Indian hero, William Somerset Chandran, boasts that "foreign critics began to see in me the spiritual
source of *The Razor's Edge.*"[18] Naipaul uses passages from that novel and
from *A Writer's Notebook* to describe Maugham's visit to India in 1938.

Maugham has had less impact on contemporary authors than he did
on Orwell, Burgess and Naipaul. The younger writers all read him at an
early age but had reservations about his art, and he did not remain an

enduring influence. Anita Brookner noted that Maugham impressed her, as a young woman, "as being very sophisticated, i.e., knowing, competent but a bit mechanical." Margaret Drabble "read him when young, and very much enjoyed what seemed to me his broad canvas—he was one of the first adult writers I read, and he seemed very sophisticated. I was also interested in his stammer, and his use of it in *Of Human Bondage,* as I have a stammer myself." Drabble's sister A. S. Byatt "was entranced as a schoolgirl by the economy and clarity of his prose. I was also at that time impressed by his advice always to tell a story from a limited point of view—it took me a long time to see that this was both the wrong advice for me as a writer, and based on wrong premises about the god's eye view novelist.... I came to dislike the English 'well-made story'—beautifully articulated, with carefully constructed shocks and surprises—and all his seemed to me to fall into that category. There was a coldness about Maugham that left me cold."[19]

A. N. Wilson also noted his coldness, but was more positive about his work: "I admire him greatly, but—in what does this 'but' consist? Does the reader feel chilly in his presence? Is it because one can see too clearly *how it's done?* My guess is that he will be elevated in the hierarchy. He is clearly a writer interested in a wide range of topics, emotionally and geographically. He was an excellent playwright." Paul Theroux read most of Maugham's work: " 'The Outstation' is a wonderful story. I aspired to such stories, to *Ashenden* and to books like *The Gentleman in the Parlour.* In the beginning I envied Maugham for traveling in the early part of the century, when the going was good; but then I saw that he recorded his time, and that I could do the same. I attempted this in my Singapore stories—*The Consul's File* and *Saint Jack.* Maugham is underrated as a traveler—he had a strong stomach for it. . . . [He is] not given enough credit for being unbigoted. He was true to what he saw and could verify, which I admire. Hard to imagine now, but in his time his work verged on shocking." Muriel Spark "was always greatly impressed by Somerset Maugham as a storyteller. I would put him on an equal with Guy de Maupassant as one who really knew how to create an atmosphere and grip the reader from start to finish."[20]

IV

SOMERSET MAUGHAM—AS doctor, ambulance driver and nurse; linguist and secret agent in Switzerland, Samoa and Russia; propagandist and government adviser in World War II; screenwriter and film presenter; philanthropist and art connoisseur—had more various talents and wide-ranging responsibilities than any other modern writer. Never afraid to strike out in new directions, he made some sudden changes and surprising reversals in the course of his long career. He moved from the sordid realism of *Liza of Lambeth* to witty comedies, from comedies to *Of Human Bondage,* from English to Eastern stories and back again; from a deep engagement with his work to deliberately phasing out several genres: first plays and stories, then novels, and finally essays. His life was also full of dramatic turns: from medicine to literature, from Syrie to Gerald to Syrie and back again to Gerald; from the reckless Haxton to the stodgy Searle; from medical orderly to spy in Russia, where (as in Borneo) he risked and nearly lost his life.

Maugham wrote about many controversial subjects: slum life and the oppression of the working class; the defiance of sexual conventions; adultery and women's freedom; the homosexual as outcast; the predatory entanglements of American heiresses and European aristocrats; the Boer War and colonialism in Africa; the burdens of civilization and the meaningless patriotism of the Great War; the temptation of black magic and the lure of Indian mysticism; the attempt to lead a Christian life and the renunciation of God. Even in old age he was sensitively attuned to the temper of the time.

Maugham created an astonishing number of memorable characters and scenes: the joyous cartwheels, country picnic and street fight in *Liza of Lambeth;* the masochistic relations of Philip and Mildred in *Of Human Bondage;* Strickland's flight to Tahiti in *The Moon and Sixpence;* Sadie Thompson's triumph over the manic missionary in "Rain"; the cholera epidemic in *The Painted Veil;* Harrington's futile death in *Ashenden;* the satiric portrait of Alroy Kear and Willie's love affair with Rosie Driffield in *Cakes and Ale;* the forced march through Siam in *The Gentleman in the Parlour;* the analysis of El Greco in *Don Fernando;* the account of his early life and intellectual influences in *The Summing Up;* the characterization of the Fascist mentality in *Christmas Holiday;* the working of the creative imagination in *A Writer's Notebook;* the searing personal revelations in "Looking Back."

Maugham's current reputation has eclipsed that of his old rivals: Shaw, Wells, Bennett and Galsworthy. More versatile than any modern writer, he wrote outstanding works in every genre: plays, stories and novels, essays, travel books and autobiographies. His exotic settings, engaging characters and riveting plots, his clear style, skillful technique and sardonic narrator, his dramatic flair and grasp of irony continue to attract a wide audience. His dominant themes—death in childbirth, unhappy marriages and covert homosexuality, the decay of the white man in the tropics and the startling difference between appearance and reality—have a perennial interest. He "never flatters his audience," wrote Richard Aldington, "never compromises with the truth as he sees it, never plays stylistic tricks and remains quite indifferent to the ins and outs of literary fashion."[21] Maugham's books—tender and brutal, surprising and cynical—are always intelligent and entertaining. Under the sophisticated surface, they reveal in a hundred variations his essentially tragic story.

Notes

1. PARIS AND KING'S SCHOOL

1. Rudyard Kipling, "Baa Baa, Black Sheep," *Best Short Stories,* ed. Jeffrey Meyers (New York: Signet, 1987), p. 43; W. Somerset Maugham, *The Summing Up* (1938; London: Pan, 1977), p. 34; Letter from Robert Maugham, January 10, 1858, British Library; Robin Maugham, *Somerset and All the Maughams* (1966; London: Penguin, 1975), pp. 103–105.

2. Letter from Ambassador Martin Morland to Jeffrey Meyers, October 17, 2001; Robin Maugham, *Conversations with Willie: Recollections of W. Somerset Maugham* (New York, 1978), p. 22; W. Somerset Maugham, *Mrs. Craddock* (1902; New York: Penguin, 1994), p. 49; W. Somerset Maugham, *The Casuarina Tree* (Garden City, New York, 1926), p. 153.

3. Violet Hammersley, "A Childhood in Paris," *Orpheus,* 2 (1949), 186; Robin Maugham, *Conversations with Willie,* pp. 22, 137.

4. Frederic Maugham, *At the End of the Day* (Westport, Conn., 1951), p. 4 (Maugham's older brother incorrectly states that Major Snell died sixteen years later in the Indian Mutiny of 1857); Maugham, *Summing Up,* p. 15; Hammersley, "Childhood in Paris," p. 186.

5. Glenway Wescott, *Continual Lessons: Journals, 1937–1955,* ed. Robert Phelps (New York, 1990), p. 92; Frederic Maugham, *End of the Day,* p. 10; Marcel Proust, *Swann's Way,* trans. C. K. Scott-Moncrieff (1913; New York: Modern Library, 1956), p. 566.

6. Hammersley, "Childhood in Paris," pp. 186–187; Letter from Willie to

his parents at the rue d'Antin: "Dear Father, Dear Mother. On Christmas Day your little Willie is happy to send you his best wishes, and his grateful affection. Believe me, dear Papa, dear Mama, your respectful son, Willie Maugham." Charing Cross Bookshop, London, Catalogue no. 318, early 1999, sent with a letter from John Whitehead to Robert Calder, courtesy of Professor Calder.

7. D. H. Lawrence, *Letters,* ed. James Boulton et al. (Cambridge, England, 1979–2000), 8:113; W. Somerset Maugham, *Great Novelists and Their Novels* (1948; New York: Fawcett, 1962), p. 87; Jason Cowley, "Memories of My Unhappy Father," *Times* (London), August 19, 1996, p. 15.

8. Letter from Hubert Collar to the Maugham scholar Richard Cordell, August 1961, Texas A & M University, College Station, Texas; Robin Maugham, *Somerset and All the Maughams,* pp. 111, 145; W. Somerset Maugham, *Of Human Bondage* (1915; New York: Vintage, 1956), p. 21; Garson Kanin, *Remembering Mr. Maugham,* Foreword by Noël Coward (London, 1966), p. 116.

9. Wilmon Menard, *The Two Worlds of Somerset Maugham* (Los Angeles: Sherbourne Press, 1965), p. 171; Louise Morgan, "Somerset Maugham," *Writers at Work* (London, 1931), p. 57.

10. Herman Melville, *Billy Budd* (1924; New York: Signet, 1961), p. 17; Robin Maugham, *Somerset and All the Maughams,* p. 150; W. Somerset Maugham, "Some Novelists I Have Known," *The Vagrant Mood* (1952; London: Mandarin, 1998), p. 192.

11. Patrick Leigh Fermor, *A Time of Gifts* (1977; London: Penguin, 1979), p. 15, and Alan Watts, *In My Own Way* (New York, 1972), p. 98; Maugham, *Of Human Bondage,* p. 40.

12. Watts, *In My Own Way,* p. 99; Robin Maugham, *Somerset and All the Maughams,* p. 156; R. F. V. Heuston, "Lord Maugham," *Lives of the Lord Chancellors, 1885–1940* (Oxford, 1964), p. 540.

13. Ted Morgan, *Maugham: A Biography* (New York, 1980), p. 22; Ann Fleming, *Letters,* ed. Mark Amory (London, 1985), p. 184; Robert Calder, *Willie: The Life of W. Somerset Maugham* (New York, 1989), p. 26; W. Somerset Maugham, *Introduction to Modern English and American Literature* (New York, 1943), p. 423.

In *Of Human Bondage,* p. 75, Maugham changes his misdemeanor, recorded in the school's Black Book, from "Gross Inattention" to "Gross Impertinence."

14. F. J. Shirley, "William Somerset Maugham," *The Cantuarian,* December 1965, p. 17; W. Somerset Maugham, Introduction to *The Travellers' Library* (Garden City, New York, 1933), p. 6; Joseph Conrad, *Collected Letters,* ed. Frederick Karl and Laurence Davies (Cambridge, England, 1983), 1:52; 3:89.

2. HEIDELBERG AND MEDICINE

1. Richard Holmes, *Coleridge: Early Visions* (1989; London: Penguin, 1990), p. 117n; Thomas Wright, *The Life of Walter Pater* (London, 1907), 1:162; Gordon Bolitho, *The Other Germany* (London, 1934), p. 180.

2. Samuel Longfellow, *Life of Henry Wadsworth Longfellow,* 3rd edition (Boston, 1886), 1:218–219; Maugham, *Of Human Bondage,* p. 140; Bolitho, *Other Germany,* pp. 23–24.

3. Maugham, *Of Human Bondage,* p. 114; Bolitho, *Other Germany,* p. 171; W. Somerset Maugham, "Looking Back," *Show,* 2 (June 1962), 66.

4. Letter from Maugham, November 25, 1932, in Charles McIver, *William Somerset Maugham: A Study of Technique and Literary Sources* (Philadelphia, 1936), p. 2; Maugham, *Summing Up,* p. 156; Maugham, *Of Human Bondage,* p. 154.

5. Kanin, *Remembering Mr. Maugham,* p. 54. In *The Summing Up,* Maugham said he once saw Ibsen at the Maximilianerhof in Munich. W. Somerset Maugham, *On a Chinese Screen,* Introduction by H. J. Lethbridge (1922; New York: Paragon House, 1990), p. 192.

6. James Money, *Capri: Island of Pleasure* (London, 1986), p. 54; W. Somerset Maugham, *A Writer's Notebook* (Garden City, New York, 1949), p. 5, and *Of Human Bondage,* p. 144; W. Somerset Maugham, *Points of View* (Garden City, New York, 1959), 227.

7. Kenneth Allsop, "Kenneth Allsop Remembers a Meeting with Somerset Maugham Enjoying the Truce of Old Age," *Books and Bookmen,* 10 (May 1966), 19; William Somerset Maugham, "A Bad Example," *Orientations* (London, 1899), p. 41; Morgan, *Maugham,* p. 27.

8. W. Somerset Maugham, "Looking Back on Eighty Years," *Listener,* January 28, 1954, p. 173; Maugham, *Mrs. Craddock,* p. 213; Joseph Lurie,

"W. Somerset Maugham: An Appreciation and a Probe," *St. Thomas's Hospital Gazette,* 64 (Autumn 1966), 111.

9. Maugham, *Chinese Screen,* pp. 173–174; Maugham, *Writer's Notebook,* p. 15.

10. E. H. McInnes, *St. Thomas's Hospital* (London, 1963), p. 148; Mary Lee Settle, "Maugham," *Yale Review,* 76 (1987), 432; Letter from Maugham to Lord Beaverbrook, November 2, 1961, House of Lords, London.

   The massive handwritten folio "St. Thomas's Hospital—Registrations of Pupils' Attainments and Appointments, 1869–1895" lists Maugham as thirty-eighth in the class his first year and twenty-ninth in his second, and mentions his training in Outpatients, Inpatients, Post-Mortem, Skin and Eyes (Medical Library, St. Thomas's Hospital, London).

11. William Somerset Maugham, *For Services Rendered* (Garden City, New York, 1933), p. 76; William Somerset Maugham, *The Merry-Go-Round* (1904; London: Penguin, 1978), p. 126; William Somerset Maugham, *Cosmopolitans* (London, 1936), p. 114.

12. Karl Pfeiffer, *William Somerset Maugham: A Candid Portrait,* Introduction by Jerome Weidman (New York, 1959), p. 41.

13. Maugham, *Points of View,* pp. 189, 187.

14. Letter from Harry Philips to Joseph Dobrinsky, September 16, 1966, Texas A & M; Anthony Burgess, *Flame into Being: The Life of D. H. Lawrence* (New York, 1985), p. 136; Conrad, *Collected Letters,* 3:239, 241; D. H. Lawrence, *Letters,* 3:469.

15. Money, *Capri,* pp. 54; 130. The homosexuals and lesbians Robert McAlmon and Bryher, W. H. Auden and Erika Mann also contracted marriages of convenience. E. F. Benson, *Final Edition: Informal Autobiography* (New York, 1940), p. 106; E. F. Benson, *As We Were* (London, 1930), p. 291.

3. *LIZA OF LAMBETH* AND SPAIN

1. Louis Marlow, "W. Somerset Maugham," *Seven Friends* (London, 1953), p. 142; Maugham, *Of Human Bondage,* pp. 292, 329; 91; Pfeiffer, *Maugham,* pp. 23, 99–100.

2. Cecil Beaton, "The Villa Mauresque and Somerset Maugham," *The*

Strenuous Years: Diaries, 1948–1955 (London, 1973), p. 28; Maugham, *Of Human Bondage,* p. 627.

3. Letter from Maugham to Gerald Kelly, March 1, 1909, Loren Rothschild Collection, Beverly Hills, California, quoted in Derek Hudson, *For Love of Painting: The Life of Gerald Kelly* (London, 1975); Alan Chappelow, Interview with Maugham, *Daily Mail* (London), January 21, 1954.

4. Godfrey Winn, *The Infirm Glory* (London, 1967), p. 267; Louise Morgan, *Writers at Work,* p. 53; Menard, *Two Worlds of Maugham,* p. 42.

5. George Cukor, in *Remembering Maugham* (Los Angeles: University of Southern California, 1966), p. 24; W. Somerset Maugham, Introduction to *A Choice of Kipling's Prose* (London, 1952), p. xiv; Klaus Jonas, ed., *The World of Somerset Maugham* (New York, 1959), p. 10.

6. Obituary of Adney Walter Payne, *Times,* November 3, 1949, p. 7; Letter from Craig Showalter to Robert Calder, July 10, 1990, courtesy of Professor Calder; Morgan, *Maugham,* p. 32.

7. Joseph Conrad and Ford Madox Hueffer [later, Ford], *The Inheritors* (1901; New York, 1985), p. 51; Philip Unwin, *The Publishing Unwins* (London, 1972), p. 47; George Jefferson, *Edward Garnett: A Life in Literature* (London, 1982), p. 51.

8. W. Somerset Maugham, *Liza of Lambeth* (1897; London: Pan, 1978), pp. 8; 11; 98–101.

9. Conrad, *Collected Letters,* 1:361; George Orwell, *Manchester Evening News,* January 3, 1949, *Complete Works,* ed. Peter Davison (London, 1998), 18:9; V. S. Naipaul, *"Liza of Lambeth,"* *Queen's Royal College Chronicle* [Port of Spain, Trinidad], 23:11 (1948), 42–43.

10. Niccolò Machiavelli, *Florentine History,* trans. W. K. Marriott (London: Everyman, 1909), pp. 356–357; Jefferson, *Edward Garnett,* p. 52.

11. W. Somerset Maugham, *The Land of the Blessed Virgin: Sketches and Impressions in Andalusia* (1905; New York, 1924), pp. 58; 146, 148; 237; 12; 233.

4. STRUGGLING AUTHOR

1. William Somerset Maugham, *The Hero* (London, 1901), p. 44; Raymond Toole Stott, *A Bibliography of the Works of W. Somerset Maugham* (Edmonton: University of Alberta Press, 1973), p. 28.

2. Frederick Whyte, *William Heinemann: A Memoir* (London, 1928), p. 103n; Maugham, *Mrs. Craddock,* pp. 52–53; 127; 131, 134; 198; 240; 255; 219, 224; 116; 77. In act II of *The Unknown* (1920) Mrs. Littlewood, who has lost two sons in the war, also swears (like Mrs. Craddock) that she'll never forgive God.

3. Maugham, *Merry-Go-Round,* pp. 213–214.

4. Whyte, *William Heinemann,* p. 123; Stott, *Bibliography of Maugham,* p. 42.

5. Maugham alluded to Lövberg in Ibsen's *Hedda Gabler* in *Land of the Blessed Virgin,* p. 218, when he wrote that Bacchus was "a beautiful youth with vine-leaves in his hair."

6. W. Somerset Maugham, Preface to *The Collected Plays* (1931; London, 1952), 1:xv; ix; Leslie Rees, "A Meeting with Somerset Maugham," *Meanjin,* 26 (Summer 1967), 45.

7. Maugham, Preface to *Collected Plays* 1:xiv; Jonathan Swift, *Collected Poems,* ed. Joseph Horrell (Cambridge, Mass., 1958), p. 246; W. Somerset Maugham, *Lady Frederick* (London, 1912), act III.

8. Plays:

Plays:	Novels and Stories:
A Man of Honour (written 1898; produced 1903)	*The Merry-Go-Round* (1904)
The Explorer (1899; 1908)	*The Explorer* (1908)
Lady Frederick (1903; 1907)	"Lady Habart" (1900)
Loaves and Fishes (1903; 1911)	"Cupid and the Vicar of Swale" (1900) and *The Bishop's Apron* (1906)
The Tenth Man (1909; 1910)	"Pro Patria" (1903) and "The Making of a Millionaire" (1906)
Grace (both 1910)	*The Merry-Go-Round* (1904)
The Unknown (both 1920)	*The Hero* (1901)
The Letter (1926; 1927)	"The Letter" (1924)
Sheppey (both 1933)	"A Bad Example" (1899)

9. Interview with Maugham's niece, Diana Marr-Johnson, London, October 3 and 4, 2001; Robin Maugham, *Somerset and All the Maughams,* p. 199.

5. Bohemia and Fame

1. Frank Harris, *Oscar Wilde: His Life and Confessions* (1916; London, 1938), p. 171; Sir John Wolfenden, *Report of the Committee on Homosexual*

Offences and Prostitution (London, 1957); Morgan, *Maugham,* p. 38; Philip Hoare, *Noël Coward: A Biography* (London, 1995), p. 495.

2. Ada Leverson, *The Limit* (London, 1909), p. 184; Richard Ellmann, *Oscar Wilde* (New York, 1987), p. 415; D. H. Lawrence, *Aaron's Rod* (1922; New York, 1965), pp. 211–213; Letter from Harry Philips to Joseph Dobrinsky, September 16, 1966, Texas A & M University. Maugham appreciated this witty put-down and repeated it many years later when he recalled Reggie saying: "My rare editions are my *second* ones. They just don't seem to exist" (Letter from Francis King to Jeffrey Meyers, September 7, 2001).

3. Douglas Goldring, *Odd Man Out* (London, 1935), p. 54; Letters from Harry Philips to Joseph Dobrinsky, September 16 and November 14, 1966, Texas A & M. Philips married in 1911, was a captain in the Northumberland Fusiliers in the Great War and was awarded an M.B.E. in 1921. He died in Windsor in 1969.

4. Maugham, *Of Human Bondage,* p. 219. In *Purely for My Pleasure* (Garden City, New York, 1962), p. 22, Maugham writes that he bought these pictures when he first met O'Conor in 1905. Though the date of one picture is illegible, two others are clearly dated 1923 and 1926.

5. Clive Bell, *Old Friends* (London, 1956), p. 142; Peter Inchbold (October 1975) and S. C. Hutchinson (July 30, 1982), handwritten accounts of Kelly, Rothschild Collection; W. Somerset Maugham, Preface to *Exhibition of Paintings by Sir Gerald Kelly* (London: Leicester Galleries, 1950).

6. Sir Gerald Kelly, "Old Friends," *Sunday Times,* January 24, 1954, p. 6; Arnold Bennett, *Journal* (New York, 1933), p. 209; Maugham, *Vagrant Mood,* p. 187.

7. Peter Daubeny, *My World of Theatre* (London, 1971), p. 26; W. Somerset Maugham, *Don Fernando, or Variations on Some Spanish Themes* (1935; New York: Paragon, 1990), p. 105; Maugham, *Vagrant Mood,* pp. 166; 167. Maugham also wrote negatively about James in *The Gentleman in the Parlour* and *Cakes and Ale* (both 1930), *Introduction to Modern English and American Literature* (1943), *The Razor's Edge* (1944), *A Writer's Notebook* (1949) and *Points of View* (1952).

8. Calder, *Willie,* p. 70; Morgan, *Maugham,* p. 121.

9. The rarest of Maugham's books include *Orientations* (1899); *The Hero* (1901); the play *A Man of Honour* (1903), of which only a few copies

were bound in paper to be used in rehearsals and sold in the theater; and *My South Sea Island* (1936), a minor newspaper article reprinted as a pamphlet in Chicago.

10. W. Somerset Maugham, *The Explorer* (1901; London: Penguin, 1969), pp. 119; 88; 89; 50; 122.

11. Ernest Hemingway, *A Moveable Feast* (New York, 1964), pp. 87–88; Roy Foster, *W. B. Yeats: A Life* (Oxford, 1997), 1:232; Christopher Isherwood, *Diaries: Volume One, 1939–1960,* ed. Katherine Bucknell (New York, 1997), p. 558.

12. Morgan, *Maugham*, p. 126; W. Somerset Maugham, *The Magician* (1908; New York: Penguin, 1967), pp. 99; 199; 140; Susan Roberts, *The Magician of the Golden Dawn: The Story of Aleister Crowley* (Chicago: Contemporary Books, 1978), p. 107.

13. *H. L. Mencken's "Smart Set" Criticism,* ed. William Nolte (Chicago, 1987), p. 45; W. Somerset Maugham, "Tribute to Marie Tempest," *Souvenir Programme,* Theatre Royal, Drury Lane, May 28, 1935; Hilary Spurling, *Ivy: The Life of I. Compton Burnett* (New York, 1984), p. 275.

14. Maugham, *Of Human Bondage,* p. 305; George Doran, *Chronicles of Barabbas, 1884–1934* and *Further Chronicles and Comment* (New York, 1952), p. 150; George Tyler, *Whatever Goes Up* (Indianapolis, 1934), p. 210.

15. Basil Dean, *Seven Ages: An Autobiography, 1888–1927* (London, 1970), p. 177; Irene Vanbrugh, *To Tell My Story* (New York, 1949), p. 78.

16. Morgan, *Maugham*, pp. 147; 158; W. Somerset Maugham, *Smith: A Comedy* (London, 1913), act III; Morgan, *Maugham*, p. 169.

17. Michael Swan, "Conversations with Maugham," *Ilex and Olive: An Account of a Journey Through France and Italy* (London, 1949), p. 75; Harold Acton, Interview with Anthony Curtis, "The Faces of Maugham," BBC-Radio 3, January 25, 1974, courtesy of Anthony Curtis and Loren Rothschild; Maugham, *Vagrant Mood,* pp. 175, 177.

18. Arthur Mizener, *The Saddest Story: A Biography of Ford Madox Ford* (New York, 1971), pp. 142, 145; Barbara Belford, *Violet* (New York, 1990), p. 116; Morgan, *Maugham,* p. 95; Alec Waugh, "W. Somerset Maugham: RIP," *My Brother Evelyn and Other Profiles* (New York, 1967), pp. 272–273.

19. Wells' ardent young mistress Odette Keun also cordially dedicated a book to Maugham, *I Discover the English* (1934), in which she wrote:

"During a time of great bewilderment, you showed me a fearless, wise and steadfast friendship for which I do not cease to be grateful." Quoted in David Smith, *H. G. Wells: Desperately Mortal* (New Haven, 1986, p. 411); W. Somerset Maugham, *The Moon and Sixpence* (1919; New York: Modern Library, n.d.), pp. 21–23.

6. SUE JONES AND SYRIE

1. Maugham, *Writer's Notebook*, p. 22; W. Somerset Maugham, *The Constant Wife* (Garden City, New York, 1926), p. 84; Menard, *Two Worlds of Maugham*, pp. 9–10, 24.

2. Doris Arthur Jones [Sue's sister], *What a Life* (London, 1932), p. 224; Morgan, *Maugham*, p. 130, and Calder, *Willie*, p. 96. The portraits of Sue are reproduced in Frederic Raphael, *Somerset Maugham and His World* (New York, 1976), p. 75, and in Calder, *Willie*, following p. 110. John Mander and Joe Mitchenson, *Theatrical Companion to Maugham* (London, 1955), p. 41, has a photo of Sue as the maid in *Penelope*.

3. Maugham, *Writer's Notebook*, p. 84; Hudson, *Gerald Kelly*, p. 51; Kanin, *Remembering Maugham*, p. 100; W. Somerset Maugham, *Cakes and Ale* (1930; London, Penguin, 1983), pp. 140, 145–146.

4. Helen Turner, *Henry Wellcome: The Man, His Collection and His Legacy* (London, 1980), p. 39; Reginald Pound, *Selfridge: A Biography* (London, 1960), p. 235; Richard Fisher, *Syrie Maugham* (London, 1978), p. 19.

5. Robert Rhodes James, *Henry Wellcome* (London, 1994), p. 308; Maugham, "Looking Back," *Show Magazine*, 2 (July 1962), 44; Compton Mackenzie, *My Life and Times: Octave Four* (London, 1965), p. 233.

6. Maugham, "Looking Back," July 1962, p. 96. The authenticity of this letter has been questioned, and some scholars claimed that it was manufactured ex post facto as late as 1962. I have examined the original draft of this letter in the Rothschild Collection and compared it to the printed version in "Looking Back." I believe it is genuine and was written in the mid-1920s, at the end of their marriage.

7. Leonard Lyons, "Maugham-By-the Sea," *Saturday Review*, October 14, 1961, p. 74; Lord Robert Boothby, *Recollections of a Rebel* (London, 1978), pp. 191–192.

8. Kanin, *Remembering Maugham*, p. 46; Morgan, *Maugham*, pp. 204; 244.

9. Maugham, *Of Human Bondage,* p. 593; W. Somerset Maugham, *The Hour Before the Dawn* (1942; New York: Popular Library, 1962), p. 138; Robin Maugham, *Conversations with Willie,* p. 140.

10. Osbert Sitwell, obituary of Syrie Maugham, *Times* (London), August 1, 1955, p. 9; Winn, *Infirm Glory,* p. 258; Fisher, *Syrie Maugham,* p. 18.

11. Cecil Beaton, *The Glass of Fashion* (Garden City, New York, 1954), p. 247; Philip Hoare, *Serious Pleasures: The Life of Stephen Tennant* (London, 1990), p. 143.

12. W. Somerset Maugham, *Six Stories Written in the First Person Singular* (Garden City, New York, 1931), p. 151; Beverley Nichols, *A Case of Human Bondage* (London, 1966), pp. 82; 133.

13. Maugham, *Chinese Screen,* pp. 105–106; Kanin, *Remembering Maugham,* p. 227; Gerald McKnight, *The Scandal of Syrie Maugham* (London, 1980), p. 137.

14. Morgan, *Maugham,* p. 225; Michael Holroyd, *Lytton Strachey: A Biography* (1967–68; London: Penguin, 1971), p. 923; Robert Bruce Lockhart, *Diaries, 1915–1938,* ed. Kenneth Young (London, 1973), pp. 312–313, 362. Barbara Back is identified in the manuscript of Lockhart's *Diaries,* in the House of Lords.

15. W. Somerset Maugham, *The Land of Promise* (1913; London, 1922), act III; Billie Burke, with Cameron Shipp, *With a Feather on My Nose* (New York, 1949), p. 116.

16. W. Somerset Maugham, *Our Betters* (London, 1923), pp. 88; 44; 145; 29; 137; Kanin, *Remembering Maugham,* p. 88.

7. THE GREAT WAR AND GERALD HAXTON

1. Samuel Rogal, *A W. Somerset Maugham Encyclopedia* (Westport, Conn., 1997), p. 234; Desmond MacCarthy, *Experience: With the Red Cross, 1914–1915* (New York, 1935), p. 202; W. Somerset Maugham, *The Gentleman in the Parlour: A Record of a Journey from Rangoon to Haiphong* (1930; New York: Marlowe, 1989), p. 179.

2. Maugham, *Writer's Notebook,* pp. 92; 94.

3. This new information on Gerald and his parents comes from: "Sketch and Portrait of Mrs. H. R. Haxton," *San Francisco Call,* April 26, 1891; H. R. Haxton, "The Reverend John Craig," *Overland Monthly,* N.S., 13

(1889), 106; W. A. Swanberg, *Citizen Hearst* (New York, 1961), p. 56 (on Henry's heroism); *San Francisco Examiner,* April 6, 1917 (on Henry's journalism and friendship with Bierce); and *San Francisco Chronicle,* September 17, 1923, p. 14 (on Sara's death). The Bancroft Library at the University of California, Berkeley, has twenty-seven letters from Sara Haxton to Louise Sharon.

Ted Morgan, p. 220, cites the article of June 1, 1918, but does not connect Gerald to his father, Henry R. Haxton. He also takes the information on Gerald's parents (probably supplied by Maugham from memory) from his New York death certificate. In fact, his father Henry (not George) was English (not American); his mother was American (not English). Though Gerald was brought up in England, Maugham calls him "a young American," and no one ever mentioned his English accent. Morgan also inaccurately states that "Gerald was sent to South Africa for training," rather than, after leaving the army, to take up a job in Java.

4. Nichols, *Case of Human Bondage,* p. 18; Dwight Taylor, "Maugham and the Young Idiot," *Vogue,* 122 (September 1, 1953), 212; Maugham, *Our Betters,* p. 32.

5. Maugham, "The Ant and the Grasshopper," *Cosmopolitans,* p. 124. The title comes from La Fontaine's *Fables,* which little Willie recited to his mother's guests in Paris. Robin Maugham, *Somerset and All the Maughams,* p. 56; Robin Maugham, *The Search for Nirvana* (London, 1975), p. 26; Letter to Jeffrey Meyers from Oliver Lendrum, Record Management Services, Home Office, October 4, 2001.

6. Letter from Francis King to Jeffrey Meyers, January 20, 2002; Klaus Jonas, ed., *The Maugham Enigma* (New York: Citadel, 1954), p. 59; Maugham, *Modern English and American Literature,* p. 600; Maugham, *Vagrant Mood,* p. 80.

7. Daphne Fielding, *Emerald and Nancy: Lady Cunard and Her Daughter* (London, 1968), p. 130; Letter from Francis King to Jeffrey Meyers, October 31, 2001; Wescott, *Journals,* p. 91; Morgan, *Maugham,* p. 538.

8. Wescott, *Journals,* pp. 97; 155.

9. Morgan, *Maugham,* pp. 466; 278; 275; 225. I've quoted letters to Morgan from people now dead, but have given my own interpretations of this important material.

10. Morgan, *Maugham,* p. 382; Robin Maugham, *Escape from the Shadows: An Autobiography* (New York, 1973), p. 227.

11. Maugham, "Prose and Dr. Tillotson," *Points of View,* p. 158; Gore Vidal, "Maugham's Half & Half," *United States: Essays 1952–1992* (New York, 1993), p. 231; Graham Greene, "Some Notes on Somerset Maugham," *Collected Essays* (New York, 1979), p. 200.

12. Maugham, *Six Stories,* p. 148; Lawrence, *Letters,* 2:90.

13. For Ribera's picture, see John Moffitt, *Spanish Painting* (London, 1973), p. 107; E. J. Trelawney, *The Last Days of Byron and Shelley* (1858; New York: Anchor, 1960), p. 197; Francis King, Review of Frederic Raphael's *Somerset Maugham and His World, Sunday Telegraph,* February 20, 1977, p. 16.

14. Maugham, *Of Human Bondage,* pp. 450, 471; 669; 261.

15. Maugham, *Of Human Bondage,* pp. 330; 358; W. Somerset Maugham, *Creatures of Circumstance* (London, 1947), p. 165.

16. Letters from Harry Philips to Joseph Dobrinsky, September 16 and November 14, 1966, Texas A & M.

17. Maugham, *Of Human Bondage,* pp. 481; 759; Benedict de Spinoza, *A Spinoza Reader: The "Ethics" and Other Works,* trans. and ed. Edwin Curley (Princeton, 1994), p. 197; Wescott, *Journals,* p. 77; Thomas Mann, Introduction to *The Works of Schopenhauer,* ed. Will Durant (1939; Unger, 1955), p. xx.

18. Henry James, *Stories of Artists and Writers,* Introduction by F. O. Matthiessen (New York, 1965), p. 293; Maugham, *Of Human Bondage,* pp. 654–655.

    Maugham's annotations in his copy of Spinoza's *Ethics* (1910) reverse Spinoza's argument and anticipate the conclusion of *Of Human Bondage:* "If all that happened is inevitable, regret in considering the past is absurd, and regret has meaning only as a motive of future action. . . . If there are no necessary truths, there is no form of eternity" (King's School Library).

19. Anthony Curtis and John Whitehead, *W. Somerset Maugham: The Critical Heritage* (London, 1987), pp. 132–133.

20. W. Somerset Maugham, *Ashenden: or The British Agent* (1928; London, 1951), pp. xiii; 4; Joseph Conrad, *Under Western Eyes,* Introduction by Jeffrey Meyers (New York: Modern Library, 2001), pp. 106, 213.

21. Sir Basil Thomson, *The Scene Changes* (Garden City, New York, 1937), p. 278; Calder, *Willie,* p. 136; Maugham, *Hour Before the Dawn,* pp. 24–25.

8. SECRET AGENT

1. Maugham, *Of Human Bondage,* p. 752; Samuel Johnson, *A Journey to the Western Islands of Scotland,* ed. R. W. Chapman (Oxford, 1984), p. 3; Maugham, *Of Human Bondage,* p. 583.

2. Jonas, *Maugham Enigma,* p. 58 (this passage was omitted when Maugham's letter was reprinted in *World of Maugham,* 1959); Marshall Dill, Jr., *Germany* (Ann Arbor, 1961), p. 186; Maugham, *Gentleman in the Parlour,* p. 13.

3. Aldous Huxley, "Wordsworth in the Tropics," *Collected Essays* (New York, 1958), p. 2; Jonas, *World of Maugham,* p. 97.

4. Burton Rascoe, "A Chat with Somerset Maugham," *A Bookman's Daybook* (New York, 1929), p. 148; Frederic Raphael, *Personal Terms: The 1950s and 1960s* (Manchester, 2001), p. 22; Lawrence, *Letters,* 4:286.

5. W. Somerset Maugham, *The Moon and Sixpence,* Introduction by Jeffrey Meyers (New York: Signet, 1995), p. 227; S. N. Behrman, *People in a Diary* (Boston, 1972), p. 296; Lockhart, *Diaries, 1915–1938,* p. 411.

6. Morgan, *Maugham,* p. 227; Rhodri Jeffreys-Jones, "Maugham in Russia," *American Espionage: From Secret Service to CIA* (New York, 1977), p. 87; Maugham, *Ashenden,* p. xi.

7. Brian Boyd, *Vladimir Nabokov: The Russian Years* (Princeton, 1990), p. 126; Nicholas Riasonovsky, *A History of Russia,* 3rd ed. (New York, 1977), pp. 507–509; Robert Bruce Lockhart, *Memoirs of a British Agent* (1932; new edition: London, 1974), p. 171.

8. Rupert Hart-Davis, *Hugh Walpole* (1952; London, 1985), p. 159; Hugh Walpole, "W. Somerset Maugham: A Pen Portrait by a Friendly Hand," *Vanity Fair: A Cavalcade of the 1920s and 1930s,* ed. Cleveland Amory and Frederic Bradlee (New York, 1960), p. 41.

9. George Woodcock and Ivan Avakumovic, *Peter Kropotkin: From Prince to Rebel* (Montreal: Black Rose, 1990), p. 240; George Bernard Shaw, *Collected Letters, 1911–1925,* ed. Dan Laurence (New York, 1985), p. 343; Maugham, *Ashenden,* p. 274.

10. Emmanuel Voska and Will Irwin, *Spy and Counter-Spy* (New York, 1940), p. 20.

In America Sasha wrote articles for the *Freeman,* published two Russian cookbooks, translated *War and Peace* and *The Brothers Karamazov* into English, and, with Boris Lebedev, Shaw's *Androcles and the Lion* and *Pygmalion* into Russian. Her memoir, "Pleasant Memories of Bernard Shaw," *New American Mercury,* 72 (January 1951), 23–29, was reprinted in the *Independent Shavian,* 38 (2000), 51–56. She became an American citizen and died in New York, at the age of seventy-nine, in 1966. Paul Avrich's interview with Sasha appeared in *Anarchist Voices* (Princeton, 1995), pp. 16–18.

11. Henry Wickham Steed, *Through Thirty Years, 1892–1922: A Personal Narrative* (Garden City, New York, 1924), 2:42; Thomas Masaryk, *The Making of a State: Memories and Observations, 1914–1918,* edited, with an introduction, by Henry Wickham Steed (New York, 1927), p. 189; Winston Churchill, "Boris Savinkov," *Great Contemporaries* (1937; London: Fontana, 1972), p. 102.

12. W. Somerset Maugham, "The Terrorist," *Redbook* (October 1943). For another allusion to Savinkov, see W. Somerset Maugham, *The Razor's Edge,* Introduction by Anthony Curtis (1944; London: Penguin, 1978), p. 271.

In 1925 Savinkov, a shrewd survivor, was lured back to Russia by his old enemies. The Bolsheviks promised an amnesty, but on his arrival they immediately arrested him, sentenced him to ten years in prison and killed him by pushing him out of a window. Lockhart thought that "behind that tortured brain there was some grandiose scheme of striking a last blow for Russia and of carrying out a spectacular *coup d'état*" (*British Agent,* p. 182).

In a photo taken during his rigged trial, the bald Savinkov, standing before the Stalinist court in an ill-fitting double-breasted suit, is surrounded by twelve uniformed guards, one of whom peers at him from behind a flag. In the left foreground a clerk and a woman wearing a peasant-style kerchief seem to be taking notes of the proceedings. Four stern military officials, seated at a cloth-covered table, are about to condemn him to a certain death. Savinkov played an important role in the biography of Sidney Reilly, *Ace of Spies* (1967) by Lockhart's son Robin, and in the excellent British television film series, based on the book, starring Sam Neill.

13. Warren Walsh, *Russia and the Soviet Union: A Modern History* (Ann Arbor, 1958), p. 378; Lockhart, *British Agent,* p. 176; W. B. Fowler, *British-American Relations, 1917–1918: The Role of Sir William Wiseman* (Princeton, 1969), p. 116.

14. Robert Lorin Calder, *W. Somerset Maugham and the Quest for Freedom* (Garden City, New York, 1973), pp. 287; 288–289.

15. Boyd, *Nabokov,* p. 132; Hart-Davis, *Hugh Walpole,* p. 164; Letter from Maugham to Kerensky's secretary, October 14, 1962, Ransom Humanities Research Center, University of Texas, Austin. In 1917 the two pro-peace and pro-Soviet Labour members of Lloyd George's cabinet were Arthur Henderson and George Barnes (1859–1940). Kerensky must have been referring to Barnes, who replaced Henderson on August 8. See Peter Rowland, *Lloyd George* (London, 1975), p. 411.

16. Keith Neilson, " 'Joy Rides'?: British Intelligence and Propaganda in Russia, 1914–1917," *Historical Journal,* 24 (1981), 905; Lockhart, *Diaries,* p. 256; Conrad, *Under Western Eyes,* p. 101.

17. Jeffreys-Jones, *American Espionage,* pp. 99–101; Mander, *Theatrical Companion,* p. 303.

18. Morgan, *Maugham,* p. 236.

9. Malaya and China

1. W. Somerset Maugham, *The Circle* (New York, 1921), pp. 78; 81; 55; 91; George Powell, *The Victorian Theatre, 1792–1914: A Survey* (Cambridge, England, 1978), p. 148.

2. Maugham, *Moon and Sixpence,* pp. 52; 214; Joseph Conrad, *Lord Jim* (1900; New York, 1931), p. 214.

3. Maugham, *Moon and Sixpence,* pp. 50; 1; 56; 54; 146.

4. Katherine Mansfield, "Inarticulations," *Novels and Novelists,* ed. John Middleton Murry (1930; Boston: Beacon, 1959), pp. 18, 20; Hart Crane, *Letters, 1916–1932,* ed. Brom Weber (1952; Berkeley, 1965), p. 29; Kim Townsend, *Sherwood Anderson: A Biography* (Boston, 1987), p. 161.

5. Maugham, *Summing Up,* pp. 138–139; Edgar Allan Poe, *Selected Prose,*

Poetry and "Eureka," ed. W. H. Auden (New York, 1950), p. 450; W. Somerset Maugham, *Selected Prefaces and Introductions* (Garden City, New York, 1963), p. 110; Maugham, *Modern English and American Literature,* p. 526.

6. W. Somerset Maugham, *Ah King* (Garden City, New York, 1933), pp. 250; 259. In his famous preface, Conrad emphasized the appeal to the senses and wrote that "my task ... is by the power of the written word, to make you hear, to make you feel—it is, before all, to make you *see*" (Joseph Conrad, *Three Great Tales,* New York: Modern Library, 1960, p. ix); Maugham, *Modern English and American Literature,* p. 322; Conrad, "Heart of Darkness," *Three Great Tales,* pp. 270–271; Maugham, *Of Human Bondage,* p. 520.

7. Menard, *Two Worlds of Maugham,* p. 28; Conrad, *Letters,* 1:171; Frederic Prokosch, *Voices: A Memoir* (New York, 1983), p. 259.

8. *The Lyttleton Hart-Davis Letters,* ed. Rupert Hart-Davis (London, 1983), 5:126; Frances Donaldson, *P. G. Wodehouse: A Biography* (New York, 1982), p. 297; Angus Wilson, Introduction to *A Maugham Twelve* (London, 1966), p. x.

9. Conrad, "An Outpost of Progress," *Tales of Heroes and History,* ed. Morton Zabel (Garden City, New York: Anchor, 1960), p. 251; W. Somerset Maugham, *The Trembling of a Leaf* (New York, 1921), pp. 111; 128; 139; 143.

10. Maugham, *Trembling Leaf,* pp. 199; 188; 191; 271–272; 301.

11. Curtis, *Critical Heritage,* p. 153; Maugham, *Trembling Leaf,* p. 103; Graham Greene, *Journey Without Maps* (1936; New York: Compass, 1961), p. 205; Graham Greene, "Some Notes on Somerset Maugham," p. 197.

12. Sheridan Morley, *John Gielgud: The Authorized Biography* (London, 2001), p. 102; Dean, *Seven Ages,* p. 250.

13. Maugham, *Chinese Screen,* pp. 231; 113; W. Somerset Maugham, *East of Suez* (New York, 1922), pp. 95; 134–135.

10. DANGEROUS JOURNEYS, DANGEROUS FRIENDS

1. G. V. de Freitas, Introduction to Maugham's *Borneo Stories* (Hong Kong: Heinemann Asia, 1976), p. 9; W. Somerset Maugham, *Letter from Singapore* (Stanford: Stanford University Libraries, 1979), n.p., courtesy of Robert Trujillo.

2. Maugham, *Casuarina Tree,* p. 225; Maugham, *Gentleman in the Parlour,* p. 182; William Hazlitt, "On Going on a Journey" (*Table Talk,* 1821), *Selected Writings,* ed. Ronald Blythe (London: Penguin, 1970), pp. 136, 144.

3. Maugham, *Gentleman in the Parlour,* pp. 149–150; 45; 291.

4. Rascoe, "A Chat with Somerset Maugham," p. 150; Lawrence, *Letters,* 8:111; 7:615; W. Somerset Maugham, *The Mixture as Before* (New York, 1940), pp. 177–178.

5. Frieda Lawrence, *Not I, But the Wind* (New York, 1934), p. 147; Lawrence, *Letters,* 5:157; D. H. Lawrence, *Phoenix,* ed. Edward McDonald (London, 1936), p. 387; Maugham, *Modern English and American Literature,* p. 241; Frieda Lawrence, *Not I, But the Wind,* p. 199. See Maugham, *A Writer's Notebook,* p. 261, for an almost verbatim repetition of Frieda's anecdote.

6. Hoare, *Noël Coward,* p. 123; Nichols, in Vidal, *United States,* p. 234; Nichols, *Case of Human Bondage,* pp. 137; 67; John Halperin, Interview with Maugham's niece Clarissa Farrell, London, July 9, 1986, on Syrie's love, courtesy of Professor Halperin; Nichols, *Case of Human Bondage,* pp. 27–28.

   A newspaper clipping (with no citation), pasted into the British Library's copy of Nichols' book, printed this squib:

   > Though scorn was the norm
   > For Somerset Maugham,
   > A creature of passions and prickles,
   > At least he hit out
   > While his friends were about
   > Not later, like Beverly Nichols.

7. Maugham, *Don Fernando,* p. 130; Maugham, Introduction to Noël Coward's *Bittersweet and Other Plays* (London, 1929); Noël Coward, *Point Valaine* (London, 1935), p. 97; Noël Coward, "Nature Study," *To Step Aside* (London, 1938), pp. 226–227; Noël Coward, *South Sea Bubble* (London, 1956), pp. 5, 9, 44.

8. W. Somerset Maugham, *The Painted Veil* (1925; London: Penguin, 1952), pp. 39, 49. Kitty's father, Bernard Garstin, bears a striking resemblance to Willie: "he was a little, wizened man, with tired eyes, a long upper lip, and a thin mouth. . . . The down-turned corners of his

mouth and the dejection of his eyes gave him an air of mild depression" (pp. 21–22); Robin Maugham, *Somerset and All the Maughams,* p. 211; Interview with Diana Marr-Johnson; Peter Burton, "Interview: Robin Maugham," *Gay Sunshine,* 33–34 (Summer–Fall 1977), 23, courtesy of Peter Burton.

9. Arthur Marshall, "In Gratitude," *New Statesman,* 93 (February 25, 1977), 251; Robin Maugham, *Somerset and All the Maughams,* pp. 203, 205; Wescott, *Journals,* p. 155.

10. Loren Rothschild and Deborah Whiteman, eds., *William Somerset Maugham: A Catalogue of the Loren and Frances Rothschild Collection of Manuscripts, Letters, Printed Books, Pamphlets, Periodicals, Art and Ephemera,* Introduction by Paul Theroux (Los Angeles: Heritage Book Shop, 2001), p. 62; Kelly, "Old Friends," *Sunday Times,* p. 6.

11. Dante Alighieri, *"The Divine Comedy,"* *The Portable Dante,* trans. Laurence Binyon, ed. Paolo Milano (New York: Viking, 1947), p. 213; Dante Alighieri, *Purgatorio,* trans. with commentary by Charles Singleton (Princeton, 1973), p. 107.

See also Henry Francis Carey, translation and notes to Dante, *Purgatorio and Paradiso,* Illustrated by Gustave Doré (1814; London, 1988), p. 43. Pia "is said to have been a Siennese lady, of the family of Tolommei, secretly made away with by her husband, Nello della Pietra, of the same city, in Maremma, where he had some possessions." Samuel Rogers, *Italy: A Poem* (London, 1836), notes p. 295, mentions the unhealthy region: "It was somewhere in the Maremma, a region so fatal to so many, that the unhappy Pia, a Siennese lady of the family of Tolommei, fell a sacrifice to the jealousy of her husband. Thither he conveyed her in the sultry time, having resolved in his heart that she should perish there." T. S. Eliot quotes this passage, without explication, in his essay on Dante (1929).

12. This scene may have influenced Hemingway's *To Have and Have Not* (New York, 1937), in which the husband actually opens the bedroom door and watches his wife having sex with her lover. The wife, ignoring the intrusion, urges the lover to continue by exclaiming: "Don't mind him. Don't mind anything. Don't you see you can't stop now. . . . He knows all about these things" (p. 189).

13. Maugham, *Painted Veil,* pp. 67; 85; 93; 168. These sentences may have

inspired a similar passage in André Malraux's *Man's Fate:* "There is always a need for intoxication: this country [China] has opium, Islam has hashish, the West has woman. . . . Perhaps *love* is above all the means which the Occidental uses to free himself from man's fate" (trans. Haakon Chevalier, 1933; New York: Modern Library, 1934, p. 241, my italics).

14. Maugham, *Painted Veil,* pp. 237; 238; Stott, *Bibliography of Maugham,* p. 86.

11. VILLA MAURESQUE

1. Bennett, *Journals,* p. 874; Maugham, *Summing Up,* pp. 66–67; J. E. Cirlot, *A Dictionary of Symbols,* trans. Jack Sage, 2nd edition (New York, 1972), p. 271.

2. Cecil Roberts, *Sunshine and Shadow, 1930–1946* (London, 1972), p. 40; Beaton, *The Strenuous Years,* p. 26; Roderick Cameron, *The Golden Riviera* (London, 1975), p. 43.

3. *Daily Express* file, quoted in Morgan, *Maugham,* p. 310; Rylands, Interview for "Faces of Maugham."

4. Maugham, *Razor's Edge,* pp. 126–127; Beaton, *Strenuous Years,* p. 27; Edouard MacAvoy, *Le Plus clair de mon temps: 1926–1987* (Paris: Editions Ramsay, 1988), p. 150, my translation; Behrman, *People in a Diary,* pp. 290–291.

5. Arthur Marshall, in Anthony Curtis, "The Faces of Maugham: A Portrait for His Centenary," *Listener,* 91 (February 7, 1974), 169; John Weightman, "Poor Willie," *Times Educational Supplement,* April 25, 1980, p. 23; Menard, *Two Worlds of Maugham,* p. 178.

6. Raymond Mortimer, Interview for "Faces of Maugham"; David Pryce-Jones, Introduction to Cyril Connolly, *Journal and Memoir* (New York, 1984), p. 12; Cameron, *Golden Riviera,* p. 43.

7. Jonas, ed. *World of Maugham,* p. 34; Klaus Jonas, *The Gentleman from Cap Ferrat* (New Haven, 1956), p. 22; Hugh and Mirabel Cecil, *Clever Hearts: Desmond and Molly MacCarthy* (London, 1991), p. 295.

8. Kenneth Clark, Interview for "Faces of Maugham"; Kenneth Clark, *The Other Half* (New York, 1977), p. 115; Cameron, *Golden Riviera,* p. 42.

9. Colefax, in James Lees-Milne, *Harold Nicolson* (London, 1980), 1:365;

Maugham, Introduction to *Kipling's Prose,* p. xxiv; Cameron, *Golden Riviera,* p. 46; C. P. Snow, Interview for "Faces of Maugham."

10. Doran, *Chronicles of Barabbas,* p. 152; Maugham, *Vagrant Mood,* p. 158; Settle, "Maugham," p. 432.

11. W. Somerset Maugham, "Cupid and the Vicar of Swale" (1900), *Seventeen Lost Stories,* ed. Craig Showalter (Garden City, New York, 1969), p. 141; Dadie Rylands, Interview for "Faces of Maugham"; Winn, *Infirm Glory,* p. 264.

12. Victor Purcell, *The Memoirs of a Malayan Official* (London, 1965), p. 271; Maugham, *Ah King,* p. 171.

13. Maugham, *Casuarina Tree,* p. 242. See Margaret Shennan, *Out in the Midday Sun: The British in Malaya, 1880–1960* (London, 2000), p. 65. See also John Butcher, *The British in Malaya, 1880–1941: The Social History of a European Community in Colonial South East Asia* (Kuala Lumpur: Oxford University Press, 1979), pp. 233–238.

14. Maugham, *Casuarina Tree,* pp. 251; 284; Eugene O'Neill, *Selected Letters,* ed. Travis Bogard (1988; New York: Limelight, 1994), p. 262; Mander, *Theatrical Companion,* p. 209.

15. Agate, in Leslie Halliwell, *Halliwell's Film Guide,* 7th edition (New York, 1989), p. 593; Christopher Isherwood, *Lost Years: A Memoir, 1945–1951,* ed. Katherine Bucknell (New York, 2000), p. 38.

16. Morgan, *Maugham,* p. 287; Maugham, *Constant Wife,* p. 77; W. Somerset Maugham, *Home and Beauty* (London, 1923), act III.

17. Calder, *Willie,* pp. 199–200; Morgan, *Maugham,* pp. 319; 447; Winn, *Infirm Glory,* p. 254.

12. "Stately Homo"

1. Wescott, in Morgan, *Maugham,* p. 192; Robin Maugham, *Search for Nirvana,* p. 52; Jane Kelly, Interview for "Faces of Maugham."

2. Letter on Marshall from Francis King to Jeffrey Meyers, February 20, 2002; Curtis, *Listener,* p. 169; Marshall, "In Gratitude," p. 251.

3. Nichols, *Case of Human Bondage,* p. 16; Morgan, *Maugham,* p. 316; Jonas, *Gentleman from Cap Ferrat,* p. 23; Interview with Diana Marr-Johnson.

4. The younger friends were, in order of appearance in Maugham's life:

Harry Philips, Carl Van Vechten, Noël Coward, Beverley Nichols, Godfrey Winn, Hugh Walpole, Osbert Sitwell, Raymond Mortimer, Arthur Marshall, Dadie Rylands, Chips Channon, Christopher Isherwood, Karl Pfeiffer, George Cukor, Robin Maugham, Glenway Wescott, Jerome Zipkin, John Lehmann and Harold Acton.

5. Quentin Crisp, *The Naked Civil Servant* (New York, 1968), p. 169; Victoria Glendinning, *Rebecca West: A Life* (New York, 1987), p. 111; Behrman, *People in a Diary,* p. 303; Frank Swinnerton, Interview for "Faces of Maugham."

6. G. Lowes Dickinson, "Oscar Browning," *Dictionary of National Biography, 1922–1930,* ed. J. R. H. Weaver (London, 1937), p. 127; Prokosch, *Voices,* p. 256; Morgan, *Maugham,* p. 288.

7. Frank Swinnerton, *Figures in the Foreground* (Garden City, New York, 1964), p. 90. Wyndham Lewis' drawing of the handsome Ivor, in surgical gown and menacing rubber gauntlets, is reproduced in Walter Michel, *Wyndham Lewis: Paintings and Drawings* (London, 1971), plate 103. Morgan, *Maugham,* p. 475.

In his *Diaries,* p. 674 (August 26, 1948), Robert Lockhart reported Moura Budberg (another of Wells' mistresses) stating that Maugham "had had an *affaire* with X. He was not really in love with her, but he could not resist keeping her on a string because she was very smart. Then suddenly he just shut down the whole relationship. There was no quarrel. He just ignored her. . . . He made her very unhappy—and quite unnecessarily so." "X" was Barbara, and the gossip, typical of the malice directed at Maugham, was false. He did not, in fact, have sexual relations with her. Their friendship remained close and lasted till the end.

8. Maugham, *Six Stories,* pp. 24, 27; Morgan, *Maugham,* p. 405; Maugham, *Constant Wife,* pp. 81; 78; 90; 92–93.

9. Morgan, *Maugham,* p. 207; Peter Henderson, "W. Somerset Maugham, 1889–1989," *The Cantuarian,* August 1989, p. 173n; Maugham, *Ashenden,* pp. 6; 47; 158; 244.

10. Morgan, *Maugham,* p. 313; Lockhart, *British Agent,* p. 117.

11. W. H. Auden and Louis MacNeice, *Letters from Iceland* (London, 1937), p. 221; W. H. Auden, *Collected Poetry* (New York, 1945), p. 18; John Fuller, *W. H. Auden: A Commentary* (Princeton, 1998), p. 162.

12. Maugham, *Ashenden,* p. 51; Preface to *Ashenden,* p. xiii (in one of the

three new paragraphs added to the original version); *Die Tagebücher von Joseph Goebbels,* ed. Elke Fröhlich, Teil I, Band 7 (München: K. G. Sauer Verlag, 1998), p. 246, and Wilfred von Oven, *Wer War Goebbels?: Biographie aus der Nähe* (München: Herbig Verlag, 1987), pp. 54, 203 (my translations). There are no references to Maugham in *Goebbels-Reden [Speeches]: 1932–1945,* 2 vols., ed. Helmut Heiber (Düsseldorf: Droste Verlag, 1971).

13. Julian Symons, review of Eric Ambler's *The Case of Time, New York Times Book Review,* September 13, 1981, 3; *Raymond Chandler Speaking,* ed. Dorothy Gardiner and Katherine Walker (1962; Berkeley, 1997), pp. 84–85.

   In a presentation copy of a 1948 reprint of *Ashenden,* Maugham wrote: "To Raymond Chandler, who has given the author of this book both in sickness and in health, many hours of undiluted happiness" (courtesy of Dennis Wills).

14. John Pearson, Interview for "Faces of Maugham"; Graham Greene, *The Pleasure Dome: Collected Film Criticism, 1933–1940,* ed. John Russell Taylor (London, 1972), pp. 74–75; Graham Greene, *The Quiet American* (1955; New York, 1962), p. 199; Morgan, *Maugham,* p. 313.

   In a letter to me (November 1, 2001) about Maugham's "mission to Moscow," le Carré confuses Moscow with Petrograd and gets the facts completely wrong. He gives Maugham no credit for his exceptional bravery and insight, and merely recycles malignant gossip: "I know that he was held to have made a complete hash of it, and behaved with a marked absence of courage." Maugham is condemned, as usual, even after doing brilliant work.

13. REPUTATIONS: *CAKES AND ALE*

1. Maugham, *Cakes and Ale,* p. 187; T. S. Eliot, *Selected Essays, 1917–1932* (New York, 1932), pp. 7–8.

2. Maugham, *Cakes and Ale,* pp. 181; 34; Maugham casually mentions the name of his subject when he notes that the "English are a hardy as well as a conservative race" and quotes Mallarmé's sonnet: *"le vierge, le vivace et le bel aujourd'hui"* (the virginal, hardy and beautiful today), p. 190; Robert Gittings, *Thomas Hardy's Later Years* (Boston, 1978), p. 213.

3. Maugham, *Cakes and Ale,* pp. 187–189; R. H. Goodsall, Interview for "Faces of Maugham"; Maugham, *Cakes and Ale,* p. 167.

4. Letter from Hubert Collar to Richard Cordell, August 1961, pp. 18–19, Texas A & M; Letters from Dennis Kemp, grandson of Arthur Albert Kemp, to Stuart Hunt, September 11, 2001, and from Stuart Hunt to Jeffrey Meyers, September 12, 2001.

5. Maugham, *Cakes and Ale,* pp. 202; 107; Leon Edel, *Henry James* (Philadelphia, 1953–72), 4:316; Maugham, *Cakes and Ale,* p. 20; Waugh, *My Brother Evelyn,* p. 129; Swinnerton, *Figures in the Foreground,* p. 93.

6. Hart-Davis, *Hugh Walpole,* pp. 318–319; Virginia Woolf, *Diary, Volume 3, 1925–1930,* ed. Anne Bell (New York, 1980), p. 328; Virginia Woolf, *Letters, Volume 4, 1929–1931,* ed. Nigel Nicolson and Joanne Trautmann (New York, 1978), pp. 250–251; Alec Waugh, *My Brother Evelyn,* pp. 137; 131.

7. Hart-Davis, *Hugh Walpole,* p. 317; Edmund Wilson, *The Fifties,* ed. Leon Edel (New York, 1986), p. 145.

8. Behrman, *People in a Diary,* p. 304; Nancy Mavity, "Somerset Maugham, 75," *Oakland Tribune,* January 30, 1949, p. C-5; Thomas Brady, "The Eighty Years of Mr. Maugham," *New York Times Magazine,* January 24, 1954, pp. 52–53.

9. "A. Riposte" [Elinor Mordaunt], *Gin and Bitters* (New York, 1931), p. 5; Hart-Davis, *Hugh Walpole,* pp. 323–324. See Alec Waugh, *My Brother Evelyn,* after p. 198. Secker, in Rothschild, *Maugham Catalogue,* p. 73.

10. Hugh Walpole, *Captain Nicholas* (London, 1934), p. 257; Hugh Walpole, *John Cornelius* (London, 1937), pp. 235–236.

11. Curtis, *Critical Heritage,* pp. 191; 188–189; Noël Coward, *Diaries,* ed. Graham Payn and Sheridan Morley (Boston, 1982), p. 512; Marlow, *Seven Friends,* p. 147.

12. Maugham, *Six Stories,* pp. 53; 241.

13. Maugham, *Ah King,* p. 241; Curtis, *Critical Heritage,* p. 203.

14. W. Somerset Maugham, *The Narrow Corner* (1932; London: Penguin, 1963), p. 179. Maugham's inscription in Diana Marr-Johnson's copy of this book expressed a strain of self-pity and suggested that the fiction—"stories of some people the author has known in his long and sad life"—was based on real events. See Jeffrey Meyers, "Conrad:

Victory," *Homosexuality and Literature, 1890–1930* (London: Athlone, 1977), pp. 76–89.

15. Maugham, *Narrow Corner,* pp. 37; 70, 86; 112–113; 177; 121; 211; 201; 204.

16. Maugham, Preface to *Collected Plays,* 3:xvi; Raphael, *Maugham and His World,* p. 79; Siegfried Sassoon, "Does It Matter?" *Collected Poems, 1908–1956* (London, 1984), p. 76.

17. Maugham, *Modern English and American Literature,* p. 158; Beverley Nichols, *Twenty-Five* (London, 1925), p. 236; Ernest Hemingway, *A Farewell to Arms* (1929; New York, 1969), pp. 184–185; Maugham, *For Services Rendered,* p. 70.

18. Rees, "Meeting with Maugham," p. 455; Winn, *Infirm Glory,* pp. 249–250; Richard Eyre and Nicholas Wright, *Changing Stages* (New York, 2001), p. 110; John Russell Taylor, *The Rise and Fall of the Well-Made Play* (New York, 1967), p. 104.

14. INDIA AND ETERNAL YOUTH

1. Morgan, *Maugham,* p. 420; Robert Rhodes James, *Robert Boothby: A Portrait of Churchill's Ally* (New York, 1991), p. 170.

2. Kanin, *Remembering Maugham,* p. 47; W. Somerset Maugham, *Letters to Juliet Duff,* edited with an introduction by Loren Rothschild (Pacific Palisades, California: Rasselas Press, 1982), p. 5; W. Somerset Maugham, *The Mixture as Before* (Garden City, New York, 1940), pp. 25–26.

3. Carl Justi, "Die Anfänge des Greco" (1897), *Miscelleneen aus drei Jahrhunderten spanischen Kunstlebens* (Berlin, 1908), 2.203; Max Dvorak, "Über El Greco und Manierismus," *Kunstgeschichte als Geistesgeschichte* (München, 1928), trans. John Coolidge in *Magazine of Art,* 46 (1953), 14–23; Ernest Hemingway, *Death in the Afternoon* (New York, 1932), p. 204; Maugham, *Don Fernando,* pp. 214–215.

4. Maugham, *Great Novelists,* pp. 189–190; Greene, *Collected Essays,* pp. 198, 197.

5. Maugham, *Trembling Leaf,* p. 103; Graham Greene, *The End of the Affair* (1951; New York: Viking, 1963), p. 186.

6. Graham Greene, *Evening Standard,* August 17, 1945; Isherwood, *Diaries,* p. 558; Ludovic Kennedy, *On My Way to the Club* (London,

1989), p. 219; Michael Meyer, *Words Through a Window Pane: A Literary Life in Theatrical London* (New York, 1989), p. 136n.

7. Kenneth Clark, Interview for "Faces of Maugham." Christopher Hassall, *A Biography of Edward Marsh* (New York, 1959), pp. 691–702, lists many examples of Marsh's useful comments.

8. Dadie Rylands, Interview for "Faces of Maugham."

9. Swan, *Ilex and Olive*, p. 72; Eliot, *Selected Essays*, p. 250; Maugham, *Summing Up*, p. 123.

10. Cowley, "Memories of My Unhappy Father," p. 15; Maugham, *Chinese Screen*, p. 178; Maugham, *Cosmopolitans*, p. 76.

11. Maugham, *Gentleman in the Parlour*, pp. 294–295; George Santayana, *Letters*, ed. Daniel Cory (New York, 1955), p. 320; Maugham, *Modern English and American Literature*, p. 580. See also *Writer's Notebook*, p. 341.

12. W. Somerset Maugham, *Theatre* (1937; New York: Vintage, 2001), pp. 292; 204; 238; Curtis, *Critical Heritage*, p. 310.

13. Holroyd, *Lytton Strachey*, p. 1050; Maugham, *Ashenden*, p. 34; Maugham, *Summing Up*, pp. 147–148; 145, 143. "Clever young men" specifically alluded to Hugh Walpole's "Tendencies of the Modern Novel," *Fortnightly Review*, 134 (October 1933), 407–415, which deliberately ignored Maugham.

14. Harold Nicolson, *Diaries and Letters*, ed. Nigel Nicolson (London, 1966–68), 1:350; Curtis, *Critical Heritage*, p. 323; Maugham, Preface to *Creatures of Circumstance*, p. 4.

15. Maugham, *Great Novelists*, pp. 198–199; Maugham, *Vagrant Mood*, p. 198; Maugham, "A Fragment of Autobiography," *The Magician*, p. 5.

16. Lonely Planet, *India*, 6th ed. (Hawthorne, Victoria, Australia, 1997), pp. 1063–1065; Maugham, Preface to *Selected Novels* (London, 1953), 3:x–xi; Maugham, *Points of View*, p. 75.

17. Maugham, *Points of View*, pp. 88–89; Maugham, *Writer's Notebook*, p. 15.

18. Swan, *Ilex and Olive*, p. 70; Brian Finney, *Christopher Isherwood: A Critical Biography* (London, 1979), p. 180; Christopher Isherwood, *Christopher and His Kind* (1976; New York: Avon, 1977), p. 327.

19. Christopher Isherwood, *Prater Violet* (1945; London, 1949), p. 15; Isherwood, *Diaries*, pp. 142–143; 559, 558; Isherwood, *Lost Years*, p. 40.

20. Behrman, *People in a Diary,* p. 311; Woolf, *Diary,* 5:185; Jonathan Fryer, *Isherwood* (Garden City, New York, 1978), p. 250.

21. F. Scott Fitzgerald, "One Trip Abroad," *Afternoon of an Author,* ed. Arthur Mizener (New York, 1957), p. 161; Patrick McGrady, *The Youth Doctors* (New York, 1968), p. 72. Thomas Mann is often included on this list, but there is no evidence in his letters or biographies that he ever took the Niehans treatment.

22. Calder, *Willie,* p. 339; Coward, *Diaries,* p. 515; Kanin, *Remembering Maugham,* p. 140; Harold Acton, *More Memoirs of an Aesthete* (1970; London: Hamish Hamilton, 1986), p. 328.

15. WAR PROPAGANDA AND HOLLYWOOD

1. Morgan, *Maugham,* p. 413; Interview with Diana Marr-Johnson; Evelyn Waugh, *Diaries,* ed. Michael Davie (1976; London: Penguin, 1982), p. 657; Robert Bruce Lockhart, *Comes the Reckoning* (London, 1947), p. 77. See Maugham, *Strictly Personal,* pp. 128–129.

2. Maugham, Preface to *Selected Novels,* 3:ix; W. Somerset Maugham, *Christmas Holiday* (Garden City, New York, 1939), pp. 162; 62; 213.

3. Evelyn Waugh, "The Technician," *Essays, Articles and Reviews,* ed. Donat Gallagher (Boston, 1984), pp. 247–248; Wescott, in Jonas, ed., *World of Maugham,* pp. 173–174; Maugham, *Christmas Holiday,* pp. 314; 250–251.

4. Maugham, *Letters to Juliet Duff,* p. 20; Maugham, *Vagrant Mood,* p. 77; Maugham, *Strictly Personal,* p. 83.

5. W. Somerset Maugham, *France at War* (London, 1940), pp. 1, 4; Maugham, *Strictly Personal,* p. 214; Wescott, *Journals,* p. 90.

6. Maugham, *Strictly Personal,* pp. 166; 257; Jeremy Lewis, *Cyril Connolly: A Life* (London, 1997), p. 339; Julian Maclaren-Ross, *Memoirs of the Forties* (London, 1965), p. 78.

7. Maugham, *Vagrant Mood,* p. 81; George Orwell, *A Collection of Essays* (Garden City, New York: Anchor, 1954), pp. 140, 144.

8. P. N. Furbank, *E. M. Forster: A Life* (New York, 1978), 2:179; Walter Allen, *As I Walked Down New Grub Street* (London, 1981), p. 66; Woolf, *Diary,* 5:184–185; Swan, *Ilex and Olive,* p. 75.

9. Ellen Doubleday, in *W. Somerset Maugham: An Appreciation with Biographical Sketches and a Bibliography* (Garden City, New York, 1965), p. 9; Paul

Horgan, "Luncheon with Somerset Maugham," *American Scholar,* 62 (1993), 100.

10. Maugham, *Letters to Juliet Duff,* p. 18; Winn, *Infirm Glory,* p. 248; Daubeny, *My World of Theatre,* pp. 68–69.

11. Joan Givner, *Katherine Anne Porter: A Life* (New York, 1982), pp. 275, 274; Wescott, *Journals,* p. 57; Behrman, *People in a Diary,* pp. 279, 291.

12. Enid Nemy, "Jerry Zipkin, Who Lunched and Listened, is Dead at 80," *New York Times,* June 9, 1995, p. B–11; Rothschild, *Maugham Catalogue,* p. 65; Michael Korda, *Another Life* (New York, 2000), p. 84.

13. Interview with Don Bachardy, Los Angeles, March 1, 2002; Don Bachardy, in *The Isherwood Century: Essays on the Life and Work of Christopher Isherwood,* ed. James Berg and Chris Freeman (Madison, 2000), p. 93; Cameron, *Golden Riviera,* p. 44; Roberts, *Sunshine and Shadow,* p. 41.

14. Morgan, *Maugham,* pp. 557; 467.

15. Maugham, *Mixture as Before,* p. 187; Lionel Trilling, *Prefaces to "The Experience of Literature"* (1967; New York, 1979), p. 91; Maugham, *Mixture as Before,* p. 84; V. S. Pritchett, in Jonas, ed., *Maugham Enigma,* pp. 188–189.

16. W. Somerset Maugham, *Up at the Villa* (1941; New York: Vintage, 2000), pp. 64–65; 91; 129; Curtis, *Critical Heritage,* pp. 343–345; Anthony West, "New Novels," *New Statesman,* 21 (May 31, 1941), 562.

17. John Kobler, *Damned in Paradise: The Life of John Barrymore* (New York, 1977), p. 355; Swan, *Ilex and Olive,* p. 71; Maugham, *Letters to Juliet Duff,* p. 33.

18. Harold Clurman, *All People Are Famous* (New York, 1974), p. 252; John Halperin, Interview with Liza Maugham (Lady Glendevon), London, July 3, 1986, courtesy of Professor Halperin; Kanin, *Remembering Maugham,* p. 98; Morgan, *Maugham,* p. 476.

16. YEMASSEE AND HAXTON'S DEATH

1. Maugham, *Letters to Juliet Duff,* p. 35; Wescott, *Journals,* p. 96; Ellen Doubleday, in *Maugham: An Appreciation,* p. 9.

2. Max Eastman, *Love and Revolution* (New York, 1964), p. 471; Maugham, *Letters to Juliet Duff,* p. 41; Morgan, *Maugham,* pp. 389; 566; 571–572; 474. Posner—who later married, published some poetry and died in

1985—was drawn to elderly homosexual writers. He once told me that he had courted Thomas Mann in Princeton.

3. Maugham, *Hour Before the Dawn,* p. 89; Maugham, *Letters to Juliet Duff,* pp. 36, 32; Maugham, *Strictly Personal,* p. 232; Maugham, *Hour Before the Dawn,* pp. 8; 41; 78.

4. Maugham, *Razor's Edge,* pp. 51; 305; *Time,* February 12, 1945, p. 96; Berg, ed., *Isherwood Century,* p. 225; Christopher Isherwood, *Vedanta for Modern Man* (New York, 1951), p. 250, and Christopher Isherwood, *Exhumations* (New York, 1966), p. 120.

5. *"Chips": The Diaries of Sir Henry Channon,* ed. Robert Rhodes James (London, 1967), p. 392; Marcel Proust, *The Past Recaptured,* trans. Andreas Mayor (1970; New York: Vintage, 1971), p. 102; Maugham, *Razor's Edge,* pp. 239; 119; 84; Maugham, *Don Fernando,* p. 215.

6. Maugham, *Razor's Edge,* p. 74; Ernest Hemingway, "Cat in the Rain," *Short Stories* (New York, 1953), p. 170; W. Somerset Maugham, *A Traveller in Romance: Uncollected Writings, 1901–1964,* ed. John Whitehead (New York, 1984), p. 166.

7. Maugham, *Razor's Edge,* pp. 294; 164; 79; 223.

8. W. Somerset Maugham, Preface to *The Partial View* (London, 1954), p. xi; Maugham, *Razor's Edge,* pp. 263; 276; Brady, "The Eighty Years of Mr. Maugham," p. 12.

9. Curtis, *Critical Heritage,* pp. 358, 360; *Raymond Chandler Speaking,* p. 86, and Raymond Chandler, *Selected Letters,* ed. Frank MacShane (New York, 1981), p. 355.

10. Stott, *Bibliography of Maugham,* p. 145; Letter from George Cukor to an unknown correspondent, May 29, 1961, Texas A & M; Maugham, *Purely for My Pleasure,* p. 50.

11. Emanuel Levy, *George Cukor: Master of Elegance* (New York, 1994), p. 158; Patrick McGilligan, *George Cukor: A Double Life* (New York, 1991), p. 180; Rudy Behlmer, ed., *Memo from Darryl F. Zanuck* (New York, 1993), p. 94; Pauline Kael, *5001 Nights at the Movies* (New York, 1991), p. 617.

12. Winn, *Infirm Glory,* pp. 263–264, 282; Morgan, *Maugham,* p. 486; Maugham, *Letters to Juliet Duff,* p. 46; Morgan, *Maugham,* p. 487.

13. Behrman, *People in a Diary,* p. 286; Winn, *Infirm Glory,* p. 282; Morgan, *Maugham,* p. 487; Roberts, *Sunshine and Shadow,* p. 376.

17. ALAN SEARLE AND ART

1. Maugham, Preface to *Partial View*, p. x; Maugham, Interview with R. H. Waithman, *News Chronicle*, November 21, 1953.

2. Nicolson, *Diaries and Letters*, 3:154; Leonard Lyons, Interview with Maugham, *Philadelphia Enquirer*, August 3, 1953; Morgan, *Maugham*, p. 461; Pfeiffer, *Somerset Maugham*, pp. 141, 100.

3. Strachey may have been alluding to Bronzino's *Allegory of Venus and Cupid* (1545, National Gallery, London), in which Venus is embraced by a cute, curly-haired Cupid with prominent bare buttocks.

   Letter from Magistrate Sarah Curtis to Jeffrey Meyers, December 28, 2000, on prison visitors; Bryan Connon, *Somerset Maugham and the Maugham Dynasty* (London, 1997), p. 94; Behrman, *People in a Diary*, p. 298.

4. Morgan, *Maugham*, p. 494; Wescott, *Journals*, p. 161; Morgan, *Maugham*, p. 495; Interview with Diana Marr-Johnson; Letter from Alan Searle to Bert Alanson, January 12, 1950, Stanford.

5. Rothschild, *Maugham Catalogue*, p. 59; Letter from Searle to Alanson, October 8, 1952, Stanford; Newspaper clipping, no citation, Rothschild Collection.

6. Letters from Searle to Jerome Zipkin, August 24, 1955; June 24, 1950; May 7, 1956, Rothschild Collection.

7. Morgan, *Maugham*, p. 494; Letter from Searle to Alanson, November 30, 1955, Stanford; Arthur Marshall, Interview for "Faces of Maugham"; Levy, *George Cukor*, p. 311.

8. Morgan, *Maugham*, p. 540; Maugham, *Summing Up*, p. 54.

9. Curtis, *Critical Heritage*, p. 363; Diana Trilling, *Reviewing the Forties* (New York, 1978), pp. 179–180; *Edmund Wilson: The Man in Letters*, ed. David Castronovo and Janet Groth (Athens, Ohio, 2001), p. 76. Maugham's speech is published in *Traveller in Romance*, pp. 129–134.

10. Edmund Wilson, *Classics and Commercials* (1950; New York: Vintage, 1962), pp. 321, 326; Morgan, *Maugham*, pp. 586; 548.

11. Maugham, *Christmas Holiday*, p. 6; Kenneth Clark, Interview for "Faces of Maugham." For Maugham's art collection, see *Purely for My Pleasure* and *Catalogue of the Collection of Impressionist and Modern Pictures Formed by W. Somerset Maugham* (London: Sotheby's, April 10, 1962).

12. Maugham, *Purely for My Pleasure,* pp. 80; 17; Maugham, *Vagrant Mood,* p. 64.

13. Jacob Epstein, *Epstein: An Autobiography* (London, 1963), p. 235; MacAvoy, *Le Plus clair de mon temps,* pp. 149; 176; Interview with Don Bachardy; MacAvoy, *Le Plus clair de mon temps,* p. 188 (my translations).

14. Sutherland, in Leon Edel, "The Figure Under the Carpet," *Telling Lives,* ed. Marc Pachter (Washington, D.C., 1979), p. 34; Roger Berthoud, *Graham Sutherland: A Biography* (London, 1982), pp. 141–142.

15. Behrman, *People in a Diary,* p. 308; Berthoud, *Graham Sutherland,* p. 142; Letter from Maugham to Sutherland, quoting Kenneth Clark, March 18, 1950, Tate Gallery Archives.

18. THE LIZARD OF OZ

1. Ann Fleming, *Letters,* p. 291; Evelyn Waugh, *Letters,* ed. Mark Amory (New Haven, 1980), p. 249.

2. Maugham, *Creatures of Circumstance,* pp. 44; 271; 272–273.

3. Maugham, *Creatures of Circumstance,* pp. 307; 308; 312; 311; 305; 314; V. S. Pritchett, "Mr. Maugham," *New Statesman and Nation,* 34 (August 2, 1947), 94.

4. Ann Fleming, *Letters,* p. 184; Behrman, *People in a Diary,* p. 305; Calder, *Willie,* p. 355.

5. Kanin, *Remembering Maugham,* p. 161; Maugham, *Great Novelists,* p. 19.

6. Maugham, Introduction to *The Travellers' Library,* pp. 4, 409; 144; Maugham, *Great Novelists,* p. 36.

7. Jean Cocteau, *Past Tense: Diaries,* trans. Richard Howard (New York, 1988), 2:52; Robin Maugham, *Conversations with Willie,* pp. 164–165.

8. For plays adapted from Maugham's works, see Mander, *Theatrical Companion,* p. 295, and Stott, *Bibliography of Maugham,* pp. 218–220; for the forty-eight films based on his work, see my Filmography. He also inspired musical works, and in 1957 John Gardner composed an opera based on *The Moon and Sixpence.*

9. The dedications to Maugham were rather scanty and may have discouraged his own: Violet Hunt's *White Rose and Weary Leaf* (1908), Odette Keun's *I Discover the English* (1934), Noël Coward's *Point Valaine* (1935) and Barbara Back's *Back Chat* (1935).

10. G. B. Stern, *And Did He Stop and Speak to You?* (London, 1957), p. 126; Morgan, *Maugham,* p. 157; Maugham, Introduction to *Travellers' Library,* pp. 2–3, 1.

11. Morgan, *Maugham,* p. 501, quotes Maugham saying in *The Summing Up:* "I know just where I stand. In the very first row of the second-raters," but this remark does not appear in that book. Hamilton Basso, "Very Old Party—I," *New Yorker,* 20 (December 30, 1944), 32; Charles Goren, "Maugham Never Forgot the Day I Trumped His Ace," *Sports Illustrated,* 24 (January 17, 1966), 50; Pfeiffer, *Somerset Maugham,* p. 106.

12. Morgan, *Maugham,* p. 539; Basso, "Very Old Party—I," p. 27; Maugham, in *Nelson Doubleday, 1889–1949* (privately printed, 1950), n.p.

13. Lockhart, *Diaries,* p. 637; Channon, *Diaries,* p. 436; Frances Partridge, *Everything to Lose: Diaries, 1945–1962* (London, 1985), p. 131.

19. ROYALTY AND HONORS

1. Maugham, *Choice of Kipling's Prose,* pp. ix, xxvii; Maugham, *Points of View,* pp. 177–178; Maugham, "Looking Back," *Show,* August 1962, p. 99.

2. Swan, *Ilex and Olive,* p. 68; Wescott, in Morgan, *Maugham,* pp. 545; 556; Nicolson, *Diaries,* 1:351; Beaton, *Strenuous Years,* p. 26.

3. Philip Ziegler, *Diana Cooper: A Biography* (London, 1981), p. 266; Waugh, *Letters,* pp. 371–372; Robin Maugham, *Conversations with Willie,* p. 115.

4. John Pearson, *The Life of Ian Fleming* (1966; London: Companion Book Club, n.d.), pp. 211; 240; Rothschild, *Maugham Catalogue,* p. 46.

5. Ann Fleming, *Letters,* p. 105; Rothschild, *Maugham Catalogue,* p. 46; Ann Fleming, *Letters,* pp. 137; 184; 185; Interview with Patrick Leigh Fermor, Kardamyli, Greece, May 28, 2002.

6. Ann Fleming, *Letters,* p. 42; Anthony Powell, *Journals, 1982–1986* (London, 1995), p. 245; Andrew Lycett, *Ian Fleming: The Man Behind James Bond* (Atlanta: Turner, 1995), p. 179.

7. Maugham, *Letters to Juliet Duff,* p. 70; Peter Quennell, *The Wanton Chase* (New York, 1980), pp. 162–164.

8. Robin Maugham, *Conversations with Willie,* p. 14; Anthony Powell, *To Keep the Ball Rolling: Memoirs* (1976–1982; London: Penguin, 1983), p. 240; Quennell, *Wanton Chase,* pp. 163–164.

9. Morgan, *Maugham,* p. 561; Lyons, Interview with Maugham, *Philadel-*

phia Enquirer. Velázquez did many portraits of Philip IV (not Philip II). The most likely royal painting was the virtuoso costume study *Philip IV in Brown and Silver* (c. 1634, National Gallery, London).

10. D. L. Edwards, *A History of the King's School, Canterbury* (London, 1957), p. 183; Shirley, *Cantuarian,* p. 21; Prokosch, *Voices,* pp. 257–258; Morgan, *Maugham,* p. 580.

11. Jeffrey Meyers, *The Enemy: A Biography of Wyndham Lewis* (London, 1980), pp. 326; 308; Jonas, ed., *Maugham Enigma,* p. 51; Letter from Sir Gerald Kelly to Bert Alanson, March 3, 1953, Stanford.

12. Arthur Marshall, "In Gratitude," p. 251; Marshall, Interview for "Faces of Maugham"; Morgan, *Maugham,* p. 569.

13. Letters from Searle to Alanson, January 29, 1953; May 18, 1958; July 31, 1952; January 29, 1953, Stanford; Isherwood, *Diaries,* p. 559.

20. THE OLD PARTY

1. Harold Acton, Interview for "Faces of Maugham"; W. Somerset Maugham, "Books of the Year," *Sunday Times* (London), December 25, 1955; Harry Ritchie, *Success Stories: Literature and the Media in England, 1950–1959* (London, 1988), p. 71; Amis, "Faces of Maugham," *Listener,* p. 168.

2. Kingsley Amis, *Letters,* ed. Zachary Leader (London, 2000), pp. 243–244; Amis, "Faces of Maugham," *Listener,* p. 168; Kingsley Amis, *I Like It Here* (1958; London: Penguin, 1968), pp. 34; 77; 132.

3. Letter from Alan Searle to A. S. Frere, May 26, 1958, Rothschild Collection; Letter from Searle to Klaus Jonas, May 19, 1958, Texas; *Letters of Evelyn Waugh and Diana Cooper,* ed. Artemis Cooper (New York, 1992), p. 261.

4. Maugham, *Purely for My Pleasure,* p. 44; Morgan, *Maugham,* p. 579; Letter from Searle to Bert Alanson, July 18, 1956, Stanford; Letter from Searle to Patricia Frere, February 12, 1961, Rothschild Collection.

5. *Lyttleton Hart-Davis Letters,* 3:170; King, Interview for "Faces of Maugham"; Letter from Francis King to Jeffrey Meyers, November 19, 2001. For more on Francis King, see Jeffrey Meyers, *Privileged Moments: Encounters with Writers* (Madison, 2000), pp. 102–121.

6. Francis King, *Yesterday Came Suddenly* (London, 1993), p. 182; Letter

from King to Meyers, September 7, 2001; King, Interview for "Faces of Maugham"; Letter from King to Meyers, September 7, 2001.

7. Letter from Searle to Jerry Zipkin, November 10, 1959, Rothschild Collection; Letter from John Lloyd, Far Eastern agent of Heinemann, to Robert Calder, January 21, 1990, courtesy of Robert Calder; King, *Yesterday Came Suddenly,* p. 183; Letter from Searle to Zipkin, June 23, 1960, Rothschild Collection.

8. Letter from Lloyd to Calder, January 21, 1990; Ilsa Sharp, *There Is Only One Raffles: The Story of a Grand Hotel* (London, 1981), p. 108; George Orwell, *The Road to Wigan Pier* (1937; London: Penguin, 1962), p. 108.

9. Maugham, *Points of View,* p. 216; Maugham, *Travellers' Library,* p. 1319; Maugham, *Modern English and American Literature,* p. 464; Maugham, *Points of View,* p. 208.

10. Wescott, *Journals,* p. 166; Letter from Searle to Joseph Dobrinsky, November 23, 1966, Texas A & M; Yuri Nagibin, *An Unwritten Story by Somerset Maugham,* trans. S. Kotlobye (Moscow: Raduga, 1988), p. 424.

11. Raphael, *Personal Terms,* p. 23; W. Somerset Maugham, "Why D'You Dislike Us?," *Saturday Evening Post,* 214 (April 11, 1942), 60; Shirley, *Cantuarian,* p. 19.

12. Morgan, *Maugham,* p. 574; Letter from Searle to Alanson, January 10, 1958, Stanford.

13. Ernest Samuels, *Bernard Berenson: The Making of a Legend* (Cambridge, Mass., 1987), p. 569; Letter from Searle to Patricia Frere, January 10, 1961, Rothschild Collection.

14. Robert Boothby, Interview for "Faces of Maugham"; MacAvoy, *Le Plus clair de mon temps,* p. 182; Maugham, "Looking Back," *Show,* August 1962, p. 98.

15. Ann Fleming, *Letters,* p. 207; A. S. Frere, Interview for "Faces of Maugham,"; Letter from Searle to Alanson, January 28, 1958, Stanford; Behrman, *People in a Diary,* p. 308.

21. FAMILY VALUES

1. Maugham, Preface to *Sotheby's Catalogue,* n.p.; Morgan, *Maugham,* pp. 531; 598; Susannah Clapp, *With Chatwin: Portrait of a Writer* (New York, 1997), p. 84.

2. James, *Robert Boothby,* p. 47; Conrad, *Victory,* p. 164; Raymond Mortimer, "Fame and Fortune," review of *Purely for My Pleasure,* clipping with no citation, Texas.

3. Wescott, *Journals,* p. 359; Letter from Alan Searle to Jerry Zipkin, August 13, 1959, Rothschild Collection; Behrman, *People in a Diary,* p. 302.

4. Morgan, *Maugham,* p. 602; Liza, Interview in *Pittsburgh Press,* December 29, 1962; Morgan, *Maugham,* p. 564.

5. Cowley, "Memories of My Unhappy Father," *Times,* p. 15; Morgan, *Maugham,* p. 595; Interview with Diana Marr-Johnson.

6. Morgan, *Maugham,* p. 608; Letters from Searle to Zipkin, July 14, 1962, and August 26, 1963, Rothschild Collection.

     In his unpublished autobiography, p. 107, the eminent lawyer F. A. Mann, who represented Maugham, explained why they lost the case: "Just before I came on the scene Mr. Maugham had adopted Alan Searle before a notary in Nice. Under the law of France where both parties were domiciled the adoption was valid only in the absence of legitimate children. Lady John Hope intervened on the ground of her alleged status as Mr. Maugham's legitimate daughter. . . . But Somerset Maugham, who in January 1964 reached the age of ninety, was loath to fight and withdrew the appeal" (courtesy of Sir Lawrence Collins).

7. A. S. Frere, Interview for "Faces of Maugham"; Letter from Searle to Patricia Frere, February 12, 1961, Rothschild Collection.

8. Hoare, *Noël Coward,* p. 494; Graham Greene, *Yours Etc.: Letters to the Press, 1945–1989* (London, 1989), p. 129; Robert Boothby, Interview for "Faces of Maugham."

9. Arthur Marshall, Interview for "Faces of Maugham"; Marlow, *Seven Friends,* p. 169; Kenneth Clark, Interview for "Faces of Maugham."

10. Coward, *Diaries,* pp. 382; 504, and Hoare, *Noël Coward,* p. 474.

11. Coward, *Diaries,* p. 511, and Kanin, *Remembering Maugham,* pp. 170–171.

     Ogden Nash, *Saturday Evening Post,* 224 (December 15, 1951), 38, also wrote a clever limerick on Maugham:

> There was a young lady from Guam
> Who peddled her charms, charm by charm,
> Inspired I suppose
> By the classical prose
> Of W. Somerset Maugham.

12. Sheridan Morley, Interview for "Faces of Maugham"; Noël Coward, "*A Song at Twilight*," *Suite in Three Keys* (London, 1967), pp. 41; 50, 52; 59.

13. Coward, *Song at Twilight*, pp. 64; 68; Hoare, *Noël Coward*, p. 496; Connon, *Somerset Maugham and the Maugham Dynasty*, p. 255; Sheridan Morley, Interview for "Faces of Maugham"; Hoare, *Noël Coward*, p. 497.

14. Raphael, *Personal Terms*, p. 23; Maugham, *Letters to Juliet Duff*, p. 77; Allsopp, "Meeting with Somerset Maugham," 55.

   See Plato, *The Republic*, translation with introduction and notes by Francis Macdonald Cornford (Oxford, 1941), p. 4: "I remember someone asking Sophocles, the poet, whether he was still capable of enjoying a woman. 'Don't talk in that way,' he answered; 'I am only too glad to be free of all that; it is like escaping from bondage to a raging madman.' "

15. Winn, *Infirm Glory*, p. 252; Morgan, *Maugham*, p. 532; Letter from Searle to Monroe Wheeler, December 15, 1963, Yale University.

16. Letter from Searle to Jim Dobell, May 29, 1964, Texas A & M; Cukor, in the *Remembering Mr. Maugham* symposium, p. 24; Stephen Coulter, "Maugham at Ninety," *Sunday Times* (London), January 19, 1964, p. 31.

17. Harold Acton, Interview for "Faces of Maugham"; Michael Moynihan, "At the Villa Mauresque," *Sunday Times* (London), September 12, 1965, p. 48; Alec Waugh, *My Brother Evelyn*, p. 292; Morgan, *Maugham*, p. 603.

18. Morgan, *Maugham*, pp. 609–610; Bryan Connon, *Beverley Nichols: A Life* (London, 1991), p. 295.

19. Robin Maugham, *Conversations with Willie*, p. 152; Calder, *Willie*, p. 380; Letter from Searle to Zipkin, April 5, 1965, Rothschild Collection; Coward, *Diaries*, p. 607.

20. Calder, *Willie*, p. 384; Georges Rosanoff, "William Somerset Maugham," *Racontez . . . Docteur!: Un demi-siècle de souvenirs et d'anecdotes vécues*, Préface par Graham Greene (Paris: Guy le Prat, 1977), p. 150, my translation; Maugham, *The Explorer*, p. 191.

22. AFTERLIFE

1. Jonas, ed., *Gentleman from Cap Ferrat*, p. 21 (for Maugham's claim, see *Traveller in Romance*, p. 265); Boswell, *Life of Johnson*, p. 707.

   In his will Maugham specified that none of his unpublished writings should be printed after his death and that no assistance should be given to his biographer. Though the Royal Literary Fund has received all his royalties, they felt no moral or legal obligation to follow the terms of his bequest, and contravened his will by authorizing a biography and by granting permission to publish his letters. Donors who leave money to the fund should be warned that the explicit terms of their will may be completely ignored.

2. Liza died in December 1999. Her son Nicolas Paravicini lives in Wales; her daughter, Camilla Paravicini, married Bluey Mavroleon and then Count Frédéric Chandon, and lives in Klosters, Switzerland. Julian Hope inherited the Glendevon title in 1964 and lives in London.

   The contents of Searle's auction at Sotheby's on November 20, 1967, included Maugham's autograph letters and manuscripts; first editions and presentation copies; Impressionist and modern paintings; Tang horses and Ming tilework figures; Cypriot terra-cotta statues and Ivory Coast dance masks; icons and carved wood figures; carpets; English, Spanish and Italian furniture.

3. Drew Middleton, obituary of Maugham, *New York Times,* December 16, 1965, p. 50; MacShane, *Raymond Chandler,* pp. 182–183; Peter Daubeny, *Stage by Stage* (London, 1952), p. 69; Gore Vidal, in Kenneth Tynan, *Diaries,* ed. John Lahr (New York, 2001), pp. 226–227.

4. Leon Edel, "Of Willie's Bondage," *Saturday Review,* 36 (March 15, 1980), 36; Lionel Trilling, *Experience of Literature,* pp. 89–90.

5. Frances Spalding, *Stevie Smith: A Biography* (New York, 1988), p. 175; Letter from Francis King to Jeffrey Meyers, February 20, 2002; Raphael, *Personal Terms,* p. ix; Gordon Bowker, *Pursued by Furies: A Life of Malcolm Lowry* (1993; London: Picador, 1994), p. 157; Robert Boothby, Interview for "Faces of Maugham."

6. Frederic Raphael, "The Skins of an Exotic Fruit," *Times Literary Supplement,* March 31, 1989, p. 329.

   Maugham's influence on Lawrence, Coward, Isherwood, Greene and Amis, and of *Ashenden* on Chandler, Ambler, Fleming and le Carré has already been noted. Georges Simenon called Maugham, who invented the term "Whodunit," "my friend and master." The title of Maugham's *The Trembling of a Leaf* (1921) was echoed in Yeats' autobiography *The Trembling of the Veil* (1922). Maugham's long anecdote about a futile attempt to escape a rendezvous with death in *Sheppey*

(1933) was used as the title and epigraph of John O'Hara's novel *Appointment in Samarra* (1934). Golightly, the name of two characters in *Penelope* (1908), became the name of Truman Capote's flaky heroine, Holly Golightly, in *Breakfast at Tiffany's* (1958). *The Explorer* provided the title of Paul Scott's novel of India, *The Jewel in the Crown* (1966).

Maugham's works inspired Alec Waugh's and Robin Maugham's travel books about the South Seas and the Far East. Like Maugham, Bruce Chatwin, another innovative travel writer, used marriage to disguise his homosexuality (which he never publicly acknowledged) and expressed his homosexual themes covertly. In William Faulkner's early story "Yo Ho and Two Bottles of Rum" (1925), "the situations are Conradian, the sentiments Maugham's." The roguish hero, pathetic spinster and seedy ambience of the seaside boardinghouse in Maugham's story "The Round Dozen" (1924) influenced Terence Rattigan's play *Separate Tables* (1955), which carried on the theatrical tradition of Maugham and Coward. In Philip K. Dick's *Dr. Bloodmoney* (1965), Walt Dangerfield, a disc jockey stranded on a satellite and circling the globe, distracts himself by reading *Of Human Bondage*.

See John Whitehead, "'Whodunit' and Somerset Maugham," *Notes & Queries,* 21 (October 1974), 370; Pierre Assouline, *Georges Simenon,* trans. Jon Rothschild (New York, 1997), p. 313; Frederick Karl, *William Faulkner: American Writer* (New York, 1989), p. 204.

7. George Orwell, "Autobiographical Note" (1940), *Collected Essays, Journalism and Letters* [*CEJL*], ed. Sonia Orwell and Ian Angus (New York, 1968), 2:24; Maugham, *Summing Up,* p. 34; Orwell, "Such, Such Were the Joys" (1950), p. 45.

8. Maugham, *Summing Up,* p. 43, and Maugham, *Of Human Bondage,* p. 98; Morgan, *Maugham,* p. 126; Orwell, *CEJL,* 4:205; W. Somerset Maugham, Preface to Francis de Croisset, *Our Puppet Show* (New York, 1929); Orwell, "Confessions of a Book Reviewer" (1946), *CEJL,* 4:183.

9. Maugham, *Summing Up,* p. 29; Orwell, "Why I Write" (1947), *Collection of Essays,* p. 320; Henderson, "W. Somerset Maugham," *Cantuarian,* August 1989, p. 174; Orwell, "Why I Write," p. 315.

10. Maugham, *Chinese Screen,* p. 142; Orwell, *Road to Wigan Pier,* pp. 112–113.

11. Orwell, "Inside the Whale" (1940), *Collection of Essays,* p. 232;

Maugham, *Gentleman in the Parlour,* p. 52; Orwell, *Road to Wigan Pier,* p. 97; Maugham, *Chinese Screen,* p. 229; George Orwell, "A Hanging" (1931), *Decline of the English Murder* (London: Penguin, 1965), p. 16.

12. Maugham, *Chinese Screen,* p. 62; George Orwell, *Burmese Days* (1934; New York: Popular Library, 1958), p. 84; Maugham, *Casuarina Tree,* p. 183; Orwell, *Road to Wigan Pier,* p. 128.

13. Maugham, *Cakes and Ale,* p. 103; Orwell, "Boys' Weeklies" (1940), *Collection of Essays,* p. 299; Maugham, *Cakes and Ale,* p. 179; George Orwell, *Coming Up for Air* (1939; London: Penguin, 1962), pp. 200, 209.

14. Maugham, *Explorer,* p. 121; George Orwell, *Homage to Catalonia* (1938; New York, 1952), p. 231.

15. Maugham, *East of Suez,* p. 95, and Maugham, *Summing Up,* p. 38 (see also Maugham, *Don Fernando,* p. 180); Orwell, "Benefit of Clergy" (1944), *Decline of the English Murder,* p. 20.

16. Anthony Burgess, *Little Wilson and Big God* (New York, 1986), p. 402; Anthony Burgess, *Earthly Powers* (1980; New York: Avon, 1981), pp. 2; 11; 14.

17. Bruce King, *V. S. Naipaul* (New York, 1993), p. 96; V. S. Naipaul, Review of Christopher Isherwood's *Exhumations, New Statesman,* March 18, 1966, p. 381; Paul Theroux, Afterword to *Sir Vidia's Shadow* (Boston, 2000), pp. 361–362.

 Just as Graham Greene told Maugham that *The Sacred Flame* was "the worst play ever written," so Naipaul told Theroux that Maugham's "Salvatore" was "the worst story ever written" (conversation with Paul Theroux, October 15, 2001).

18. *Conversations with V. S. Naipaul,* ed. Feroza Jussawalla (Jackson, Miss., 1997), p. 156; V. S. Naipaul, *Half a Life* (New York, 2001), p. 5.

19. Letters to Jeffrey Meyers from Anita Brookner, May 5, 2002; Margaret Drabble, May 2, 2002; and A. S. Byatt, April 30, 2002.

20. Letters to Jeffrey Meyers from A. N. Wilson, May 27, 2002; Paul Theroux, September 10, 2002; and Muriel Spark, May 12, 2002.

21. Richard Aldington, "Somerset Maugham," *Selected Critical Writings, 1928–1960,* ed. Alister Kershaw (Carbondale, Illinois, 1970), p. 32.

Maugham's Travels

WINTER 1888—*in Hyères*

WINTER 1889—*in Hyères*

SUMMER-FALL 1890–SPRING 1892—*Heidelberg*

SPRING 1894—*Italy*

SUMMER 1895—*Capri*

DECEMBER 1897–APRIL 1899—*Seville*

LATE 1904—*trip to France*

FEBRUARY–JUNE 1905—*Paris*

JULY–AUGUST 1905—*Capri*

JANUARY–MARCH 1906—*Greece and Egypt*

FALL 1910—*first trip to America*

OCTOBER 1914–FEBRUARY 1915—*with the Red Cross in France*

JULY–SEPTEMBER 1915—*in Rome with Syrie for birth of Liza*

SEPTEMBER 1915–SUMMER 1916—*secret agent in Switzerland*

NOVEMBER 1916–MAY 1917—*San Francisco, Hawaii, Samoa, Tahiti*

MAY 1917—*marries Syrie in New Jersey*

JULY–NOVEMBER 1917—*secret agent in Petrograd*

SEPTEMBER 1919–MARCH 1920—*China*

OCTOBER 1920—*New York, Los Angeles, San Francisco*

FEBRUARY–JULY 1921—*Hawaii, Australia, Malaya, Borneo*

OCTOBER 1922–JULY 1923—*Burma, Siam and Indochina*

SEPTEMBER 1924–JANUARY 1925—*New York, Mexico and Guatemala*

SUMMER 1925—*visits Syrie in Le Touquet*

OCTOBER 1925–FEBRUARY 1926—*Malaya*

OCTOBER 1926—*buys Villa Mauresque at Cap Ferrat*

LATE 1929—*Greece and Egypt*

JANUARY 1932—*Berlin*

MARCH 1934—*Spain*

DECEMBER 1935–JANUARY 1936—*Haiti and penal colony in French Guiana*

MAY–JULY 1937—*Scandinavia and Germany*

EARLY 1938—*India*

SEPTEMBER 1938—*first visit to Niehans Clinic in Vevey, Switzerland*

FEBRUARY–MARCH 1939—*America*

JUNE 1940—*escapes from France to England*

OCTOBER 1941–MAY 1946—*war years in New York, South Carolina, Martha's Vineyard and Hollywood*

JUNE 1946—*returns to Villa Mauresque*

APRIL 1948—*Spain*

JANUARY 1949—*visits Nelson Doubleday, just before his death, in New York*

APRIL 1950—*Morocco*

NOVEMBER 1950—*lectures in New York*

SEPTEMBER 1952—*hernia operation in Switzerland*

SPRING 1953—*Greece and Turkey*

JANUARY 1956—*Egypt*

APRIL 1959—*Munich, Badgastein, Vienna and Venice*

OCTOBER 1959—*Japan and Singapore*

MAY 1961—*made honorary senator at Heidelberg*

Iconography

—Several of Kelly's thirty portraits have been reproduced: with bow tie, high collar, mustache and hair parted in middle, 1907 (Mander, frontispiece); *The Jester,* 1911, Tate Gallery (Mander, p. v); four portraits between 1932 and 1962 (Curtis, *Somerset Maugham,* pp. 158–159); undated portrait (*Writer's Notebook,* frontispiece); three late portraits (Curtis, *Somerset Maugham,* p. 187). Fifteen of them are now at the University of Texas in Austin.

—H. Huggler Wyss, wood carving of Maugham's head, 1920.

—Alfred Wolmark, ink portrait of Maugham's head, 1926 (Rothschild, *Catalogue,* p. 350).

—Alfred Wolmark, oil portrait, 1930.

—Philip Steegman, oil portrait, 1931, National Portrait Gallery.

—David Low, caricature of Maugham seated, with crossed legs, 1935 (*New Statesman and Nation,* supplement to January 6, 1934 issue).

—Marie Laurencin, oil portrait vaguely resembling Maugham, with mustache, jacket and open collar, 1936 (*Purely for My Pleasure,* p. 45).

—William Rothenstein, pencil drawing, 1937 (Rothenstein, *Contemporaries: Portrait Drawings,* London, 1937, pp. 63–64).

—Laurence Tompkins, bronze bust, 1941 (Morgan, *Maugham,* sec. II, no. 35).

—H. Andrew Freeth, pencil drawing of Maugham wearing a pin-striped suit, with hands clasped, standing behind a chair, 1946 (Curtis, *Somerset Maugham,* back of dust jacket).

—H. Andrew Freeth, etching of Maugham's head, n.d. (Curtis, *Somerset Maugham,* p. 167).

—Edouard MacAvoy, oil portrait, 1947, Museum of Fine Arts, Nice (*Purely for My Pleasure,* frontispiece).

—Zsigmond Kisfaludi Strobl, bust, 1949.

—Graham Sutherland, pencil study of Maugham's head, 1949, Fitzwilliam Museum, Cambridge, England (*The Explorer,* back cover of Penguin edition).

—Graham Sutherland, pencil drawing of Maugham's head, 1949, Beaverbrook Museum, Fredericton, New Brunswick, Canada (Michael Wardell, "A Visit to Somerset Maugham," *Atlantic Advocate,* April, 1962, p. 74).

—Graham Sutherland, oil portrait, 1949, Tate Gallery (Berthoud, *Graham Sutherland,* after p. 160).

—Graham Sutherland, black and red chalk study for lithograph, 1953 (Berthoud, *Graham Sutherland,* after p. 160).

—Jacob Epstein, bronze head, 1951 (Rothschild, *Catalogue,* frontispiece).

—Ronald Searle, pencil drawing of Maugham with one hand in pocket, the other holding a cigarette, 1954 (Curtis, *Somerset Maugham,* frontispiece).

—Vasco Lazzolo, n.d., private collection.

—Ivor Roberts-Jones, bronze head, n.d., Beaverbrook Museum.

—Andrew Rhodes, lithograph, with crossed arms, wearing double-breasted suit and striped tie, 1960 (Rothschild, *Catalogue,* dust jacket).

—Leslie Tryon-Tratorian, caricature, 1981 (*Los Angeles Times Book Review,* August 23, 1981).

Bibliography

Behrman, S. N. "W. Somerset Maugham." *People in a Diary: A Memoir.* Boston: Little, Brown, 1972. Pages 276–312.

Burgess, Anthony. Introduction to *Maugham's Malaysian Stories.* Hong Kong: Heinemann Asia, 1969. Pages vi–xvii.

Calder, Robert. *W. Somerset Maugham and the Quest for Freedom.* Garden City, New York: Doubleday, 1973.

———. *Willie: The Life of W. Somerset Maugham.* New York: St. Martin's, 1989.

Connon, Bryan. *Somerset and the Maugham Dynasty.* London: Sinclair-Stevenson, 1997.

Coward, Noël, *Diaries.* Ed. Graham Payn and Sheridan Morley. Boston: Little, Brown, 1982.

Curtis, Anthony. *The Pattern of Maugham.* London: Hamish Hamilton, 1974.

———. *Somerset Maugham.* New York: Macmillan, 1977.

Curtis, Anthony, and John Whitehead, eds. *W. Somerset Maugham: The Critical Heritage.* London: Routledge & Kegan Paul, 1987.

Epstein, Joseph. "Is It All Right to Read Somerset Maugham?" *Partial Payments.* New York: Norton, 1989. Pages 185–209.

Fleming, Ann. *Letters.* Ed. Mark Amory. London: Collins, 1985.

Greene, Graham. "Some Notes on Somerset Maugham." *Collected Essays.* New York: Viking, 1979. Pages 197–205.

Isherwood, Christopher. *Diaries: Volume One, 1939–1960.* Ed. Katherine Bucknell. New York: HarperCollins, 1997.

Jeffreys-Jones, Rhodri. "Maugham in Russia." *American Espionage: From Secret Service to CIA.* New York: Free Press, 1977. Pages 87–101, 233–235.

Kanin, Garson. *Remembering Mr. Maugham.* Foreword by Noël Coward. London: Hamish Hamilton, 1966.

King, Francis. *Yesterday Came Suddenly.* London: Constable, 1993.

Mander, Raymond, and Joe Mitchenson. *Theatrical Companion to Maugham.* London: Rockliff, 1955.

Maugham, Frederic. "Early Days." *At the End of the Day.* Westport, Conn.: Heinemann, 1951. Pages 3–21.

Maugham, Robin. *Somerset and All the Maughams.* 1966; London: Penguin, 1975.

———. *Escape from the Shadows: An Autobiography.* New York: McGraw-Hill, 1972.

———. *Conversations with Willie.* New York: Simon & Schuster, 1978.

Morgan, Ted. *Maugham.* New York: Simon & Schuster, 1980.

Pfeiffer, Karl. *W. Somerset Maugham: A Candid Portrait.* Introduction by Jerome Weidman. New York: Norton, 1959.

Powell, Anthony. "Somerset Maugham." *Under Review: Further Writings on Writers, 1946–1989.* Pages 290–295.

Raphael, Frederic. *Somerset Maugham and His World.* New York: Scribner's, 1976.

Rothschild, Loren, and Deborah Whiteman, eds. *William Somerset Maugham: A Catalogue of the Loren and Frances Rothschild Collection.* Los Angeles: Heritage Book Shop, 2001.

Sotheby's. *Catalogue of the Collection of Impressionist and Modern Pictures Formed by W. Somerset Maugham.* London: Sotheby's, April 10, 1962.

Stott, Raymond Toole. *A Bibliography of the Works of W. Somerset Maugham.* Edmonton: University of Alberta Press, 1973.

Swan, Michael. "Conversations with Maugham." *Ilex and Olive: An Account of a Journey Through France and Italy.* London: Home & Van Thal, 1949. Pages 67–76.

Vidal, Gore. "Maugham's Half & Half." *United States: Essays, 1952–1972.* New York: Random House, 1993. Pages 228–250.

Waugh, Alec. "W. Somerset Maugham: RIP." *My Brother Evelyn and Other Profiles.* New York: Farrar, Straus & Giroux, 1990.

Wescott, Glenway. *Continual Lessons: The Journals of Glenway Wescott, 1937–1955.* Ed. Robert Phelps. New York: Farrar, Straus & Giroux, 1990.

Whitehead, John. *Maugham: A Reappraisal.* London: Vision, 1987.

Wilson, Angus. Introduction to *A Maugham Twelve.* London: Heinemann, 1966. Pages vii–x.

Filmography

The Explorer, 1915, Dorothy Davenport and Lou Tellegen

The Land of Promise, 1917, Billie Burke and Thomas Meighan

Smith, 1917, Elizabeth Risdon and Fred Groves

The Divorcée (Lady Frederick), 1919, Ethel Barrymore and E. J. Ratcliffe

Jack Straw, 1920, Carol McComas and Robert Warwick

The Ordeal, 1922, Agnes Ayres and Clarence Burton

East of Suez, 1924, Pola Negri and Edmund Lowe

Infatuation (Caesar's Wife), 1925, Corinne Griffith and Percy Marmont

The Circle, 1925, Eleanor Boardman and Creighton Hale

The Canadian (The Land of Promise), 1926, Mona Palma and Thomas Meighan

The Magician, 1926, Alice Terry and Paul Wegener

Sadie Thompson ("Rain"), 1928, Gloria Swanson and Lionel Barrymore

The Letter, 1929, Jeanne Eagels and Herbert Marshall

The Sacred Flame, 1929, Pauline Frederick and George Brent

Charming Sinners (The Constant Wife), 1929, Ruth Chatterton and William Powell

Strictly Unconventional (The Circle), 1930, Catherine Dale Owen and Tyrell Davis

Rain, 1932, Joan Crawford and Walter Huston

The Narrow Corner, 1933, Douglas Fairbanks Jr. and Ralph Bellamy

Our Betters, 1933, Constance Bennett and Gilbert Roland

Of Human Bondage, 1934, Bette Davis and Leslie Howard

The Painted Veil, 1934, Greta Garbo and George Brent

The Right to Live (The Sacred Flame), 1935, Josephine Hutchinson and Colin Clive

*The Secret Agent (Ashenden), 1936, Madeleine Carroll, Peter Lorre and Robert Young

Isle of Fury (The Narrow Corner), 1936, Humphrey Bogart and Margaret Lindsay

The Tenth Man, 1936, Antoinette Collier and John Lodge

The Beachcomber ("The Vessel of Wrath"), 1938, Elsa Lanchester and Charles Laughton

*The Letter, 1940, Bette Davis and Herbert Marshall

Too Many Husbands (Home and Beauty), 1940, Jean Arthur and Fred MacMurray

The Moon and Sixpence, 1943, George Sanders and Herbert Marshall

Christmas Holiday, 1944, Deanna Durbin and Gene Kelly

The Hour Before the Dawn, 1944, Veronica Lake and Franchot Tone

Of Human Bondage, 1946, Eleanor Parker and Paul Henreid

The Razor's Edge, 1946, Gene Tierney, Tyrone Power and Clifton Webb

Dirty Gertie from Harlem U.S.A. ("Rain"), 1946, all-black cast

The Unfaithful ("The Letter"), 1947, Ann Sheridan and Lew Ayres

*Quartet ("The Facts of Life," "The Alien Corn," "The Kite," "The Colonel's Lady"), 1948, Mai Zetterling and Dirk Bogarde

*Trio ("The Verger," "Mr. Know-All," "Sanatorium"), 1950, Jean Simmons and Michael Rennie

*Encore ("The Ant and the Grasshopper," "Winter Cruise," "Gigolo and Gigolette"), 1952, Kay Walsh and Nigel Patrick

*Miss Sadie Thompson ("Rain"), 1953, Rita Hayworth and José Ferrer

The Beachcomber ("The Vessel of Wrath"), 1954, Glynis Johns and Donald Sinden

Three Cases of Murder ("Lord Montdrago"), 1954, Orson Welles and Alan Badel

Three for the Show (Home and Beauty), 1955, Betty Grable, Marge and Gower Champion

The Seventh Sin (The Painted Veil), 1957, Eleanor Parker and George Sanders

Adorable Julia (Theatre), 1962, Lilli Palmer and Charles Boyer

Of Human Bondage, 1964, Kim Novak and Laurence Harvey

Overnight Sensation ("The Colonel's Lady"), 1983, Louise Fletcher and Robert Loggia

The Razor's Edge, 1984, Catherine Hicks and Bill Murray

Up at the Villa, 2000, Kristin Scott-Thomas and Sean Penn

* = best films

Index

Acton, Harold, 70, 235, 312, 337
Aga Khan, 306
Agate, James, 181
Alanson, Bertram, 120–121, 185, 271–272; and Searle, 276, 277, 310
Aldington, Richard, 159, 222, 340, 351
Allen, Walter, 243
Ambler, Eric, 194, 293
Amis, Kingsley, 288; *I Like It Here,* 313; *Lucky Jim,* 312–313
Anderson, Sherwood, 140
Ashenden, Leonard, 191
Auden, W. H., 37; "His Excellency," 193; *Letters from Iceland,* 193
Austen, Jane, *Mansfield Park,* 109

Bachardy, Don, 248
Back, Barbara, 89, 91, 104, 171, 188–191, 363n14, 373n7
Back, Ivor, 188–189
Bankhead, Tallulah, 147, 149
Barnardo, Thomas John, 80–81
Barrie, Sir James, 198, 307; *Peter Pan,* 72
Barrymore, Ethel, 190
Barrymore, John, 252
Beaton, Cecil, 88–89, 168, 170, 186, 301
Beaverbrook, Lord, 249, 273, 324, 331
Beerbohm, Max, 72, 174, 231, 287, 306

Behrman, S. N., 205, 246–247, 276, 307
Bell, Clive, 61
Benét, Stephen Vincent, 228
Bennett, Arnold, 15, 53, 62, 166
Benson, E. F., 33, 83, 186
Berenson, Bernard, 323
Boothby, Robert, 324, 327, 331–332
Bowen, Elizabeth, 227
Brenan, Gerald, *South from Granada,* 46
Bright, Reginald, 70
Bronzino, Agnolo, *Allegory,* 381n3
Brookner, Anita, 349
Brooks, John Ellingham, 24–25, 32–34, 36, 83, 109, 186, 249
Brooks, Romaine, 32–33
Browning, Oscar, 187
Bruce, Nigel, 181
Buchanan, Sir George, 193
Burgess, Anthony, 32, 343; *Earthly Powers,* 347–348; *Time for a Tiger,* 347
Burke, Billie, 94
Butler, Samuel, 108
Byatt, A. S., 349
Byron, Lord George, 108

Cameron, Roderick, 175
Capote, Truman, 247

Chambrun, Jacques, 247
Chandler, Raymond, 194, 264, 341, 374n13
Channon, Henry "Chips," 261–262, 298
Chatwin, Bruce, 326
Chekhov, Anton, 140–141, 299
Chiaramello, Annette, 169–170
Churchill, Winston, 9, 48, 127, 193, 222, 234, 273, 287, 308, 309, 324
Clark, Kenneth, 174, 222, 282, 287, 332
Clurman, Harold, 253
Cocteau, Jean, 171, 174, 285–286, 295
Colefax, Sybil, 175
Colles, William Morris, 52–53, 247
Colvin, Sir Sidney, 198
Compton, Fay, 190
Connolly, Cyril, 72, 172, 241, 264
Conrad, Joseph, 20, 32, 42, 53, 118, 176, 227, 348; *Almayer's Folly,* 142; *Heart of Darkness,* 66, 137, 142, 144; *The Inheritors,* 40; *Lord Jim,* 137; *The Nigger of the "Narcissus,"* 141, 268n6; *Nostromo,* 52; *Outcast of the Islands,* 142; "An Outpost of Progress," 143–144, 179; *The Secret Agent,* 142, 192; *Typhoon,* 141; *Under Western Eyes,* 114, 126; *Victory,* 211–212, 327
Constant, Benjamin, *Adolphe,* 112
Cooper, Diana, 301, 315
Cooper, Douglas, 337–338
Cooper, Gladys, 69, 181
Cordell, Richard, 274
Cornell, Katharine, 181
Coward, Noël, 59, 91, 159, 186, 207, 233, 306, 332–333, 338; and Niehans, 234–235; "Nature Study," 161, 334; *Point Valaine,* 160–161; *A Song at Twilight,* 334–335; *South Sea Bubble,* 161–162
Crane, Hart, 139–140
Crowley, Aleister, 66–68, 109
Cukor, George, 246, 265–267, 336
Cunard, Emerald, 94, 104

Dante, *Purgatorio,* 164–165, 370n11
Dean, Basil, 70, 149
Dickens, Charles, 108
Doran, George, 69, 112, 172, 176
Doubleday, Ellen, 255
Doubleday, Nelson, 244, 254, 260, 265, 280, 297–298, 331
Douglas, Norman, 66
Drabble, Margaret, 349
Dreiser, Theodore, 112–113, 252
Dumas, Alexandre, *La Dame aux camélias,* 54
Dvorak, Max, "El Greco and Mannerism," 219

Eagels, Jeanne, 147
Eakins, Thomas, *The Gross Clinic,* 28
Eastman, Max, 256
Edel, Leon, 342
Eisenhower, Dwight, 296
Eliot, T. S., 199, 222, 227, 307, 308, 370n11; "The Metaphysical Poets," 223; "Prufrock," 150, 223; "Tradition and the Individual Talent," 197, 223
Elizabeth II, Queen, 308
Epstein, Joseph, 283
Eyre, Richard, 216

Fermor, Patrick Leigh, 16, 303–304
Fischer, Kuno, 23–24
Fitzgerald, F. Scott, 234, 252; *Tender is the Night,* 167
Flaubert, Gustave, *Madame Bovary,* 108
Fleming, Ann, 291, 301, 302–304, 324
Fleming, Ian, 194, 301–302, 304
Ford, Ford Madox, 73, 198; *The Inheritors,* 40
Ford, Richard, *Handbook for Travellers in Spain,* 45
Forester, C. S., *The African Queen,* 209
Forster, E. M., 50, 174, 241, 242–243, 307, 309; *Howards End,* 243; *The Longest Journey,* 108

Francis, David Rowland, 193
Frere, Alexander, 222, 314, 331
Frohman, Charles, 70, 246
Fuller, John, 193

Garnett, Edward, 40, 44
Gauguin, Paul, 117, 119–120, 136, 137–138; *Eve in Paradise,* 120; *Nevermore,* 138
Gautier, Théophile, *Journey to Spain,* 45
Gide, André, 319
Gielgud, John, 147–148
Gittings, Robert, 198
Goebbels, Joseph, *Diaries,* 194
Goldring, Douglas, 60
Goren, Charles, *Standard Book of Bidding,* 296
Graves, Robert, 46
Greco, El, 109, 111, 219, 281; *Laocoön,* 220; *St. Sebastian,* 219
Greene, Graham, 107, 194, 307, 331; *The End of the Affair,* 221, 259; *The Heart of the Matter,* 147, 221; *The Human Factor,* 221; *The Living Room,* 221; *Our Man in Havana,* 195; *The Power and the Glory,* 147, 221; *The Quiet American,* 195; *The Tenth Man,* 221

Hall, Radclyffe, 73
Hammersley, Violet, 6–8, 10
Hardy, Emma, 198
Hardy, Florence, 198–199
Hardy, Thomas, 374n2; *Jude the Obscure,* 197–198
Hare, Augustus, 39–40
Harris, Frank, 58
Hauptmann, Gerhart, 72
Haxton, Gerald: character, 101–102, 116, 144, 186; deportation, 102–103, 113; family background, 98–101, 363n3; illness and death, 267–268; in Maugham's works, 94–95, 101–102, 251, 331;

relationship with Maugham, 83, 92, 96, 105, 118, 120, 160, 167, 182, 184–188, 217, 239, 244, 247, 253, 269–270, 274, 277, 334–335; sex life, 247, 252; travels with Maugham, 149–150, 152–3, 157, 158, 229, 291; wartime, 121, 241, 254
Haxton, Henry, 98–100, 363n3
Haxton, Sara Thibault, 98–99, 100–101
Hazlitt, William, 154–155
Heard, Gerald, 106, 232, 233, 252
Heinemann, William, 49, 50, 246, 255, 331
Hemingway, Ernest, 252, 295; "Cat in the Rain," 263; *Death in the Afternoon,* 219; *A Farewell to Arms,* 97, 214–215; *A Moveable Feast,* 66, 332; "The Short Happy Life of Francis Macomber," 210, 289; *To Have and Have Not,* 370n12
Hichens, Robert, 59
Hofmannsthal, Hugo von, *Der Rosenkavalier,* 54
Hope, Lord John, 291, 329
Horgan, Paul, 244
Horizon, 241–242
Housman, A. E., 104
Housman, Laurence, 59, 73
Hunt, Violet, 64, 73, 76, 97, 109; *White Rose of Weary Leaf,* 74
Huxley, Aldous, 252; "Little Mexican," 193; *Time Must Have a Stop,* 253, 280; "Wordsworth in the Tropics," 118
Huyshe, Wentworth, 39, 40

Ibsen, Henrik, 24, 53
Isherwood, Christopher, 181, 231, 252, 260–261, 285, 311; *Christopher and His Kind,* 232; *Diaries,* 232–233; *Prater Violet,* 232; *Vedanta for the Western World,* 261; *The World in the Evening,* 233

James, Henry, 62, 64, 73, 94, 118, 141, 202, 299, 359n7; *The Ambassadors*, 63; "The Figure in the Carpet," 112; *Guy Domville*, 63
Johnston, Edward, 45
Jonas, Klaus, 307
Jones, Ethelwyn (Sue), 76, 77–80, 91–92, 95, 199
Justi, Carl, "The Novice El Greco," 219

Kanin, Garson, 95, 218, 246
Karsh, Yousuf, 175
Kelly, Gerald, 61–62, 76, 82, 109, 163, 191–192, 308; portraits: Sue Jones, 78; Sasha Kropotkin, 124, 125; Maugham, 74, 283, 286
Kelly, Princess Grace, 322–323
Kelly, Jane, 184
Kelly, Rose, 66, 67
Kerensky, Alexander, 123, 125, 128–130, 131, 194, 367n15
King, Francis, 104, 105, 108, 288, 316–318, 343
King's School, 16–20, 306–307, 322, 339
Kipling, Rudyard, 3, 118, 177, 229, 299; *France at War*, 240; "The Ladies," 293; "Mandalay," 151
Kirke, Major Walter, 115
Knoblock, Edward, 132
Kropotkin, Alexandra (Sasha), 76, 125–126, 191, 238, 366n10
Kropotkin, Prince Peter, 125, 126

Lane-Poole, Stanley, *The Moors in Spain*, 45
Lang, Andrew, 43
Laurencin, Marie, 171, 248
Lautrec, Henri de Toulouse, *Le Polisseur*, 282
Lawrence, D. H., 11, 32, 46, 107, 119, 140, 198; meeting with Maugham, 156–158; *Aaron's Rod*, 59; *Lady Chatterley's Lover*, 50, 51, 259; "Odour of Chrysanthemums," 51;

The Plumed Serpent, 158; *The Rainbow*, 156, 159; "The Rocking-Horse Winner," 209; *Sons and Lovers*, 111, 159; *Women in Love*, 214
Lawrence, Frieda, *Not I, But the Wind*, 157–158
Lawrence, T. E., 198
Lebedev, Boris, 125, 126
le Carré, John, 195, 288, 374n14
Legrand, Louis, 185
Lenin, Vladimir, 128, 129
Leopold II, King of the Belgians, 168
Leverson, Ada, 246; *The Limit*, 59
Lewis, Sir George, 82
Lewis, Sinclair, 112, 252
Lewis, Wyndham, 307; *Tarr*, 136
Lloyd George, David, 130, 367n15
Lockhart, Bruce, 91, 121, 123, 128, 130, 193, 237, 298, 373n7
Longfellow, Henry Wadsworth, 21, 22

MacAvoy, Edouard, 170, 283, 285, 324
MacCarthy, Desmond, 97, 112, 173, 228
Machiavelli, Niccolò, *History of Florence*, 43–44; *La Mandragola*, 279
Mackenzie, Compton, 83, 84, 204–205, 306
Malraux, André, *Man's Fate*, 149, 371n13
Mann, Thomas, 37, 112, 378n21; "Death in Venice," 136; *The Magic Mountain*, 132
Mansfield, Katherine, 139, 140, 299, 319–320; "The Garden-Party," 178; *In a German Pension*, 23
Marchand, Leslie, 207
Marsh, Edward, 186, 222, 265
Marshall, Arthur, 171–172, 185, 278, 309
Masaryk, Thomas, 126, 127, 194
Matisse, Henri, 171; *Woman Seated in an Armchair*, 283
Maugham, Camilla (granddaughter), 328, 388n2
Maugham, Charles Ormond (brother), 7, 54, 61, 223–224

Maugham, Diana (niece), 162, 186, 330, 337

Maugham, Edith Snell (mother), 7–8, 10–12, 131

Maugham, Frederic Herbert (brother), 7, 9, 12, 18–19, 236–237, 308, 336; disapproval of homosexuality, 102–103, 162–163, 256–257

Maugham, Rev. Henry Macdonald (uncle), 12

Maugham, Henry Neville (brother), 7, 39, 56–57

Maugham, Honor (niece), 236

Maugham, Liza (daughter), 186, 271, 276, 309; birth, 84, 96; family, 388n2; marriages, 236, 253, 291; and Maugham, 223–224, 311, 325–327, 328–330, 331, 341, 386n6; and Syrie, 86, 90–91, 183

Maugham, Nicolas (grandson), 328

Maugham, Robert (grandfather), 4–5

Maugham, Robert Ormond (father), 5–7, 10, 12

Maugham, Robin (nephew), 162, 184, 185, 236, 256–257; on Maugham, 102, 103, 105, 106, 213, 305, 335; *The Servant,* 258; *Somerset and All the Maughams,* 333–334

Maugham, Sophie Scheidlin (aunt), 14, 21

Maugham, Syrie Barnardo Wellcome (wife): background, 80–81; character 81–82, 85; death, 309–310; decorator, 88–89; divorce, 182–183; marriage to Maugham, 83–88, 91–92, 96, 103, 113, 117, 121, 160, 167; in Maugham's work, 76, 89, 94–95, 133, 144, 164, 182, 331, 332; relationship with Liza, 90–91, 183

MAUGHAM, WILLIAM SOMERSET (1874–1965)

CHARACTER
ambitious, 35, 56, 57, 83, 96, 220
athletic, 175–176

bisexual, 20, 30, 46, 86, 91–92
capacity for love, 3, 184–185, 267, 335
cold and remote, 35–36, 70, 115, 174, 175, 327, 341
competitive, 204–205
confident, 35–36, 47
cynical, 165, 174, 203
dominant, 36, 105, 174, 305
generous, 170, 340
hardworking, 7, 38
modest, 222
repressed, 3, 106, 305–306
sad, 305–306
self-controlled, 56, 248–249, 342
self-disciplined, 35–36, 47, 60, 175, 247, 342
short-tempered, 36, 175
shrewd, 69, 265–266, 297, 306
shy, 15, 35–36, 167
stammer, 3, 15–16, 19, 20, 35, 103, 151, 232, 243, 248, 305; treatment for, 247–248
unpopularity, 342–343
views: Jews, 225, marriage, 76–77, 83–84, 155, 165, 190–191, 253, other writers, 62–63, 228–229, 252, 299, 319–320, 359n7, politics, 272–273, on religion, 30–31, 33, 98, 122, 227, 230–231, 264

LIFE
affairs with women, 91–92; Syrie Barnardo, 76, 81–82, 92, Violet Hunt, 73, 76, Sue Jones, 76, 92, 95, Sasha Kropotkin, 76, 125
agents, 52–53, 70, 172, 247
appearance, 7, 35, 156, 175, 205, 244, 298, 300, 315, 323
art collecting, 9, 61, 120, 169, 266, 281–283, 325–330
birth, 8
bridge-playing, 296
cellular therapy, 234, 314–315, 337
childhood, 3, 9–12, 14–16, 37
death, 19, 339–340
death of mother, 11–12

MAUGHAM, WILLIAM SOMERSET
(1874–1965)
LIFE *(continued)*
divorce, 182–183, 331, 332
earnings, 56, 69–70, 149, 167, 170,
265, 294, 306, 321–322, 331,
340
education: Heidelberg, 21–25; King's
School, 16–20; St. Thomas's
Hospital, 26–31, 356n10
family background, 3–11
fictional portraits of, 59, 160–162,
205–206, 334–335, 347–348
friendships: 72–73, 186, 246, 360n19,
373n4; Alanson, 120–121, Barbara
Back, 89, 104, 171, 188–190, 373n7,
Beaverbrook, 324, Brooks, 24–25,
32–34, Churchill, 9, 308, 324,
Coward, 159, 207, 306, 332–335,
338, Ann and Ian Fleming,
301–304, Hare, 39–40, Huyshe, 39,
40, Isherwood, 231–233, Kelly,
61–62, 76, 82, 308, Nichols, 90,
159–160, Payne, 38–39, 40, 47,
Philips, 60, Wescott, 105, 245–246,
Winn, 91–92, 176, 187, Zipkin,
247
funeral, 339
homes: London, 86, Villa Mauresque,
167–170, 173, 176, 217–218,
232–233, 273, 278–279, 285, 301,
321, 325, 328, 341, Yemassee,
254–255
homosexual life: concealment, 3, 34,
35, 57, 58–59, 111, 115, 167, 233,
335, creativity, 134, fights against,
86, 112, 220, 327, friends, 159, 186,
202, 373n4, milieu, 103–106, 176,
184–186, 301, 315
honors, 307–308
jobs: clerk, 25–26; Intelligence Agent,
96, 113–115, 117, 121–131, 249;
Red Cross, 96–98
illnesses: dementia, 330, 332, 337–338,
fainting, 230, 253, pleurisy, 19,
tonsillitis, 28, tuberculosis, 131–132

knowledge of languages: French, 10,
12, 167, German, 23, Italian, 32,
Russian, 121–122, Spanish, 44
marriage, 83–88, 91–92, 96, 103, 113,
117, 121, 133, 160, 167
name, 9
places: Capri, 32–34, 64, 83,
Edgartown, 255–256, Geneva,
113–114, Hollywood, 252–253,
Hyères, 19, 21, Paris, 8–10, 60,
Seville, 44–46, Whitstable, 12–14
portraits, 393–394; Epstein, 283,
Karsh, 175, Kelly, 74, MacAvoy,
283, 285, Sutherland, 175, 286–287
reading, 15, 23, 24, 31, 45, 116–117,
241
relationship with Haxton, 83, 92, 96,
98, 105, 118, 120, 121, 144, 158,
160, 167, 184–188, 217, 239, 244,
253, 269–270, 274, 277, 331,
334–335
relationship with Liza, 90, 183,
223–224, 253, 291, 311, legal
action, 325–330, 331, 386n6
relationship with Searle, 274–279,
310–311, 318, 326, 327–330, 336,
338
role in General Strike, 166–167
Somerset Maugham prize, 288–289,
313
speeches, 244, 247, 248–249, 280
travels, 116, 117–118, 391–392;
America, 244, Burma, 154,
Cambodia, 154, China, 149–150,
French Guiana, 218, India,
229–231, Indo-China, 154, Italy,
315, Japan, 315–318, Malaya, 176,
Morocco, 45, Russia, 122, Sarawak,
152–153, Siam, 154, South Seas,
116–117, Spain, 44–46, 218,
Switzerland, 113–115
will, 330, 340–341, 388n1

WORK
dedications, 78, 294–295, 374n13,
382n9

disguised homosexual characters, 59,
111, 135–136, 211–212, 289–290
historical fiction, 43–44, 294
influence of medical training, 27, 31,
33–34, 41–42, 45–46
influence on other writers, 193–195,
209, 221–222, 259, 343, 388–389n6;
Burgess, 347–348, Coward, 335,
Fleming, 301, Naipaul, 348, Orwell,
343–347
literary influences: Chekhov, 140–141,
Conrad, 66, 118, 137, 141–144, 176,
211, Dumas, 53, Eliot, 197,
Hemingway, 219, 263, Ibsen, 53,
James, 94, 112, 141, Kipling, 118,
Lawrence, 259, Maupassant,
140–141, Poe, 68, Proust, 262,
Wells, 68, Wilde, 53
methods of composition, 37–38,
118–119
narrative skill, 137, 140–143, 207,
238–239, 250
planned phases of career, 295
plays, 53–56
prose style: mannered, 36–37, plain,
106–107, 211, 214–215, 222, 226
281, 345, 349
rarest books, 359n9
real-life models for characters, 25,
60–61, 109, 111, 189–191, 192, 198,
199, 201–206, 238, 249, 260–261.
See also Haxton, Gerald, and
Maugham, Syrie
reputation: attacks on, 205–206, 221,
225, 251–252, 258, 274, 279–281,
334–335, 342, popularity, 229, 343,
350–351, praise, 228
satire, 47, 48, 53, 94–95, 133, 196–198,
201–206
self-portraits, 191–192, 196, 207–208,
263, 320, 370n8
source of creativity, 106, 305–306
themes: 350, 351; artist, 136–140,
betrayal and retribution, 142, guilt,
260, literary reputation, 196–197,
200–201, 228 204, homosexual,

211–213, 219–221, 226–227, 237,
261–262, love and art, 226–227,
love and suffering, 11, 41, 143, 146,
love vs. honor, 65, marriage, 50, 52,
155, 182, 190–191, 210–211,
mysticism, 264, self-deception, 143,
sexual desire vs. social constraints,
49–51, social conflict, 209, white
man in the East, 66, 118, 142,
150–151, 152, 177–181, 211–213,
289, 343, women as victims of
colonial life, 178–179
titles, 250
wit, 196, 207, 263

WORKS

AUTOBIOGRAPHY
"Looking Back," 25, 90, 91, 309, 320,
324, 331–333, 350, 361n6
Notebooks, 38, 78, 128
Strictly Personal, 237, 240–241, 259, 295
The Summing Up, 25, 83, 84, 95, 102,
151, 167, 223, 227–228, 265, 279,
293, 295, 320, 332, 344, 350
A Writer's Notebook, 25, 140–141, 153,
159, 225, 295, 320, 348, 350

ESSAYS
Books and You, 252
"The Decline and Fall of the
Detective Story," 241–242
Great Novelists and Their Novels,
220–221, 291–293, 302, 328
"Introduction" to Coward's *Bittersweet
and Other Plays,* 160
"Introduction" to *Choice of Kipling's
Prose,* 299
*Introduction to Modern English and
American Literature,* 319–320
Points of View, 295, 299, 319–320
"Preface," to *Collected Works,* 68
"Preface" to *Creatures of Circumstance,*
228–229
"Prose and Dr. Tillotson," 319
Purely For My Pleasure, 327
"The Saint," 230, 319

MAUGHAM, WILLIAM SOMERSET
(1874–1965)
WORKS *(continued)*
ESSAYS *(continued)*
"The Short Story," 299, 319
Tellers of Tales, 141
"Three Journalists," 319
"The Three Novels of a Poet," 319
Travellers' Library, 319
The Vagrant Mood, 222, 229, 242
"Why D'You Dislike Us?," 280
The World's Ten Greatest Novels, 229

FILMS
Encore, 294
The Hour Before the Dawn, 260
Quartet, 293
The Razor's Edge, 261, 265–267
Three Cases of Murder, 250
Trio, 294
Up at the Villa, 252
filmography, 398–400

NOVELS
The Bishop's Apron, 64–65, 68, 201, 344
Cakes and Ale, 76, 80, 295, 346, 350;
    autobiographical, 9, 182, 196–206,
    339, review, 207
Catalina, 294
Christmas Holiday, 77, 218, 237–239,
    265, 281–283, 295, 350
The Explorer, 49, 65–66, 68, 78, 260,
    339, 344, 346–347
The Hero, 47–49, 65, 68, 260
The Hour Before the Dawn, 86, 115,
    258–260
Liza of Lambeth, 29, 40–43, 47, 345,
    350; dedication, 39
The Magician, 66–68, 106
The Making of a Saint, 43–44, 68
The Merry-Go-Round, 30, 51–52, 55, 68,
    92, 136
The Moon and Sixpence, 74, 76, 119–120,
    134, 136–140, 144, 177, 320, 350;
    opera, 382n8, reviews, 139–140
Mrs. Craddock, 6, 27, 49–51, 104

The Narrow Corner, 142, 211–213, 295,
    375n14
Of Human Bondage, autobiographical,
    3, 19, 24, 30, 35–36, 95, 107–112,
    136, 212, 219, 339, characters, 23,
    25, 60–61, 86, 104, 109–111, 350,
    plot, 144, 345, reviews, 112–113,
    sales, 264, 265, 340, style, 106–107,
    title, 112, 191
The Painted Veil, 147, 150, 162,
    163–165, 180, 228, 350
The Razor's Edge, 133, 170, 175, 237,
    261–265, 295, 348; mystical theme,
    264–265, plot, 144, 260, preface,
    230, reviews, 264, sales, 340
Theatre, 194, 226–227, 295
Then and Now, 279–280
Up at the Villa, 250–252, 295

PLAYS
Caesar's Wife, 23
The Circle, 134–136, 216
Collected Plays, 71
The Constant Wife, 77, 182, 189–191,
    194, 216
East of Suez, 150, 151
The Explorer, 69
For Services Rendered, 30, 213–215, 216,
    260
Grace, 55
Home and Beauty, 133, 182
Jack Straw, 69, 70
Lady Frederick, 54–55, 69
The Land of Promise, 92, 94
Landed Gentry, 71
Love in a Cottage, 133
A Man of Honour, 55, 71
Mrs. Dot, 69
Our Betters, 76, 94–95, 96, 101, 133,
    182, 216
Penelope, 70, 78
The Sacred Flame, 221
Sheppey, 215, 295
Smith, 71
The Tenth Man, 71, 221
The Unattainable, 96, 133

PROPAGANDA
France at War, 240

STORIES
Ah King, 209–211, 295
Ashenden, 57, 76, 113–115, 125, 126,
   128, 142, 191–195, 238, 295, 350;
   influence of 301, reviews, 158
The Casuarina Tree, 142, 177–181
Collected Stories, 340
Complete Stories, 155
Cosmopolitans, 222, 224, 225
Creatures of Circumstance, 289–290, 295
The Mixture as Before, 249, 295
Six Stories Written in the First Person
   Singular, 207–209
The Trembling of a Leaf, 140, 142, 147,
   295

"The Alien Corn," 207, 208–209, 225,
   293
"The Ant and the Grasshopper," 102
"The Back of Beyond," 210–211
"A Bad Example," 25–26
"Before the Party," 177–178
"Behind the Scenes," 193
"The Book-Bag," 177, 209
"The Buried Talent," 263
"A Casual Affair," 110, 143
"The Colonel's Lady," 293–294
"The Door of Opportunity," 210
"Episode," 289–290
"The Escape," 84
"The Facts of Life," 250
"The Fall of Edward Barnard," 144,
   147
"Flotsam and Jetsam," 289
"Footprints in the Jungle," 210
"The Force of Circumstance," 6, 179
"The Hairless Mexican," 193–194
"His Excellency," 193
"Honolulu," 178
"The Human Element," 107, 207,
   208, 250
"Jane," 76, 89
"The Judgement Seat," 31

"The Kite," 289, 290, 293
"The Letter," 55, 147, 178, 180–182
"Lord Montdrago," 157, 249–250
"The Lotus Eater," 249
"Mackintosh," 143–144, 180
"A Man with a Conscience," 218
"A Marriage of Convenience," 155
"Masterson," 155
"Mirage," 155
"Mr. Harrington's Washing," 192
"Mr. Know-All," 224–225
"Neil MacAdam," 141, 209–210
"The Outstation," 179–180, 348, 349
"P. & O.," 178
"The Pool," 145–146
"Rain," 146–147, 149, 350
"Red," 144–145
"Sanatorium," 132–133
"The Treasure," 250
"Unconquered," 289
"The Vessel of Wrath," 209
"Virtue," 189, 207, 208
"The Yellow Streak," 153–154

TRAVEL BOOKS
Don Fernando, 106, 151, 218–221, 350
The Gentleman in the Parlour, 6,
   117–118, 154–155, 225, 246, 345,
   350
The Land of the Blessed Virgin, 44–46,
   74, 106
On a Chinese Screen, 150, 223, 224,
   345–346
Orientations, 45, 68

Maupassant, Guy de, 140–141, 299;
   "The Necklace," 224–225
Melville, Herman, 292; *Billy Budd,* 220;
   Omoo, 116; *Redburn,* 220; *Typee,* 116
Mencken, H. L., 69
Meyerbeer, Giacomo, 23
Millay, Edna St. Vincent, 186
Mishima, Yukio, 317
Mordaunt, Elinor [Evelyn Wiebe], *Gin*
   and Bitters [Full Circle], 205–206

Morgan, Ted, 337
Mortimer, Raymond, 172, 217–218, 222, 228, 306, 327
Munch, Edvard, *Dead Mother and Child,* 11

Nabokov, V. D., 129
Naipaul, V. S., 43, 288, 343; *A Bend in the River,* 348; *Half a Life,* 348
Nash, Ogden, 386n11
Neilson, Keith, 130
Nichols, Beverley, 90, 101, 185, 282; *A Case of Human Bondage,* 159–160, 369n6
Nicholson, Harold, 185, 301
Niehans, Dr. Paul, 233–235
Nuttall, Zelia, 158

O'Conor, Roderick, 60–61, 109, 119, 359n4
Old Heidelberg, 21–22
O'Neill, Eugene, 181
Orwell, George, 43, 343, 348; "Boys' Weeklies," 346; *Burmese Days,* 345–346; *A Clergyman's Daughter,* 344, 345; *Coming Up for Air,* 346; "England, Your England," 347; "A Hanging," 345; *Homage to Catalonia,* 347; *Keep the Aspidistra Flying,* 344; "Raffles and Miss Blandish," 242; *The Road to Wigan Pier,* 318, 345; "Such, Such Were the Joys," 344; "Without Benefit of Clergy," 347

Paravicini, Nicolas, 224, 250, 253, 291
Partridge, Frances, 298
Payne, Adney Walter, 38–39, 40, 47, 69, 111, 144, 212
Pfeiffer, Karl, 274
Philips, Harry, 60, 65, 111, 359n3
Picasso, Pablo, *La Grecque,* 282, 310
Pinker, J. B., 53, 67, 247

Plomer, William, 211, 242, 306
Poe, Edgar Allan, 68, 140
Porter, Katherine Anne, 245–246
Posner, David, 258, 276, 379n2
Powell, Anthony, 304, 305, 306
Pritchett, V. S., 250, 288, 290
Prokosch, Frederic, 187
Proust, Marcel, *The Guermantes Way,* 71; *The Past Recaptured,* 262; *Swann's Way,* 9–10

Quennell, Peter, 305, 306

Rainier, Prince, 171, 322
Raphael, Frederic, 214, 321, 343
Rascoe, Burton, 156
Read, Herbert, 242–243
Rembrandt, *The Anatomy Lesson,* 28
Renoir, Pierre Auguste, *Andrée,* 282
Ribera, José de, *Boy with a Clubfoot,* 108
Roberts, Cecil, 248, 269
Romer, General Cecil, 103
Rosanoff, Georges, 234, 338
Ross, Robert, 59
Rylands, George "Dadie," 170, 176, 187, 222

Santayana, George, 225–226
Sassoon, Siegfried, 198, 214
Savinkov, Boris, 125, 126–128, 366n12
Schopenhauer, Arthur, 112
Searle, Alan, 235, 287, 289, 323; after Maugham's death, 320, 341, 388n2; character, 275–276; relationship with Maugham, 105, 248, 270, 273, 274–279, 310–311, 314–315, 318, 321, 324, 326, 327–330, 336, 338
Secker, Martin, 206
Selfridge, Gordon, 81, 82, 84, 94, 133
Shaw, George Bernard, 72, 125
Sherriff, R. C., 293
Shirley, Canon F. J., 306–307, 322

Sitwell, Osbert, 37, 86–87, 91, 222–224
Snell, Anne (grandmother), 7
Snell, Major Charles (grandfather), 7
Snow, C. P., 175
Spark, Muriel, 349
Spinoza, Benedict, *Ethics,* 112, 364n18
Stanley, H. M., 65
Steevens, Christina, 78
Stendhal, 11
Stern, G. B., 246, 295, 340
Stevenson, Robert Louis, 43, 117, 119
Strachey, Lytton, 91, 228, 275
Sutherland, Graham, 175, 286–287, 307, 324
Swan, Michael, 104–105
Swift, Jonathan, "The Lady's Dressing Room," 54
Swinnerton, Frank, 9, 187, 203

Taylor, John Russell, 216
Tchelitchew, Pavel, 105
Tempest, Marie, 69, 70
Theroux, Paul, 348, 349; *Sir Vidia's Shadow,* 21
Thesiger, Ernest, 69
Thompson, Basil, 115
Towne, Charles, 163, 172–173, 247
Trilling, Diana, 279–280
Trilling, Lionel, 250, 342–343
Turner, Reggie, 59, 72, 186, 246, 359n2
Tyler, George, 69–70

Unwin, Fisher, 40, 49

Vanbrugh, Irene, 70
Velázquez, Diego, *Philip IV in Brown and Silver,* 306, 384n9
Vidal, Gore, 107, 113, 342
Voska, Emmanuel, 126, 130

Wallinger, Sir John, 113, 115
Walpole, Hugh, 16, 124, 129–130, 201–205, 322; *Captain Nicholas,* 206; *John Cornelius,* 206
Watt, A. P., 247
Waugh, Alec, 74, 202–203, 204, 301
Waugh, Evelyn, 237, 238–239, 288–289, 301, 303; *A Handful of Dust,* 71, 182
Weightman, John, 172
Wellcome, Henry, 81, 82, 84, 329
Welles, Orson, 250
Wells, H. G., 72, *Boon,* 73, *The Island of Doctor Moreau,* 68
Wescott, Glenway, 112, 184, 239, 245–246, 255, 276, 300, 320, 327; *Calendar of the Gods,* 105; *Journals,* 232, 246
West, Anthony, 252; *Heritage,* 332
West, Rebecca, 73, 106, 147, 186, 234
Wheeler, Monroe, 105, 242, 245, 282
Wilde, Oscar, 53, 58–59
Wilson, A. N., 349
Wilson, Angus, 143
Wilson, Edmund, 204–205; *Memoirs of Hecate County,* 280–281
Windsor, duchess of, 217–218
Windsor, duke of, 217–218, 234
Winn, Godfrey, 91–92, 176, 187, 267
Wiseman, Sir William, 122, 129, 131
Wodehouse, P. G., 143
Wolf, Max, 246
Wolfenden Report, 58–59
Woolf, Virginia, 203–204, 228, 231, 241, 243–244

Yeats, W. B., 66, 227, 234

Zabel, Morton, 251–252
Zanuck, Darryl, 265–267
Zipkin, Jerome, 247, 277, 278, 318

Compiled by Valerie Meyers